Writing in Transit

by DENISE K. COMER

FOUNTAINHEAD
PRESS

As a textbook publisher, we are faced with enormous environmental issues due the large amount of paper contained in our print products. Since our inception in 2002, we have worked diligently to be as eco-friendly as possible.

Our "green" initiatives include:

Electronic Products
We deliver products in nonpaper form whenever possible. This includes PDF downloadables, flash drives, and CDs.

Electronic Samples
We use a new electronic sampling system, called Xample. Instructor samples are sent via a personalized web page that links to PDF downloads.

FSC Certified Printers
All of our Printers are certified by the Forest Service Council, which promotes environmentally and socially responsible management of the world's forests. This program allows consumer groups, individual consumers and businesses to work together hand in hand to promote responsible use of the world's forests as a renewable and sustainable resource.

Recycled Paper
Almost all of our products are printed on a minimum of 10-30% post-consumer waste-recycled paper.

Support of Green Causes
When we do print, we donate a portion of our revenue to Green causes. Listed below are a few of the organizations that have received donations from Fountainhead Press. We welcome your feedback and suggestions for contributions, as we are always searching for worthy initiatives.
Rainforest 2 Reef
Environmental Working Group

Cover and text design: Ellie Moore

Copyright © 2015 Fountainhead Press

Stock images provided by Shutterstock.

For information, please call or write:
1-800-586-0330
Fountainhead Press
Southlake, TX 76092

Website: www.fountainheadpress.com
E-mail: customerservice@fountainheadpress.com

ISBN: 978-1-59871-803-4

Printed in the United States of America

Contents

Acknowledgments

Many people have contributed to the shaping and development of *Writing in Transit*. My particular gratitude goes to Scott Timian, whose leadership and vision moved the book forward from the beginning through to publication. Felix Frazier's insights and conceptual ideas were foundational to generating the manuscript. Thank you to both Scott and Felix for believing in me. Amy Salisbury, my fantastic developmental editor, provided crucial feedback and encouragement throughout the entire process. My friend and colleague Aftab Jassal offered incredibly astute insights on the manuscript. The inimitable Ellie Moore has granted her creative genius to designing *Writing in Transit*. Shelley Smith has provided her scrupulous eye toward copyediting.

The approach to writing transfer that informs *Writing in Transit* has been shaped through many years of working with the multidisciplinary faculty who comprise the Duke University Thompson Writing Program; exchanges with these talented colleagues have helped make visible cross-disciplinary convergences and divergences, and I am deeply grateful to all past and present Thompson Writing Program faculty. In particular, many productive conversations grounded on writing transfer have emerged through conversations among participants in the Postdoctoral Summer Seminar in Teaching Writing, which I have co-taught for nearly a decade (first with Joseph Harris and more recently with Marcia Rego). Special appreciation goes to my friend Joseph Harris, founding director of the Thompson Writing Program, whose approach to teaching writing has been integral in shaping my writing pedagogy. Kristen Neuschel's mentorship and support over the past several years have helped me come to understand writing itself in much more nuanced ways.

I am extremely thankful for the many writers from around the world who have enrolled in English Composition I: Achieving Expertise and engaged in cross-disciplinary and intercultural conversations about writing. These conversations have greatly enhanced my thinking about writing transfer. My appreciation extends especially to those who have graciously contributed Writer Insights throughout this book.

My close friends and family provide ongoing motivation, inspiration, strength, and space for my writing. They express interest in and enthusiasm for my projects, reassuring, insightful advice, and compassion for my quandaries. My immense gratitude goes to Parag Budhecha; Patty and Mike Comer; David, Paige, Amanda, and Lauren Gotterer; Emily Robbins; Rebecca Ryslik; and Jonathan Wolitz. Particular appreciation goes to Ray and June Wolitz for their guidance. I am also grateful to my mother, Barbara

Gina Garrett, for her ideas and support. My three curious and creative children, Owen, Ethan, and Drew Comer, also deserve special recognition for their patience, interest, and insights. And, to my rock-star husband, David Comer: you have provided honest feedback, helped create time and energy for me to write, and offered courage, inspiration, and laughter.

Preface to Instructors

Archaeoastronomy and Writing Transfer

Each chapter of *Writing in Transit* opens with a different archaeoastronomical site from around the world. Offering a unifying thread for the book—and a metaphor for writing transfer—these chapter openings each include a brief site description and a writing prompt that invite students to consider that particular archaeoastronomical site through the lens of that particular chapter's area of focus. Archaeoastronomy provides an apt inroad for *Writing in Transit* in part because it infuses writing with curiosity and wonder, but also because it holds much in common with writing transfer. As archaeoastronomical sites forge intersections and emphasize difference across disciplines, cultures, time, and space, so too does the kind of active consideration of writing transfer central to *Writing in Transit*. Therefore, with each new chapter of *Writing in Transit,* instructors and students can use the archaeoastronomical sites to sponsor and inform conversations about writing transfer: How do culture, time, discipline, and space yield unique yet intersecting contexts for writing, learning, and knowledge? In what ways do context and individual dispositions shape, reflect, and refract the kinds of questions writers ask and the knowledge writers create? How do writing-related practices and approaches align and depart across, through, and in between the enormous range of contexts writers encounter in academia and beyond?

Writing Transfer

Perhaps more than ever before, twenty-first century college students need to become adept at writing within and across disciplinary boundaries and navigate increasingly complex, overlapping, and varied landscapes of writing. In short, they need to cultivate habits of mind grounded on transfer.

Transfer, according to Linda Darling-Hammond and Kim Austin of the Stanford School of Education, is "the ability to extend what one has learned in one context to new contexts." Writing-related transfer involves students reflecting on what they learn in one context about writing and about themselves as learners and writers, and then applying, extending, rejecting, or otherwise modifying this knowledge for other disciplinary, interdisciplinary, and transdisciplinary contexts.

Writing in Transit foregrounds writing transfer, making explicit the changing, intersecting, and disparate contexts of writing across, within, and beyond our institutions. *Writing in Transit* invites students to actively engage with, reflect on, and position themselves within those varying and overlapping domains so they can become better at transferring their writing-related knowledge, practices, approaches, and skills to whatever contexts they encounter.

Research into writing transfer has a long history, reaching back at least as far as Aristotle's *Rhetoric* in the fourth century B.C.E. (Nowacek). Writing transfer is often based on inquiries into the connected yet divergent values and practices within particular disciplines. David Russell's notion of "activity theory," for instance, suggests that each discipline—and each discipline's (sometimes overlapping) approach to writing—has a highly contextualized and historically grounded set of practices, motives, and approaches:

> [Activity theory develops] metaphors of interlocking, dynamic systems or networks. These systems embrace both human agents and their material tools, including writing and speaking.... An activity system is any ongoing, object-directed, historically-conditioned, dialectically-structured, tool-mediated human interaction: a family, a religious organization, an advocacy group, a political movement, a course of study, a school, a discipline, a research laboratory, a profession, and so on. These activity systems are mutually (re)constructed by participants using certain tools and not others (including discursive tools such as speech sounds and inscriptions). ("Rethinking")

As you can see in Figure 1, Russell maintains that writing thus reflects, shapes, and is shaped by the particular network(s) from which it emerges.

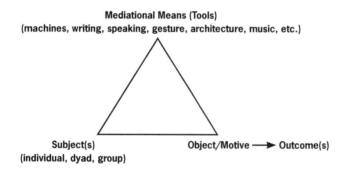

FIGURE 1 An Activity System (Fundamental Unit of Analysis of Social Practices).
From Russell, "Rethinking," 510.

Contemporary research into writing transfer often invokes and builds on Russell's notions of activity systems, or what others have since termed "communities of discourse" (Carter) or "language socialization" (Duff).

One of the most important recent ideas about transfer is that it is a highly dynamic process (Bransford, Brown, and Cocking). It can occur deliberately or unconsciously, directly or indirectly, positively or negatively (knowing what *to do* or what *not to do* in particular circumstances). Anne Beaufort's research shows that competing values in discourse communities can sometimes stymie students' abilities to effectively enact writing transfer. Elizabeth Wardle emphasizes the importance of reflection and meta-awareness for transfer. Dana Lynn Driscoll and Jennifer Wells examine "the role of learners' dispositions" in transfer. They emphasize that learners' personalities, dispositions, and identities impact their approach to transfer and that this can shift with time as well. This means that students should reflect meaningfully on their work as learners, thinkers, and writers on a continuing basis. Kathleen Blake Yancey, Liane Robertson, and Kara Taczak's recent work in *Writing across Contexts* emphasizes the importance of designing curriculum in first-year writing courses with an explicit emphasis on enabling students to "foster transfer in writing."

Rebecca Nowacek's research on writing transfer yields particular insights into how students engage with writing transfer. She has resituated binary conceptions of transfer (low-road/unconscious or high-road/deliberate; positive or negative) to unpack a more matrixed approach: "four avenues of connection, four resources that individuals employ as they draw connections among various contexts: knowledge, ways of knowing, identity, and goals." Nowacek foregrounds the agency involved with transfer to emphasize that students are not merely conduits moving from context to context but are instead "agents of integration" who actively reconstruct writing-related knowledge and practices through transfer.

Of significance to point out is that a transfer-based approach to writing is not equivalent to promoting interdisciplinarity. Those involved with transfer acknowledge that activity systems enable scholars to advance knowledge within their disciplines because they can build on the work of others and move forward long-term conversations premised on shared knowledge, conventions, and outcomes. These discourse communities are vitally important, and cultivating attention to transfer does not mean that disciplinary boundaries should necessarily become more porous. Rather, a transfer-based approach encourages students to cultivate the meta-awareness to recognize and participate in and across these discourse communities more effectively.

The diversity and complexity of discourse communities helps us understand why writing, and more broadly academic inquiry, can be so challenging for undergraduates as they move between activity systems. Gerald Graff, for instance, decries that students' perception of their college education can too often seem "a disconnected series of courses." It can be difficult even for faculty to help students make connections across courses because faculty themselves sometimes struggle with or resist developing a more integrated approach to research and writing. Michael Carter suggests that faculty can be so immersed in their particular discipline's activity systems that they may be unlikely to notice the situatedness of writing in their field, much less acquire the perspective to help students understand these contexts: "[B]ecause professors typically learn to write in their disciplines not by any direct instruction but by a process of slow acculturation through various apprenticeship discourses, they are unable to see that writing itself is specific to the discipline." The result, Carter argues, is that faculty may conceive of their discipline's approach toward and values about writing as universal: "Consequently, faculty in the disciplines continue to conceive of writing as generalizable to all disciplines and therefore distinct from disciplinary knowledge, to be learned as a general skill outside the disciplines." This conception of writing as generalizable can then, according to Carter, give way to the idea that learning how to write is primarily only about mastering grammar, punctuation, and spelling rather than about higher order abilities such as posing questions, engaged reading, critical thinking, and effective argumentation.

One way writing faculty and students can move more deliberately and productively among various networks of discourse is by designing courses that integrate transfer-based approaches to learning, writing, and assessment. Informed by these conversations, *Writing in Transit* invites first-year students and faculty to foster just such a transfer-based approach toward writing through pointed areas of focus (see Table 1).

TABLE 1 Pointed areas of focus.

Disciplinary Epistemologies	What kinds of knowledge production and strategies for learning and knowing operate within and across disciplines? What counts as worthwhile, effective questions in particular contexts, and how can we reframe these questions for other contexts?
Discourse Conventions	How can we transfer our awareness of discourse conventions, including matters of genre, voice, tone, and citation, from one writing context to others? How can we transfer our abilities to identify particular discourse conventions as we encounter different contexts?
Individual Epistemology	What kinds of learning work best for us as individuals? How can we learn more about ourselves as learners based on our work in first-year writing? What kinds of approaches to inquiry, peer engagement, collaboration, and research work best for us as individuals and under what circumstances? How might these preferences or affinities change across time as we grow and change?
Writing Process/Practices	Which aspects of the writing process (i.e. research, pre-writing, drafting, feedback, revision, and editing) can be applied and adapted from one context to other writing and learning occasions?
Writing Moves and Skills	How can specific writing moves, such as developing arguments, engaging with the work of others, integrating evidence, crafting introductions and conclusions, structuring arguments, and writing effective sentence-level prose be adapted from one context to other writing and learning occasions?
Content	In what ways might the content-based knowledge we acquire through texts, writing, and research impact concurrent and subsequent learning and writing occasions, be they in the academy or outside?

Writing in Transit invites students to cultivate this transfer-based approach to writing by examining texts and writing practices from across disciplines. The framing material for these texts, though, guides students not towards a prescribed set of conventions, but instead towards thinking about disciplinary epistemologies, asking what we can learn about values and approaches to writing in disciplines. And, even as *Writing in Transit,* draws from the work of scholars in linguistics, such as Charles Bazerman, who identify patterns across texts, it also embraces Carter's notions of "disciplines as ways of knowing."

By providing example texts from across disciplines, and writing concepts situated in a disciplinary based context, *Writing in Transit* can accustom students to think with transfer-based habits of mind, facilitating the agency students have in transfer, and thereby empowering them to find more value and integration in their education, especially through the centrality of writing and writing-related transfer.

Whom *Writing in Transit* is for

This book is primarily aimed toward first-year writing students, but it would also be valuable for writers at other stages of their educational journeys—undergraduates through graduate students, and faculty who are integrating writing (in large or small ways) into their discipline-based courses. It would also offer useful materials for interdisciplinary or multidisciplinary faculty learning communities.

Transfer-Based Features of *Writing in Transit*

Writing in Transit facilitates your exploration of writing transfer with students by providing key pedagogical elements specifically designed to promote a transfer-based approach to writing and learning.

Archaeoastronomical chapter openers

Students' journey exploring the many moving parts of writing finds a corollary journey with each chapter opener, which orients students to the chapter content through a different archaeoastronomical site from around the world. Together, these sites provide a unifying thread across *Writing in Transit*, operating as an alignment in much the same way as the features of writing included in the text. Even beyond this form of alignment, however, archaeoastronomy is a field of inquiry and contains structures that—like writing transfer—transverse disciplines, cultures, and individuals, retaining some common characteristics but also bending slightly (or drastically) in response to these varying contexts.

Opportunities for writing and reflecting

Writing in Transit includes numerous opportunities for writing and reflecting, opportunities that are specifically infused with a transfer-based approach so students can actively engage in the process of writing transfer.

"Write Here"

Appearing with and emerging from each archaeoastronomical site, Write Here writing prompts locate students both geographically within the particular site and position them as writers within the area of focus for that particular chapter. Write Heres invite students to begin thinking and writing about the feature of writing that will be addressed in that chapter.

"Write Now"

Interspersed throughout each chapter and consisting of opportunities for brief writing and reflecting, Write Now writing prompts ask students to engage with elements of writing transfer connected to a particular chapter's area of focus.

"Write Away"

Located at the close of each chapter, Write Away projects invite students to embark on a slightly more substantive writing experience related to that chapter's content and ask students to draw upon your transfer-related skills and practices. Write Aways are individual opportunities for writing as well as occasions where students can collaborate with a small group of peer writers.

Together, these occasions for writing and reflecting sponsor opportunities for students to transfer writing knowledge within and across disciplinary contexts and writing occasions.

Maps guiding students through each chapter

Since *Writing in Transit* is steeped in movement, it becomes ever more crucial to occasionally pause and take stock, to consider how ideas build on one another and where ideas may lead. Two elements of the text in particular help map this dynamic terrain.

"Pinpointing Chapter [Number]"

Located early in each chapter, these sections show how the elements of writing transfer being addressed in the current chapter build on preceding chapters and how subsequent chapters will, in turn, extend them as well. These Pinpointing sections also provide an overview of the chapter material so students can see the direction in which they are heading as writers.

"Transferring [Chapter Name]"

Appearing at the end of each chapter, these sections re-emphasize how writers transfer the aspect of writing addressed in that chapter to many and diverse writing occasions. These sections also highlight how students can transfer what they have learned in prior chapters to the aspect of writing addressed in that chapter and how they can transfer what they have learned in the current chapter to subsequent chapters. In this way, students can see how writing transfer operates across *Writing in Transit* as a dynamic series of interlocking, sequenced, and recursive concepts and practices.

Multi-disciplinary examples

Within chapters, explorations of the writing feature under consideration are grounded in multi-disciplinary and multi-contextual perspectives. As *Writing in Transit* illustrates how writers transfer—borrow, adapt, and reject—aspects of writing from one occasion to others, each chapter brings multiple disciplines and contexts to bear on the aspect of writing under consideration.

Occasions to connect with others

Through "Transfer Hubs," students will have occasion to engage in productive exchanges about writing with others beyond the immediate course setting. The Fountainhead Press Transfer Hub (fountainheadpress.com/transferhub) invites students to visit a wider networked site to contribute their ideas and see what others have written, thereby facilitating even greater degrees of transfer and exchange. Many of the writing and reflecting opportunities are also in and of themselves opportunities for connecting through collaborations with peers.

Insights about writing

National and international writers share their experiences with writing throughout *Writing in Transit*. These Writer Insights provide glimpses into writing from across professions, disciplines, and contexts. The real-world people who contributed provide authentic perspectives on transfer-based aspects of writing.

Amidst all of these transfer points, your students, as writers, will travel, moving through disciplines and writing occasions by exploring and discovering writing in transit.

Why You Should Introduce Students to *Writing in Transit*

Academic writing is hard, even for those of us who are purportedly experts at it. First-year writing students deserve the chance to actively interrogate the ways in which academic inquiry, writing values, expectations, and conventions are shaped by and reflected in the writing that exists within disciplines. They also deserve to contribute to these conversations by learning how to pose meaningful questions and engage with the work of others in ways that are situated within, across, and against disciplinary perspectives.

Perhaps most importantly, students should have the space to think about themselves within, outside of, and alongside these domains. Framing first-year writing around these disciplinary practices and questions will illustrate for students that academic writing itself is dynamic, animated by the shifting, often recursive and overlapping aims, methods, purposes, and ideas scholars bring to their writing.

Your Integral Role with *Writing in Transit*

One of the most important aspects of writing transfer to keep in mind is that faculty have a strong role encouraging, or discouraging, students' aptitude with transfer:

> The rich evidence of longitudinal studies also indirectly supports what we have learned from studying the research on transfer, namely, that transfer depends heavily, although not exclusively, on our teaching: when we teach with analogies, encourage metacognition, scaffold student learning, motivate our students effectively, and provide sufficient time for the learning to 'take,' our teaching potentially enables transfer." (Boone, et al.)

Writing in Transit anticipates that you will, and makes room for you to, bring your expertise as a teacher of writing, and your own disciplinary lens, to bear on these texts and ideas as you encounter them with students. *Writing in Transit* relies on your teaching as a key mechanism for supporting and encouraging writing transfer.

You do not, however, need gain expertise in writing for every discipline. Just as writers write better when they write about something they care about, the best writing pedagogy occurs when we teach writing from within our own scholarly perspectives. Students learn best when texts, teachers, circumstances, and they themselves all work together, colliding, intersecting, and overlapping.

Writing in Transit encourages you, therefore, to find your own path through the materials, and to supplement these materials with others that you have created and collected. You and your students can also find a variety of other valuable resources and supplements at the Fountainhead Press website.

About the Author

Denise Comer, Assistant Professor of the Practice of Writing Studies and Director of First-Year Writing at Duke University, has worked with a multidisciplinary first-year writing faculty for more than fifteen years.

Duke University's award-winning and nationally recognized first-year writing program recruits faculty with Ph.D.s across the social sciences, natural sciences, and humanities to teach first-year writing. The program is founded on the premise that cross-disciplinary conversations about first-year writing improve the teaching of writing and help first-year writers learn how to navigate more effectively the variegated landscape of academic writing.

Approaching first-year writing pedagogy as an intellectual endeavor and fostering conversations about writing that actively consider disciplinary perspectives have helped earn Duke University's Thompson Writing Program national recognition with the 2006 CCCC Writing Program Certificate of Excellence and through the 2012 *U.S. News & World Report*, which commended Duke for "making the writing process a priority at all levels of instruction and across the curriculum."

Denise has collaborated on several initiatives for Duke and the Durham community that demonstrate her investment teaching writing to *all* learners: launching a writing course for students who need more time and preparation with college-level writing, many of whom are first-generation or low-income; integrating responsiveness to English Language Learners across all first-year writing courses; developing writing workshops for low-income, high-potential urban middle-school children; and creating a writing-based program for chronically and fatally ill children residing at the Ronald McDonald House of Durham. In 2013, she launched a Massive Open Online Course, English Composition I: Achieving Expertise, funded largely through a grant from the Bill & Melinda Gates Foundation and offered in partnership between Duke University and Coursera. Currently in its third iteration, to date over 200,000 learners from around the world have enrolled in that course. Prior to teaching at Duke, she taught writing at public universities, community colleges, and a military base.

Denise's scholarship explores writing transfer with multidisciplinary inquiries into writing pedagogy, writing program administration, and the intersections between technology and the teaching of writing. Her book, *It's Just a Dissertation: Transforming Your Dissertation from Daunting to Doable to Done,* co-written with Barbara Gina Garrett (Fountainhead Press, 2014), provides guidance to graduate students across disciplines on how to write and complete a dissertation. Her articles, attentive to multidisciplinary perspectives and often grounded on a transfer-based approach, have appeared in such journals as *Writing across the Curriculum*, *Teaching/Writing*, *Pedagogy*, and *WPA: Writing Program Administration*. She has also given presentations about, offered keynote addresses on, and worked as a consultant on multidisciplinary writing pedagogy and writing transfer.

Writing Transfer

Pinpointing Chapter 1

As the introductory chapter of the text, Chapter 1 introduces transfer as a way of approaching writing and as a strategy for learning. To provide you with strategies for *writing transfer*, this chapter addresses the following concepts:

- What is Writing Transfer?
- The Dynamic Nature of Discourse Conventions
- A Transfer-Based Approach to Writing
- Writing Practices that Align, Modify, and Differentiate across Contexts
- Strategies for Becoming Better at Writing Transfer
- Why Writing Transfer Matters

Subsequent chapters each feature and explore a key writing practice that writers align, modify, and differentiate across contexts. These key writing practices align across disciplines and writing occasions, even while also refracting, shaping, and reflecting distinct perspectives and approaches.

Chaco Canyon is one of the most impressive examples of ancient engineering, astronomy, and architecture. Located in what is now a relatively remote area of New Mexico, the structures in Chaco Canyon were built by the Chaco Anasazi people of the Pueblo culture between 850 and 1250 C.E.

Representing the accomplishments made possible through interdisciplinary collaboration, Chaco Canyon fuses "architectural designs, astronomical alignments, geometry, landscaping and engineering." Connecting more than 150 communities together, the site stands among "[m]ore than four hundred miles of interlocking ancient roads," suggesting it was a hub of intercultural activity ("Chaco"; Gibson).

Chaco Canyon is especially well known for its Great Houses, which were enormous complexes, multiple stories high, some of which included as many as 750 rooms. Archaeologists believe Great Houses functioned primarily as "important focal point[s] for ritual activity" rather than as residences. While each Great House contained unique characteristics, they also all shared several features in common. One such feature—a precise astronomical alignment between windows and walls—enabled Anasazi people to recognize the summer and winter solstices ("History"; Malville; Ward).

One of Chaco Canyon's most exceptional structures is the Sun Dagger, which consists of three sandstone slabs and spiral petroglyphs that, until recently due to a settling of the rock slabs, marked solstices and equinoxes: "[At summer solstice,] a vertical shaft of light passed through the center of the spiral…At winter solstice, two noonday daggers framed the large spiral. During the equinoxes, the smaller spiral was bisected at midday by a lesser dagger" ("Fajada"). With its precise use of shadows to track time, the Sun Dagger remains an exemplar of ancient knowledge, collaboration, and achievement.

Chaco Canyon makes visible the complex intersections between things that may otherwise seem discrete: Great Houses were each distinctive, yet they all shared certain key structural features; Chaco roads each led to a different place, but interlocked to enable movement between and through these locales; people with unique disciplinary knowledge each contributed toward realizing a shared goal of developing Chaco Canyon; the stone slabs around the Sun Dagger existed independently, but then aligned, if only for a moment, to mark time.

Moving, diverging, and intersecting parts—which together generate the marvel that became Chaco Canyon—illustrate the value of forging connections and adapting knowledge even as difference is preserved. Chaco Canyon thus exemplifies the achievements possible through disciplinary and cultural collaboration, but at the same time reaffirms the value of deep disciplinary and culturally-based knowledge production.

Similar to the alignments transecting Chaco Canyon's Sun Dagger or Great Houses, academic writers, across overlapping and disparate disciplines and writing occasions, engage in many of the same writing-related moves, strategies, and practices, even as discipline and context shape each writer's unique approach to any given writing occasion.

The kind of thinking required by this terrain of academic writing is known as transfer. Transfer consists of the ability to establish connections, notice confluences, and adapt prior knowledge amidst different concepts and contexts, even those that may at times seem widely disconnected.

Writing in Transit will help you become more effective at transfer, especially, though not exclusively, within the context of academic writing. A transfer-based approach to writing will enable you to more effectively transfer knowledge, ideas, and practices about and across writing contexts. Gaining acumen with writing transfer will facilitate your growth as a writer, thinker, and global citizen and empower you to contribute ideas to ongoing conversations, advance knowledge, achieve your goals, and make a meaningful difference in the world around you.

Write Here

Chaco Canyon exemplifies the collaboration and exchange that often occurs across disciplines and cultures. What other structures or sites—historical and/or contemporary—can you think of that exhibit this kind of fusion, transfer, and exchange? For several of the sites or structures you name, identify also the various component cultures, disciplines, or concepts that intersect and align to create that structure/site.

 Transfer Hub: Contribute your ideas and see what others have written at fountainheadpress.com/transferhub.

What is Writing Transfer?

Writing transfer entails customizing your knowledge, practices, and approaches to learning and writing from one writing occasion to other writing occasions. Writing transfer relies on complex, higher-order thinking skills and emerges through practice, awareness, and reflection. With writing transfer, you can adapt what you have learned about writing, and about learning itself, from one context to others.

Navigating possible intersections and divergences across writing occasions, however, can be quite challenging, especially in the context of academic writing, for the dynamic and varied landscape of academic writing does not readily lend itself to a compact set of guidelines

Writer Insights

What values or priorities influence your writing across and within different disciplinary perspectives?

I've written throughout my life, and one pattern that I have noticed is that I write in order to understand my world. When I was younger, "truth" came in the form of political criticism. I remember giving a speech in 8th grade on parallels between America and the fall of Rome...In high school, influenced by my history teacher, I read Chomsky and wrote several essays critical of American hegemony....By my junior year, I joined the debate team and competed in national tournaments. One day...someone introduced me to Richard Feynman, an incredibly brilliant physicist, and [I] was blown away. "This was real truth. Scientific truth!" I applied (and got into) UC Davis Physics. I stopped writing about politics, but I didn't stop writing. For nearly a decade, I wrote peer reviews for scientific papers, published papers in journals, maintained a research blog, and even churned out a doctoral thesis....When I graduated, I continued to write for my job, but now I "wrote" Powerpoint presentations. I was a data scientist for an analytics startup....Recently, I've decided to...write about data analysis on social issues. I still write to understand the world, but my focus is now closer to home and towards bringing about positive changes in my community.

~Jesse Singh, Physicist,
Oakland, California, U.S.

for how to be a good academic writer. Instead, conventions and expectations for writing shift across and within various fields of inquiry, or **disciplines**.

These disciplines, and the writers within them, create knowledge through shared (though shifting) understandings about how to pose questions, how to pursue research, and how to communicate ideas as effectively as possible. In order to write in a way that carries purchase with readers in their disciplines, those writing from within a given disciplinary perspective generate texts whose features coalesce to form what scholar James Porter refers to as a **discourse community**, "a local and temporary constraining system, defined by a body of texts (or more generally, practices) that are unified by a common focus. A discourse community is a textual system with stated and unstated conventions [and] a vital history." *Apuli frame*

Together, the "stated and unstated conventions" within discourse communities generate patterns that help readers and writers in those disciplines advance knowledge (Bazerman). These conventions are known as **discourse conventions**, and they influence the choices people make when writing. When you write a paper for a psychology class, for instance, you will likely invoke writing practices that both resonate with and differ from those you might summon while writing an essay in an English course. Similarly, when you write a biology lab report, you are working within yet another disciplinary context comprised of some unique writing features and some crossover elements.

These discourse conventions can even impact seemingly minute aspects of writing. For example, in a study by Ken Hyland, data shows that writers in the disciplines of Philosophy and Marketing refer directly to themselves in their writing (with "I," "we," or the impersonal pronoun) 550% more frequently than writers in the discipline of Mechanical Engineering. Amidst so many different disciplinary contexts and writing occasions, the criteria for what makes writing effective can seem confusing, if not arbitrary.

Discourse conventions, however, are about much more than just pronouns. Instead, they reflect the values, priorities, and customs for how people in disciplines create and advance knowledge. Discourse communities shape and reflect the values writers embrace, and the expectations and conventions writers bring to writing, reading, and research.

Connecting discourse conventions with the creation of knowledge, Gordon Wells, Professor of Education at University of California, Santa Cruz, writes:

> Each subject discipline constitutes a way of making sense of human experience that has evolved over generations and each is dependent on its own particular practices: its instrumental procedures, its criteria for judging relevance and validity, and its conventions of acceptable forms of argument. In a word each has developed its own modes of discourse.

These **modes of discourse**, therefore, which emanate from and govern writing within and across disciplines, thus reflect and shape the arguments most valued by members of those disciplines. Being able to navigate among these discourse communities requires becoming more sophisticated at writing transfer, adapting prior knowledge, experiences, and strategies to each new writing occasion you encounter.

Write Now

Think of two or three different writing experiences you have had within different disciplinary perspectives. Options might include an English paper, a history essay, a journalistic piece, a math proof, a lab report—any experiences with writing that you believe were influenced by a disciplinary perspective. Reflect in writing about the discourse conventions operating within each of these experiences. How would you describe these instances in terms of discourse conventions? Did you notice any shared discourse conventions? Any unique ones? Did anything surprise you in terms of the expectations or conventions for the writing occasions?

The Dynamic Nature of Discourse Conventions

As you consider the nature of discourse conventions, however, it becomes crucial to recognize that they are dynamic rather than static. Discourse is dynamic because disciplines are created and sustained by human beings. This sounds simple enough, but it is worth emphasizing: humans in disciplines create knowledge, rethink approaches, change assumptions, and move ideas forward (or sometimes backward). For that reason, disciplinary writing, by its very nature, grows and changes.

Not only do disciplinary conventions shift, but different people also hold varying individual expectations and values about what constitutes effective writing. These individualistic preferences can be shaped by disciplinary history and context, as well as by particular scholars' unique dispositions, experiences, and approaches to learning, thinking, and writing.

Making discourse communities even more complex, these values, conventions, and expectations about writing shift not only within and between disciplines and people, but often across historical and cultural contexts as well. Twenty years ago, for example, writing in online environments was not as prevalent in academic contexts; today, nearly every discipline has modes of writing that operate in digital environments. Similarly, what people agreed upon as effective writing in 1820 is not necessarily what we would agree upon now. Scholars in different places around the world can have a diverse and sometimes conflicting range of expectations, approaches, and conventions. Janice Walker, a scholar of writing studies, uses citation as an example to illustrate just how heterogeneous these writing practices can be:

> Strict attribution of sources has not always been necessary, and indeed in many cultures and contexts, it is still not (necessarily) required. Ancient texts often did not follow any formal rules of attribution, since it was assumed that the audience would already be familiar with the body of scholarly work. I have also heard…that in Chinese culture, the words of others are used without attribution as a way of honoring those whose words were considered so important that they needed no attribution.

Walker goes on to outline the many changes in citation practices that have occurred over the past ten years, including shifting rules about italics, citation of online sources, and what does or does not constitute "common knowledge." Walker, herself an expert in writing studies and a highly accomplished writer, exclaims at one point: "I'm *so* confused!"

While disciplinary perspectives, historical context, and writers themselves all occupy important roles in shaping and reflecting discourse conventions, other layers of transfer are at play in this landscape as well, for even within particular disciplines, writing expectations and conventions can shift dramatically across and between writing projects.

A writer's particular purpose, for example, significantly impacts what constitutes an effective approach to writing. Depending on whether writers hope to persuade, inform, critique, or define, their discourse conventions shift accordingly. When writers have multiple, overlapping, or even perhaps contradictory purposes, their decisions about how to write effectively become even more complex.

Discourse conventions also change in relationship to whether writing is meant to be more private, professional, scholarly, widely accessible, or some combination therein. Increasingly, writers across disciplines produce and share knowledge not only in scholarly settings but also in more public contexts, including such forms of writing as blogs, verbal presentations, op-eds, captions for museum exhibits or online archives, magazine articles, or reviews of books or films.

Pointing out the ways in which writers transfer writing practices between public and scholarly contexts (distinctions which are themselves frequently blurred), Professor of English Mike Rose suggests that this approach entails "bilingualism." Bilingualism of the sort Rose names hinges on a transfer-based approach to writing and learning.

Writer Insights

What different writing occasions have you traversed through in your life?

[I]n high school…I wrote several reports and opinions about classical books. In college [I wrote everything from] book reports to final exams. Today, as a notary, I'm writing constantly: contracts, descriptions of facts and persons, different kinds of affidavits. Also, I have written two monographs, one about trust and [the] other about patrimonial aspects of marriage. Both of them [were] published in legal journals.

~Gonzalo Toro, Public Notary,
Jujuy, Argentina

Each writing occasion presents unique opportunities and challenges for writers regarding how they might adapt, modify, extend, or otherwise reconsider—in essence, how they will *transfer*—the choices they make about writing from one writing occasion to others. And, because discourse is so dynamic, it would be nearly impossible to articulate precisely what the rules are for writing in particular disciplines or for particular writing occasions, nor can a text such as *Writing in Transit* provide you with neat and tidy formulas for writing in each discipline. What can happen, however, is that writers can invoke a transfer-based approach to writing and learning in order to bring prior knowledge, practices, and experiences to bear on each new writing occasion.

Write Now

Create a timeline documenting your writing history. Begin your timeline with your earliest memories involving writing (even if these entailed "pretend" writing while you were a child, for example), and move through the years to the present day, documenting memorable or meaningful (or mundane) writing experiences. Plot out on your timeline all the many different occasions in which you have written, whether in school, in your personal experiences, and/or in your professional encounters.

A Transfer-Based Approach to Writing

Writing in Transit will help make the complexities of discourse conventions, disciplinary perspectives, and context more manageable for you by preparing you to more effectively transfer your knowledge, practices, goals, individual dispositions, and ideas from one writing context to others. Adopting a transfer-based approach to writing, the concepts in this text will bring to your attention varying disciplinary approaches to writing, illustrating how writers create knowledge and how their dynamic values and priorities inform writing practices and discourse conventions.

This approach embraces a premise whereby disciplines operate as "ways of knowing" (Carter). As such, *Writing in Transit* models the dynamic nature of academic writing. Exploring writing as a network of shifting inquiries, this book invites you to consider the kinds of questions scholars in various disciplines ask and the values about writing that scholars across disciplines hold. A transfer-based approach to writing will enable you to anticipate the dynamic nature of discourse conventions and prepare you for these twists and turns, honing your transfer acumen and equipping you to explore new writing occasions with curiosity and confidence rather than with confusion and frustration.

But this transfer-based approach not only asks you to reflect on others' writing choices, but equips you with the ability to transfer *your* writing practices across disciplinary contexts. You will learn, for example, strategies for creating knowledge within and between diverse disciplinary perspectives, by turn shaping your inquiries and arguments to these perspectives and also at times deliberately infusing different perspectives into particular discourse communities. Writing with a transfer-based approach will therefore position you to participate actively in ongoing academic conversations, contribute your ideas effectively, and advance knowledge meaningfully in the world around you.

Writing Practices that Align, Modify, and Differentiate across Contexts

A transfer-based approach to writing explores how writers forge key intersections across writing contexts, even though discipline, writing occasion, and individual disposition will continue to impact how writers approach any given writing occasion. As Dawn Youngblood maintains, "No discipline is an island entirely in itself.... [D]isciplines are by no means discrete entities—they necessarily overlap, borrow, and encroach upon one another." Similarly, within, across, and beyond disciplines, the writing you encounter may seem to be (or actually be) quite discrete, but it too will "necessarily overlap, borrow, and encroach upon" other writing occasions.

Exploring in more detail these overlaps and encroachments across writing occasions, each chapter of *Writing in Transit* showcases a key feature of academic writing that aligns across context. Specifically, each chapter considers one of the following aspects of academic writing that transverse context, alternately overlapping, intersecting, and diverging across disciplines and writing occasions:

- Research and Writing as a Process
- Posing Meaningful Questions
- Reading
- Summary
- Synthesis
- Analysis
- Framing Arguments
- Constructing Arguments
- Designing Arguments
- Choosing and Integrating Evidence
- Citing Evidence

Discovering the ways in which these key aspects of academic writing align across disciplines will enable you to more effectively transfer, modify, and apply your writing-related knowledge from one writing occasion to others.

Keep in mind, though, that despite the ways in which writers might be able to transfer these writing practices across context, *Writing in Transit* cannot offer one perfect, go-to strategy for these writing practices. Instead, this transfer-based approach prepares you to identify which practices (or parts of practices) might work best within particular contexts, and invites you to take into account disciplinary discourse conventions, individual priorities and dispositions, and other relevant aspects of writing occasions to tailor your practices and approaches accordingly.

Strategies for Becoming Better at Writing Transfer

Writing in Transit offers you a transfer-based framework for becoming a better academic writer, preparing you for the complex and multifaceted exigencies of college-level writing across disciplines and writing occasions. But this opportunity hinges on the degree to which you actively engage with transfer as a habit of mind and as an approach to writing and learning. As you explore *Writing in Transit,* you learn to deploy certain strategies that improve your writing transfer skills (see Table 1.1).

TABLE 1.1 Strategies to improve writing transfer skills.

Consider how people in various disciplines create knowledge.	What kinds of questions do scholars ask in various disciplines? What forms of research do they conduct? What purposes and aims do various writers have within and across disciplines?
Identify shared and unique patterns of writing across disciplines and writing occasions.	As you encounter texts across disciplines and contexts, identify general patterns as well as features that seem unique to a particular discipline or writing occasion. Assess what seems non-transportable as well: are there, for instance, any conventions or expectations within certain disciplines or occasions that you believe might be counterproductive in other contexts?
Reflect on your own writing approaches and values.	What are your individual dispositions and inclinations with regard to writing? What approaches seem most meaningful to you when you encounter writing projects? What values do you hold about effective writing? How do your values shift according to context? Which kinds of questions most often spark your curiosity?
Think about yourself as a writer.	Reflect actively on how you as a writer are changing and growing, and identify periodically what is working more or less effectively for you as a learner. Which approaches and practices seem to come more readily to you? As you read others' writing, think about which aspects you would like to emulate, modify, or reject. Keep in mind that your learning and writing approaches will shift across time and context.
Consider this the beginning stage of a lifelong journey enriched through transfer.	Writing is a lifelong enterprise, and you are the individual best positioned to know and track your writing experiences, your writing ambitions, and your writing strengths and limitations. The goal of *Writing in Transit* is to help you cultivate a habit of mind in which you can rely on transfer as you move forward in your education, career, and life.

Carrying these strategies with you as you move within, across, and among all the many writing occasions you will encounter in college and beyond will prepare you to approach each new writing occasion with transfer-based thinking and writing practices.

Why Writing Transfer Matters

A transfer-based approach to writing and learning—the ability to establish connections, notice confluences, and adapt prior knowledge amidst what at times may seem widely disparate concepts and contexts—has particular value in our increasingly connected twenty-first century. Future studies expert William H. Newell emphasizes just how interconnected the world is becoming:

> Most public intellectuals as well as experts in future studies would agree that the increasingly global society of the first half of the twenty-first century will be characterized by increasing connectivity, diversity, scale, and rapidity of change....
> [S]tudents will face challenges in the next several decades unlike those in the past. In general, small events on one part of the planet and in one sphere of human existence can now end up having large and relatively rapid effects on other parts of the planet and in other spheres of human existence.... Coping with this complexity will require a new way of understanding—one that does not rely on having only a single viewpoint.

The increasing "connectivity, diversity, scale, and rapidity of change" to which Newell refers will ask us, perhaps more than ever before, to sharpen and rely on our abilities to engage in transfer-based thinking.

Your educational path—whatever it may be—will likely involve moving within and between courses across a wide range of disciplines, and each of these disciplines will likely present many diverse writing occasions. According to a study of 179 syllabi from 17 different disciplines, professors assigned 40 different kinds of "papers" in one academic year. The same study found that 83% percent of undergraduates submitted, in one academic year, at least 60 pages of final-draft writing across all of their classes (Graves, et al.).

These figures demonstrate that, throughout your undergraduate experience, you will likely be expected to do a lot of writing across many different contexts, each of which will likely carry different criteria for success. Faculty assign many different kinds of papers, and their expectations about what effective writing looks like are contingent on the genre of the writing assigned, the purpose of the writing, established discourse practices within their disciplines, and individual dispositions.

Writer Insights

What different writing occasions have you traversed through in your life?

I am currently a sophomore in college....Back in my elementary school days, most of my writing was done in pencil/pen. Around third grade, I learned to write in cursive, but since middle school began, I have always been writing in print or typing everything out. Throughout elementary and middle school, I mostly only wrote whenever my teachers assigned...In 8th grade, I got a Facebook account, and that was when I started posting or commenting on statuses....[In] 11th grade...my brother taught me the importance of a good thesis. [Now] I am searching for internships, which reminds me that I need...good speaking skills. In order to get these speaking skills, I need to learn how to be a better writer. This will help me express my points in a better way when talking to other people, including my friends.

~Dan Hoang, College Student,
Cupertino, California, U.S.

Have students think this out.

Gaining acumen in transfer—an essential and complex habit of mind—will enable you to strengthen your abilities in all sorts of domains (not only writing), so you can be better prepared for the demands and opportunities of the twenty-first century. A transfer-based approach to writing will provide you with the opportunity to more effectively transfer your knowledge, ideas, and practices about and from writing to other contexts, thereby increasing your growth as a writer, thinker, and global citizen.

Transferring Writing Knowledge, Practices, and Approaches

> *Writer Insights*
>
> **Why is writing important in your life across different contexts and occasions?**
>
> I've been a…writer for many years…at school and university, at work and at home. In my childhood I often…was at the top of the class [for] writing essays, I wrote many letters to my relatives and friends, [and] I had a personal diary. Now I write emails, different kinds of papers for my job (reports, instructions, etc.)…I remember [once] I was asked to write a special thank you letter for an American school principal. To be honest it was not easy at all [but] thanks to collaboration with other people I managed to do it! It was my small success in writing.
>
> ~Marina Leonova, Vice Principal, Russia

This text foregrounds the ways in which writing is highly dynamic, moving and shifting across context. Chapter 1 offers an orientation to the text and to writing transfer, emphasizing how transfer will enable you to reflect on your learning abilities, gain increased awareness of what strategies work more or less effectively for you, and strengthen your intellectual acumen. With this approach, *Writing in Transit* empowers you to more effectively contribute your ideas, realize your dreams, and advance knowledge through writing across your undergraduate experience and beyond.

Each of the subsequent chapters builds on the foundation established in Chapter 1 by focusing on a key aspect of academic writing that aligns—with its own unique elements—across complementary writing contexts. Through these chapters, you can move through *Writing in Transit*, engaging with such aspects of writing as reading, research, and argumentation, across deeply distinct though overlapping disciplinary perspectives and writing contexts. Far from providing one perfect, universal approach, writing transfer instead involves cultivating a habit of mind where you learn to apply, modify, and revisit writing practices from one writing occasion to others, even as you also discover new approaches and strategies.

Consider the content of this book, then, an invitation for you to explore, read, discuss, and write about ideas that matter to you and others, and to discover how writing shifts across and within disciplines, time, and context. Consider *Writing in Transit* an invitation to learn more about yourself as a writer, thinker, learner, and citizen.

ℰ ℰ ℰ

Chapter 1 Key Terms

Transfer

Writing transfer

Disciplines

Discourse conventions

Discourse communities

Writing occasions

Modes of discourse

Write Away

Just as Chaco Canyon's Great Houses contained distinctive features as well as alignments, so too will your writing experiences. Essentially, your journey from one writing occasion to others throughout your college career and beyond will in some ways resemble a visit to a Great House, where you will move from room to room through aligned features. As a writer, you will find yourself transferring various writing practices, approaches, and skills to each new writing "room" you come to occupy, as well as discovering new approaches to writing along the way. This activity invites you to imagine your own writing trajectory as a "Writing Great House" by creating a visual depiction of all the different writing rooms—aligned and yet also discrete—that you will likely encounter across your college career and beyond.

Build or sketch out the beginnings of a Writing Great House. You can shape your great house any way you choose. Be as creative as you are inclined to be, selecting colors and design features that resonate with or reflect your experiences with and attitudes about writing.

Gradually add on writing rooms to your Writing Great House. Add "rooms" for all the different writing experiences you have had and that you anticipate having over the next few years of your education and beyond. To identify prior writing experiences, you can return to the Write Now timeline on page 7. To imagine future writing possibilities, consider any core education requirements you will be completing, as well as any potential majors or minors you might choose. Consider as well the writing you will engage in as construed more broadly, such as verbal presentations, online writing, professional writing, and personal writing. Label each writing room clearly to indicate what kind of writing experiences it has housed or will house.

Forge connections among rooms. Create connections—passageways, routes of exchange and transfer—among the rooms you have created. Which ones have more overlap than others? Which ones are located farther apart from one another? You, as a writer, will traverse the Great House through these connections and intersections.

Reflect on writing transfer. Reflect in writing about what skills or approaches you think you will need in order to be prepared as you move through all these writing rooms across your college career and beyond, finding alignments but also noticing distinctions. What aspects of writing are you already equipped to draw upon as you move within and between various writing occasions? What features of writing do you anticipate needing to strengthen, or perhaps even discard, as you encounter writing in transit throughout your Writing Great House?

Research and Writing as a Process

Building J, located at Monte Albán, in Oaxaca, Mexico, has been described as "one of ancient Mesoamerica's most enigmatic structures." Shaped like an arrow, Building J holds 40 stone slabs decorated with upside down heads and place names, believed to signify Zapotec conquests of different cities and regions. Building J has long puzzled scholars because it is "a rarity in Zapotec architecture…set at a 45-degree angle to the site's main axis [and opening] to the northeast." Aligned with "the rising position of Capella, the sixth-brightest star in the sky," Building J is often referred to as the 'observatory' (Aveni; Ching, Jarzombek & Prakash; Marcus; "Zapotec").

Monte Albán has earned status as a World Heritage Site in part because its buildings and structures were "literally carved out of the mountain." Architectural historians maintain that the "Zapotec elite constructed [Monte Albán as] a new administrative center" around 500 B.C.E. This date, however, marks only the beginning of an extended, phased process of construction and development across approximately 1500 years. Throughout these centuries, Monte Albán became, by turns, home to several different groups of people, at one point housing as many as 30,000 residents. In 850 C.E., for reasons that are still unknown, people began to abandon the area (Ching, Jarzombek & Prakash; "Historic"; Urcid & Joyce).

This lengthy trajectory wherein people built, expanded, and rebuilt Monte Albán foregrounds the iterative nature of progress and knowledge, the impact of context, and the complexity of process.

Changes in context and knowledge across time, for example, influenced site construction regarding agriculture. To contend with seasonal variations and slope erosion in the land surrounding Monte Albán, farmers "buil[t] terraces [which] retained sufficient soil and moisture to assure adequate and predictable production" (Garcia). To better forecast these seasonal shifts, farmers may have relied on astronomical indicators, perhaps explaining in part Building J's compelling architecture.

Likewise demonstrating the impact of long-term process and the importance of adapting approaches, be it with farming practices or knowledge itself, one Monte Albán scholar

revised his research claims about Building J after recognizing the centuries-long, phased construction of the site. In 1972, Anthony Aveni argued that Building J was aligned with the five brightest stars and also worked in concert with Building P to track the sixth brightest star, Capella. Subsequently realizing that different stars gained or lost visibility across the centuries of development, Aveni had to modify his claim to argue instead that Building J only tracked Capella and did so alone rather than with Building P ("Mound J"; "Zapotec").

The extended, iterative, adaptive, and recursive development process of Monte Albán mirrors in important ways people's research and writing processes. Rarely do writers produce discrete writing projects in linear, uninterrupted moments. Instead, and much like Monte Albán, research and writing processes often involve starts and stops, reflections, reconsiderations, adaptations, and additions over long periods of time.

Similarly, the growth process for writers themselves involves long-term effort, reconsideration, and adaptation. People are not generally born "good" writers. Even established writers like Maya Angelou acknowledge that writing is a long-term process: "Some critics have said I'm a natural writer. Well, that's like being a natural open-heart surgeon."

And here's the really tough news: being an effective writer requires this level of effort every time you write and even, retrospectively, after each writing occasion.

Of course, writers grow and improve over time, but writing remains challenging in part because nearly every writing occasion carries different expectations and conventions. Although writing and research processes have some relatively stable components across contexts, writers must tailor their processes with every writing project and thereby build a long-term trajectory of experiences and proficiencies that they can then transfer, adapt, and build on for new writing occasions.

Write Here

Monte Albán represents a centuries-long, iterative developmental process. Brainstorm a few other examples of a structure, concept, or place that has undergone a similarly long and complex developmental process. Choose one of these to explore further by reflecting in writing about the aspects of this structure, concept, or place that have been revised, expanded, or otherwise adapted across time.

 Transfer Hub: Contribute your ideas and see what others have written at fountainheadpress.com/transferhub.

Overview of the Research and Writing Process

Generally speaking, the academic research and writing process involves four recursive phases, all of which include research and feedback, and which, together, ultimately yield a final product: pre-writing, drafting, revising, and editing.

FIGURE 2.1 Phases of the writing process.

There are several defining features of these phases of the writing process—the way by which writers arrive at that final product—to keep in mind as you move through them.

The writing process is dynamic

Disciplinary context largely shapes the writing process, along with individual preferences and experience. Writers vary their processes across time, experimenting with different versions and reflecting on what works well in a given situation with a particular project, or what might need to be adjusted. Because the research and writing process is so dynamic, it is vital to reflect on your process continually so you can make choices more deliberately and evaluate how best to proceed on any given occasion.

The writing process is recursive

Writers rarely proceed in a linear manner from one phase of the research and writing process through to another. Instead, they circle back or jump ahead in a **recursive** manner as illustrated in Figure 2.1. As I wrote this book, for example, I spent time researching, pre-writing, then drafting, then back to pre-writing, and then included more research throughout. While I was revising I would sometimes edit, then continue drafting or return to pre-writing or to more research.

The writing process is social

The idea of a writer sitting alone, toiling away tirelessly at a document may be compelling, but more often than not, the research and writing process is intensely social. It involves interacting with others at nearly every stage. Sometimes this involves reading and engaging with others' texts, and other times it involves talking with readers, writers, and other scholars. In many disciplines, the social nature of writing and research emerges because of intensive collaboration and co-authorship. But even those disciplines that privilege single-authored texts still include a social component as writers solicit and provide feedback from others and engage with the work of others.

The writing process is context-dependent

The context of a particular writing project helps determine the shape of the research and writing process. Some writing occasions require longer processes, some shorter, some focus more heavily on one phase over another. Context involves many different components, including but not limited to assignment, discipline, timeline, expertise, purpose, and goals.

Writer Insights

Describe your research process.

Whenever I am asked to translate an article or a document, the same systematic process starts. First of all, I focus on gathering as much information as possible. I read and analyze data from related books, newspaper articles, and journals, both in English and Spanish.... [W]e, translators have to understand the message properly and... have detailed knowledge of the subject area.

~Lucía Inés Martinez, Translator and EFL Teacher, Tigre, Buenos Aires, Argentina

The writing process is individualized

While it is true that every writer has a research and writing process, that process varies drastically across writers. Different writers enjoy different parts of the process, and find different strategies for moving a piece of writing forward more or less effective. It's important to be experimental in one's approach and be willing to adapt and try new approaches, but it's also important to be aware of one's own preferences and strengths, even as they may change over time and across disciplinary context.

Research across Disciplines

Research is perhaps the most critical and ongoing component of academic writing and is deeply nested in disciplinary context.

An ethnomusicologist, for instance, might conduct research by listening to music, talking with people in musical groups, and then listening to the transcripts of those conversations. A literary scholar may instead conduct research by reading literature closely and critically and by locating and reading what other scholars have already written about that literature. A chemist, on the other hand, conducts much of her research through experiments in a lab.

Often, researchers invoke several different kinds of research for a project. In the examples above, for instance, it is likely that all three of those scholars, not only the literary scholar, would spend time researching published relevant scholarship so they could build on, push against, or otherwise advance what others have already written.

Research includes many different practices; some of the most common ones include:

- reading, listening to, or viewing the work of others
- analyzing texts, sounds, textures, or images
- conducting fieldwork (i.e. observations, interviews, data collection)
- gathering data and performing quantitative analysis
- conducting experiments and measuring and analyzing the results
- visiting an archive of materials

Each of these research strategies asks that the writer follow accepted conventions for what are known as **research methodologies**. Research methodologies are often rooted in disciplinary perspective. While they are highly complex (there are entire graduate-level courses devoted to research methodology!), they can be generally grouped into in one of three overlapping categories: qualitative research, quantitative research, and mixeed-methods research.

Qualitative research

Research that is **qualitative** relies primarily on observation and analysis of non-numerical data. According to Professor Michelle A. Saint-Germaine, Professor of Public Policy and Administration at California State University, Long Beach, qualitative methodologies are often used by "psychologists, anthropologists, sociologists, and program evaluators." Literary scholars and ethnographers also use qualitative research.

Writer Insights

Describe your research process.

I find research a great tool to detect and solve teaching and learning difficulties. Research is a systematic inquiry to understand something and make sense of issues of contemporary significance. So, to carry out a valid research project, we must develop some stages for effective research. First of all, this journey starts with a research question that allows us to focus on the matter we want to undertake. Secondly, we must carry out a literature review to support the topic or subject areas we want to develop. Then, we design the appropriate methodology and instruments to measure the study. Finally, it is relevant to analyze the data and come up with relevant conclusions. For developing these significant conclusions and the whole stages of the research project, writing is crucial for the scholar to outline the project. By doing this, the researcher is able to be focused, objective, reflective, and above all to share his/her research work with a specific community.

~ *Alexander Izquierdo Castillo,*
EFL Teacher and Researcher,
Bogotá, Colombia

Quantitative research

Quantitative research methodologies involve measurements and observation or analysis of numerical and *quantifiable* data. Disciplines that rely extensively on quantitative research might include statistics, computer science, engineering, biology, chemistry, and mathematics.

Mixed-methods research

This research relies on both qualitative and quantitative methods. Increasingly, researchers across disciplines are making use of **mixed-methods** approaches, either in their own research or through collaboration. Disciplines such as sociology, health-related professions, education, and business, for instance, are among those whose researchers regularly adopt mixed-methods approaches.

Another way research can be organized is through what are often overlapping categories between primary, secondary, or tertiary sources.

Primary sources

These are direct, firsthand sources. Examples of **primary sources** are interviewees for a survey in political science; art for an art history analysis course; or a novel in an English literature course.

Secondary sources

Secondary sources include materials that address a primary source. These might include scholarly or popular writing about a topic or subject, such as criticism about a novel.

Tertiary sources

Tertiary sources include compilations of primary and secondary sources that survey a particular area of research. These might include encyclopedias, almanacs, dictionaries, indexes, or other types of reference materials.

Decisions about which methodology to employ or how to navigate between primary, secondary, and tertiary sources will be shaped largely by the disciplinary context in which you are writing. Different disciplinary contexts use different approaches to research as a means of forwarding knowledge; disciplinary context and writing occasion can also impact how a particular source might be categorized. For instance, in an analysis of websites, a website would be primary, whereas in another writing occasion that same website might be considered secondary or tertiary. Being effective at research means not only that you can transfer not only specific research skills from one context to another, but also that you can transfer the ability to identify research methodologies and source distinctions within particular disciplines.

Write Now

Read one of the excerpted examples of argument located in Chapter 9: Constructing Arguments, and try to identify what kinds of research went into generating that argument. What methodology or methodologies do you think the author has employed? Where and when do you imagine the research was conducted? Can you tell if the research involved primary, secondary, and/or tertiary sources?

Pre-Writing Strategies across Disciplines

Pre-writing involves everything the writer thinks and writes before actually drafting the writing project. It blends deeply with the drafting phase and also overlaps with research. Pre-writing may entail thinking about a writing project, posing questions, reading, and conducting research. The purpose of pre-writing is to gather evidence, generate ideas, and explore topic ideas in order to move toward the drafting phase. Pre-writing also helps to "prime the pump" (Elbow), or get a writer in the mode of writing, and help the writer overcome writing blocks or difficulties getting started. There are many pre-writing strategies, some of which lend themselves more fittingly to particular disciplines. Review some of the more common pre-writing strategies and their guidelines to discover the approaches you can take to accomplish the pre-writing phase of the writing process.

Outlining

Use Roman numerals to outline the major and minor aspects of a topic or line of inquiry.

Journaling

Using paper or an electronic device, record your thoughts about a writing project in brief journal entries over an extended period of time, including random observations and ideas as they come to you. If you are more visually oriented, you could choose to draw images or take photographs that will help you develop your concept further. If you prefer to talk, then create audio journals using a recording device.

Reading

Read extensively in related texts, materials, or images. Seek out scholarly texts (academic journals and websites) as well as more popular texts (blogs, newspaper articles, other non-scholarly online sources), and related visual, aural, and tactile materials.

Note-taking

Many disciplines ask writers to take notes as part of the research pre-writing phase, such as interview notes in oral history, journalism, or sociology, and field notes in cultural anthropology or biology.

If you are in a discipline that does not use field notes or lab notes, or if you are writing a project that does not necessitate formal notes, you can write notes as you read related texts or encounter related events, by documenting what strikes you as significant, erroneous, interesting, and/or curious. Jot down anything that reminds you of something else someone argued or that seems to contradict another scholar's assertions or approaches. Identify gaps in the field where you can contribute to the conversation. Your notes can be in the form of text, audio, or visuals—be as creative as you wish. There are countless ways to compose notes; take a look at some of the various strategies you can use to achieve useful notes.

Talking

Spend several minutes talking about a writing project with another person or into a recording device. Address your main ideas, what you would like to accomplish, where you may be feeling stuck, and what you would like to include. Ask your listener to repeat back to you what she/he heard, and/or replay what you have recorded.

Walking

Sometimes getting outside and moving around while thinking or talking about your project can help generate progress.

Freewriting

Write for five minutes about anything that is in your head. You will not be sharing this writing, so don't worry about grammar or consistency. Try not to stop writing for the entire five minutes; if you run out of something to write, just write "I'm out of ideas" until the next idea rolls into your head.

Directed quickwriting

Spend five to ten minutes writing about a topic. Don't stop writing no matter what, even if you have to write "I feel stuck."

Looping

Do a directed quickwrite, then re-read it and pick one key term; use that key term as the beginning topic for another iteration of directed quickwriting. Repeat as many times as needed in order to explore a concept more fully. See Figure 2.2.

Directed freetalking

This is a modified version of directed quickwriting and entails one writer talking about his/her project for three full minutes to another individual. If possible, the listener then spends one full minute repeating back to the writer what he/she heard (note: not a response that includes what he/she thinks about it, but just repeating back what he/she heard). Then, the partners can reverse roles.

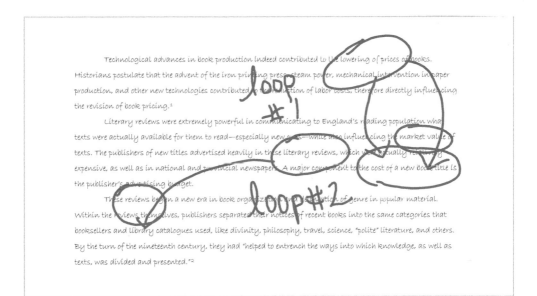

FIGURE 2.2 Example of looping.

FIGURE 2.3 Example of a Collaborative Brainstorm by a group generating ideas for a writing mashup project.

Brainstorming

Jot down as many ideas and thoughts as possible as quickly as possible. See Figure 2.3.

Concept mapping

Either on paper, or a document, or through an online concept-map generator, write down a main concept and draw a box or circle around it; then, branch out all around it with ideas; continue branching into sub-ideas. See Figure 2.4.

FIGURE 2.4 Example of a concept map about social media.

Data analysis

Examine the data you have collected and identify trends, patterns, divergences, significant findings, etc.

Posing questions

Use a heuristic, or guided template, to generate as many questions as possible about your area of inquiry. One useful heuristic is the journalist's 5 Ws and H.

Formulating hypotheses

Based on what you know or think about a given project, spend time writing down what you anticipate will be the outcome and why.

Writer Insights

How do you use concept maps?

[When] brainstorming for ideas, I use Mind Maps, which use bubbled maps to generate and record ideas and thoughts. One uses bubbles to jot down ideas and thoughts and connects them to similar ideas branching out of it. This creates a wide networked bubbled map and it makes the flow of ideas very easy and naturally without the need to write long sentences that may cause delay in the flow of thoughts. It makes it very easy to select relevant ideas and plots and the rest is easily discarded.

~Sweta Lal,
Creative Writer/Management Research Candidate,
Bentleigh East, Melbourne Area, Australia

Write Now

Think about a writing project you will be completing this term. Choose two of the above pre-writing strategies that make sense given the context of the writing occasion (discipline, project, timeline, aims, etc.) and spend five minutes trying out the technique.

Regardless of which pre-writing strategy a writer chooses, there are several critical factors that can help make pre-writing strategies more effective. Depending on the context, different writing occasions sometimes warrant different pre-writing strategies. For instance, if you are writing a personal narrative for a Creative Writing course about a difficult moment in your life, you may decide to do some freewriting just to get yourself mentally prepared to tackle a difficult subject. If you are writing about an electrical engineering research study for your Introduction to Engineering course, you probably want to generate a hypothesis and pose questions. If you are writing an historical analysis of the civil rights movement for an African and African-American Studies Course, you might opt for a concept map so you can think through the many aspects of this movement and decide where you want to focus your attention.

Think as creatively as possible so you can have lots of possible ideas to consider. Avoid questioning or limiting your pre-writing because you never know if an idea might be worthwhile. The point of pre-writing is often to generate as many possibilities and gather as much data as is reasonable given the project scope and timeframe of your endeavor.

Context helps writers determine which pre-writing strategies to adopt. **Context** includes such elements as the following:

- **Discipline:** What is the disciplinary context for this writing project?
- **Genre:** What options do you have for the genre of writing with this project? What genre makes the most sense?
- **Aims/Purpose:** To whom are you primarily writing? Why? What do you hope to accomplish with this writing project?
- **Timeline:** When is this writing project due? When should the various phases of the project be completed? When would you like to finish it?
- **Other:** Is this a collaborative or individual writing project?

Write Now

Think about a writing project you will be completing this term. Write for five minutes about your aims and purpose: What do you hope to accomplish with this piece of writing? Who do you hope reads it? Why? Where are you planning on sending/publishing the final version? How will your awareness of purpose and aims help shape your pre-writing plans for the writing project?

Transfer Hub: Contribute your ideas and see what others have written at fountainheadpress.com/transferhub.

Drafting across Disciplines

Drafting occurs when a writer moves from primarily pre-writing activities such as researching or brainstorming to composing the sentences and paragraphs of a piece of writing. This phase overlaps significantly with research, pre-writing, and revision. As with all parts of the writing process, there is no "right" or "wrong" way to draft. Some writers choose to draft an entire piece before revising; other writers will draft a portion of a text, then start revising that section before the whole project is written. Others might start in the middle of a piece of writing, and save the beginning or end for the end of the process.

Disciplines also impact how writers approach the drafting phase. In Archaeology, for instance, scholars spend most of their time with research and pre-writing, and then may "write-up," or draft, their findings in a relatively short period of time. By contrast, American Literature scholars may spend most of their time drafting as a means of discovering new insights into a period of literature or particular writing. A person writing a public-policy memo may find herself generating a succinct document in a very brief period of time; in that case, the entire process, drafting included, is abridged. Regardless of where on the continuum of drafting you find yourself for a writing occasion, there are a few tips for successful drafting to keep in mind.

Begin drafting early

Writers often delay the drafting phase because they feel like they need to spend more time doing research, analyzing data, or thinking about the project. In fact, drafting can often help solidify a project, and writers can often begin drafting certain parts of a project fairly early in the process. Starting sooner rather than later helps you get your ideas down and gets a writing project moving forward.

Establish a writing ritual

Whether you know it or not, you likely have writing rituals that you adopt when you write. Some people prefer to write to music, others in silence. Perhaps you have a favorite place to write, or a favorite writing implement or equipment. Or maybe you have an activity you engage in prior to writing that offers you a writing transition, such as going for a walk, or preparing a cup of tea or coffee.

These habits are not merely quirks but are important rituals writers use in order to be ready to engage with their writing. Sometimes these habits are static for a writer; other times they shift depending on the kind of writing a writer engages in. They also make writing fun.

Writer Insights

What is your writing process?

My writing process includes conversations with research providers; data analysis and development of business implications. I start by creating an outline of key points for the topic at hand. Then I compose a section for each point that details the research findings, explains how they would affect business decisions made by my colleagues, and illustrates the data with graphs. When all topics are complete, I compose a summary that introduces the general topic and touches the main points and their business implications. The next step is editing the draft, removing extraneous details, rewriting sentences to be understandable to both junior and senior colleagues, subtitling each section, and making sure the ideas flow logically and are relevant. The summary is presented at the start of the final version. It is emphasized by enclosing it in a box with a bold border that separates it from the rest of the text. Most of my colleagues will only read the report if they think it affects their own job, so it's important to grab their attention with the summary box at the start or they won't take the time to read beyond the first few paragraphs.

~Liz N., Advertising Research Director,
New York City, U.S.

Write Now

What are your writing habits or rituals? Do you engage in any activities that help transition you into writing? Where do you prefer to write? When? Write for five minutes on your writing rituals and habits. Share your ideas and see what others have written.

Transfer Hub: Contribute your ideas and see what others have written at fountainheadpress.com/transferhub.

Start anywhere and jump around

You don't need to start at the beginning of a writing project (unless you want to). Feel free to dive in anywhere in the project and move around as you wish. Drafting does not have to be a linear, sequential process.

Quiet your "inner critic"

Writing is already difficult, but it is often made more difficult by our own misgivings, insecurities, and ambivalences. Our "inner critic" is the negative voice inside our own heads that challenges our ideas, questions our capabilities, and sometimes prevents us from making progress on our writing. Kathleeen Kendall-Tackett, Acquisitions Editor for Hale Publishing, describes the "inner critic":

> For most writers, getting started is the hardest part. You may be bursting with good ideas. But somehow, what comes out on paper is…horrible. Because of that disconnect, it's easy to put writing off. A major reason writers procrastinate is that little voice inside our heads. It's the voice that tells you your writing is awful and will never improve. Talk with other writers and you'll find out what a common experience this is.

Kendall-Tackett, like many others, relies on the advice of author Anne Lamott, who emphasizes in *Bird by Bird*, that all writing begins needing work: "Almost all good writing begins with terrible first efforts. You need to start somewhere. Start by getting something—anything—down on paper."

Don't get stuck with details

Avoid focusing on the details such as grammar or perfect word choice. You can work on these aspects later in the revision and editing phases. Getting bogged down in the details during the drafting phase may hamper your progress. If you find yourself stuck on a detail, just insert a bracket with "return later" inside, and instead keep writing the rest of the sentence.

"Park on the downhill slope"

We all need breaks when writing, sometimes just to stretch or move around, other times to sleep, or most often because other aspects of our life need attending to. Busy college students may not have time to work on one writing project at a time in sustained ways. Expert writing advisor Joan Bolker urges writers to "park on the downhill slope" in order to make it easier to return and pick up the writing project again:

> [Y]ou'll come to a point at which you start to tire and feel like there's not much left in your writing reservoir for the day. This is the time to begin to summarize for yourself where you've been, to write down your puzzlements or unanswered questions, to do what Kenneth Skier, who taught writing at M.I.T. many years ago, calls "parking on the downhill slope": sketching out in writing what your next step is likely to be, what ideas you want to develop, or follow, or explore when you pick up the writing again the next day. This step will help you get started more easily each day, and it will save you an enormous amount of energy and angst.

Breaks are important. Writers need them to regain energy and to take a step back and think through the writing project. So take breaks, but try to plan your next writing steps proactively.

Revising across Disciplines

Writing is, at its core, about rewriting. **Revision** involves a writer rethinking his or her text. Revision generally involves global rethinking and restructuring, whereas editing involves smaller, more sentence-level changes and proofreading. Revision involves making changes to the structure, organization, and content of a project. Take a look at some strategies that can make your revising more effective.

Allow time and distance

Revision generally requires that a writer have time to rethink a text; this might involve stepping away from a text for a day, or several days, and returning to it with a fresh perspective.

Read aloud

Find a quiet place to read your text aloud. Mark moments in the text where you notice an aspect you would like to adjust. Read to make sure that you have accomplished what you hope to have accomplished, or that you have communicated the significance of your ideas. Think about structure, organization, and evidence.

Get feedback

Feedback is crucial to the revision process. An extended section on feedback is provided on p. 30, but for now, we suggest that you find several people you trust to read your draft and provide feedback on it to help you make it stronger.

Create a reverse outline

You are likely familiar with what an outline is. This version is called a "reverse outline" because it happens after a piece is written rather than before. A writer notes beside each paragraph a key phrase that captures what that paragraph communicated. After writing a phrase next to each paragraph, the writer can reflect on and perhaps reconsider such aspects of writing as overall organization, paragraph unity, and overall cohesion.

Overall organization

Does the sequence of paragraphs make sense? Is there anything missing? Does any material seem tangential or unnecessary? If so, that material might be deleted or connected more explicitly. Should the piece be organized differently?

Paragraph unity

Was it possible to develop a word or phrase to capture a paragraph? If not, the paragraphs might need to be divided differently.

Overall cohesion

Do all the parts of the paper work together to advance your main point and overarching purpose?

Writer Insights

Why is revision important in your writing?

Writing is the physical manifestation of thoughts, concepts and ideas. Words give form to abstractions bubbling out of the imagination. Laid side by side, these create sentences whose sole task is to impart the reader with a sense of pace and, if all goes to plan, drama. Getting at those right words and placing them in the right order takes time. Writing becomes re-writing, which becomes re-re-writing. All this calls for patience and trust that with a sustained effort, your initial idea will be captured out of abstraction and laid out for all to see.

~Benoit Detalle, Animation Scriptwriter and Animator, Belgrade, Serbia

Be open to change

Perhaps one of the biggest barriers to revision is the writer him- or herself. We get attached to a turn of phrase or concept, and may resist considering a new direction for our writing project. Be willing to rethink your piece. Sometimes revision can be frustrating as well because it unravels some of what you have accomplished, or makes you realize that you are not as far along as you may have hoped. This messiness and recursivity, though, is part of the writing process and rather than responding with denial or dismay, expect and embrace it.

Perhaps you have other revision strategies. No matter what strategy you adopt, be sure to engage in revision. Revising makes your writing stronger.

Figures 2.5, 2.6, and 2.7 show a writer, Katharine Krieger, moving through the drafting and revision process of an introduction to an article.

Notice in Figure 2.7 how much material Krieger changes during the process of revising.

Draft: Nov 23, 2010

Dating back almost a century, scientists have been interested in the behavior of animals. Information such as their habitat, reaction to environmental changes and interactions with other animals of the same and different species has been little understood until the past decade. The field of biologging has increased and improved exponentially with the improvements in technology. Tracking animals has gone from observing and taking notes on land mammals that could be seen, to satellite and other tracking technologies on marine animals, providing us with, in some cases, real time information of the temperature, salinity, depth and pressure of the water, along with their location, heart rate, and consumption (Roupert-Coudert, Wilson, pp. 438, 2005).

Biologging is defined as the study of animals' behavior, physiology, and ecology of free-ranging animals, especially that which cannot easily be observed (Davis, pp.12, 2008). More specifically, biologging is the study of animals, which are not easily observed, for example nocturnal animals, marine animals or very small animals. Each of these groups cannot be observed using conventional method's as there are restrictions on human's ability to see them for long periods of time.

Google Earth is a virtual globe that brings the user a 3-D interactive view of the earth containing endless information. The newest version, Google Earth 5, now allows users to explore beneath the oceans surface, seeing things such as coral reefs, trenches, and the movements of GPS-tracked marine life (Butler, para. 1, 2009). The importance of this science lies in the advancements that can be made in protecting the animals that are studied. The more that is understood regarding habitat and environments that endangered animals live, and how they react to stimuli such as global warming and pollution will undoubtedly lead to better protection of the animals.

The purpose of this article is to highlight the advancements in biologging marine animals, and show how Google Earth is helping this field to further develop and increase awareness of the issues surrounding these animals.

FIGURE 2.5 Early draft of Katharine Krieger's introduction to "Google Earth's Role in Marine Conservation through Biologging."

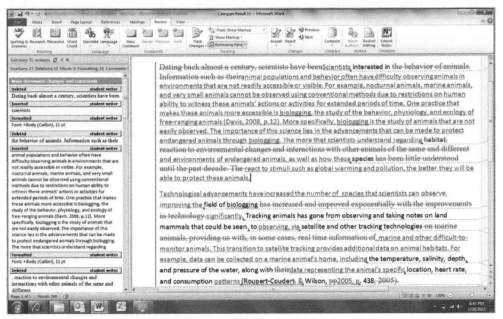

FIGURE 2.6 Krieger's revisions to the introduction to "Google Earth's Role in Marine Conservation through Biologging" (depicted through Microsoft Word's Compare Document Feature).

Published: Oct 28, 2011

Scientists interested in animal populations and behavior often have difficulty observing animals in environments that are not readily accessible or visible. For example, nocturnal animals, marine animals, and very small animals cannot be observed using conventional methods due to restrictions on human ability to witness these animals' actions or activities for extended periods of time. One practice that makes these animals more accessible is biologging, the study of the behavior, physiology, and ecology of free-ranging animals (Davis, 2008, p.12). More specifically, biologging is the study of animals that are not easily observed. The importance of this science lies in the advancements that can be made to protect endangered animals through biologging. The more that scientists understand regarding habitat and environments of endangered animals, as well as how these species react to stimuli such as global warming and pollution, the better they will be able to protect these animals.

Technological advancements have increased the number of species that scientists can observe, improving the field of biologging significantly. Tracking animals has gone from observing and taking notes on land mammals that could be seen to observing, via satellite and other tracking technologies, marine and other difficult-to-monitor animals. This transition to satellite tracking provides additional data on animal habitats. For example, data can be collected on a marine animal's home, including the temperature, salinity, depth, and pressure of the water, along with data representing the animal's specific location, heart rate, and consumption patterns (Roupert-Coudert & Wilson, 2005, p. 438). Until recently, however, technology allowing the spatial representation of this breadth of data has not kept up with advances in data collection technology.

FIGURE 2.7 Krieger's final version of the introduction to "Google Earth's Role in Marine Conservation through Biologging."

Write Now

What did Krieger change through the course of her revision? Can you identify the ways in which she improved her introduction?

Editing across Disciplines

Editing, as opposed to revision, generally involves smaller, local changes to a piece of writing. The editing phase occurs as a piece of writing is nearing the final version. Some depictions of the writing process include a final phase, termed proofreading, but we have decided to include proofreading in the editing phase. Commonly, writers work on the following aspects of writing as they edit:

- clarity
- grammar
- word choice/diction
- proofreading
- titles
- opening sentences
- closing sentences
- topic sentences

Editing usually involves short, small changes in order to polish a piece of writing and make it ready to share in a final version. Try to reserve editing until the latter stages of a piece of writing so that you don't spend valuable time getting the words of a sentence just right only to learn later as you revise that you are deciding to take out that sentence altogether.

Feedback Mechanisms within and across Disciplines

Feedback is one of the most crucial parts of the writing process, and, like research, is best located throughout every stage of the writing process. Feedback can be verbal or written, it can involve your own feedback to yourself or be from others, and it can be formal or informal. Throughout the process during which you receive feedback, keep certain strategies in mind to make feedback its most useful.

Integrate feedback throughout the writing process

Avoid waiting until you have a polished draft before asking for feedback. You can share writing or ideas at earlier stages in the process in order to help develop a piece of writing. You can also ask for feedback towards the end of a process.

Choose readers purposefully

Different readers will offer different strengths and perspectives Perhaps there is a disciplinary perspective that you would like to include. Perhaps you know someone who is working on a related project. Or, perhaps you've admired an aspect of writing or thinking in another and you would like his or her input. We can't always choose who is giving feedback to us, but if you have any input in the selection process, try to do so purposefully. Also aim for getting feedback from multiple readers. Each reader should have the potential to offer something valuable.

Sharing can be uncomfortable

If you are comfortable sharing your writing with others, good for you! But, if you are like many of us, you may feel nervous sharing your writing. Getting used to sharing your writing,

though, will make you a better writer. Receiving feedback helps you grow as a writer overall, and it helps you improve a particular writing project. Writers at all levels in all disciplines, especially professors or researchers, must submit their writing to peers for review before their work is published in academic journals or books. See Figure 4.2 on p. 63 to learn more about this process.

Write Now

Think back to moments in the past where you have provided or received feedback on a piece of writing. The feedback could be from a peer, friend, colleague, or teacher. What makes feedback more or less effective? Do you remember any particular feedback you received? What makes this feedback stand out? What's hard about providing feedback to others? Share your ideas and see what others have written.

Offer your readers feedback guidelines

When you ask for feedback, avoid just asking "What do you think?" Also try to avoid asking yes/no questions. Instead, share with them what your main concerns are, what you would especially like feedback on, where you were stuck or uncertain as a writer. For example, you might ask any of the following questions: Which evidence did you find most effective? What other evidence would be helpful for my argument? I struggled on page 4 with the [insert specific] section; what do you think that paragraph is trying to accomplish or communicate? Which elements of my introduction enable you to become interested in the writing project? As much as possible, try to avoid asking readers to copyedit (at least not until later in the process); substantive feedback should really be more about the

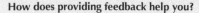

Writer Insights

How does providing feedback help you?

I am a biomedical scientist, and my latest writing task is a systematic review paper. Since English is my second language, writing in English has been an exciting challenge. The same way English is language of the academic world, written communication is the most common form of communication in science. In addition to writing letters, scientific papers and course assignments, I also review the writing of my co-workers which is a great opportunity to improve my writing skills and help people with theirs.

~D., Biomedical Scientist,
Porto Alegre, Brazil

ideas and substance of the writing, not the more surface aspects.

Be open and flexible

If you think you've written a perfect final version and then you share it with others, you will likely be disappointed with their feedback. Feedback involves more than just putting a stamp of approval on it. Be willing to consider others' ideas and be open to change.

Make productive use of feedback

If a writer doesn't make productive use of feedback, then the feedback is not being put to good use. Try to listen carefully to what your readers are saying and think about how you might respond to their feedback in order to strengthen your writing.

Don't forget the more challenging suggestions

Sometimes academic writers might be inclined to focus on feedback that is easier to address than that which is more complicated. For instance, it is fairly easy to fix typos, change words, or even revise a first sentence or final sentence. Much more challenging would be to delete an entire section that seems tangential, or reframe the argument more completely. Making meaningful use of feedback entails a willingness to address the more complicated aspects.

Take time reviewing feedback, and let it digest

After you receive feedback, consider waiting a little while before you implement the suggestions. Read and re-read the feedback so you can let it digest and you can think about how you are going to revise. Sometimes feedback can seem overwhelming, but waiting a few days usually enables you to find renewed energy to revise a writing project.

If the feedback is unclear, ask for more feedback

Do not settle for less than satisfactory feedback. If you can return to the reader, do so, or find another reader who will provide more substantive feedback. While we may all as writers like to hear "It's great." However, that kind of feedback on its own will not necessarily help us revise. If different readers provide contradictory feedback, accept that this is part of readers as individuals rather than thinking one person is right or one person is wrong. Different readers respond differently. You can arbitrate between contradictory feedback and/or get another opinion entirely.

If the feedback is harsh, revise it in your own mind

Sometimes writers encounter overly negative feedback and respond by ignoring the feedback. For instance, if a responder says that your writing is "awkward and choppy," you can revise that comment in your head to, "Your writing will work better with longer sentences and careful word choice."

If you disagree with feedback, you can reject certain portions of it

You are the writer, after all, and you can decide what you ultimately want to do with your text.

You can provide your own feedback, too

When you allow yourself to gain some distance from your text, you can also revise a writing project and provide feedback on your own writing.

Feedback is always valuable

Writing transfer emphasizes that you will move forward as a writer even after individual pieces of writing are completed. Accept and solicit feedback even on a final product so you can use that feedback as a way to move forward with related projects, extend ideas, or grow as a writer.

Providing feedback helps you become a stronger writer

Offer to provide feedback to others! Doing so not only helps their writing, but helps your writing too. You can identify ideas and aspects of writing that you would like to continue thinking about or extend, or model your own work on.

Transfer and The Final Product

In academic writing, a final product is not an end, necessarily, so much as the moment when your writing becomes more public so that others can engage with your ideas and thereby continue the conversation. Of course, some writing is meant only to be read by the person who wrote it, and some writing is written without even the intention of being read at all. But academic writing, for the most part, is generally read by others so that scholars can contribute to and advance knowledge based on engaging with others' texts.

Academic writing takes many shapes and forms across disciplines. Some writing appears in books (or as books), as articles in

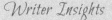

Writer Insights

How do you know when you have a final product?

I just received notice that a scientific manuscript for which I am lead author was accepted for publication in a respected peer reviewed journal. The acceptance came after the editor requested a substantial rewrite, which led me to reconsider and reconceptualize the way I presented my study. Applying the peer feedback, engaging in critical thinking and articulating a compelling rebuttal letter were important steps that helped turn a possible rejection into a publication. I am left with a physical feeling of accomplishment and growth.

~Deirdre Dingman,
Postdoctoral Fellow with Public Health Law Research,
Temple University, Philadelphia, Pennsylvania, U.S.

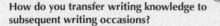

Writer Insights

How do you transfer writing knowledge to subsequent writing occasions?

I am a writer working in Tokyo. Since I first became a copywriter in 1989, I have been changing my writing style and focusing area. I wrote in advertising for about a decade, then I became a writer for a history magazine. After working in the editorial office, I started a web design business by myself in the 2000s. And in recent years, I have co-authored web articles and books with scientists. These works may look similar, but they are diverse in backgrounds, interests, and cultures. So each time I moved to another field, I had to take on a new challenge. Now I am engaged in another one: becoming a writer in English. Through my experience, I think that switching to a new field has only good effects for improving writing skills. I anticipate that it will bring the most revolutionary reform to my writing.

~Rue Ikeya, Writer, Research Administrator,
Tokyo, Japan

scholarly journals, or in more popular forms of writing such as op-eds, blogs, memos, policy papers, and reviews. But across all these possible formats, academic writing, at its best, sponsors more writing and research, be it by the original authors or by others encountering that text.

But, even though academic writing participates in an ongoing conversation, a final product does mark an ending point of a kind. Sometimes writers may not feel ready for a writing project to be finished, but a deadline might demand that it be finished. Or, sometimes a writing project has just reached its natural conclusion. Regardless, it is important to acknowledge that a piece of writing does at some point live as a final product, a material artifact of your thoughts and research at a given moment in time (even if in cyberspace).

However, even as you take a moment to acknowledge this moment of closure, it is vital that you also recognize that you will encounter subsequent writing projects. Because writing transfer hinges in large part on your ability to adapt, modify, reject, or translate what you learn from a previous writing occasion when a new writing occasion occurs, it is important to reflect on your experience with writing at this final juncture. As King Beach advises, transitions are not all created equally, and for a transition to be meaningful, it should include reflection: "A transition is *consequential* when it is consciously reflected on, struggled with, and shifts the individual's sense of self or social position."

To help make your writing transitions as "consequential" as possible, reflect on what you have learned and how you are planning to move forward.

Post-project reflection questions

- What did you like best about the process of writing this text?
- What did you like least about the process of writing this text?
- What did you learn about yourself as a writer from this writing experience?
- Identify several upcoming writing projects, in or out of school, that you intend to complete. How do you think you can draw from this most recent writing experience to strengthen your approach to each of these next ones?
- What do you hope to continue working on in terms of your writing for subsequent writing occasions?

Addressing these questions thoughtfully as you complete writing projects will help you cultivate a habit of mind grounded in writing transfer, one that enables you to navigate more successfully through the many writing occasions you will encounter both in and outside of school settings.

Transferring the Research and Writing Process

These phases of the research and writing process provide writers with a way to navigate through writing projects that may otherwise seem daunting or overly complex. Pre-writing, drafting, revising, and editing, with research and feedback throughout, enable writers to develop worthwhile final products that advance knowledge and contribute to ongoing conversations.

As indicated throughout this chapter, it is crucial to keep in mind the ways in which context impacts the research and writing process. With some writing projects, you may find it necessary to focus most of your energies and time on research; with others, revision might take precedence. Still other writing occasions may demand that writers compress these phases into a shorter overall timeframe. Becoming effective at transfer means that you can draw on these general phases of the research and writing process but customize them to meet the particular needs and constraints of any given writing occasion.

Building on what you have learned in this chapter about the research and writing process, the next chapter invites you to consider how writers pose meaningful questions. Questions are often that which actually animate the research and writing process, providing the jumping-off points for research, pre-writing, and drafting, and the anchor points for revising, editing, and feedback. As Chapter 3 illustrates, questions are also that which sponsor ongoing inquiry that builds on final, published products.

ℰ ℰ ℰ

Chapter 2 Key Terms

Writing process	Mixed-methods research	Drafting
Recursive	Primary sources	Revising
Research methodologies	Secondary sources	Editing
Quantitative research	Tertiary sources	Feedback
Qualitative research	Pre-writing	

Write Away

Context deeply impacts the research and writing process. This chapter's activity asks you to conduct and produce an interview of another writer in which you find out about his or her research and writing process. Follow these steps (notice that these steps themselves involve phases of the research and writing process).

Find a writer to interview (pre-write and research). Think about a person you might interview in order to learn more about his or her research and writing process from the perspective of his or her particular discipline or context. This writer can be a faculty member, administrator, or graduate student at your institution whom you would like to get to know, or it can be a peer acquaintance. You might interview a family member, friend, or other acquaintance, someone younger or older than you, and you can conduct the interview virtually, by phone, or in person.

Develop interview questions (pre-write, research, and feedback). To develop your interview questions, work in small teams with your classmates. Think about what questions you will ask (and how many) that will enable the interviewee to share specific details about his or her research and writing process. Since your interviewee is likely to write across several different contexts, you might invite him or her to think in particular about one or two recent writing occasions as they describe their process. Keep in mind as well that your interviewee might not know as much about the phases and features of the research and writing process as you do!

Select an interview format (pre-write, research, and feedback). Decide, in consultation with your interviewee, what format you would like to use for creating your interview: a brief written article, a PowerPoint or Prezi, an audio account (such as a podcast), a video, or some other format or combination. Deciding in advance will enable you to procure any necessary technology. Use a format in which you have some experience, so that you are not taking on too many new challenges at once.

Conduct the interview (research). Conduct the interview using your interview questions as a guide, but allowing yourself the flexibility to also let the conversation move forward organically. During the interview, take particular care to understand the context (genre, discipline, aims, audience, etc.) surrounding the particular research and writing process your interviewee is describing. Be sure to have a way of archiving the interview so you will not lose the material.

Create and develop your final product (draft, revise, edit, and feedback). Create and develop the final version of your interview, using the format you have decided upon. Verify with your interviewee whether you should use his/her name or use a pseudonym. Share a somewhat polished draft of the interview with your interviewee and invite that individual to make any adjustments or changes they believe would better capture what they had to say.

Share your interview (feedback). Share the interview final product with your classmates.

 Transfer Hub: Contribute your ideas and see what others have written at fountainheadpress.com/transferhub.

Reflect (transfer). After you have examined the interviews created by your classmates, write for ten minutes to reflect on what you have learned from this experience about the interview process and/or what you have learned from the interviews about how you might transfer portions of the research and writing process across contexts and disciplines.

Posing Meaningful Questions

Pinpointing Chapter 3

Chapter 3 deepens and extends the ideas from Chapter 2 by addressing how writers develop and pose questions as part of their research and writing process. The parameters of questioning and the process for developing them may vary extensively, but writers throughout all disciplines pose questions, sometimes explicitly and sometimes implicitly. To provide you with strategies for *posing questions in transit*, this chapter addresses the following concepts:

- Disciplinarity and Questions
- Writers Posing Questions: Examples from across Disciplines
- Characteristics of Effective Questions
- Strategies for Posing Meaningful Questions

Chapter 4 advances these strategies by exploring how academic writers read others' texts and, in so doing, have occasion to see how writers actually pursue the questions they pose through their research and writing.

The Egyptian pyramids at Giza, constructed between 2600 and 2450 B.C.E., have fascinated humans for centuries. The largest pyramid on the site, the pyramid of Khufu, is composed of "2½ million blocks of limestone, which weigh from 2 to 70 tons each." The pyramids' enormity and precision have prompted some people, known as "alternative theorists," to surmise that the pyramids were built by "aliens or by people from the mythical land of Atlantis." Most scholars, however, agree that the pyramids were built as part of a royal undertaking ("Giza"; "Introduction"; Magli).

Herodotus, in one of the earliest known writings about the pyramids, claims that King Khufu enslaved the laborers who built the pyramids and, to help pay for the enormous construction costs, "put his own daughter in a brothel and made her charge a fee." Modern Egyptologists, however, have suggested that Herodotus's narrative of Khufu's oppression and cruelty was erroneous, and that those involved with the pyramids' construction did so on a voluntary basis in order to be affiliated with an endeavor they believed to be glorious and worthwhile (Clark).

Whether Khufu motivated those who built the pyramids through cruelty or inspiration, most scholars agree that the Great Pyramid of Khufu served as his royal tomb. Mathematical physicists have noted that the pyramid, oriented precisely to true north, aligns with the sun to create symbolic significance: "[T]he complex was called Akhet Khufu because it actually was precisely that: the Akhet—the horizon—belonging to [King] Khufu" ("Giza"; Magli).

As scholars learn more about who built the pyramids and why, remaining mysteries endure, prompting scholars to pose and pursue new questions about the pyramids. Recently, a team of engineers and computer scientists curious to learn what was in the depths of the pyramids, used a "climbing robot named 'Djedi'" to explore hidden areas, revealing long-unseen hieroglyphics (Richardson, et al.). Physicists, wondering how Egyptians moved the heavy limestone, recently determined that Egyptians could have transported building materials with far fewer people than previously believed by adding water to sand and thereby enabling greater "sliding friction" (Fall, et al.). And archaeologists, seeking to learn more about how ancient Egyptians used the pyramids, have recently identified buildings that likely served as grain silos or bakeries, and they have discovered "numerous bones from the forelimbs of cattle," likely indicating that ancient cult worship and offerings took place at the pyramids (Jarus).

Questions from many different disciplinary perspectives, as illustrated by this research, persist regarding the pyramids: Classics Professor Donald Redford asks questions about how the pyramids were built; Professor of Theology and Religious Studies, Jeremy Naydler, poses questions about the intersections between religion and Egyptology; Professor of Oriental Studies, Kate Spence, pursues questions about how the Egyptians were able to so accurately align the pyramids to true north (McCauley).

But the pyramids are not unique in sponsoring this preponderance of questions. Scholars across all fields spend much of their time posing questions about all sorts of ideas, entities, people, periods, and texts. Answers, when discovered, serve more often than not as jumping-off points for new questions: "[I]n research," remarks Nobel Laureate Salvador Edward Luria, 1969 Winner for Physiology or Medicine, "there are no final answers, only insights that allow one to formulate new questions."

Asking meaningful questions, pursuing avenues of curiosity, and discovering new areas of **inquiry** are among the most important and rewarding aspects of academic writing. Unfortunately, many students become accustomed instead to teachers posing questions, such as with assignment prompts or essay exams. These students may then perceive that questions are not part of their own work. These students may regrettably assume that their main responsibility is not only to drum up answers, but to find the right answers and defend them as vigorously as possible.

Writing in Transit works against that model by showing how writers across disciplines—at all levels of experience—pose questions in order to advance knowledge.

Write Here

What research questions might a biologist ask about the pyramids? An anthropologist? An economist? Brainstorm as many questions, from as many different disciplinary perspectives as you can, about the Giza Pyramids.

 Transfer Hub: Contribute your ideas and see what others have written at fountainheadpress.com/transferhub.

ᗰ ᗰ ᗰ

Disciplinarity and Questions

Disciplines are in many ways defined by **questions**. According to the website physics.org, for instance, "Physicists ask really big questions like: How did the universe begin? How will the universe change in the future? How does the Sun keep on shining? What are the basic building blocks of matter?" Similarly, the website for the English Department at Illinois State University describes its discipline in the form of questions: "In English Studies multiple and interdisciplinary perspectives are used to examine and produce texts for audiences communicating in English: how do cultures shape language and how does language shape culture; how do intersections of cultures affect communication across borders; what forms can we

Writer Insights

What current research questions are you focusing on?

The questions that occupy my thoughts are those about ways to empower students to learn a new language in an unprivileged context. Also, those about how to teach English to students in an EFL context and how to help them change their lives in the process! As a teacher trainer, I ask myself about how to help teachers become better professionals who can generate change in our nation. I wonder about how to make a better country every day and I know it is through education and better opportunities!

~Carolina R. Buitrago, Lecturer and Researcher,
English Language Teaching Master's Program,
Universidad de La Sabana, Bogotá, Colombia

create to connect and enter into dialogue with each other?"

Many questions, of course, traverse disciplinary boundaries. John Brockman, founder of *edge.org*, poses these kinds of more universally applicable questions each year, inviting prestigious thinkers from different fields to share their thoughts on such queries as, "What should we be worried about?"; "What have you changed your mind about? Why?"; and "What are you optimistic about?"

While widely applicable questions sponsor engaging cross-disciplinary conversations, they offer only a partial glimpse of the role of questions in academic writing. Most academic questions, that is, emerge from within and are shaped by disciplinary context.

Brockman's 1998 query, in which he asked, "What Questions Are You Asking Yourself?" illustrates how disciplinary perspective shapes academic questions. Notice in each of the following "answers" how each scholar poses a question that emerges from within his or her disciplinary frame.

Christopher Stringer
Research paleoanthropologist at the Natural History Museum, London; Author, *Lone Survivors;* **Co-Author of In Search of the Neanderthals; Co-Author of** *African Exodus*

"What was the key factor in the success of Homo sapiens compared with other human species such as the Neanderthals?"

Charles Simonyi
Chief Architect, Microsoft Corporation; Software Engineer; Computer Scientist; Entrepreneur; Philanthropist

"Does reality have real numbers?"

Elaine Pagels
Harrington Spear Paine Professor of Religion at Princeton University; Author, *Revelations;* **Author,** *The Gnostic Gospels;* **Author,** *The Origin of Satan*

"Why are religions still vital?"

Of course, sometimes scholars step outside of disciplinary boundaries, as in the following question submitted by technology correspondent Katie Hafner, who opts to ask about history.

Katie Hafner

Technology Correspondent, *New York Times;* **Author,** *Where Wizards Stay Up Late*

"Why does history matter?"

But Hafner's case and others like it aside, most scholars' questions emerge from within a disciplinary context.

Notice in the following excerpts from different disciplines the many different questions scholars ask about one topic, in this case Pompeii art by way of example.

As you read these four excerpts, look for implicit and explicit questions, as well as for the ways in which each excerpt illustrates how academic writers in disciplines advance knowledge through questions and how they articulate the significance of their lines of inquiry.

> ### *Writer Insights*
>
> **What's important about posing effective questions?**
>
> Science is a field where writing is a very powerful tool. A well-written question is the key for a complete research in fact, everything orbits around the right question, so a mistake using a wrong verb or noun, can mean a disaster.... [W]riting is not only a combination of words, but also a collection of interpretations. A question can be grammatically correct, even elegant, and fail when other researchers read it. That makes language a complex process.
>
> ~ *Alma Dzib Goodin, Neuroscientist, Chicago, Illinois, U.S.*

Write Now

I wonder...? What if...? How does...? Why did...? What are you curious about? What questions matter to you? Why? Brainstorm several general questions—about anything or several things—that you find interesting and/or important. Then, for each of these questions, identify a smaller subset of questions that might emerge from various disciplinary perspectives, as a way of gaining practice refining and tailoring questions inflected by perspective.

Writers Posing Questions: Examples from across Disciplines

Example 1: Disciplinary Questions, Chemistry, and Pompeii Art

Excerpt from "Evaluation of Corrective Measures Implemented for the Preventive Conservation of Fresco Paintings in Ariadne's House (Pompeii, Italy)" by P. Merello, F. Garcia-Diego, and M. Zarzo

The long-term preservation of wall paintings in open-air sites or semi-confined environments is a challenge due to the difficulty in providing optimum ambient conditions. In such cases, the deterioration process of paintings is determined by many factors such as petrographical and chemical characteristics of the materials, presence of mineral salts and organic substances on the surfaces, air pollution, sunlight, heating, water content of the surface, etc.... The house of Ariadne or dei capitelli colorati (of the colored capitals) is one of the most interesting places in ancient Pompeii (Italy).... Although most interior walls were originally ornamented with frescoes, the paintings have suffered severe damages since the excavation of Ariadne's house in 1832-1835. At present, original frescoes are only conserved in three rooms that were sheltered with transparent polycarbonate sheets in the 1970s...Mural paintings of Ariadne's house have undergone deterioration processes in the last decades, and a research project was launched in 2008 to assess their conservation state by means of microclimate monitoring, thermography, study of materials, solar radiation, characterization of salt efflorescence, etc.... The present work performs a comparative statistical analysis of data recorded in 2008 and 2010 (summer periods) aimed at evaluating the effect of roof change on the microclimate conditions surrounding the valuable fresco paintings. Results provide guidelines for additional corrective measures.

> Merello, Garcia-Diego, and Zarzo are asking questions here about how chemicals in the atmosphere impact the deterioration process of Pompeii art.

> In 2008 researchers in chemistry asked, How can we assess the "conservation state" of murals in Ariadne's house?

> Here they are asking, what is the effect of roof change on microclimate conditions around the paintings?

> We learn that these chemists care about this question in order to advance long-term preservation through chemical "corrective measures."

From *Chemistry Central Journal*, 2013.

Example 2: Questions in Disciplines, Art History, and Pompeii Art

Excerpt from "Before Pornography: Sexual Representation in Ancient
Roman Visual Culture" by J. Clarke

The study of ancient visual representations of sexual activity reveals the modernity of the
term 'pornography.' Not only is pornography a modern word, its genesis
lies in modern collecting practices that so isolated ancient erotic objects
from their contexts as to render them meaningless.

> Clarke is here asking, what is the history of erotica collection in museums?

Beginning with the Renaissance, wealthy collectors assembled collections of Greek and Roman sculptures, vase paintings, mosaics, ceramics, small bronzes and gems with sexual representations, calling them

> Clarke asks, what are the origins of the term pornography and how have people decided to categorize certain art as pornographic?

'erotica.' The discovery of Herculaneum (1738) and Pompeii (1748) brought about an explosive proliferation of such objects.... We have the German scholar, Karl Otfried Müller, to thank for the term 'pornography,' borrowed from the Green word *pornographos*. We know that *pornographos* was literally a 'whore-writer,' that is, an author who wrote about the famous accomplished prostitutes of the time, called *pornai*.... What prompted Müller to coin the word 'pornography' was embarrassment. With increasing rapidity the excavations of the cities buried by Vesuvius turned up paintings, mosaics, bronze objects and terracottas that shocked the excavators.... In 1819, during the period of the Bourbon restoration, Ferdinand, King of the Two Sicilies, ordered his curator of antiquities, Michele Arditi, to sequester all objects that could be considered obscene by

> Clarke here is interested in the following questions: what are the social and cultural influences on museum collecting practices? How do social and cultural influences shape collecting practices?

> Clarke asks, what were ancient Roman attitudes toward sexual images?

the standards of his time. In 1823 the name of this collection was changed to the Cabinet of Secret Objects and sealed with a brick wall for good measure.... [A]t about the same time the British Museum formed the so-called Museum Secretum, and the museums in Florence, Madrid and Dresden followed suit. All of these rooms were filled with ancient Greek and Roman objects considered to be obscene. Rather than seeing this as a common-sense curatorial decision, I would like to question the social and cultural forces that or-

From *Pornographic Art and the Aesthetics of Pornography*, 2013.

phaned these objects, separating them not only from their architectural and archaeological contexts, but also keeping them from public view...My main concern in both of my books on ancient sexual representation was to understand ancient Roman attitudes towards sexual images with Roman eyes...I wanted to put aside modern notions of pornography and the obscene. One of my strategies was to find out where the sexually explicit objects in the Pornographic Collection in Naples came from and put them back into their original settings. In this way, I could reconstruct the ancient experience, the situations where men, women, and children originally looked at what we today consider pornographic.

> Clarke explains that his questions are significant because they enable us to "reconstruct the ancient experience."

Example 3: Questions in Disciplines, Literature, and Pompeii Art

Excerpt from "Imperial Decadence: The Making of the Myths in Edward Bulwer-Lytton's The Last Days of Pompeii" by W. St Clair and A. Bautz

> St Clair and Bautz ask, how have excavations been depicted and represented in art and artistic productions?

Ever since the discovery in 1749 of the remains of Pompeii, ... the excavations have yielded rich materials for understanding the daily life of the Roman Empire. They also featured as themes in contemporary European design, art, and music, including opera. In the nineteenth century, previously diverse elements were unified into a romantic mythic narrative, fixed in material form, disseminated, consolidated, imported to Pompeii, naturalised, and then re-exported.

> St Clair and Bautz are asking questions about publication history of a novel.

This process is evident in the publication history of Edward Bulwer-Lytton's novel, *The Last Days of Pompeii* (1834). Taking in the spin-offs and feedbacks of theatre, songs, opera, pantomime, the circus, high and popular art, and book illustrations, we use quantified information about readerships and viewerships from archival and other primary sources to show how, within the economic and technological governing structures of the Victorian age, cultural consumers cooperated with producers to invent myths and clichés still vigorous today.

From *Victorian Literature and Culture,* 2012.

The *Last Days of Pompeii* begins with a scene of wealthy Pompeians sauntering through the streets of Pompeii where they encounter Nydia, a blind slave girl selling flowers. This casual meeting between her and the rich Greek Glaucus introduces the storyline. Nydia, who soon loves Glaucus across the insuperable social divide, is purchased by him and presented as a gift to the beautiful and virtuous Greek heiress, Ione, who is the ward of Arbaces, an Egyptian priest of the religion of Isis.... Suddenly the volcano erupts and buildings shake and fall to the ground as the city is torn open by earthquakes.... In the darkness and confusion of the last day only the blind Nydia can find her way through the rubble-strewn streets, and she leads Glaucus and Ione to the port. On the voyage to Athens, however, Nydia throws herself into the sea, suicide being allowed by ancient eth-

> St Clair and Bautz ask, what are the traditions within which authors position themselves and from which they draw?

ics.... Her death makes way for the socially matched, newly converted, Christian couple to live together happily ever after.

When Bulwer wrote and published *The Last Days of Pompeii*, he was inserting himself into a tradition ... He was able to draw on and adapt a wealth of cultural production relating to Pompeii and its destruction as offered to different types of cultural consumers in a variety of media across Europe. And in some cases it can be shown from the biographical record that he had direct knowledge of his predecessors, both ancient and recent. Among recent predecessors were paintings, volcanic spectacles, literature and travel writing, and opera, yet none of these, either individually or to-gether, came close to being as influential as his novel was to become.

> Here, St Clair and Bautz ask direct questions about the text and its publication history, and indirect questions about the reception and influence of "adaptations and spin-offs."

The main focus of this essay is on the materialities of the production and diffusion of the ideas in the *Last Days*, asking questions such as how did the text come to be written in the form that it was, who had access to the book, when, in what numbers, in which versions, and with what consequences? The essay also explores the materiality of the adaptations and spin-offs—theatre, songs, opera, pantomime, the circus, high and popular art, and book illustrations—that both influenced the text of the novel by being anticipated, and then helped to shape readerly and viewerly respons-es and interpretations.

> St Clair and Bautz show that the significance of their questions is that art can shape our responses to and interpretations of historical events.

Example 4: Questions in Disciplines, Archaeology, and Pompeii Art

Excerpt from "Painted Birds at Pompeii" by B. A. Sparkes

Birds come in all shapes and sizes, and the evidence for their study is similarly diverse. When studying birds for archaeological purposes, the remains of the actual bones are obviously of the utmost significance. However, it is also important to consider written evidence from previous periods to see what earlier writers observed or inferred about the appearance, habits and habitats of birds. Allied to this is the visual evidence in the form of objects such as stone carvings, bronze figurines, coin dies, gem engravings, mosaics and paintings on different materials such as wood, canvas, silk, and terracotta. When we turn our attention to the visual images of the Mediterranean cultures of the Greeks and Romans in classical antiquity (1000 BC to AD 500), we see that the Greeks showed a serious interest in birds in their literature and art. They appear as the 'familiars' of the gods and goddesses, such as Zeus's eagle, Athena's owl and Aphrodite's doves, and they are also part of their myths and legends, such as Leda and the swan, and Prokne and Philomela as nightingale and swallow. Their coins carry birds as symbols of various cities; their tombstones show birds as pets of children and adults or as symbols of another life; and vase-paintings include birds as elements in patterns and as characters in narratives of myth and everyday life. When we move down to the Roman period, the evidence is equally full. We have Roman writers such as Varro, Columella and Pliny the Elder, who give basic information on the varieties of birds and their habitat, and the artists of the day had a much greater interest than the Greeks in representing nature for its own sake in their art. Trees, plants, animals and birds form the subject matter of many of their works of art, particularly their wall-paintings. In the cities, towns and country villas of Roman Italy in the first centuries BC and AD, house and villa owners were enthusiastic in having the walls in the different rooms of their houses covered with complex wall-paintings: dining rooms, bedrooms, halls, courtyards and others. The wall-paintings acted as one way of demonstrating their status and position in society. The best preserved examples of this decoration are to be found in Pompeii and the other Campanian towns that were buried by the volcanic eruption of Vesuvius in AD 79.

> Sparkes is asking, what evidence can we use to learn more about ancient birds?

> Sparkes wonders, what roles did birds play in ancient civilizations?

> Sparkes asks, what kinds of wall-paintings existed and in what ways were they markers of social status?

From *International Journal of Osteoarchaeology*, 1997.

Write Now

Using a research-based text of your choosing, identify the main questions informing that text. What explicit questions are included in the text? What are the underlying, or implicit, questions sponsoring the research?

Although none of these examples fully represents the discipline from which it emerges (disciplines are far too varied and dynamic), we can nonetheless glean a considerable amount about how scholars pose questions and construct knowledge within disciplinary contexts. From these examples, we learn that chemists (these chemists anyway) ask questions about chemical elements and test which ones are most effective for their purposes; art historians ask questions about museum collecting practices and about the role of social and cultural forces in shaping perceptions about art; literary scholars ask about how events are represented in art and literature, and about the publication history of literature; finally, archaeologists ask questions about ancient civilizations and how we can learn more about them through the artifacts we find. All of the scholars locate their questions within a larger frame of questioning, and all articulate the significance of their questions. They also all have larger and smaller questions. Perhaps most evident from these excerpts is just how very *many* questions are being asked.

Characteristics of Effective Questions

Although you may have heard before that no question is a bad question, the truth is (sorry to have to tell you…), in academic writing, some questions are in fact more effective than others. Jane Agee writes, "Good questions do not necessarily produce good research, but poorly conceived or constructed questions will likely create problems that affect all subsequent stages of a study." Becoming a better academic writer requires learning how to develop strong, meaningful questions.

Originate from a disciplinary context

Meaningful academic questions often emerge from within a **disciplinary context** and take into account prior disciplinary knowledge so scholars can continue advancing knowledge.

This can take many forms. It might be that a scholar borrows questions from one discipline and applies it to his or her own. One can imagine, for instance, that St Clair and Bautz raise questions that might be applicable as well to performance or theatre studies. Situating questions within a disciplinary frame may also entail a scholar using prior questions to generate new questions, such as when Merello, Garcia-Diego, and Zarzo build on a 2008 research study. Linking questions within disciplinary frames can also sometimes involve a scholar duplicating or revisiting prior questions. The questions Clarke asks, for example, are steeped in cultural context, and so might need to be revisited across time and culture as attitudes toward pornography shift.

The way in which a question is posed should likewise be connected to a disciplinary context—scholars phrase their questions to fit into, or sometimes to deliberately resist, a disciplinary model.

It should also be noted that over time, certain questions will seem to *trend* within a discipline, where scholars will become occupied with a particular set of questions. For instance, before artifacts began to erode, chemists such as Merello, Garcia-Diego, and Zarzo likely would have been asking different questions. It is likely due to advancements in knowledge about preservation practices and a growing urgency for preserving artifacts in the light of rapidly changing environmental conditions prompting them to undertake these questions. As time moves forward, chemists may still be asking these same questions, but they will also discover new kinds of questions to ask.

Maintain significance

Good questions can be simple or complicated, but they should always have **significance**. They do not need to be of significance to everyone—but they should at least be significant to some subset of people. A good example of this is in the bird excerpt above; not everyone may care as much about birds as Sparkes, but birds are linked in his article to larger questions about how we can reconstruct the ancient experience. One can imagine that at least a larger subset of people may be interested in recreating the ancient experience more broadly conceived, and can appreciate birds as one piece of that larger effort.

Sometimes the significance of a question is fairly self-evident, as with questions about how chemicals can improve long-term preservation methods. Other times, though, academic writers may need to convince others that a question is important. Perhaps, for instance, Clarke may have needed to make a case at some point as to why learning more about ancient views on sexuality is of significance.

Perhaps of most importance is that the questions you ask should matter to you. Figure out what you care about and why you think others should care as well. Doing so will enable you to feel motivated to pursue a question and invested in learning and writing more about it.

Keep a pointed scope

Even as meaningful questions have larger significance, they are also manageable, addressing one part of a larger question. St Clair and Bautz, for instance, look at Bulwer's novel *The Last Days of Pompeii*, which is one part of Bulwer's larger set of writing, and which is one part of the larger set of literature about Pompeii and Pompeii excavations. St Clair and Bautz have opted to treat a smaller part of this larger set of inquiries in order to achieve depth in pursuit of their research question about the publication history and reception of Bulwer's novel.

Even book-length texts focus in on one part of a larger set of questions. Clarke, for example, alludes to his books on Roman attitudes toward sexuality; one can see that this project is part of a larger set of questions about cultural attitudes toward sexuality across other moments of time and place.

Returning briefly for inspiration to the Pyramids at Giza, one helpful way of thinking about how writers tailor and narrow questions to make them more effective is through the very notion of a pyramid, whereby the most general questions are located at the bottom, and increasingly specific questions emerge towards the top. In this way, one might think about Clarke's research questions as involving a general question, at the bottom of the pyramid, about cultural attitudes toward sexuality in general, and a more specific question, in the middle of the pyramid about Roman attitudes toward sexuality, and even more specific questions, at the top of the pyramid about erotica collecting in museums or about visual erotica from Pompeii (see Figure 3.1).

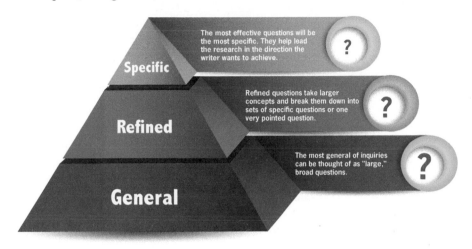

FIGURE 3.1 Pyramid of narrowing questions.

Spur further research

A question should be sufficiently complex that it could sponsor at least some degree of multiplicity and complexity, perhaps even disagreement, in the ways in which people might approach that question. That is, meaningful questions have multiple branches of inquiry leading from and to them. For example, the questions Sparkes asks about the role of birds in ancient civilizations might be examined through other means than wall-paintings; inquiries into literary artifacts, or animal husbandry practices may lead to different ideas about the role of birds. Similarly, scholars could pick up on where St Clair and Bautz stop by examining the publication and reception history of other novels aside from Bulwer's about Pompeii excavations.

Write Now

Add to this list of criteria for effective questions by reading several texts of your choosing, perhaps from different disciplines, and identifying the components of questions that make them more or less effective. Why are certain questions more engaging? What, if anything, makes certain questions less effective?

Transfer Hub: Contribute your ideas and see what others have written at fountainheadpress.com/transferhub.

Strategies for Posing Meaningful Questions

Learning how to pose effective questions is of critical importance to the work of academic writing. It can be difficult as well. To help you learn the process of generating your own questions, you might try implementing some strategies to help you compose your most meaningful questions.

Examine other writing

Use a subject-specific database (for example, PubMed, International Index to the Performing Arts, or Political Science Complete—ask a librarian for help!) to find several examples of recent academic writing from the discipline in which you are writing. Skim through these examples to identify the kinds of questions scholars are asking in that discipline, and how they are posing those questions. Do they tend to ask questions directly or indirectly? What kinds of questions are being asked in that discipline over the most recent five-year period? How do these scholars articulate the significance of their questions? Because disciplines can be so amorphous and dynamic, there will always be variation and overlap, but if you read enough examples with questions in mind, you will likely be able to identify some trends or approaches that you can adopt and/or modify for your own questions.

Consider publication medium and platform

Examining the kinds of questions asked by scholars in a particular discipline will get you only so far because even within disciplines, the publication medium affects the ways in which questions are asked. Are you writing a piece intended for scholarly readers only or is it geared towards a broader public? Will you be writing for an online or print format? Who do you imagine is likely to read your writing? How much do they already know or not know about your line of inquiry? The kinds of questions a neuroscientist asks in a peer-reviewed research journal such as the *Journal of the American Medical Association* will look different from the kinds of questions he or she might ask when writing for WebMD or Medicine Net. More popular kinds of publication mediums tend to ask more widely applicable questions and make the significance of those questions more self-evident. Digital platforms also often hold different expectations from print platforms.

Use a question heuristic

A question **heuristic** is a general template or guide for generating questions. Heuristics often include a specific set of questions designed to explore the many facets of a general area of inquiry or topic. These can offer good beginning points to help you explore an idea and identify which questions are more

Writer Insights

How do you design and develop your research questions?

I work on experimental condensed matter physics, and developing research questions in writing in my field not only depends on our personal understanding of general topics such as plasmonics, quantum dots, nano-photonics, thin magnetic films, etc., but also relies on the specific experimental process, especially on our experimental data. The final answer of a research question is a resonant explanation of the underlying physics which is well-supported by our experimental data.

~Yikuan Wang, Associate Professor, Physics, Yancheng, Jiangsu Province, China

relevant or valuable to you. With heuristics, though, it is important to adapt them to better fit your particular writing occasion.

Question Heuristic #1: Journalists' "Big Six" Questions

These questions enable writers to explore various dimensions of a topic. In the examples below, I infuse a disciplinary dimension to the big six by exploring journalistic 'big six' questions about Pompeii artwork from the perspective of Economics.

> **Who?**
>
> *Example: Who collects Pompeii art now? Who were art collectors in Pompeii? Who decides the value of Pompeii art?*

> **What?**
>
> *Example: What was the economic impact of the production and distribution of art in ancient civilizations such as Pompeii?*

> **Where?**
>
> *Example: Where are the most valuable collections of Pompeii art located?*

> **When?**
>
> *Example: When have the peak periods of value for Pompeii art occurred? When did the large-scale production and distribution of art in ancient Pompeii begin to impact its economy?*

> **Why?**
>
> *Why has the value of Pompeii art fluctuated?*

> **How?**
>
> *How was art produced and distributed in Pompeii?*

Question Heuristic #2: Interpretive Questions

Librarian Holly Samuels has developed a framework for brainstorming and designing what she has labeled "interpretive questions." In the examples that follow, I have included a series of interpretive questions from the perspective of someone in Environmental Studies exploring Pompeii art.

> **"Hypothetical:** How would things be different today if something in the past had been different?"

> *Example: How might slight shifts in intensity, duration, or direction of the volcanic eruption have impacted Pompeii, its structures, and its art? How might*

the preservation of Pompeii's art have been different if climatic conditions had been different in the centuries following the eruption?

"**Prediction:** How will something look or be in the future, based on the way it is now?"

Example: What will happen to Pompeii's sculptures and wall paintings as the climate continues to change? If carbon dioxide levels rise, how will that impact the long-term preservation of art in Pompeii?

"**Solution:** What solutions can be offered to a problem that exists today?"

Example: How could environmental conditions be improved in Pompeii so as to better preserve the city? What can be done to ensure that climate change does not negatively impact Pompeii?

"**Comparison or Analogy:** Find the similarities and differences between your main subject and a similar subject, or with another subject in the same time period or place."

Example: In what ways was the impact of Mt. Vesuvius on Pompeii's structures and art similar to or different from its impact on Herculaneum? What are the differences between the preservation of art in Pompeii and the preservation of art in other areas of the world under different environmental conditions?

"**Judgment:** Based on the information you find, what can you say as your informed opinion about the subject?"

Example: How has the environment impacted Pompeii's structures and art? How have changing climatic conditions shifted preservation methods for Pompeii's art and structures?

Question Heuristic #3: "Fundamental Disciplinary Questions"

Table 3.1 is from Michael Quinn Patton's book, *Qualitative Research and Evaluation Methods*, is organized by discipline to show the kinds of questions scholars in particular disciplines tend to ask. Since Patton is dealing with qualitative research, he has focused primarily on disciplines that make heavy use of qualitative research methods.

TABLE 3.1 Patton's Fundamental Disciplinary Questions.

Anthropology	What is the nature of culture? How does culture emerge? How is it transmitted? What are the functions of culture?
Psychology	Why do individuals behave as they do? How do human beings behave, think, feel, and know? What is normal and abnormal in human development and behavior?
Sociology	What holds groups and societies together? How do various forms of social organization emerge and what are their functions? What are the structures and processes of human social organizations?
Political science	What is the nature of power? How is power organized, created, distributed, and used?
Economics	How do societies and groups generate and distribute scarce resources? How are goods and services produced and distributed? What is the nature of wealth?
Geography	What is the nature of and variations in the earth's surface and atmosphere? How do various forms of life emerge in and relate to variations in the earth? What is the relationship between the physical characteristics of an area and the activities that take place in that area?
Biology	What is the nature of life? What are variations in the forms of life? How have life forms emerged and how do they change?

You might use Patton's fundamental disciplinary questions to generate possible questions for your area of inquiry (Table 3.1). For instance, if you were writing a research essay for a Psychology course and were interested in Pompeii art, you could model your questions on the questions Patton provides for that discipline:

> *Example: Why did ancient Romans collect art? How might Pompeii art reveal how ancient Romans behaved?*

Question Heuristic #4: Quantitative Questions

Researchers Burke Johnson and Larry Christensen have developed a guideline for developing questions in disciplines that make considerable use of quantitative research methods. For the following quantitative questions, I continue to draw out our illustration by providing an example of someone writing about Pompeii art in a Statistics course.

Descriptive Questions: "Descriptive research questions seek answers to 'How much?', 'How often?,' or 'What changes over time or over different situations?'"… They also seek to identify the degree of relationship between two variables."

Example: How much have particular pieces of Pompeii art eroded over the past 1500 years? What is the relationship between the number of visitors to Pompeii and levels of deterioration?

Predictive Questions: "Predictive questions are questions that seek to determine whether one or more variables can be used to predict some future outcome."

Example: Does income level predict the likelihood of members of ancient Roman civilizations producing or collecting art?

Causal Questions: "Causal questions…compare different variations of some phenomenon to identify the cause of something."

Example: Does variation in the amount and duration of sunlight produce a change in the long-term preservation of Pompeii art?

Transferring Questions

One of the most important aspects to note with developing effective questions is that writers across disciplines pose and pursue questions that matter to them. In the same way, as you develop questions, try to identify ones that matter to you. Not every question will matter equally to you or to your readers, and your motivations for asking certain questions might sometimes be varied. But do try to ask questions about which you harbor at least some degree of curiosity. Following your intellectual interests will enable you to create more meaningful academic writing. This chapter has also illustrated that it is entirely possible to apply your own particular areas of interest to multiple different disciplinary inquiries. It's even possible, for instance, to bring an interest in Pompeii art into a statistics course. Using questions as a framework for academic writing enables writers to capture their own interests and use a disciplinary lens to discover, explore, and learn about ideas from a wide variety of perspectives. In the subsequent chapter, you will see, through reading, how writers develop scholarship based on the meaningful questions they pose.

℘ ℘ ℘

Chapter 3 Key Terms

Questions   Significance   Heuristic

Inquiry   Disciplinary context

 Write Away

Form a team with three to five classmates to engage in pyramid building with questions. In so doing, you will gain experience with the process of developing and narrowing questions and with the ways in which questions are influenced by disciplines.

Establish a pyramid base. Person A writes down a general question that matters to him or her, along with the kind of research one would need to conduct in order to pursue that question. This question will serve as the pyramid's base.

Add a second layer to your pyramid. Person B takes Person A's question and refines it in order to create another level of the pyramid, narrowing the question and inflecting it with a related disciplinary perspective and also indicating what kind of research would now need to be done in order to successfully pursue that question.

Continue building your pyramid. Person C takes Person B's question, and so on, repeating the process until all members of the group have had the opportunity to refine and reshape a question.

Round two. Repeat the process again, using a different Person A and beginning with a different question to build a second pyramid. Or, as an optional challenge, instead see how high you can get your first pyramid to go, by adding on increasingly specific questions with each new turn.

Transfer Hub: Contribute your ideas and see what others have written at fountainheadpress.com/transferhub.

Reflect. As a group, reflect together on how the questions shifted across context and what you learned about the process of posing meaningful questions (what was challenging, surprising, inspiring, etc.)

Reading

Pinpointing Chapter 4

Chapter 4 expands on Chapter 3 by providing you the opportunity to explore how to use the questions you develop for your writing to motivate your choices about which texts to read and how to read them. To provide you with strategies for *reading in transit*, this chapter addresses the following concepts:

- Choosing What to Read: Primary, Secondary, and Tertiary Reading Materials
- Deciding How to Locate Reading Materials
- Deciding How to Read: Shallow and In-Depth Reading Strategies
- Invoking Discipline-Specific Reading Skills

After exploring reading, the next chapter addresses summary, one of several specific ways in which writers respond to, extend, challenge, and otherwise make use of the reading they engage with throughout the research and writing process.

Chichén Itzá, located in the Yucatan Peninsula, was once a thriving city. The Mayans settled there in the sixth century C.E. The Pyramid of Kukulcan, also known as El Castillo, is one of the seven wonders of the world, in part because of the precise astronomical features of its design. On the first day of spring and the first day of fall (the Vernal Equinoxes), the setting sun casts a shadow across the stairs in the image of a long snake that appears to be "slithering" down the stairs. This snake is said to represent the god for whom the temple is named: "The feathered snake, Kukulcan, was the most important god for the people who lived here" (Lopata).

Other buildings at Chichén Itzá also illustrate Mayan expertise with astronomy: El Caracol, "the observatory," has "narrow shaftlike windows [that] frame important astronomical events. One...window marks an appearance of Venus at a particular point on the horizon...once every eight years" ("About Alignments").

Another well-known structure at Chichén Itzá is the Great Ball Court, where Mayans played tlachtli, or in Mayan, pok-ta-pok. This game involved a ball that players kept in the air "by hitting it with the hips, thighs or upper arms and bouncing it off the side walls. Use of the hands or feet was forbidden." Scholars hypothesize that the ball had symbolic astronomical significance: "preventing the ball from hitting the ground may have represented maintaining the orbit of the Sun or Venus."

Tlachtli was violent. The ball was so heavy that it killed some players upon impact. Myth holds that "the winning Capitan would present his own head to the losing Capitan, who then decapitate[d] him" as an act of great honor to facilitate his entry to heaven ("Great Ball Court"). Depictions of the game found on three detailed stone carvings on site, however, suggest, that it was actually the losing team's captain who faced beheading. Whomever actually was decapitated at the end of a game, their bones apparently may have been crushed to create a white powder that was then used as a dusting to cover a flint game ball known as "White Flint" ("General"; "Great Ball Court"; "Mayan Ball Game").

Scholars have been able to acquire this knowledge about Chichén Itzá by *reading* all sorts of *texts:* anything from wall carvings, hieroglyphics, and Maya Codices to bones, ancient chronicles, travel narratives, prior scholarship, and architecture itself. Reading such as this, of all kinds, is a cornerstone academic writing, and scholars across disciplines read numerous kinds of texts in the course of their research. They build on, extend, examine, modify, revisit, rebut, and otherwise respond to what others have written or produced. They read evidence and data to draw conclusions and make arguments.

Still, as ubiquitous as reading is, it nevertheless can present deep challenges. Nicholas Carr, himself an author of several books, confesses that sustained reading, for him, can be difficult: "[M]y concentration often starts to drift after two or three pages. I get fidgety, lose the thread, begin looking for something else to do. I feel as if I'm always dragging my wayward brain back to the text."

Reading closely, as Carr suggests, requires energy and sustained concentration. But another issue that makes reading especially challenging is that nearly everything about how we read and what we read can shift depending on our disciplinary perspective, the writing occasion, and our aims and purposes. Reading well demands that academic writers be reflective and deliberate in taking context into account on a continuing basis.

Fostering this kind of deliberateness requires an approach to reading that centers on making choices… choices about what to read, how much to read, how closely to read, when to read, and whom to read.

Write Here

Archaeologists read all sorts of texts for their research—stones, bones, buildings, images, garments, etc. Imagine that you are an archaeologist thousands of years from now and have just discovered your campus, perfectly preserved though without human presence. What different kinds of texts, broadly defined to include words, material artifacts, and abstract concepts, would you read to understand the campus? What might you learn from reading each of these different texts? Might any of these texts yield conflicting or contradictory insights about your campus?

Choosing What to Read: Primary, Secondary, and Tertiary Reading Materials

What do academic writers read? Everything! If you think academic reading only involves specialized texts with elevated language, minimal pictures or images, and scores of footnotes, think again. While these kinds of texts certainly do accomplish important work and play a significant role in academic writing, academic writers read a broad and varied array of texts.

They read visual images, websites, datasets, social media, newspapers, magazines, novels, speeches, poetry, comics, artwork, policy briefs, musical soundtracks,

Writer Insights

What kinds of texts do you read?

I read cartoons for a living. People often say: "You get to just look at cartoons all day—that's not work!" But it is—and lots of it. I research nearly 5000 editorial cartoons: one artist's body of work for the last 20 years of South African democracy. Visual analysis is serious stuff. Not all political cartoons are funny, and my goal is to better understand them. I'm looking for links, patterns, trends—none of which I know for sure I'll find. They're there, but will I see them? It can be daunting, exciting, sobering, terrifying—some days all four.

~Gregory Paitaki, Ph.D. Candidate, Film & Media Studies, Cape Town, South Africa

"READ"

performances, and even human and animal actions and interactions. Scholars 'read' numbers, solids, liquids, gasses, and earth matter.

Choosing what to read for a particular writing project is largely contingent on the context within which you are working. There are four questions you can use to help you determine more specifically your writing context so that you can make reading choices that best fit your aims.

1. What is the disciplinary context for your writing project?

If you are working within a particular discipline, it's likely a good idea to read texts that emerge from that discipline. The psychology student writing the paper we imagined earlier, for instance, would likely read scholarly articles about violence and video games that are written from a psychological perspective; and he would engage in research methods that are consonant with psychology research. Academic writers also will apply frameworks from one discipline to another, or engage with multiple disciplinary perspectives, but in these cases they nevertheless also ground their research in some way within their disciplines.

2. What are your research questions?

Your research questions will help you make choices about what to read. For instance, our psychology student will likely be searching library databases and internet search engines for materials that have to do with video games and with violent behavior among adolescents. He will need to decide how to define violent (only extreme or also mild?), and may decide to narrow the research question to an age range of 13 to 15-year-olds or only adolescents with a particular socio-economic background. Posing a specific and meaningful research question (see Chapter 3: Posing Meaningful Questions), will enable you to identify a more manageable range of potential reading materials.

3. What is your research methodology?

Chapter 2: Research and Writing as a Process, discusses different kinds of research methodologies (quantitative, qualitative, or mixed). If you were writing the psychology paper, would you plan to conduct interviews, distribute surveys, engage in observation, or conduct a review of existing research? If you decided to conduct interviews, you'd expect to analyze the interviews and also read other examples of interviews in psychology so you can build on and draw from that research. As you decide upon your research methods, you will be better able to choose the kinds of readings with which you may want to engage.

4. What kind of writing project are you creating?

The amount and type of reading you do depend on the length, style, and tone of your writing project. Writing projects that are more scholarly in nature (see p. 63 for definition of scholarly literature) require more scholarly reading. The writer in psychology would likely draw on a variety of sources, reading about how popular culture portrays violence in video games alongside reading interview transcripts and actual scenes from video games, as well as more scholarly articles and books about violence and video games.

Once you have asked and reflected on these questions, you will be in a better position to actually choose your reading materials. The three main categories of reading from which academic writers choose, each outlined in more detail, are as follows: primary materials, secondary materials, and tertiary materials.

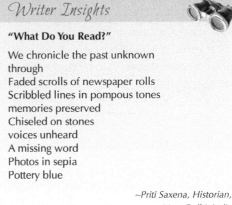

Writer Insights

"What Do You Read?"

We chronicle the past unknown through
Faded scrolls of newspaper rolls
Scribbled lines in pompous tones
memories preserved
Chiseled on stones
voices unheard
A missing word
Photos in sepia
Pottery blue

~*Priti Saxena, Historian, New Delhi, India*

Primary Materials

Primary materials are direct, original, firsthand sources, texts or data. They include data sets, statistics, letters, novels, speeches, photographs, artifacts, etc. The writer working on violence in video games might read any number of primary materials, like:

- transcripts from interviews with adolescents
- results from a survey sent to people in mental health care, adolescents, parents, people affiliated with the K-12 public school system, or members of the judicial system
- images and scenes from actual video games, such as Call of Duty or Grand Theft Auto;
- data from a heart-rate monitor or blood-pressure cuff measuring the rates of people before, during, and after playing the games
- statistics on violence and video games
- posts in an online gaming forum such as gtaforums.com

Secondary Materials

Secondary materials are those written about a particular question or idea. The University of California at Berkeley Library describes secondary materials in this way: "Secondary sources describe, interpret, analyze, evaluate, explain, comment on, or develop theories related to a topic. They are often written after-the-fact, with hindsight." Secondary materials can further be differentiated along the continuum of popular to scholarly as shown in Figure 4.1.

Popular Secondary Sources	Public Scholarship Secondary Sources	Scholarly Secondary Sources

FIGURE 4.1 Continuum of secondary materials.

Keep in mind, though, that texts will rarely be located at either end of the spectrum; they instead are usually perched somewhere along the continuum, and there is usually some measure of overlap and multiplicity.

Popular secondary sources can appear online or in print; nearly all disciplines have some set of materials that are popular in nature. Popular secondary sources can be written by scholars, members of the general public, or professional writers. They often have one or more of the following characteristics:

- absence of (or limited) documentation, bibliographic citations, and footnotes
- geared more towards the general public in tone, style, and content

The writer who is working on the video games and violence research essay in her Psychology course might use any or all of the following as popular secondary sources:

- A "60-Minutes" broadcast titled "Can a Video Game Lead to Murder? Did *Grand Theft Auto* Cause One Teenager to Kill?"
- An article from *Newsweek*, "This is Your Brain on Alien Killer Pimps of Nazi Doom," by journalist Karen Springen
- A blog post on computerworld.com by freelance writer Darlene Storm, "Not Again: Stop Blaming Violent Video Games for Mass Shootings"
- A book by writers Dave Grossman and Gloria DeGaetano titled *Stop Teaching Our Kids to Kill: A Call to Action against TV, Movie & Video Game Violence*

Public scholarship is becoming increasingly prevalent as scholarship becomes more accessible through online platforms. Public scholarship is geared towards a general readership, but is written, created, or produced by a scholar and contains some attentiveness to documentation, bibliography, and citation. It is not what we might label fully *scholarly*, though, because public scholarship usually does not go through as rigorous or as official a peer review process.

Our student writing on video games and violence in Psychology may use the following kinds of public scholarship sources:

- a podcast titled "Violent Video Games—What Does the Research Say?" by Michael (Ph.D. Psychology) on the website "PsychFiles"
- an article by Professor of Psychology at San Diego State University, Jean M. Twenge, published in *Psychology Today*, titled "Yes, Violent Video Games Do Cause Aggression"
- a video titled *Game Over: Gender, Race and Violence in Video Games*, by Nina Huntemann, Associate Professor of Media Studies at Suffolk University
- a brief summary of previous research on this topic, titled "Violence in the Media— Psychologists Study TV and Video Game Violence for Potential Harmful Effects," posted on the American Psychological Association website (apa.org)

Scholarly secondary sources appear online or in print, and are, like public scholarship, written by academics. Scholarly secondary sources, however, are distinguished by the following characteristics:

- published by university presses or scholarly organizations
- documented extensively with citations and footnotes
- geared in tone, style, and content toward a postsecondary reader
- vetted through the formal peer review process. This process (depicted in Figure 4.2) involves review and approval of a manuscript by peer experts. These peers decide whether a manuscript deserves to be published by whether it meets publication and disciplinary standards for research and academic integrity

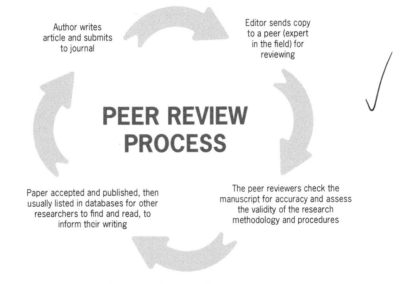

FIGURE 4.2 Peer review process.

Our student writer researching violence in video games might read the following scholarly sources:

- An article by scholars Brad J. Bushman and L. Rowell Huesmann published in the peer-reviewed journal *European Psychologist*: "Twenty-Five Years of Research on Violence in Digital Games and Aggression Revisited: A Reply to Elson and Ferguson (2013)"
- An article by scholar Tobias Greitemeyer published in the *Journal Of Experimental Social Psychology:* "Intense Acts of Violence During Video Game Play Make Daily Life Aggression Appear Innocuous: A New Mechanism Why Violent Video Games Increase Aggression"

- A book by scholars Craig A. Anderson, Douglas A. Gentile, Katherine E. Buckley, published by Oxford University Press: *Violent Video Game Effects on Children and Adolescents: Theory, Research, and Public Policy*

Tertiary materials

Tertiary materials include reference works about a certain area of research. They can include such items as encyclopedias, dictionaries, or indexes. The writer working on violence in video games might read any of the following kinds of tertiary materials:

- The *Encyclopedia of Video Games: The Culture, Technology, and Art of Gaming*, edited by Mark J. P. Wolf. This encyclopedia has over 300 entries on terms, games, and people related to the video game industry
- The *Encyclopedia of 20th-century technology*, edited by Colin A. Hempstead and William E. Worthington
- The *Wikipedia: WikiProject Video games/Reference library*
- The *Guinness World Records Gamer's Edition*
- *A Dictionary of Video Game Theory* by Jesper Juul

Write Now

Think about a research question you will be exploring this term. For that question, brainstorm several ideas for primary, secondary, and tertiary materials that you might choose to read. Be sure, for the secondary materials, to include a range of texts that exist all throughout the continuum of popular writing, public scholarship, and scholarly writing.

Deciding How to Locate Reading Materials

Whether you are seeking primary materials, popular secondary materials, public scholarship, or scholarly secondary materials, you will likely be making use of some of the following search strategies to explore and discover reading materials.

Direct experiments or data collection

Through these mechanisms, you will be able to amass primary reading materials, such as datasets, field notes, and results. The type of collection, research, or experimentation method depends on the discipline in which you are working. The Psychology student might, for example, set up a controlled experiment whereby he measures heart rate and blood pressure of users during violent moments of a particular video game.

Visiting archives/field sites

Some scholars locate reading materials by visiting important archives of materials, such as the Archives of African American Music and Culture at Indiana University, Bloomington.

Scholars in other disciplines might visit certain field sites in order to collect their primary reading materials. An evolutionary anthropologist, for example, might travel to South America to research primate behavior. Our writer in Psychology, as another example, might decide to include some archival research by visiting the Computer and Video Gaming Archive at the University of Michigan to "use and play a wide variety of games from the 1970s to the present" (Carter) or to conduct field research by attending a video game convention such as PAX, the Penny Arcade Expo, to interview manufacturers and users.

Internet search engines

Although internet searching is not alone sufficient for research in most academic contexts, it might be a useful starting point for some research endeavors. You can find a range of primary and secondary materials through an internet search engine such as Google or Bing. Choose your key terms carefully and precisely in order to maximize the likelihood that the results will be related to your topic, and be mindful of authenticity. Again, even with an internet search, you will need to move on from internet searching to one or more of the following search strategies.

General research databases

General research databases are a step more specific than a general internet search engine in that they identify more scholarly research than does the general search engine. These general research databases include, for example, Google Scholar, JSTOR, ProQuest, or AcademicOne.

Library guides

Library Guides are resource pages created by academic librarians at various postsecondary institutions about particular disciplines or topics. They are often created as a supplement or guide for a particular course. Library Guides, which are often made publicly available, can help lead you to specialized research databases and resources where you can find secondary materials to read about a particular topic. Figure 4.3 is an example of library guide for Psychology at the University of Washington, created by librarian John Holmes.

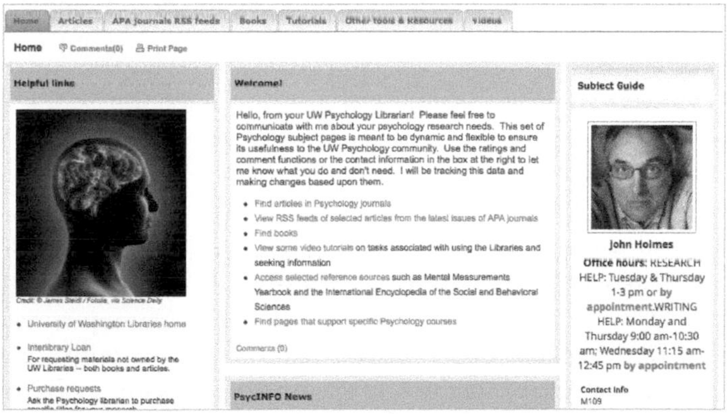

FIGURE 4.3 University of Washington library guide.

Writer Insights

Why is knowing how to conduct research important in your field?

Compared to other literary genres, perhaps Historical Fiction is the most tedious to write. In my work, I spend most of my time doing research. I want to make sure that my story sticks to accurate historical facts up to the smallest detail—like what kind of soap did eleventh century Europeans use; and did they use the same soap to wash their clothes? If you know how to do proper research, you'll find the answers you seek—I did.

~Anna Teodoro-Suanco, Novelist,
Manila, Philippines

From this library guide, our violence and video games writer could find articles, books, or specialized journals in psychology.

Ask a librarian!

Academic librarians welcome the opportunity to help students find secondary materials to read. It's part of their job and they are generally delighted when undergraduates ask them for research assistance. They are highly skilled at information science and can help you find the reading materials that will best fit with your writing occasion.

Discipline-specific research databases

These databases will provide a range of sources pertinent to a particular discipline. You can identify discipline-specific research databases through one of the library guides mentioned above or by asking a librarian. When you search in a discipline-specific research database, you can narrow results to return only popular (i.e., magazines and newspapers) or only peer reviewed, or a mix, or you can specify a certain date range for results. In contrast to more general research databases, these databases will likely offer a larger set of relevant materials and offer more flexibility with tailoring your search. For example, databases relevant to video games and violence in Psychology might include any the following: Psycinfo, Web of Science, PubMed, or PsycCRITIQUES. From here, the writer would use one of these discipline-specific research databases to search for articles and materials on violence and video games.

#followthebreadcrumbs

One of the savviest ways to identify and locate readings is to follow the bread crumbs from other scholars. Look to see what others working in your area of research have been reading and use these as a starting point for your own research. You might think of process of interconnection as resembling a hashtag in Twitter or tag on a blog. For instance, if another scholar has used a particular secondary source, you can then follow that source to see what kinds of sources that person has used.

Search for an annotated bibliography or literature review

Although you must be cognizant of how recent research is and how reliable, a search for a literature review may yield several promising results that can offer you starting points for your own secondary material search. In our example case, a literature review on violence and video games was prepared for the Australian government by the Attorney General's Office. It is titled, "Literature Review on the Impact of Playing

Violent Video Games on Aggression." It describes the current research on video games and violence. Another helpful source that can lead you to others' bread crumbs is an **annotated bibliography**, which is a list of relevant sources with brief summaries or descriptions.

Browse around a relevant book

If you find one book that fits your research topic, you can locate it on the shelves of a library and look around it for related books.

Follow the "cited by" or "related articles" link

When you conduct a database search and get a list of results, you will likely encounter a "cited by" or "related articles" link in one of the databases or search engines. These show you other relevant texts that are connected to one another. Following this trail can lead you to identify a variety of different kinds of other relevant materials.

Read others' bibliographies

As you find articles and materials that are relevant, look through their bibliographies to see what choices their writers made with readings. You can then use this as a point of departure for your work. Doing so will also give you a sense of who the major figures are in a given conversation. For instance, in the field of violence and video games, Douglas A. Gentile, a Developmental Psychologist at Iowa State University, Ames, and editor of the book *Media Violence and Children,* is one of the more well-known scholars in this area. I learned this because several bibliographies mention his work and because Google Scholar shows that his research is "cited by" many hundreds of people. It's likely that our student writer would probably want to make use in some capacity of Gentile's work since he is likely a major figure in this area of research.

Deciding How to Read: Shallow and In-Depth Reading Strategies

Given how very much there is available to read, academic writers must not only choose what to read, but they must make continual choices about which materials to devote considerable energy to and which materials they can devote less energy to. While you may have thought that all academic reading requires intense concentration and effort, academic writers often make use of other reading strategies. Sometimes they need to get up to speed quickly on a topic, or sometimes they are looking for one particular portion of a text that is more closely relevant to their research.

The bottom line is this: you cannot possibly read everything about a topic, and academic writers make continual choices about where to devote their reading energy. Key is learning to make good decisions about what warrants different levels of reading effort.

This set of choices creates a continuum of reading practices that can be usefully differentiated by the terms shallow and in-depth as shown in Figure 4.4.

Shallow Reading

In-Depth Reading

FIGURE 4.4 Continuum of reading practices.

It's important to note that the most effective academic writers likely combine these reading strategies rather than practicing only one kind of strategy.

Shallow reading

The name might seem derogatory, but **shallow reading** really does play a large, important role in academic writing. Alice Horning offers the following explanation for the importance of learning how to read faster while at the same time demonstrating how fast reading does not equate to sloppy or poor reading: "People need to read faster, just because the amount of material is growing exponentially. People need to read better, too, because it's no good to read fast if readers can't recall and use the information. That is, readers must be able to go beyond main ideas to analysis, synthesis and evaluation." While the in-depth reading strategies outlined will offer additional ways of getting "beyond main ideas," readers also need to hone their skills with shallower reading practices. Anne Mangen, a Professor at the Reading Centre in the University of Stavanger, Norway, describes "shallower" forms of reading as being characterized by "scanning and browsing." Ziming Liu, Professor of Library Science at San Jose State University, further describes shallower forms of reading as that which includes "browsing and scanning, keyword spotting, [and] one-time reading."

> *Writer Insights*
>
> **How do you ready shallowly?**
>
> I read IT blogs at mssqltips.com and sqlbog.com, twitter feeds #SQLHelp, and *ComputerWorld* magazine. I read the first 2 paragraphs first and the last 2 paragraphs next. Then I skim the middle.
>
> ~Ameena Lalani, Database Administrator, Chicago, Illinois, U.S.

This kind of shallower reading occurs in our daily lives as we browse the sports, news, or entertainment sections of a website, or as we scroll through social networking sites. But academic writers also make use of shallower forms of reading quite often. We skim through texts or data sets quickly for various reasons:

- to determine if the texts or data are relevant for our research
- to identify the main points, arguments, or key terms
- to look for the portions that are of most importance for our research
- to get a quick sense of the landscape of research on which we can build

How to read in shallower ways

Reading a text quickly and efficiently, or shallowly, often involves:

- reading the abstract
- reading the signposts of the text (i.e., title, section headings)
- looking for signals of phrases indicating significance, such as: I argue that…or the main point is
- reading the introduction and conclusion

Write Now

Reflect for ten minutes on what kinds of texts you have recently read in shallower ways and what kinds of texts you have recently read in more in-depth ways. What drove your decision on how to read these texts? Which kinds of reading practices worked more effectively for you to accomplish your particular purposes?

In-depth reading

At the other end of the reading spectrum, and also a strategy of great importance, is what Liu calls "**in-depth reading** [or] concentrated reading" (700). This form, Liu maintains, is characterized by "sustained attention…[a]nnotating and highlighting" (700). We engage with in-depth reading, also sometimes called active reading, in our leisure reading as well, if we come across, for instance, a post or image that we have particular interest in or that we want to understand more deeply. Academic writers make use of in-depth forms of reading quite often, particularly when we want to really grapple with ideas or think carefully about the ideas in the readings. We read texts or data sets through in-depth strategies in order to:

- interpret and analyze
- remember more carefully that which we are reading
- find quotes or data to integrate into our own arguments
- pose questions

How to read in-depth

2ND step

To read materials in more in-depth ways, first start with the shallow reading practices named above, but reading in-depth requires that writers read material multiple times. These multiple encounters with a text will enable you to process ideas more completely, taking the time to think about the ideas and let them percolate. Reading in more in-depth ways often includes annotating readings and writing about what you read.

Writer Insights

What are some of your in-depth reading practices?

When writing for research, I read and take notes, organize my notes thematically, and write reflections.

~Y., *English as a Foreign Language Teacher, Kyiv, Ukraine*

Annotating

Annotating a text, also known as marginal note-taking, involves taking notes while reading. As you read, engage with the text as though you were having a conversation with the author(s). Think about your annotations not only in terms of noting main points, but of creating a visible record of your thinking while reading. Figure 4.5 is a page of text illustrating annotations. The page is a selection of text from an article called "Arts of the Contact Zone," by Mary Louise Pratt. The specifics of the annotations might not make complete sense to you, but the point is not for you to be able to understand another's annotations so much as get a general sense of how a scholar engages with a text during in-depth reading. Note that annotations do not entail merely highlighting sentences but active thought through your reading of the text. The annotations address points such as:

- questions you have about the text
- words/terms with which you are unfamiliar
- connections you are noticing between this text and other texts
- points of tension within the text/moments of contradiction
- key terms/ideas from the text
- aspects/ideas that elicit some kind of emotion or affect from you (i.e., surprise, frustration, happiness, agreement, disagreement)

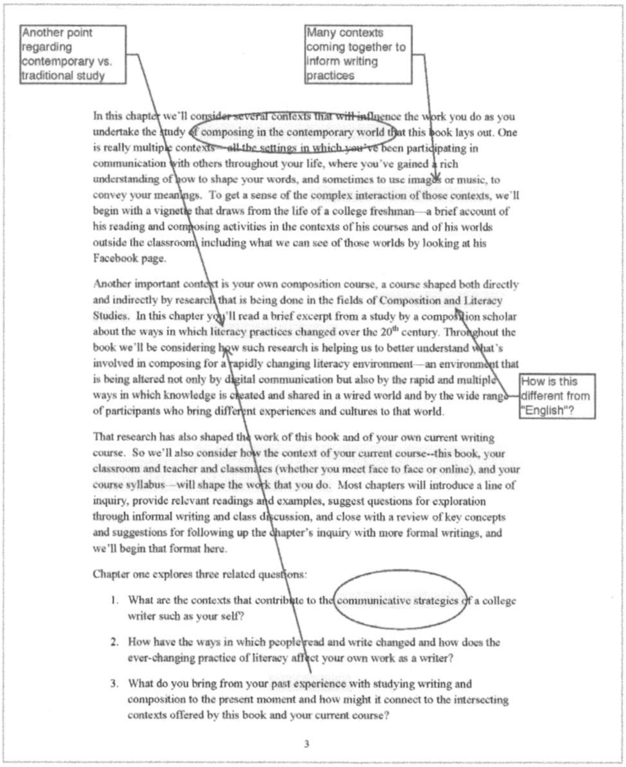

FIGURE 4.5 Annotating during in-depth reading.

Again, Figure 4.5 is not intended to be entirely transparent—it's one writer's personal notes in a personal form of in-depth reading. Instead, the image is intended to illustrate what the kind of deep engagement with text looks like that in-depth reading requires. As a student, you can also engage deeply in this manner in handwritten contexts, or by making a separate record of reading notes in a document of your own. If you do use your own document, though, make sure to make specific notes of page numbers or locations of significant passages so that you can recall later when reviewing your notes where the passages in question can be found.

Write Now

Choose a text you are currently reading, and practice annotating the text. After annotating, reflect for ten minutes about the experience. What did you find challenging about annotating? What worked really well? What do you think you might do differently if you were annotating a different sort of text, for a different course, for example?

Writing about what you read

Spending time writing about what you read enables you to discover, analyze, and explore ideas. Whereas notes such as those in Figure 4.5 amount to brief moments of writing, sustained writing over a period of five or 10 minutes (or longer) can further enable you to process what you read.

Exactly what you choose to write about when you read depends on why you are reading a particular text. Some of the following general questions are possibilities for ways that you can write about what you read.

- What do you take to be the author's purposes?
- What themes do you notice across the dataset or fieldnotes?
- What worked well?
- What seemed confusing?
- What seems significant and why?
- What questions do you have and why?
- Which portions shed new light on your research questions?

Two specific strategies for in-depth reading are important to feature here in that they are generally applicable to and important for academic writers across disciplines.

Featured in-depth reading strategy: Read like a writer

Composition scholar Mike Bunn argues that students who are interested in developing as academic writers should not only read for content, but should also read texts as writers. Bunn describes the process in this way:

> [I]dentify…the choices the author made so that you can better understand how
> such choices might arise in your own writing. The idea is to carefully examine

the things you read, looking at the writerly techniques in the text in order to decide if you might want to adopt similar (or the same) techniques in your writing…. You are reading to learn about writing.

Bunn's point is that the texts we read must always serve two purposes: to help us learn about and explore a line of inquiry and to provide a model of writing that we can then follow, adapt, or reject in our own work as writers. Reading like a writer focuses on the latter of these purposes, asking that you conduct in-depth reading strategies on the writing choices themselves as made by the author(s). In-depth reading as a writer might include making notes in the text and in a writer's journal of your own about such aspects of the text like:

- overall structure and organization
- types of secondary and primary sources
- integration of evidence
- use of quotes or data
- approaches to introductions and conclusions
- articulation of the argument or position
- integration of visual elements (graphs, charts, tables, images, media, etc.)
- use of signposts. Signposts are phrases that indicate to readers where a writing project is moving. Signposts include such phrases as *For instance…In this essay I will argue …To summarize…Historically…More recently…*
- other, as inspired by discipline and/or writing occasion

One helpful strategy for in-depth reading of a text's overall structure and organization would be to do a reverse outline on the text (for guidelines on reverse outlining, see Chapter 2, p. 27). Use the texts you are reading as an opportunity to gain more familiarity with writing in particular disciplines and/or in particular writing contexts. For example, if you are learning how to write in the discipline of history, as you read historical scholarship, make note of features of historical research and writing. Likely, you will discover a range of (perhaps even conflicting) approaches that you can consider as you develop your own writing acumen.

Again, consider keeping a writer's journal (print or electronic) for you to track ideas about writing that emerge as you read like a writer. Note down the text, the page or section, and what you noticed about the writing. You may not know at a given moment how you might put one of these ideas to use in your own writing, but you will have them collected together. Keeping a writer's journal will also help you acquire the habit of mind of thinking of yourself as a writer.

Featured in-depth reading strategy: Reading rhetorically

Rhetoric can be understood to be the art of persuasion. Reading rhetorically asks that readers approach a text by thinking about how and why the text is attempting to persuade or influence readers. Compositionists Christina Haas and Linda Flower define rhetorical reading as "an active attempt at constructing a rhetorical context for the text as a way of making sense of it" (167-8). Reading rhetorically empowers readers not only to develop a deeper understanding of a text, but also to generate meaning within the text. Reading rhetorically invites readers to consider the rhetorical situation from which the text has emerged. (Chapter 7: Analysis and Chapter 8: Framing Arguments, both expand on the concept of rhetorical reading.)

To explore rhetorical reading, let's look at how to utilize the following three aspects of reading rhetorically: exigence-audience-constraints, rhetorical triangle, and the argumentative appeals.

Exigence-audience-constraints

Lloyd Bitzer, a rhetorician and professor emeritus at University of Wisconsin-Madison argues that there are three aspects to what he terms the "rhetorical situation":

- **Exigence:** the problem that gives rise to an argument
- **Audience:** who can or will be in a position to hear the argument and/or be influenced by the argument
- **Constraints:** the limitations, form, and context within which the argument will be developed and delivered. This includes such matters as discipline, publication context, form limitations, time constraints

All of these elements shape an argument. The exigence impacts how a writer defines his or her area of inquiry; the audience and constraints work together to shape what a writer chooses to include in his or her argument, and how they make the argument.

Rhetorical triangle

Another way of reading rhetorically is through what is known as the **rhetorical triangle** (Fig. 4.6).

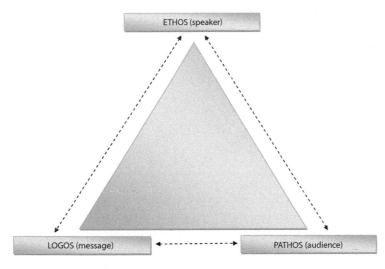

FIGURE 4.6 Rhetorical triangle.

Considering the rhetorical triangle enables readers to understand more about how and why an argument emerged through considering the elements of the triangle. Reading rhetorically means asking questions about these elements in order to construct and create meaning in a text as well as to understand the text more thoroughly.

- **Author:** Who is the author? Why does she care about this topic? What may be influencing her perspective or approach?

- **Audience:** Who is being or can be influenced by a particular text? How is the text shaped in ways that are directed toward these readers? Who do you think is the intended audience and why?

- **Purpose/Message:** What do you understand to be the aim of the text? What is it attempting to accomplish? What are the messages of the text? How is the text organized? What evidence does the writer use to convey the message(s)? How does the writer situate the message(s) within ongoing research and current debates? What might the message(s) reveal about the writing occasion or rhetorical context?

Reading through the Lens of Aristotle's Argumentative Appeals
(*ethos, pathos, logos*) and *kairos*

Aristotle developed a scheme for the ways that rhetoricians can persuade their audiences.

Ethos: persuasion by appealing to readers on the basis of the author's character and authority

Pathos: persuasion by appealing to readers' emotions

Logos: persuasion by appealing to readers' sense of reason and logic

Depending on the context of a particular writing occasion, one or more of these appeals might be more or less relevant or apparent. Reading rhetorically in this vein, though, asks that readers consider these appeals even if it is only to recognize that one is privileged over the others.

Another term was central to how Aristotle approached rhetoric: *kairos*. Kairos is roughly translated as time, which in this context would mean that an argument should emerge at the appropriate time, ostensibly when an argument can succeed at persuading its audience.

According to Phillip Sipiora and James Baumlin, *kairos* can be thought of in two ways: (1) Adhering to matters of propriety in terms of writing in such a way as to observe the expectations of any given context and (2) Demonstrating timeliness in that the text is

---

Writer Insights

How do you integrate *ethos* in your writing?

How I write cover letters by midnight:

- Off Tweets and onto research in the target company, especially "About Us" page and qualification requirements

- Drafting time: remember to sound polite but not affected, confident but not pompous, neither above nor below who I am

- Review and ask myself: does it sound good to my ear?

- If not, make changes; if yes, chances are my readers may like it, too

~Jing Hu, Freelance Translator, Urumqi, Xinjiang, China

---

shown to emerge at a "uniquely timely" moment. Kairos might thus be understood as the way that a writer situates his or her argument within an awareness of time (timeliness for the argument itself and a sense of being contemporary in recognizing the historical moment in which he or she is writing).

Translating these four concepts into a way of reading rhetorically would direct readers to ask the following about a given text (see Table 4.1).

TABLE 4.1 Argumentative appeals questions.

Ethos	How does the writer establish her credibility and/or expertise? What gives him or her the right to construct and deliver this argument? Why would readers be inclined to consider being persuaded by her?
Pathos	What emotions does the writer invoke for readers? Does the writer appeal to readers' sense of justice, sympathy, love? How does the writer encourage readers to become emotionally invested in the argument?
Logos	What elements of reason and logic are included in the text and how do they work to persuade readers? How does the writer address opposing or modified views?
Kairos	How does the writer attend to content, format, style, and structure in ways that adhere to, modify, or reject conventions and expectations of the discipline, publication context, etc.? How does the writer establish the timeliness of the argument?

These approaches to rhetorical reading can work together as a range of concepts for you to use with in-depth reading. As you can see, they require time and patience, and re-reading.

Example of Rhetorical Reading

Review this annotated article about video games to demonstrate rhetorical reading. In this annotation, several approaches to rhetorical reading are fused as a means of illustrating a blended approach. The article, written by undergraduate student Obaid Rashed Aleghfeli at Kaist University in South Korea, was originally published in the *Undergraduate Research Journal for the Human Sciences*. Note that not every rhetorical aspect is annotated here, just a few to provide an example. It is also possible to argue that a rhetorical feature can have multiple components at once. For instance, a particular aspect of the text could be appealing to *logos* and *kairos* simultaneously, or message and purpose could overlap.

Rhetorical reading of "Video Games" by O. Aleghfeli

At the root of the notion of video games is the word "video," which orig-inally meant a kind of electronic device that can show images (Stiles, 2010). In fact the first video games were sometimes called TV games. Having appeared as an experiment for human interaction, video games have changed dramatically and now have become an example of art and a form of business industry (Gladwell, 2000). All you need to have to play a video game is an input device, a joystick (or any other kind of game controller, such as a keyboard, a mouse etc.), and a particular video game. Speakers and headphones are not obligatory; they just make the effects more impressive.

Aleghfeli establishes **ethos** *by invoking others' published scholarship and, later in this paragraph, well-known writers such as Malcolm Gladwell. This shows he has conducted research and has expertise.*

Since Aleghfeli begins with a general overview and physical description of video games, he assumes his audience includes those who are very unfamiliar with video games. It also suggests that his purpose is to provide an overview of video games, to inform.

Original video games could be found in a number of formats; everything depended on the electronic device it had to fit. The first widely sold game was called "Computer Space" and was created by T. Dabney and N. Bushnell. In fact, it played only on the black and white TV. This type of video game was developed and transformed into "Brown Box," which appeared in the 1960s and could be used with a standard TV. The enormous success came after the appearance of the "Space Invaders" in 1980s. The game inspired thou-sands of movie and story tellers and literally became a well-known brand. In fact, it opened a golden era of video games that is still continuing.

He establishes **kairos** *here by showing that video games are prevalent and have been since the 1980s.*

Because video games are a form of art, we can divide them into different genres due to different aspects (the level of interactivity which the game pres-ents, ways of playing this game, types of devices, the style of playing the game, etc.). Educational video games are considered to be the most useful ones. In fact, in 2009 President Barack Obama supported a pro-gram called "Educate to Innovate," which included the development of technology in the sphere of education. According to this program, video games helped students to gain knowledge in an interactive way.

Ethos *is again established through expertise on these details and with this informed historical account.* **Kairos** *emerges through the reference to Obama, suggesting an inquiry worthy of contemporary politics.*

From *Undergraduate Research Journal for the Human Sciences,* 2012.

The second type is casual games that are usually played on telephones and a PC. These types of games may seem to be useless, but some psychologists still consider them to develop skills of time management and reaction time. One more type is serious games (Winegarner, 2005), created to develop some kind of learning experience and is not usually intended for simple entertainment. They are dedicated to development of specific professional skills and knowledge. One of the most prominent examples of this type is a game called "Microsoft Flight Simulator," which was developed for the military (Roberts, 2001)....

> Throughout the article, Aleghfeli demonstrates *kairos* (as in propriety) by including a blend of scholarly citations, his own ideas, and, later in the text, popular literature such as *Forbes Magazine*. This meets readers' expectations about a topic like video games, which spans the popular to scholarly continuum.

There is no doubt that games can educate people by providing them not only pure knowledge but also skills that are hard to gain. Knowledge received from playing will not be static; this knowledge will develop "cognitive maps," which create strategies to manage time, to count resources, and to find solutions to hard problems (Layford, 2008). On the other hand, it is necessary to remember that the virtual world still differs greatly from the real one. For example, learning how to drive a car in a video game does not mean you can really drive.

> These two paragraphs demonstrate *logos* as he cites specific examples of video games that cultivate knowledge and skills and describes how video games accomplish this.

Professor B. Griffiths, from the University of Nottingham, noted that playing video games helps disabled people, in particular disabled children, to gain social and educational skills (Aarseth, 2004). In fact, some medical departments in the U.S. recover individuals' motor skills and develop coordination by giving them opportunity to play video games. What is more, research shows that playing such kinds of games make people think more creatively and faster. Children are also thought to gain some amount of self-confidence, motivation, and inspiration not to search for easy solutions while dealing with hard problems (Blodget, 2006).

> This paragraph illustrates *logos* with specific examples, *ethos*, by citing scholars and establishing expertise, and *pathos*, by appealing to readers' emotions about the education of children and people with disabilities.

> By addressing violent video games, he shows that his *purpose* is not only to show the educational purposes of video games, but also to address the potential negative impact of video games. His *ethos* emerges therefore as trustworthy and judicious.

Although there are positive outcomes of playing video games, it is also a double-edged sword. There are many educative outcomes, but what are the outcomes of violent games (Greg, 1994)? If players are killing other creatures, they may unconsciously change their psychological condition and become more aggressive and uncontrollable. Psychologists think that there is enough blood, violence, and death in movies and television for children today. They have no need to play murderers.

Too much of something can never be useful. While playing any types of video games it is extremely necessary to have a healthy environment (Miller, 2005). Many people claim video games to be the main reason of destruction of family relationships, as this kind of amusement takes too much time away from family activities that keep people close together (Crawford, 1992). Moreover, there are claims that video games are the main cause of children's mental imbalance; kids are easily addicted to playing games that keep their attention for long hours. This makes children isolated from the world of doing their homework and family duties. This is why, parents need to control and limit the time their children spend on playing this type of game. For sure, game addiction may not be compared to drinking alcohol and taking drugs, but it still destroys health (Dolan, 2009). Children and adults who are addicted to games not only fail to do their work or school duties, they also forget about sports, eating, and even sleeping.

Spending too much time eye-to-eye with a computer will also cause a "social withdrawal" effect, where a person is left out of the social circle and without friends. Moreover, it effects the development of natural talents and the amount of time spent on hobbies (Wills, 2002).

Many people working in the video game industry today become concerned about the question: "What is the future of the video games?" Making predictions about the future was never an easy task in the fast-moving video game business. Michael Noer, from *Forbes Magazine*, said that the graphics of video games will continue to develop, especially concerning colors and details. The demographics and motion-sensitive controllers are also expected to change greatly. Huge video game corporations will divide

> The focus of this paragraph and the next is largely on children and families, which suggests that his audience might include those who are parents of children who play video games.

> *Logos* appears here as he cites experts on claims about the damaging impact of video games.

> These sections invoke *pathos* as he appeals to readers' sympathy for those in the throes of addictive behavior and fear of the destructiveness of that behavior and the "social withdrawal" effect.

> Because he spends considerable time outlining the potential negative impact as well as the positive impact, Aleghfeli's audience likely includes those who are skeptical about video games as well as those who are enthusiasts. He might be offering a dual message, suggesting a middle-ground approach to video games that recognizes their potential and their drawbacks.

> This paragraph speaks to the business and industry side, suggesting that people in those sectors are also among his audience. This paragraph also invokes *kairos* by showing that video games have a future presence.

into smaller ones, and the competitiveness of producing high-quality video games will rise greatly. Games will include more possibilities to actually "feel" what you are playing, for example it will include sensitive instruments, pedals, new types of wheels, and other innovations (Noer, 2007)....

Kairos emerges here since video games are likely to play a role of some sort in our lives. This shows it is worth our while to consider the effects and use of video games.

This concluding paragraph reveals his message, that video games have positive and negative effects, and must be controlled by the user or parent. His audience is people who play video games and parents of children who do.

All in all, no matter how bad or good you think the role of video games play in present day life, they are definitely an active part of it. If one listens to the people who specialize in this industry, they will remain so. Counting all the advantages and disadvantages of playing these games gives a conclusion that a video game can have both positive and negative effects. Video games are a double-edged sword that can work in both directions; everything depends upon how you manage to use it (Lieu, 1997). One thing remains clear, individuals have to control the time they spend playing a game and be sure that the game is worth it. As to the children, parents should not only take care of how much they play, they should also watch what they are playing in order to avoid further social and health problems described in this essay. Have fun playing, but make sure not to cross the boundary between "being entertained" and "being addicted."

He ends with a clear message of playing with moderation. His purpose, thus, seems to be to help his audience (gamers and parents of children who game) play safely and have fun, while recognizing the educative potential and avoiding the risks of addiction.

[References omitted here; available at http://www.kon.org/urc/v11/aleghfeli.html]

Write Now

Choose a text you are currently reading and practice one of the above strategies: either reading like a writer or reading rhetorically (or practice a combination of each). After you have completed this in-depth reading strategy, reflect in writing for ten minutes: What did you learn about the text and/or about yourself as a writer and reader by having adopted this in-depth reading strategy?

Invoking Discipline-Specific Reading Skills

Alongside the aforementioned strategies for reading, academic writers also need to make decisions about which discipline-specific reading skills they might invoke in different contexts. Researchers have identified and developed a range of discipline-specific reading skills, to which readers should be attuned. Charles Bazerman, for example, conducted research about physicists' reading practices, and identified that they "generally do not read articles sequentially." Instead, Bazerman found that they often "looked at the introduction and conclusions," "scann[ed] figures," and often "skipped over...detailed mathematics." Understanding how you might approach texts based on these discipline-specific elements should help you become a more effective and efficient reader.

Structure

Some disciplines adopt particular kinds of structures for much of the writing in that field. For instance, one common structure for academic articles in such fields as the health sciences, known as IMRAD, involves dividing the paper into the following sections: "introduction, methods, results, and discussion" (Sollaci and Pereira). This format is so popular, in fact, that according to researchers it grew in use over the twentieth century until becoming, in the 1980s, "the only pattern adopted by original papers." Learning how to recognize structures such as this in disciplines will help you read more accurately and effectively within disciplines.

Particular questions

While research questions may vary depending on an academic writer's project, readers within particular disciplines will often pose similar kinds of questions as they read. Chapter 3: Posing Meaningful Questions, offered a sense of this. For example, in certain disciplines readers may be trained to ask what the dates of research are for secondary materials; in other disciplines readers may be trained to ask what kinds of evidence a writer is drawing upon; readers in other disciplines may be accustomed to asking where contradictions lie within a text.

Visual literacy

Many disciplines require acumen with understanding visual texts and graphics as you read. These can include images, charts, graphs, and tables, as well as other forms of media, such as videos, animations, and interactive multimedia elements. Reading visually asks that you consider how the visual elements intersect with other elements of the text, what their purpose is, and how they contribute to the overall direction of a text. Visual literacy invites you to think about the choices writers have made in assembling, curating, and developing visual elements as substantive aspects of their texts. Chapter 7: Analysis and Chapter 10: Designing Arguments, both expand on visual literacy from the perspectives of visual analysis and visual argument.

Mathematical literacy

Many disciplines also require a certain level of facility with mathematical calculations. This is true not only in math, though, but also across the social sciences in such fields as economics and sociology, as well as in the natural sciences, business, and engineering fields.

Data

Disciplines that tend to be more data driven (i.e., Chemistry, Economics, Environmental studies, etc.) require that readers understand some basic elements of data as they read. People reading in Psychology, for instance, will likely need to know what the use of a ellipsis ("…") means.

Technical vocabulary

Academic writers will often encounter a set of terms within a discipline that seem to be particular to that discipline. Those newer to reading in that discipline can expect to need to spend time learning any technical vocabulary. Proof in mathematics is one such example; other kinds of technical vocabulary might include the vocabulary needed to understand historical primary source documents.

Transferring Reading

Reading well in academic contexts requires a deliberate approach. Chapter 3 discussed how varied and numerous academic questions can be. In the same way, with every new and different question, writers face decisions about how to best pursue that question through reading. Recognizing and learning to navigate through the many different choices one can face with deciding what to read and how to read will enable you to become a more effective and efficient academic reader. Each writing occasion—each time you pose and pursue a question—necessitates that you consider carefully what kinds of text you will read and how you will read them.

And, although this chapter began with an admission that reading can be challenging, it can also be quite exhilarating: Reading enables you not only to learn from others, but also to begin to formulate your own thoughts as you move toward contributing your ideas through your writing. Helping you move in exactly this direction, Chapter 5, which addresses summary, will introduce you to the use of summary across disciplines as a way of engaging with others so you can move towards becoming a participant, through writing, in the very conversations about which you are now reading.

ᥱ ᥱ ᥱ

Chapter 4 Key Terms

Primary materials	Shallow reading	*Logos*
Secondary materials	In-depth reading	*Kairos*
Tertiary materials	Research databases	Literature review
Popular sources	Rhetorical triangle	Annotated bibliography
Scholarly sources	*Ethos*	
Public scholarship	*Pathos*	

Write Away

This activity invites you to explore and reflect on discipline-specific reading strategies so you can become more adept at approaching reading from a transfer-based perspective.

Pose a question. Pose a general research question. You can use one of those you developed in Chapter 3, or you can pose an entirely new one. Your question should be broad enough that you will be able to apply it to several different disciplines.

Find (at least) three different disciplinary perspectives. Using several different discipline-specific databases at your institution, find three different articles related to that topic, each from a different disciplinary perspective. For instance, you might find one article from an English Literature perspective, one from Sociology, and one from Chemistry. Focus specifically on scholarly articles from whichever particular disciplines you are choosing.

Read and annotate. Read and annotate in-depth each of those articles, looking specifically for moments where you as a reader find yourself using discipline-specific reading skills. For example, do you notice any particular structures? Where are you finding technical vocabulary? Do any of the articles require you to use visual, mathematical, or data-based literacy skills?

Reflect. After annotating the articles, reflect in writing for ten minutes about what you have learned about discipline-based reading strategies and about how you will transfer your approaches to reading across contexts.

Summary

Pinpointing Chapter 5

Now that you have encountered throughout Chapters 2, 3, and 4 several foundational aspects of academic writing that transverse disciplines—research and writing as a process, posing questions, and reading—our exploration now focuses in toward a more specific writing practice: summary. Chapter 5 offers you a glimpse into how academic writers across disciplines and contexts make use of the many varied forms of summary. To provide you with strategies for *summary in transit*, this chapter addresses the following concepts:

- Correcting Common Myths about Summary
- Prerequisites for Writing Summary
- Varied Components of Summary across Context
- Varied Criteria for Effective Summaries across Context
- Different Occasions for Summary

Chapter 6 focuses on synthesis, a writing strategy that uses summary as its foundation by making connections between and across different ideas and texts, thus supporting both analysis and arguments, which will then be the areas of focus for the remaining chapters.

Days 1 & 2—Kathmandu, Nepal
Arrive in Kathmandu and transfer to our hotel, where we'll gather for an orientation. Spend the following day discovering medieval Kathmandu. Venture into Pashupatinath and visit Nepal's largest Buddhist stupa, the Boudhanath Stupa, both part of the UNESCO's World Heritage site. Shangri-La Hotel (*National Geographic Expeditions*).

That these expeditioners chose to feature their visit to the Boudhanath Stupa in even the briefest of journal entries demonstrates its impressiveness and the now-iconic presence it occupies in Kathmandu, Nepal. Those on Mount Everest expeditions often stop at the Boudhanath Stupa to spin prayer wheels and, according to custom, travel the perimeter in clockwise circumnavigation.

The Boudhanath Stupa is one of a number of stupas that exist across Asia, some of which date from as early as 250 B.C.E. and which were often erected as burial monuments in honor of Buddha. Those who study and write about stupas have conveyed many intricacies about these structures. Many feature remarkable astronomical accuracy, oriented so that the moonrise and sunset can mark time and built so that the center pole, which is often the highest point, tracks the sun's zenith…each day. Looking down from the top of a stupa, one can discern an axis point, from which emerge four directions pointing east, north, south, and west ("History"; Kak; Rao; Shelby).

Nearly all the aspects of the stupa have symbolic significance, from the pyramid with 13 steps, "representing the ladder to enlightenment" to the "two circular plinths supporting the hemisphere of the stupa, symbolizing water." The route for clockwise circumnavigation along the bottom of a stupa also holds symbolic importance: "If one thinks of the stupa as a circle or wheel, the unmoving center symbolizes Enlightenment" ("Boudhanath"; Shelby).

The origins of the Boudhanath Stupa have given rise to several legends from varying cultural traditions, that have been passed down across generations and that, together, reflect the multiculturalism of Kathmandu, a city known to sponsor the "greatest intermingling" of Hindus and Buddhists in what is otherwise officially a Hindu country. One legend describes a woman outwitting a king: "[A] woman...asked the king for land to build a shrine to [B]uddha. He agreed to let her have enough land that a buffalo's skin could cover. The woman cut a buffalo's hide into strips and made a large circumference" ("Guide"), thereby winning more land than the king had anticipated.

Another legend holds that a female poultry farmer, Shamvara, and her four sons built the Boudhanath Stupa. However, according to legend, villagers began to complain about the construction but Shamvara refused to stop and died on the spot, thus attaining Buddhist salvation. Yet another legend, emerging from Hinduism, maintains that "the great stupa was built by King Manadeva I in the fifth century C.E. to absolve himself from the sin of patricide" ("Cultural").

Conveying origin myths such as these, relaying architectural features of stupas, and journaling about travel experiences all rely on one of the most valuable, pervasive, and varied features of academic writing: summary. Summary enables people to share knowledge, data, observations, experiences, and ideas.

While summaries such as a three-sentence travelogue might suggest that summary is quite easy, the reality is that summary—even the most concise versions—requires a number of complex writing decisions about what to include and how to incorporate it most effectively for a particular aim or purpose. Far from being simplistic, summary is one of the most powerful, challenging, and central skills you will encounter in academic writing across disciplines and contexts. In fact, it would be difficult to overstate just how vital summary is to academic writing, and just how varied are its forms.

The act of summarizing involves condensing another's text (or your own), into a smaller amount of text. The notion of what constitutes a text in this case, as in Chapter 4: Reading, must be broadly construed because writers routinely summarize all sorts of texts, be they written, verbal, visual, material, auditory, or some combination thereof.

With multiple, sometimes overlapping purposes, summaries can work to share key information, encourage others to examine a text for themselves, discuss the uses and limits of a text, or provide a platform of knowledge from which writers and their readers can build. Sometimes summaries stand alone, and other times they are embedded as part of larger writing projects.

Write Here

Locate two or three other travel accounts of Kathmandu, read them, and then compare them to the brief one excerpted from the *National Geographic* expedition on the first page of this chapter. What sites and experiences in Kathmandu do these other travelers document? What do you think influences the decisions different travelers make for how to summarize their experiences and how to select which experiences to include or omit as they develop their travelogues?

Correcting Common Myths about Summary

Summary can carry with it a somewhat unforgiving reputation, in part due to some common myths about what summary is and what it is not. So let's begin by debunking some of these common myths about summary.

Myth #1: Summary is objective

Summary is rarely objective. Since all humans understand texts and experiences based on their perspectives, summary looks different depending on who is writing a summary. Different individuals notice different details, and have different priorities. Summaries also emerge from within varying contexts, and this shapes what summary looks like. Summaries often reflect these individual and diverse nuances.

Myth #2: Summary is easy to write

Summary involves a number of complex choices: How much detail to include? How much background to offer? How to integrate it into a longer writing project? What kind of tone to convey? Some of these choices are determined by the publication context or disciplinary perspective. Others are determined by other elements of a writer's goals and purposes. Regardless, summary is challenging because it asks you to fully understand the text you are summarizing, capture its essence and/or other relevant aspects, and situate it within your own purposes—all within what is often a quite brief amount of text.

Myth #3: Summary isn't used in college

Since summary can sometimes be associated with book reports, people may inadvertently think that summary is not a skill worth focusing on at the postsecondary level. However, summary appears in countless ways throughout academic writing at the college level, as you will see in the final section of this chapter.

Prerequisites for Writing Summary

Approaching summary requires two critical prerequisites:

1. **Careful reading.** Writing effective summaries hinges on your critical reading skills, so you are encouraged to review Chapter 4: Reading, especially the section on Featured In-Depth Reading Strategy: Reading Rhetorically. It is exceptionally difficult to summarize a text effectively if you haven't read it thoroughly, taking into account matters of context, purpose, and other aspects of the text.

2. **Understanding the occasion for the summary.** This involves gaining a nuanced understanding of the occasion giving rise to the summary. Why are you writing the summary? What do you hope to accomplish? The following section includes several key questions writers should ask and answer before creating summaries.

Key questions for determining the occasion for summary

Since nearly every aspect of a summary is determined by the particular occasion for the summary, it is crucial for writers to understand several key aspects about the occasion for any given summary. Doing so will enable writers to craft the most effective summaries for whatever the given occasion demands.

Purpose

Is your purpose primarily to inform readers, ostensibly in lieu of their reading, viewing, or listening to the text themselves? Or, is your purpose primarily to persuade readers to read or purchase the text? Is your summary connected to a larger argument or aim in a piece of writing?

Audience

How knowledgeable are they about the subject matter and/or text you are summarizing? What do you hope your readers learn from the summary? Why might they be reading the summary?

> ### *Writer Insights*
>
> **How and when do you use summary in your writing?**
>
> As a consultant for workforce development, my writing starts with knowing my audience. For example, when I develop a curriculum, I include more instructions in simpler language if the teachers are likely to be inexperienced. If people who can easily interpret statistics are the targeted audience, I provide less explanation of the numbers than I do for a general readership. Sometimes a bulleted list is desirable as denser text would be a barrier or ignored. Most often I provide an introduction and a summary so potential readers can quickly assess whether the material is relevant to their needs.
>
> *~Laura Wyckoff, Workforce Development Consultant, Portland, Oregon, U.S.*

Requirements

The length of summaries varies considerably, ranging from 140 characters (as in a tweet) to much longer summaries that might be found in a full-length review or detailed overview. Determinations of length requirements or preferences are usually dictated by the occasion for the summary.

Write Now

Choose a long text you have read, or written, and summarize it into a 140-character tweet.

Transfer Hub: Contribute your ideas and see what others have written at fountainheadpress.com/transferhub.

General to specific

How detailed should the summary be? Is it sufficient to provide a broad, sweeping overview, or should the summary include material about evidence, methods, quotes, and/or more specifics?

Background material

All writing can be connected to contextual considerations as cultural, historical, social, and biographical matters. Most writing also can be connected to larger conversations about a subject matter—other texts that are related either similarly or dissimilarly. Summaries vary in terms of how much of this context or background material should be provided.

Disciplinary context

Effective summaries also take into account the disciplinary context of the work being summarized and the disciplinary context for the summary itself.

Tone

As indicated earlier, summary is rarely objective. Summaries can be more positive or critical in nature; they can work to encourage or discourage engagement with the text being summarized.

Varied Components of Summary across Context

Your answers to the previous questions help shape the summary you produce. Depending on how you answer these questions, you might include any or all of the following in your summary:

- main argument/features of the text
- key terms of the text
- evidence and/or main examples from the text
- significance of the text
- key quotes from the text
- purpose of the text
- methods used in the text (see "Research across Disciplines" in Chapter 2: Research and Writing as a Process)
- political, social, and cultural context or background
- assumptions guiding the text
- probable audience of the text
- tone of the text
- related texts

Criteria for Effective Summaries across Contexts

Given the drastic variation in purpose, discipline, format, and style among summaries, it would be challenging to develop an exhaustive list of criteria that make summaries more or less effective. Still, there are some general criteria that might be applied across disciplines. Effective summaries, regardless of discipline or format, will generally all include the same components and features.

Accuracy

Summaries should not misrepresent, underrepresent, or otherwise mischaracterize the text. You might be familiar with inaccurate summaries in the political arena, where those with one political priority might take a snippet of text from someone with a different political priority and put it out of context, using it as a way to mischaracterize how that individual approaches an important issue. Such a tactic is an underrepresentation and mischaracterization. One way of guarding against this is through careful and thorough reading. Another way is to imagine that the author of the text being summarized is reading the summary. Would he or she agree that the summary captures the text honestly and thoroughly?

Appropriately reduced

One major point of summary is to reduce another text. If your summary is the same length or longer than the text you are summarizing, then you have likely not achieved summary.

Contextually appropriate

Identify the purpose and occasion for the summary and match your writerly choices to that occasion, ensuring that such matters as the length, level of detail, and tone for the summary are appropriate given the context from which the summary is emerging.

Clear

Aim to make your summary clear so that readers who have not or will not actually read, view, or listen to the original text can still understand that text.

Reflective of text's main points

Even if you are focusing in more depth on another part of an argument, it's important to share the main points of the text and/or the key terms of a text before then moving in to focus on the portion of the text you aim to summarize even more thoroughly. If there are key terms in the text, include those in the summary. Ostensibly, if you find yourself summarizing a text, there must be something significant about that text. Aim to convey that significance within your summary.

Faithful to author's voice

Some disciplines and some occasions for summary value and expect more than others that a summary may convey a sense of the author's voice. You can accomplish this either through quoting portions of the author's text or by using the author's own terms as you summarize his or her text. It's important to convey a sense of the author's voice in your summary so readers get a fuller impression and understanding of the text.

Links to larger purpose

Many summaries situate the text under consideration within a larger landscape of relevant literature. This enables readers to see how this text is positioned within these larger debates and conversations. Summaries are also usually connected to a current project, and this larger purpose should shape what is or is not included in the summary.

Different Occasions for Summary

Summary occurs in many different occasions and for many different purposes across disciplines. Here are examples and discussions of the following common occasions for summary, many of which you will likely be called upon to make use of in your academic writing at various junctures:

- Summary in Reviews
- Summary as Abstracts
- Summary and Bibliographic Annotation
- Executive Summary
- Summary in Introductions
- Summary in Conclusions
- Summary as Narrative: Events and Lives

Together, these examples illustrate the degree to which summary transverses disciplinary boundaries even as it also reflects and is shaped by disciplinary context. In this way, writers must rely on transfer-based writing and reading strategies as they engage with summary across writing contexts.

Summary in reviews

In a **review**, a writer summarizes (and usually evaluates) a movie, performance, exhibit, or book. Sometimes the summary portion of the review is called a **synopsis**. You likely have some familiarity with summary through various reviews you may have encountered. You may have read, heard, or watched a review of a song, book, album, movie, or performance in order to learn more about that text or decide if you wanted to attend the event or purchase the item.

Write Now

Have you ever read a review? If so, write for a few minutes about what reviews you have read and why you did so. What were you hoping to learn from a review? How much detail did you hope was or wasn't included? What do you think are the purposes of reviews? If you haven't ever read a review, have you ever asked friends to tell you about a movie they saw or book they read? Write for a few minutes about why you did so, what you hoped to learn, and what you learned from that conversation.

Reviews vary considerably in terms of the amount of detail, opinion, and background or contextual information. Depending on the disciplinary and publication context, some of the summaries that appear in reviews are deliberately lacking in detail because the reviewer knows that his or her readers do not want to know every detail about the text or item under consideration. Take for example an online movie review; a reviewer might provide a warning like "spoiler alert" to those who haven't seen the movie yet.

Study these four examples of summary in reviews, drawn from different disciplines and demonstrating a range of approach from popular through more scholarly modes of writing.

As you read through the following examples, make note of elements that seem to move from summary into evaluation in terms of revealing the author's attitude toward or assessment of the text.

Example 1: Popular Book Review, Non-fiction

The following example of summary in a review is an excerpt from a book review of Jon Krakauer's *Into Thin Air*, a journalistic account of the May 10, 1996, Everest disaster. On this day, a blizzard killed eight climbers, making it at the time the single deadliest day in the history of expeditions on Everest. The review is written by Alastair Scott, himself a prolific writer, traveler, and photographer. That Scott is the writer of this review demonstrates that a certain degree of expertise about the subject matter is often required in order to make summary as effective as possible.

Excerpt from "Fatal Attraction" by A. Scott
(Review of *Into Thin Air* by J. Krakauer)

"With enough determination, any bloody idiot can get up this hill," observed Rob Hall, the leader of a commercial expedition, on his eighth tour of Mount Everest. "

> At the beginning of the review, Scott attempts to provide a clear and concise overview of the content.

The trick is to get back down alive." The particular descent ahead of those on the "hill" on May 10, 1996, resulted in the greatest loss of life in the history of mountaineering on Everest....

Jon Krakauer was one of the survivors, and in "Into Thin Air" he relives the storm and its aftermath...As he sees it,...the root of the problem lies in the famous explanation George Mallory gave when asked why he wanted to climb the mountain, an explanation that still holds true, albeit with a slight amendment. People climb Mount Everest because it—and the money—is there....

> Here, Scott offers a brief rendition of Krakauer's main argument in the book.

"Into Thin Air" is a step-by-step account of how a diverse group of people try to conquer a mountain whose majesty is utterly dwarfed by the hardship required to ascend it. "The expedition...became an almost Calvinistic undertaking," Mr. Krakauer remarks, adding that he "quickly came to understand that climbing Everest was primarily about enduring pain." Most people who publish mountaineering books are more skillful as adventurers than they are as writers; Mr. Krakauer is an exception....

> Summaries often, as this one does, include quotes from the text. At the end of this excerpt, Scott begins to move from summary to analysis.

From *The New York Times*, 18 May, 1997.

Example 2, Part A: Popular Review, Documentary Television Series (Longer Version)

This next example is an excerpt from a review written by Susan Stewart about a documentary television series called *Everest: Beyond the Limit*, which aired on the *Discovery Channel* November 14, 2006 to December 30, 2009. This review demonstrates how to translate something that is visual into a written summary. This review, like Scott's, also appeared in *The New York Times*. Stewart is a Professor of the Humanities at Princeton University.

Excerpt from "Why Climb a Mountain? It's There, and It's Hard to Do" by S. Stewart
(Review of *Everest: Beyond the Limits*)

Notice the details Stewart chooses to include as she orients readers to the documentary. Why do you think she chose these details as opposed to others she might have included?

"Everest" follows a crew of climbers who paid approximately $40,000 apiece to attempt the summit in the spring of 2006. The expedition is managed by Russell Brice, a silver-haired New Zealander whose rugged good looks are only partly diminished by his chapped lips, and whose machismo is not weakened by his propensity for choking up, as when he mourns the death of a favorite Sherpa guide.

Terry O'Connor, the expedition's physician, excels at describing the effects of altitude sickness, which can strike anyone at any time in the high Himalayas.

"You get used to suffering, frankly," he says. The suffering starts at advanced base camp, where insomnia and nausea accompany the men as their bodies acclimate to the thin atmosphere. Their blood thickens, which helps them not to pass out but increases the risk that they will have strokes....

Stewart quotes from the documentary even though it is not a written text. She also includes here a sense of one of the main areas of focus: personalities.

The documentary, filmed by Sherpa guides wearing helmet-mounted cameras, invests in personalities early on....

From *The New York Times*, Nov. 14, 2006.

Example 2, Part B: Popular Review, Documentary Television Series (Shorter version)

Even a review can be summarized as in this case, where Stewart's longer review is also linked on the website for *The New York Times* to a briefer overview.

Review Summary: "Why Climb a Mountain? It's There,
and It's Hard to Do" by S. Stewart
(Review of *Everest: Beyond the Limits*)

A group of climbers from all over the world and one veteran guide climb to the world's tallest peak in an attempt to reach the summit. Partially filmed with cameras mounted to Sherpas' helmets, and two camerapersons who also summited with high-altitude cameras, it offers an unflinching look at this incredible expedition through a zeroing in on the experiences of the climbers.

From *nytimes.com*, Nov. 14, 2006.

Write Now

Imagine the editor of *The New York Times* has asked you to write a "review summary" for another's review. Choose a review of either a book, performance, movie, or album and, using the above "review summary" as an example, write a review of the summary in 50-75 words.

 Transfer Hub: Contribute your ideas and see what others have written at fountainheadpress.com/transferhub.

Example 3: Public Scholarship, Academic Review of a Popular Book, Library Science

In this example of a slightly more academic book review than those that appear in *The New York Times*, Margaret Heilbrun, senior editor for *Library Journal,* reviews a coffee-table book comprised of photographs of Mount Everest. *Library Journal* emerges from the discipline of library science or information technologies.

Excerpt from M. Heilbrun's Review of *Conquest of Everest:
Original Photographs from the Legendary First Ascent*

Lewis-Jones (Arctic) clarifies in his prolog that this book was originally intended to mark the 50th anniversary of the 1953 Everest ascent, but there were delays. The foreword by Edmund Hillary, a 2007 tribute to his friend George Lowe, is one of the last pieces Hillary wrote. Lowe was the expedition's "cine cameraman." This coffee-table book is not just a treasury of Lowe's photographs; it introduces readers fully to this "forgotten man of Everest." The bulk of the text is Lowe's

> Heilbrun focuses here on the key details of the text and conveys the main significance.

From *Library Journal* (138.7), 2013.

memoir of his life as it relates to that expedition, with "portfolios" of his photographs, many not previously published, between the chapters. Lowe, who was the last surviving member of the expedition (he died last month), writes of his first encounters with fellow New Zealander Hillary as they climbed together in the years before being chosen for the expedition: 13 men (plus "an army of Sherpa") tasked with putting the two of them on the summit. A final chapter contains "Reflections" by others, including sons of Tenzing and of Hillary. Jan Morris, who as correspondent for the *Times* was attached to the expedition, provides the epilogue.

VERDICT: Essential for all Everest collections as one of the expedition's last primary sources and a deserved testament to Lowe's contributions. He proves himself, as Jan Morris puts it, "a man of sweet charm and courtesy."

> Readers of the journal likely work for libraries and make decisions about new books to purchase. Notice in this review, therefore, that Heilbrun concludes with a "verdict" that recommends libraries purchase the text.

Example 4: Scholarly Review, Environmental Studies

The fourth example of summary in a review involves a more academic book review. Here Sebastian Interlandi, from the Department of Environmental Science, Engineering & Policy at Drexel University, writes a review of a book on environmental research. Readers of the journal in which the review appears may use the summary in the review to decide whether to read the book themselves, but they are also likely interested in using reviews to stay current in recent research in their field.

Excerpt from S. Interlandi's Review of *Top of the World Environmental Research*

This book compiles a broad range of articles that concern high elevation research on the Himalayan Plateau. The contributors have been working in conjunction with a facility called the Pyramid Laboratory, established in the Khumbu Valley by Italy's Consiglio Nazionale delle Ric.erche (CNR). Most of the information presented is general in nature, and ranges from simple descriptions of Himalayan geology and biota to assessments of regional water quality.

> Notice in this paragraph that Interlandi shifts from summary to analysis. Where do you see that shift occurring?

The first two chapters detail how the Pyramid Laboratory and this book came into existence. A brief history of European exploration in the region and an overview of Himalayan geology follows. Himalayan terrestrial ecology and aquatic ecology

From *Quarterly Review of Biology* (75.2), 2000.

are discussed in a variety of chapters, including a reasonably complete paleolimnological analysis of Himalayan lake sediments including geochemistry, fossil pigments and diatom frustules. The final chapter is an overview of the development of a GIS database of the region. Unfortunately, many chapters are too general in scope. Some are merely reviews of the topic they cover (for example, chapters on high altitude organic micropollutants, exercise at high altitude, and GIS systems) and present only a few paragraphs of information on the Himalayan system in particular. While reading this book, one gets the feeling that only a few thorough studies in the Himalayas are described and placed amid some rather fluffy review material.

The editors carefully reviewed the articles for style and language. Although most authors of the book do not share English as their native language, the chapters are well structured and easily readable with few stylistic errors. Although no conceptually novel research is presented in this volume, the comprehensive coverage of an underappreciated region makes this book interesting for those concerned with alpine research or science in developing regions. In a sense, the aura of mystery surrounding the Himalayan region is unveiled here, and for those simply curious about the area, this book would be worthwhile.

> Interlandi includes here a description of what he takes to be the primary usefulness and contributions made by the volume.

Summary as abstracts

Academic writers often create **abstracts** of either their own or others' texts. The Writing Center at the University of North Carolina defines an abstract as, "a self-contained, short, and powerful statement that describes a larger work." Many academic journals require abstracts for their published articles so busy readers can skim the abstracts in order to decide whether to read an entire article or not. Abstracts can also be called by other terms, such as **précis** or synopsis.

The amount of material academic writers include in an abstract varies considerably and depends on disciplinary and publication context. Sometimes an abstract is quite brief, perhaps a sentence or two. At other times, an abstract includes a much more detailed account of one's argument, evidence, methods, and conclusions.

Abstracts are most commonly found in articles emerging from disciplines in the sciences and social sciences, though the practice is also becoming more common in the humanities. In these contexts, journals often ask authors to write abstracts of their articles for the publication because they anticipate that busy readers will want to read an abstract in order to determine

Writer Insights

When do you write annotations?

I always write annotations to help the organization of my work, main points and topics, the data and details I will include in the paper, and to guide me in all the process of research and writing. Furthermore, I write annotations to memorize important concepts for an exam or other assignment.

~*Vinicius S. Carvalho, ESL/EFL Student,
Osasco, São Paulo, Brazil*

whether to read an article more thoroughly but also to facilitate a quick skim of a journal in order to stay current in their field.

What follows is an example of an abstract that appears at the beginning of an article in a journal geared toward biology and medicine called *High Altitude Medicine & Biology*. This article involves a case study examining high-altitude amputation on Mount Everest. As you read the abstract, you might consider how the authors might have adjusted the abstract under different length requirements. For instance, what details might they have excluded if their abstract needed to be no more than 50 or 100 words?

Abstract from "Mount Everest and Makalu Cold Injury Amputation: 40 Years On"
by S. Morrison, J. Gorjanc, and I. Mekjavic

Freezing cold injuries (frostbite) of the extremities are a common injury among alpinists

The authors describe their case study.

participating in high altitude expeditions, particularly during inclement weather conditions. Anecdotally, a digit that has suffered frostbite may be at greater risk to future cold injuries. In this case study, we profile a 62-year-old elite alpinist who suffered multiple digit amputations on both his hands and foot after

Here, they offer a description of the data they provide.

historic summit attempts on Makalu (8481 m) and Mt. Everest (8848 m) in 1974–1979. We describe the clinical treatment he received at that time, and follow up his case 40 years after the first incidence of frostbite utilizing a noninvasive evaluation of hand and foot function to a cold stress test, including rates of re-warming to both injured and non-injured digits. Finger rates of recovery to the cold stress test were not different (0.8 vs. 1.0°C·min−1) except one (injured, left middle finger, distal phalanx; 0.4°C·min−1). Toe recovery rates after cold-water immersion were identi-

The authors include the conclusions they arrive at in their article.

cal between previously injured and non-injured toes (0.2°C·min−1). Thermocouple data indicate that this alpinist's previous frostbite injuries may not have significantly altered his digit rates of re-warming during passive recovery compared to his non-injured digits.

———

From *High Altitude Medicine & Biology* (15.1), 2014.

Summary as annotation

Summary in academic writing also appears in another format closely related to abstracts, known as bibliographic annotations. Unlike the prior instance, where authors write an abstract about their own work, the summaries that appear in relationship to bibliographic annotation are generally written by authors who are writing about other people's research.

A bibliographic annotation is a short summary of a text, somewhat similar to an abstract, but generally occurs as part of a longer list of texts, found perhaps in a list of references or in a library catalog or research database.

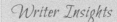

Writer Insights

How do annotations help you with your research?

When it comes to writing my thesis, ... I start by creating a list of references for all the sources I depend on. I [then] make an annotated bibliography, and [next] an outline for every chapter.

~Lubna Adel, Ph.D. Candidate & ESL Teacher, Cairo, Egypt

Example 1: Bibliographic Annotation, Annotated Bibliography

Annotated bibliographies sometimes appear in the back of books, where authors will provide summaries (annotations) of references or provide them as suggestions for further reading. Some academic writers compose annotated bibliographies as part of their research process in order to learn about relevant research in more depth. Others compose annotated bibliographies as the end product itself.

One main purpose of annotated bibliographies is to provide other researchers with a clear picture of the texts relating to a given area of inquiry. Annotated bibliographies can help researchers decide what texts they will read for their own research.

Following are two annotated bibliographic entries from one online annotated bibliography. The author, Bill Buxton, is a technology expert with a passion for mountaineering; he approaches Mount Everest scholarship from the perspectives of history and cultural anthropology. One of the entries reproduced here is longer and one is shorter, demonstrating that bibliographic annotations come in many forms.

Excerpt from "Books on History and Exploration, with a Focus on Central Asia ... [and] The History of Climbing and Mountaineering" by B. Buxton

Norgay, Tenzing & Ullman, James (1955). *Tiger of the Snow*. New York: G.P. Putnam's and Sons.

This is an autobiography of Tenzing Norgay Sherpa. See also his second autobiography, *After Everest*. As part of the 1953 expedition led by John Hunt, along with Hillary, Tenzing was

---

From *billbuxton.com*, 2014.

the first to summit Everest. While Tenzing could neither read nor write, he was clearly an exceptional man, not only for his climbing, but for his character and intelligence in general. While his story has been put down on paper by Ullman, his voice and thoughts come through convincingly.

> Here Buxton offers a concise description of who Tenzing is and his connection to Everest.

This is clearly a motivated man. He climbed and traveled in Chitral, Kashmir, Garhwal, and Tibet. His finding himself on the top of Everest was also no accident. He had been to Everest 6 times before. He went to the North Side in 1935 with Shipton, 1936 with Ruttledge, 1938 with Tilman; and 1947 with Denman. He then went to the South Side in the spring of 1952 with Swiss team led by Wyss-Dunant, and back again in the autumn on their second attempt led by Chevalley (Dittert et al., 1954).

> Notice the terms such as "convincingly" and "motivated" that convey not only a distanced perspective but also Buxton's assessment of the text.

As Ortner points out, almost all of our history of Himalayan mountaineering comes from westerners, since they were the ones with the skills and means to write the books. From the earlier period, there are only four first person accounts "from the other side," this one by Tenzing, his second autobiography *After Everest, Mémoires d'un Sherpa* by Ang Tharkay, and finally the remarkable *Servant of Sahibs*, written in 1923 by Ghulam Rassul Galwan, who had worked for Younghusband, among others. Due to their scarcity, insights, and perspective, these books make fascinating reading.

> Here, and in the paragraph above, Buxton situates Norgay's work among other related texts, and demonstrates how Norgay's work offers a unique contribution to the array of texts.

What is interesting about this book is that it spends very little time describing the actual climbing in 1953. Tenzing simply says that others have written extensively about it, so there is no need to cover the details of the expedition, other than to shed light on things that have been neglected. What he does do, which Hunt (perhaps understandably) does not, is discuss not only the issues of conflict between the Sherpa and "Sahibs," but also the repercussions (since many of these caused much controversy under the spotlight that fell on the expedition after its success.) He also talks a lot about the impact of the whole thing on his life, which was significant, given the attention given to the expedition.

> Here Buxton describes what Tenzing focuses on, and thereby enables a scholar who may be interested in the impact of the disaster on survivor's lives to see that this book would be relevant for his or her research.

Finally, one cannot read this book without being touched by the love that he had for the mountains, and the bond that he shared with those of similar spirit (not the least of whom was Lambert, of the 1952 Swiss team, with whom—despite a language barrier—he clearly had an outstanding bond.) In this there are strong echoes of Rébuffat's fellowship of the rope. For me, this spirit extended beyond the printed page, bonding author to reader.

See also Tenzing's son Jamling's book, *Touching My Father's Soul*, Tashi Tenzing's *Tenzing Norgay and the Sherpas of Everest*, Malartic's early biography, *Tenzing of Everest*, and the most recent biography, Douglas' *Tenzing: Hero of Everest*.

Excerpt from "Books on History and Exploration, with a Focus on Central Asia … [and] The History of Climbing and Mountaineering" by B. Buxton

Noyce, Wilfrid & Richard Taylor (1954). *Everest is Climbed*. Harmondsworth: Puffin (Puffin Picture Book, No. 100).

This is a brief (30 page) soft-cover picture book for children. The text is by Noyce, and the images are all drawings by Taylor.

In this second, very brief example, Buxton has chosen to summarize concisely, omitting background material or assessments of the text.

From *billbuxton.com*, 2014.

Example 2: Bibliographic Annotation, Library Catalog

The following example is a bibliographic annotation that appears in a library catalog. These kinds of annotations also sometimes appear on the back covers of books. As with many other occasions for summary, they often include an assessment of the text, or comments on its potential usefulness, because scholars are generally using these summaries to decide whether to locate and read the item on the library shelves or through an electronic distribution.

This annotation summarizes a book called *Everest and Conquest in the Himalaya*, co-written by travel writer Richard Sale and Professor in the School of Nursing at the University of Utah, George Rodway. The summary was provided to the library by a company called Syndetic Solutions, Inc., which creates "unique descriptive data components" for online catalogs ("Syndetic Solutions"). As you read, pay attention to terms and phrases in the summary that create a particular tone or convey a certain attitude—elements perhaps intended to shape readers' perceptions of the text.

Excerpt from "Title Summary"
Everest and Conquest in the Himalaya: Science and Courage on the World's Highest Mountain
by R. Sale and G. Rodway

A century ago the summits of the world's highest peaks, Everest included, were beyond reach. Pioneering attempts to overcome the dangers of climbing at extremely high altitudes ended in failure, sometimes with disastrous consequences. Yet today high-altitude ascents are frequent, almost commonplace. Everest can be conquered by relatively inexperienced mountaineers, and their exploits barely merit media attention—unless they go fatally wrong. In this fascinating study of the dramatic history of Everest climbs, Richard Sale and George Rodway describe in vivid detail the struggle to conquer the mountain and the advances in scientific knowledge that made the conquest possible. Their account gives a compelling insight into the science of mountaineering as well as the physical and psychological challenges faced by individuals who choose to test themselves in some of the harshest conditions on earth.

From *library.duke.edu*, 2014.

Write Now

Write a bibliographic annotation for a text you have recently read. Write it as though you were doing so for the back cover of the book and/or for a library catalog.

Executive summary

Executive summaries appear at the front of policy briefs or memos, and are intended to serve the exact purpose its name suggests: to provide a brief summary of the most critical aspects of a longer text so busy executives or managers can skim the material quickly. The Writing Center at Texas A&M University defines an executive summary as:

> [A] brief overview of a document's purpose, results, and conclusions condensed for the quick reading of an executive or manager. It is placed at the beginning of a longer report or proposal and summarizes specific aspects of its content. The reader of the summary is usually not interested in the technical details.

Writing that emerges from the disciplinary perspectives of public policy and business are likely to make extensive use of executive summaries.

The following example comes from the United States Department of State, Bureau of Democracy, Human Rights, and Labor. It is a 32-page single-spaced document offering details on Nepal's human rights climate for 2013. The executive summary portion, reproduced here, comprises the first one and one-half pages of this much longer report.

Excerpt from: United States Department of State, Bureau of Democracy, Human Rights, and Labor

EXECUTIVE SUMMARY

Nepal is a federal democratic republic. The political system is based on the Interim Constitution of Nepal 2063 (2007), with a prime minister as the chief executive and a Constituent Assembly, which is responsible for drafting a new constitution. On November 19, Nepal held national elections to replace the Constituent Assembly, which was suspended in May 2012 after it did not draft a new constitution by the deadline established by the Supreme Court. Domestic and international observers characterized the Constituent Assembly election results as credible and well conducted, and the Asian Network for Free Elections (ANFREL) characterized them as essentially free and fair. There were reports of political violence, intimidation, and some voting irregularities, although many fewer than in the previous Constituent Assembly elections in 2008. Authorities maintained effective control of the security forces. As in previous years, there were reports that security forces committed human rights abuses.

> For the first few sentences, the executive summary provides a general overview of Nepal's government and political system. Midway through the paragraph, the summary begins to address human rights in elections.

The most significant human rights problems were exacerbated by the country's continuing delay in promulgating a permanent constitution (reflecting the absence of an elected legislature for most of the year); the continued absence of transitional justice mechanisms, such as a truth and reconciliation commission to account for past human rights abuses; and the related failure to implement court ordered arrests of military personnel, Maoists, and other individuals accused or convicted of human rights violations stemming from the country's 10-year insurgency.

> Notice the different types of "human rights problems" addressed in this paragraph and the next and how the summary emphasizes some as more prevalent or significant than others.

Other human rights problems included poor prison and detention center conditions. Corruption existed at all levels of government and police, and the courts remained vulnerable to political pressure, bribery, and intimidation. There were problems with self-censorship by members of the press. The government sometimes restricted freedom of assembly. The government limited freedoms for refugees, particularly for the Tibetan

---

From *state.gov*, 2014.

community. Discrimination against women was a problem, and citizenship laws that discriminate by gender contributed to statelessness. Domestic violence against women remained a serious problem, and dowry-related deaths occurred. Violence against children was widespread, although rarely prosecuted, and sex trafficking of adults and minors remained a serious problem. Discrimination against persons with disabilities, some ethnic groups, and persons with HIV/AIDS continued. Violence associated with caste-based discrimination occurred. There were some restrictions on worker rights, and forced, bonded, and child labor remained significant problems.

A decreasing number of armed groups, largely in the Tarai region, attacked civilians, government officials, members of particular ethnic groups, and each other. Members of the Maoist-affiliated All Nepal National Independent Students Union-Revolutionary (ANNISU-R) were responsible for extortion, intimidation, and school bus burnings. Armed groups were responsible for abductions to obtain ransom, mainly in the Tarai region.

Impunity for conflict-era human rights violations continued to be a serious problem in the absence of a truth and reconciliation commission and a disappearances commission.

Summary in introductions

One of the most frequently found occasions for summary is in introductions. While introductions contain a number of elements, they also often include a summary of what will follow in the text. Sometimes this is in the form of a brief overview of the paper, where a writer shares in a brief sentence or two what the paper will address. In the following introductory passage, authors Robin Canniford, Professor of Business and Economics at the University of Melbourne, and Avi Shankar, Professor of Consumer Research at the University of Bath, provide an overview of the rest of their article, titled "Purifying Practices: How Consumers Assemble Romantic Experiences of Nature," which appeared in the *Journal of Consumer Research*:

> Through data gathered during an 8-year ethnography of surfing culture, we answer [our primary research question] and make three contributions to consumer research.

Other times, summaries appear in introductions to anthologies, or collections of essays, where the person writing the introduction (usually the editor) provides summaries for each of the articles or chapters in the collection.

The following such excerpt comes from the introduction to an anthology about sports and tourism edited by Mike Weed, a Professor of Applied Policy Sciences at Canterbury Christ Church University. The anthology includes a variety of reprinted texts, and in the introduction, Weed provides a summary overview of each article. This summary is for Karin

Weber's "Outdoor Adventure Tourism: A Review of Research Approaches," which is the fourth chapter of the anthology. Notice the in-depth nature of the summary Weed has written, sharing with readers Weber's main argument in extended detail.

Excerpt from "Introduction"
Sport & Tourism: A Reader, M. Weed, ed.

The fourth chapter...focuses on outdoor adventure tourism...[W]ritten in 2001, Karin Weber's paper, *Outdoor Adventure Tourism: A Review of Research Approaches* argues for a greater focus on adventure experiences in the study of outdoor adventure tourism. Weber suggests that adventure tourism has traditionally been seen as an extension of adventure recreation and, consequently, the tourism element has been overlooked.... In analyses of adventure tourism, Weber suggests that risk has been too narrowly conceived as physical risk, whereas psychological and social risk can be equally important in the adventure experience. In fact, Weber believes that adventure tourism can be conceptualized as being as much about the quest for insight and knowledge as the desire for elements of physical risk. Furthermore, Weber advocates a greater focus on interpretive qualitative methodologies in understanding adventure experiences.

From *Sport & Tourism: A Reader*, 2007.

Summary in conclusions

As with introductions, conclusions contain many different elements, and summary is often among them. Writers routinely summarize their writing projects in the conclusions, recognizing that the conclusion is the final opportunity in the text to emphasize their most important points and convey their arguments.

In the following excerpt, Linda Allin summarizes her argument about women and Mount Everest in her conclusion.

Excerpt from "Climbing Mount Everest: Women, Career and Family in Outdoor Education" by L. Allin

Summary and conclusions

This study shows the connections and disconnections for women outdoor educators in combining career and family relationships. Joint involvement in the outdoors was illustrated as

From *Australian Journal of Outdoor Education* (8.2), 2004.

> Allin reviews her findings as well as the way in which her article has built on prior knowledge.

important in maintaining some partnerships, but the findings show clearly the dilemmas and contradictions for women outdoor educators, especially after motherhood. While the issue of combining career and family is not new, the study highlights the ways in which women's ability to negotiate career and family relationships in outdoor education is made more difficult by the centrality of the body to outdoor education careers. Women outdoor educators were actively negotiating career and family relationships in a variety of ways, but tensions were compounded for women as they negotiated their career identities within outdoor organisations where the material and social realities of women's bodies were not openly acknowledged. Giddens (1991) suggests that the

> Allin summarizes another study of particular relevance to her own findings.

construction of a coherent self-identity involves an orientation towards the future as well as the past. In this study, the fragility of women's career identities in the outdoors is evident where mothers struggled to identify a coherent sense of their occupational future. As a consequence of changing legislation in the UK, as from April 2003, all workers who meet qualifying criteria in length of service are now entitled to request flexible working, something outdoor organisations will need to implement. The findings from this study suggest that outdoor organisations also need to support women, including providing time for maintaining technical competence, if they are to retain women in and through outdoor education careers.

Summary as narrative

Summary also occurs in the form of a narrative, either as a biography of a person, summarizing the person's experiences, or through a journalistic or historical summary of events. Perhaps in this format as nowhere else do the ethics involved with summarizing become evident. Notice the degree of choices writers must make when summarizing lives and events: choosing what to include and what to exclude, which perspectives to privilege, which to minimize. Summary in these occasions shapes people's impressions of others and of events.

Summary in biography

Biographical work involves many academic writing skills, summary among them. In many academic contexts, one finds occasion to summarize the life or experience of an individual or group of people.

The following example is a summary of the life of Richard William George Hingston, who served as the "medical officer and naturalist" (Pyz) for a 1924 expedition to Everest by George Mallory and Andrew Irvine. Written by Justyna Pyz, a research associate at Trinity College, Dublin, this example has a historical disciplinary perspective. Notice in the example how concisely Pyz summarizes the biography of Hingston, including only the most relevant details related to the current purpose. Another biographer, working for another purpose, might have chosen to focus on different aspects of Hingston's life.

Excerpt from "The Mallory Mount Everest Expedition of 1924: An Irish Perspective" by J. Pyz

The global career of Major Hingston

R.W.G. Hingston was born in London in 1887 but spent most of his early life in the family home at Horsehead, Passage West, Co. Cork. He was educated at University College Cork, from which he graduated with first-class honours in 1910. He subsequently passed into the Indian medical service. In 1913 he joined the Indo-Russian Pamir triangulation expedition as a surgeon and naturalist. With the outbreak of the Great War in 1914, Hingston was recalled for military service and saw action in East Africa, France, Mesopotamia, and the North-West Frontier. He was appointed medical officer and naturalist to the expedition to Mount Everest in 1924. From 1925 to 1927 Hingston acted as a surgeon-naturalist to the marine survey of India on HMS *Investigator* and then, aged 40, retired from the Indian medical service on pension and joined the Oxford University expedition to Greenland. The following year he took part in the Oxford expedition to British Guiana. In 1930 he embarked on a mission conducted by the Society for the Preservation of the Empire Fauna that took him through Rhodesia, Nyasaland, Kenya, Uganda and Tanganyika, investigating methods of preserving the indigenous wildlife. Major Hingston was recalled to military duty in India in 1939 and, after World War II, he retired to his home in County Cork, where he died in 1966.

> Notice how nearly every detail in this summary has to do with Hingston's global experiences. The summary, therefore, is shaped according to purpose. We do not learn, for example, about his personal life at all.

From *History Ireland* (19.5), 2011.

Summary of events

As with biographical writing, journalistic and historical writing involves many academic writing skills, including summary. Summaries of events are largely shaped by purpose, intended audience(s), and context.

Example 1: Historical Event Summary

The following example, written by Peter Hansen, Professor of Humanities & Arts at Worcester Polytechnic Institute, offers a summary of an historical event in which a film, *Conquest of Everest*, depicts Tenzing Norgay, Edmund Hillary, and John Hunt receiving awards and public recognition for their successful 1953 Everest summit. Thus, Hansen is simultaneously summarizing both a scene from the film and the historical event it depicts.

Excerpt from "Confetti of Empire: The Conquest of Everest in Nepal, India, Britain, and New Zealand" by P. Hansen

Kathmandu welcomed the climbers with an official parade and state reception at the Royal Palace. Newsreel footage of their arrival shows thick crowds blocking the procession as the climbers acknowledged the cheers. At the Royal Palace, Tenzing, Hillary, and Hunt received the first of their honors. As King Tribhuvan gave Tenzing the Nepal Tara, the Star of Nepal, the highest decoration not reserved for royalty, he told him in Nepali, "you have added to the prestige of Nepal." The Prime Minister, M.P. Koirala, then awarded Hillary and Hunt the Gorkha Dakshina Bahu, Order of the Gurkha Right Hand, First Class, a lesser award, telling them in English, "You have added to the prestige of Nepal and Great Britain."

———
From *Comparative Studies in Society and History* (42.2), 2000.

Example 2: Current Event Summary

What follows is a summary of the April 18, 2014, Mount Everest avalanche that killed sixteen people. The summary appears in a longer blog posting written by Jon Krakauer, author of *Into Thin Air*.

Excerpt from "Death and Anger on Everest" by J. Krakauer

On April 18th, shortly before 7 A.M. local time, an overhanging wedge of ice the size of a Beverly Hills mansion broke loose from the same ice bulge that had frightened Brice into

———
From *thenewyorkeronline.com*, 2014.

leaving Everest in 2012. As it crashed onto the slope below, the ice shattered into truck-size chunks and hurtled toward some fifty climbers laboring slowly upward through the Khumbu Icefall, a jumbled maze of unstable ice towers that looms above the 17,600-foot base camp. The climbers in the line of fire were at approximately nineteen thousand feet when the avalanche struck. Of the twenty-five men hit by the falling ice, sixteen were killed, all of them Nepalis working for guided climbing teams. Three of the bodies were buried beneath the frozen debris and may never be found.

Write Now

The choices writers make when summarizing events and people's lives have ethical and moral implications. Based on these summaries, what impressions to you have of the kind of person Hingston was, or the kind of work he did, or the circumstances surrounding the avalanche? Identify aspects of the summaries of Hingston's life and the Mount Everest avalanche that might shape readers' perceptions. What other kinds of details might have been included that could have impacted or changed your impressions of Hingston and his work? Choose either an event or a person from your life, one that is likely relatively unknown to others, and write a brief (100-150 words) summary of that event or person's experience. Imagine you are writing for general readers such as those who visit Wikipedia.

Transfer Hub: Contribute your summary and see what others have written at fountainheadpress.com/transferhub.

Transferring Summary

That which makes summary effective for one writing occasion is often not readily transportable to other writing occasions. Transferring your abilities with summary across discipline and context, therefore, requires thinking carefully about the writing occasion and your particular aims and purposes for any given summary. In this sense, summary resonates with what we learned about effective reading strategies in Chapter 4: what you read and how you read it also hinge on context.

Regardless of the particular version or form for summary, though, this skill is one of the key ways in which writers make use of what they read. Learning more about summary also paves the way for the material in Chapter 6, which builds on knowledge about summary by examining synthesis, a feature of academic writing that relies in great measure on using summary in the service of combining different ideas or concepts to create something new.

ಲ ಲ ಲ

Chapter 5 Key Terms

Summary	Abstract	Executive Summary
Review	*Précis*	
Synopsis	Annotated Bibliography	

Write Away

Choose a landmark or site in or near your locale and write several different versions of summary about that site. Doing so will help you explore how you might transfer summary across context.

Select a landmark or site. Choose a site or landmark in your area or at your institution that you can use for this Write Away. It can be one that is very well-known or one that deserves recognition but is not yet as well known. It could also be a site that may be primarily familiar only to people at your institution or in your locale. The site, though, should be one about which you can find some information fairly easily, such as background, history, significance, or other aspects of the site.

Select three-to-four versions of summary, and potential readers. Choose three to four of the different versions of summary described in Chapter 5 to use for summarizing this landmark. For instance, you might choose to write a brief abstract about the historical significance of the site, such as would go on a plaque located onsite. You might also choose to write a more extended summary of the site, such as would appear on a Wikipedia page. A third option might be an executive summary aimed at a Preservation Board or Architectural Committee considering making changes to the site. A fourth option might be a summary of the site that would appear as part of an introduction to a research essay about that landmark.

Share your summaries. Share your different summary versions with classmates and ask for their feedback about which elements of your summaries seem to work most effectively.

Reflect. Reflect in writing for ten minutes about which aspects of summary transected the different occasions for summary, and which elements of summary seemed more uniquely adapted to one particular occasion over others.

Synthesis

Pinpointing Chapter 6

Where Chapter 5 addressed how writers across disciplines engage in varied forms of summary, Chapter 6 demonstrates how writers build on summary with synthesis to advance conversations and carve out more space for writers' own perspectives. Across disciplines, writers use synthesis to generate new understandings, create new ideas, and revisit former assumptions. To provide you with strategies for *synthesis in transit*, this chapter addresses the following concepts:

- What is Synthesis?
- Purposes of Synthesis
- Questions that Shape Synthesis
- Criteria for Effective Synthesis
- Modes of Synthesis across Disciplines

After exploring synthesis here, Chapter 7 offers the opportunity to engage with the work of others and create something new by thinking in a different direction, with analysis. Synthesis, as Chapter 6 establishes, is counterpart to analysis, which invites academic writers to break apart ideas into smaller component parts for extended consideration.

Stonehenge, located near Salisbury in central southern UK is estimated to have been built in 3100 B.C.E. Theories about its purpose have ranged from a site of human sacrifice to an astronomical calculating tool. The site was constructed in stages; one of its most enigmatic aspects involves "the issue of how people achieved the almost unimaginable feat of hauling the sarsens [bluestones], weighing 25 tons or more, over 30 km from the Marlborough Downs in the north" (Ruggles). Alexander Thom provided one of the earliest investigations into the geometry of Stonehenge, observing that "Stonehenge was a lunar as well as a solar observatory," "the axis of Stonehenge pointed to the rising sostitial sun" and the "long sides of the station rectangle...indicated the moon setting in its extreme north position." Gerald Hawkins argued in a bestselling book, *Stonehenge Decoded*, "that the megaliths made up a sophisticated observatory in which the stones served to record solstices and equinoxes and even to predict lunar eclipses" ("About"; Roberts). Clive Ruggles, although acknowledging "axial alignment upon midsummer sunrise and midwinter sunset," challenged Hawkins's ideas about Stonehenge being an astronomical observatory, suggesting instead that the monument "may have symbolized cyclical time through alignments on the sun or moon, or that astronomical considerations formed part of the sacred principles." Recent research has found that as many as 240 people were buried at Stonehenge and that the site had ceremonial significance for herders and farmers. "An 'avenue' connecting Stonehenge with the River Aven is aligned with the solstice…. [Research suggests that] pigs at the site were slaughtered in December and January, suggesting that the winter solstice was marked at Stonehenge (Jarus).

One recent area of research has involved using acoustics to learn more about the purpose and use of Stonehenge.

> Researchers…tested thousands of stones on Carn Menyn in the Preseli Hills, and found a large number of the rocks ring when they are struck. Usually, stones produce a disappointing clunk when hit, with microscopic cracks making it difficult for vibrations to travel within the rock. But certain bluestones have the right microscopic structure—and sound like a metallic gong. They also found a few of the rocks remaining at Stonehenge rang as well. (Cox)

Research on what musicologist Bruno Fazendo calls "archaeoacoustics" shows that learning more about archaeological sites such as Stonehenge often involves asking questions from across disciplines. Researchers working with Fazendo have created real-life and computer-simulated models of Stonehenge to learn more about what it sounded like to stand within the structure when it existed in its entirety.

One finding is that the circular position of the stones provided "the perception…of a reverberant space,…supportive of speech activity since a speaker can be heard reasonably well from anywhere in the space." This archaeoacoustic research enhances previous research about the astronomical alignment of the site to facilitate new understanding about the site's design and function. The kind of multidisciplinary fusion engineered through archaeoacoustics, combining archaeology, musicology, and computer science, among other disciplines, illustrates the concept of synthesis, a kind of scholarly **mashup** that transects writing across disciplines. Well-known musical mashups include *The Grey Album,* a fusion of Jay-Z and the Beatles by Danger Mouse, and "Radioactive Swimming Pools," a mashup of Imagine Dragons and Kendrick Lamar. Mashups also abound in fiction with such works as *Pride and Prejudice and Zombies,* by Seth Grahame-Smith, and *William Shakespeare's Star Wars: Verily, A New Hope*, by Ian Doescher. Various academic disciplines likewise engage in mashups, such as in Computer Science, where a mashup is defined as "a web application that uses content from more than one source to create a single new service displayed in a single graphical interface [such as combining] the addresses and photographs of…library branches with a Google map to create a map mashup." In each of these cases, mashups do not merely combine elements; they do so by "mashing them together to create something new" (Fichter).

The kind of innovation engineered through mashups is part of what makes synthesis so vital in academic writing. Synthesis enables scholars to generate new ideas and create new approaches. Akin to an actual musical synthesizer, which combines "fundamental properties of sound…in a way that forms a new whole" (Harder), synthesis in academic writing involves putting together two or more ideas, concepts, or elements in order to create something new.

Write Here

Pretend you are part of a world-renowned interdisciplinary team of scholars researching Stonehenge. Form a small group with several of your peers, and appoint each person as a representative for a particular discipline (i.e., an anthropologist, a physicist, a literary scholar, etc). Ask each team member to find three or four examples of how members of their discipline have advanced knowledge about Stonehenge. After sharing with each other what you've learned, write for five minutes about disciplinary intersections and divergences around Stonehenge. What new areas of inquiry on Stonehenge might emerge from interdisciplinary collaboration?

꡷ ꡷ ꡷

What is Synthesis?

Synthesis is defined by the *Oxford English Dictionary* as "The putting together of parts or elements so as to make up a complex whole." Synthesis involves combining and integrating. It emerges across disciplines as academic writers put together two or more ideas, concepts, or materials to create new ideas, products, or entities. At its essence, synthesis is based on forging, naming, and exploring relationships—connections, overlaps, and divergences—between ideas and elements.

You are likely already familiar with synthesis through school; the art of compiling materials and ideas for a course is a form of synthesis. Your professor has synthesized concepts, theories, topics, materials, and assignments in order to create space for the class members to learn and create new knowledge.

Similarly, most academic research and writing relies heavily on synthesis as academic writers gather materials, summarize ideas, read and analyze data, and then synthesize these elements in the formation of new knowledge.

Purposes of Synthesis

Academic writers use synthesis across disciplines in myriad ways, sometimes as a stand-alone writing project, and other times as part of a larger project. The purposes of synthesis are deeply tied to the writing occasion in which synthesis emerges. Synthesis can involve one or more of the following purposes:

- to make connections between ideas
- to apply one or more ideas to one or more other contexts
- to show disagreement among ideas
- to combine ideas or concepts
- to demonstrate a gap in knowledge
- to create a fuller understanding of a concept
- to produce something new

Many disciplines have particular purposes for synthesis. For instance, according to the website *Biology Online*, synthesis is used in the natural sciences in order to accomplish the creation of new, complex entities:

Biochemistry: "The production of an organic compound in a living thing, especially as aided by enzymes"

Chemistry: "The act or process of forming a complex substance by combining or integrating two or more chemical entities, especially through a chemical reaction"

Psychiatry: "The integration of different elements of the personality" ("Synthesis")

Synthesis is also a key aspect of STEM disciplines. According to Gregory McColm, Associate Professor in the Department of Mathematics at the University of South Florida, synthesis in these disciplines serves the dual purposes of "construct[ing]...entirely new things from old parts" and in helping us come to greater "understand[ing]." In the following passage McColm describes synthesis in mechanical engineering and math:

> There are two faces of synthesis. First, creative acts usually consist of combining notions that one usually doesn't imagine having much to do with each other. For example, a carburetor is merely a very large [perfume] atomizer. ... Second, many things cannot be understood in isolation ... Consider the problem: find all solutions to:
>
> $$3x + y = 2$$
> $$-2y - z = 2$$
> $$x = 1$$
>
> This can be solved by substitution: x = 1, so y = 2 - 3 = -1, so z = 2 - 2 = 0 ... But what about:
>
> $$x - y + 2z = 2$$
> $$3x + 2y + z = 1$$
> $$x + y + z = 0$$
>
> Substitutions don't work so well here: we need to use a method that deals with the entire system at once: Cramer's rule, or the Gauss-Jordan method. (McColm)

In the field of health care, synthesis can involve examining findings from a set of studies in order to make advances in disease prevention and treatment: "Synthesis [in health-care related reviews] should...explore whether observed intervention effects are consistent across studies, and investigate possible reasons for any inconsistencies" (Center for Reviews and Dissemination).

Synthesis in the humanities and social sciences often involves application, which entails applying one theory or concept to another context. In English Literature, this might involve a theoretical reading of a text. In the social sciences, it might involve applying a theory to a new primary source, context, or culture.

Often, synthesis appears in the form of a literature review, where an academic writer makes connections among and between relevant research reports. Sometimes literature reviews function as stand-alone writing projects, designed to inform others about the field of research on a given area of inquiry. Other times, the purpose of literature reviews is to enable the writer to carve out a space for his or her own research, showing gaps, disagreements, and overlaps in knowledge. In these ways, literature reviews resonate with the ways in which academic writers use summary in referring to others' research (as discussed in Chapter 5). Synthesis, however, involves a focus on making connections between these various summaries.

Just as synthesis itself involves a combining of elements, academic writers often have numerous combined purposes for writing synthesis. This section will help you identify these purposes for yourself as you embark on synthesis.

Questions that Shape Synthesis

As you engage with your own academic writing mashups in the form of synthesis, consider utilizing several types of questions to better shape your approach.

Disciplinary context

What is the disciplinary context? Writers often approach synthesis in discipline-specific ways. In the sciences and social sciences, for instance, a literature review (which synthesizes prior research) tends to move rapidly, with a writer synthesizing numerous relevant ideas from a large quantity of sources. In the humanities, synthesis often involves a slower approach, with quotes and specific details from the various ideas, demonstrating in more specificity the connections and applications. Of course, as we are learning in this text, all disciplines have overlaps and variations in approach. As you prepare to begin a writing project using synthesis, you should review examples of synthesis in the discipline in which you are writing so you can model your approach to synthesis on these, or, if not, at least break with or modify convention in an informed and deliberate way.

Purpose

What is your purpose for the synthesis? Having a clearer sense of your aims and purpose for synthesis will help you focus your synthesis and guide your readers through it. If your purpose is to show disagreement, then you'll want to focus primarily on synthesizing opposing and/ or divergent points of view. By contrast, if your purpose is to show overlap, then you'll want to focus mainly on synthesizing ideas that are tightly related to one another.

Relationship between components

What is the relationship between component parts? What points of agreement, overlap, or connection exist among various ideas or elements? Where do various ideas or elements disagree, differ, or diverge? It might be helpful to consider the dinner conversation model described later in this chapter, where you imagine the component parts speaking to one another as a way of naming the relationships between them. Who would argue with one another? Who would become fast friends? Who would talk all night due to a spark of a new idea? The Writing and Speaking Tutorial Service at North Carolina State University has created a resource termed a "synthesis matrix" (see Figure 6.1) in order to help academic writers identify relationships among and between ideas and elements. This type of matrix might help you examine how various sources are each

Writer Insights

How does synthesis inform your scholarship?

"The original idea for [my book, *A Synthesis of Qualitative Studies of Writing Center Theory*] came when [I] prepared questions for [my] doctoral comprehensive exam in writing centers. One of the questions was, "Is there a writing center theory, and if so, what is it?" [I] found that there was no one common writing center theory, but rather a set of practices and a pattern of taking theories from other disciplines and applying them to writing centers…[I] realized that in order to find out what a unified theory of writing center tutoring would look like, it would be necessary to look at actual studies of tutoring and see what theories emerged."

~Rebecca Day Babcock, English Professor, Odessa, Texas, U.S.

approaching the same main idea. For example, if you were researching women in hip-hop, you might have Main Idea A focus on female rappers, then trace what various sources (1-4) say about female rappers. Main Idea B might be the representation of women in hip-hop songs, and you might likewise trace what each source (1-4) argues about that.

Topic: _____

Main Idea A	Source #1	Source #2	Source #3	Source #4
Main Idea B				

FIGURE 6.1 Synthesis matrix.

Write Now

Practice using a synthesis matrix with a current writing project. Identify two or more main ideas (subtopics) for the writing project, and track what four different texts argue about those main ideas. An alternative approach to experimenting with the synthesis matrix would be to formulate a question or two about your writing project (i.e., how are women represented in hip-hop?) and ask four different people. Record across the matrix what they say, and then look for connections and divergences among and between their answers.

New understandings

What new understanding, concept, or knowledge are you hoping to achieve from your use of synthesis? Synthesis, as we learned earlier in this chapter, is intended to generate something new. Having a sense of what that something new might be can help shape your approach to synthesis. Sometimes synthesis helps a writer discover a new idea or element, and in these cases, a writer may not know what that something new is at the outset. In these cases, the writer could keep the question in mind throughout the work of synthesis, and in this way, maintain focus on generating something new. Other times a writer has more of an advance idea about what the something new will be from synthesis. In these cases, the writer could focus the synthesis primarily around what is relevant for that innovation (and yet still remain open to new ideas as well).

Criteria for Effective Synthesis

Given the drastic variation in purpose, discipline, format, and style in synthesis, it would be challenging to develop an exhaustive list of criteria that make synthesis more or less effective. Still, there are some general criteria that might be applied across disciplines.

Demonstrates a connection of ideas

The main difference between summary in an annotated bibliography and the kind of work synthesis does in a literature review or other mode of synthesis is that connections are named and forged. Connections should be explicit in the synthesis you create. You should state what the relationships are among the various component elements or ideas.

Appropriately shaped for the discipline and context

Although disciplinary expectations and writing contexts overlap and many academic writers deliberately opt to modify disciplinary expectations or challenge expectations for a writing context, synthesis nonetheless should take into account disciplinary expectations and the writing context. This might involve synthesizing research that emerges from the discipline in which you are writing (and leaving out research from other disciplines), or it might involve shaping the synthesis in a way that takes disciplinary expectations into account (i.e., more or less detail, quotes or no quotes, etc.).

Represents the original text

As with conveying ideas from others in summary and analysis, effective synthesis hinges on accurately understanding and representing the component parts. This is crucial not only as a matter of ethics and academic honesty, but also so that the relationships you forge and identify between and among the elements are valid.

Integrated smoothly

Integration refers to the component parts themselves—that they are integrated with one another smoothly—and, when relevant, also that the synthesis itself is integrated more smoothly with the larger writing project. Sometimes syntheses are stand-alone writing projects. But when synthesis operates as part of a larger writing project, the writer should integrate it into his or her project as thoroughly as possible. This likely means referring back to it, starting with it as a meaningful jumping off point, or using it in some other way, rather than simply inserting it into a larger writing project as though it could stand alone.

Organized logically

Because synthesis can involve many different component parts, or an in-depth examination of complicated component parts, readers may get confused or lose track of important ideas while reading a synthesis. This is exacerbated by the likelihood that some readers of a synthesis have likely not encountered the ideas or elements being synthesized. For that reason, it is especially important to organize a synthesis in a way that makes sense and that helps readers process the connections you are making.

Focused

When synthesizing, academic writers face a risk of overdoing it because on any given topic or line of inquiry there is a vast amount of potential relevant literature or component parts. Academic writers must make sometimes difficult decisions about what to include or exclude. Sometimes, these decisions center on bringing together the most representative component parts, or the most well-known, or the least well-known. At times, once writers get in the mindset of forging connections, they get bogged down in an endless network of potential and explicit connections. While such enthusiasm is laudable, and a certain amount of discovery and exploration valuable, writers must try to remain primarily focused on those component parts that are most directly relevant to the synthesis and writing project at hand.

Advances knowledge

While we noted above that academic writers often bring a wide variety of purposes to synthesis, at its core, synthesis involves the generation of something new. The writer and his or her readers should gain new knowledge from the synthesis. Rather than making readers do the work of guessing what this something new is, academic writers should name the something new directly in the synthesis. This does not mean that readers will not sometimes generate their own new knowledge based on synthesis, that the writer may not have foreseen, but at the very least the writer should specify what he or she noticed as the something new based on the synthesis. Perhaps it is a new or fuller understanding of a concept, or perhaps it is merely a new, more pressing question or gap in knowledge that the synthesis has uncovered. Synthesis involves creating something new that likely would not have been created without those component parts being synthesized in the particular way of any given writing project. Emphasize the something new.

Modes of Synthesis across Disciplines

Numerous modes of synthesis exist across and within academic disciplines. It would be nearly impossible even to name, much less describe, all the modes of analysis that operate across disciplines.

In an article offering guidance on how to conduct literature reviews in health-care settings, the Center for Reviews and Dissemination names two primary approaches for how writers approach data synthesis: quantitative and narrative. "Synthesis involves bringing the results of individual studies together and summarising their findings. This may be done quantitatively or, if formal pooling of results is inappropriate, through a narrative approach." Within these broad categories, though, their guidelines name "descriptive synthesis," "synthesis of findings of included studies," and "quantitative synthesis of comparative studies" (CRD).

Within this large range of types of synthesis, however, there are some modes of synthesis that do emerge more commonly across disciplines. This list offers some of the most common modes of synthesis you may encounter in your undergraduate academic writing career:

- Synthesis as Literature Review
- Synthesis of Application

- Synthesis as Interdisciplinarity
- Synthesis as Curation of Collections
- Synthesis of Resources
- Synthesis as Comparison
- Synthesis as Definition
- Synthesis in Bibliographic Essays

In keeping with the overarching line of inquiry in this chapter and with the spirit of synthesis as a form of mashup, each of the included modes of synthesis contains examples that show academic writing synthesis related to hip-hop music. While each of the sections illustrates a particular mode of synthesis, the modes also intersect and overlap with one another. As you read through the examples, consider conducting a super-synthesis: a synthesis of modes of synthesis. What are the intersections and differences among and between various modes of synthesis? Where do you notice overlap? What elements seem distinctive to a particular mode of synthesis?

Synthesis as literature review

Since academic writers build on, adapt, counter, and otherwise modify the research of others in order to advance research, they must synthesize prior research through a **literature review** in order to move forward with their own projects. A literature review is also sometimes referred to as a **background synthesis** (Jamieson). Literature reviews can be stand-alone writing projects or can be part of larger writing projects. One useful way to think about synthesis in this mode is through the metaphor of a dinner conversation. Imagine two or more people sitting around a dinner table having a conversation about something. Who agrees with whom? What questions would they ask one another? Over which points might they disagree? How might their conversation lead to new areas for exploration?

Writer Insights

Describe your process of summary, synthesis, and analysis.

In our field, we design our experiment scientifically, collect data carefully, process and analyze the data correctly, and write a paper effectively. While writing, we review relevant literatures and write methods and introduction first. Then, we write result section after analyzing data in some reliable statistical software (like R). Now, we write discussion, synthesizing/interpreting our results and comparing with the previous studies, if any. We also include citations/references at the end of our paper recognizing other's work, while following the academic honesty. Lastly, we write an abstract/ summary, which includes an overall synopsis of our study.

~Subodh Adhikari, Agroecology — Ph.D. student, Montana State University, Bozeman, Montana, U.S.

A literature review, therefore, is not merely a series of summaries. They offer a new way of understanding an area of inquiry by putting others' ideas in conversation together.

Given the many directions in which a conversation can take place, one challenge with a literature review is deciding how to organize it. The Writing Center at the University of North Carolina, Chapel Hill names four methods of organizing a synthesis in the form of a literature review: chronological by publication, chronological by trend, thematic, and methodological. Since multiple forms of organization might be applicable to any given writing occasion, academic writers must choose deliberately how to organize their literature reviews.

Literature reviews can serve multiple purposes, which can often be overlapping as well. Included here are three examples, each of which demonstrates a different purpose:

- Example 1: Literature Review, Extending Others' Research, Nursing
- Example 2: Literature Review, Demonstrating a Gap in Prior Research, Business
- Example 3: Literature Review, Debates in the Field, Sociology

Example 1: Literature Review, Extending Others' Research, Nursing

The authors of the excerpt have chosen to organize their literature review by theme in order to demonstrate how they will build on existing knowledge. The excerpt illustrates a portion of the literature review from an article about using hip-hop to prevent the spread of Human Papilloma Virus (HPV). The corresponding references are also included in order to illustrate further how the writers are synthesizing the work of others through citation. (For more explanation about citing the work of others, see Chapter 12; for more discussion of integrating evidence, see Chapter 11.)

Excerpt from the Literature Review for "Hip-Hop, Health, and Human Papilloma Virus (HPV): Using Wireless Technology to Increase HPV Vaccination Uptake" by T. L. Thomas, D. P. Stephens, and B. Blanchard

> Thomas, Stephens, and Blanchard synthesize research about using technology in education and taking into account "unique cultural methods." See the next page for their references [24 - 28] as a demonstration of their synthesis.

Researchers across disciplines emphatically agree that interventions seeking to achieve changes in the attitudes toward and beliefs about racial/ethnic-minority sexuality that fail to recognize the unique cultural messages that influence these processes are likely to fail.[24] For example, young women have grown up with technologies allowing faster and more direct information consumption, particularly as it relates to health outcomes, making Internet, cell phone, BlackBerry, iPhone, and iPod devices important tools for education.[25-28] Furthermore, the ways in which these wireless technology tools and culture-specific messages influence behavioral outcomes can differ across racial/ethnic groups, making it important to integrate frameworks that reflect values and expressions relevant to these young women.[29-30] Recognizing this, we have chosen to integrate two cultural tools that that been identified as playing central roles in young adult African American women's daily lives: wireless technology tools, namely cell phones; and hip-hop culture frameworks....

From *The Journal for Nurse Practitioners* (6.6), 2010.

Next, Thomas, Stephens, and Blanchard show that hip-hop in particular is a cultural message that might have important bearing on education. Again, they synthesize multiple sources (see References).

Research on sexual health decision making and outcomes among African American adolescents and females highlights the relevance and important of integrating hip-hop specifically into sexual health promotion contexts. A growing body of psychological and public health research has examined the influence of hip-hop culture on African American women's sexual health outcomes clearly indicating their sexual health decision making processes and beliefs are influenced by this culture. Viewing hip-hop images with high levels of sexual content was also found to increase women's negative attitude toward condom use and increase their desire to conceive.[39-40] Stephens and Few [30,33] found that African American adolescents not only recognized stereotypical sexual scripts in mainstream hip-hop videos but saw them as accurate portrayals of real-life sexual behavioral guidelines for their peers.

Here Thomas, Stephens, and Blanchard show how their synthesis of prior research led them to develop this feasibility project about hip-hop as a "vehicle to send positive health promotion messages."

These research findings substantiate hip-hop's important role in health education in combination with wireless technologies as a successful vehicle for health promotion. … This feasibility project chose hip-hop music and images as the vehicle to send positive health promotion messages.

Notice through this references section, which shows the scholarship that Thomas, Stephens, and Blanchard used in their synthesis, that the authors have taken a large number of sources and put them into conversation with one another in order to develop their feasibility project.

References

[24]Kirby D. Effective approaches to reducing adolescent unprotected sex, pregnancy, and childbearing. J Sex Res. 2002; 39(1): 51-57.

[25]Donnerstein E, Smith S. Sex in the media: theory, influences, and solutions. *Handbook of children and the media.* Thousand Oaks, CA: Sage; 2001: p. 289-307.

[26]Skinner H, Biscope S, Poland B, Goldberg E. How adolescents use technology for health information: implications for health professionals from focus group studies. *J Med Internet Res.* 2003; 5(4).

[27]Stokes C. Representin' in cyberspace: sexual scripts, self-definition, and hip-hop culture in Black American adolescent girls' home pages. *Cult Health Sex.* 2007; 9(2): 169-184.

[28]Strouse J, Buerkel-Rothfuss N. Media exposure and the sexual attitudes and behaviors of college students. *J Sex Educ Ther.* 1987; 13(2): 43-51.

[29]Few A, Stephens D, Rouse-Arnett M. Sister-to-sister talk: transcending boundaries and challenges in qualitative research with Black women. *Fam Relat.* 2003; 52(3): 205-215.

[30]Stephens D, Few A. The effects of images of African American women in hip-hop on early adolescents' attitudes toward physical attractiveness and interpersonal relationships. *Sex Roles.* 2007; 56(3): 251-264.

[33]Stephens D, Few A. Hip-hop honey or video ho: African American preadolescents' understanding of female sexual scripts in hip-hop culture. *Sexuality & Culture*. 2007; 11(4): 48-69.

[39]Wingood G, DiClemente R, Harrington K, Davies S, Hook III, E, Oh M. Exposure to X-rated movies and adolescents' sexual and contraceptive related attitudes and behaviors. *Pediatrics*. 2001; 107(5): 1116.

[40]Wingood G, DiClemente R, Bernhardt J, et al. A prospective study of exposure to rap music videos and African American female adolescents' health. *Am J Public Health*. 2003; 93(3): 437.

Example 2: Literature Review, Demonstrating a Gap in Prior Research, Business

The second example of a literature review shows a writer demonstrating that many scholars have addressed a particular question from certain angles, but have omitted considering another approach or angle. Damien Arthur, lecturer in Business at the University of Adelaide, pursues the following question: how does glocalization, the process by which products or services adapt and are sold to particular cultures or people, impact consumer behavior with Australian hip-hop culture?

Excerpt from the Literature Review for "Authenticity and Consumption in the Australian Hip-Hop Culture" by D. Arthur

Over the past two decades the Australian hip-hop culture has been fighting a stigma, perpetuated by the media, that its members are imitating U.S. culture. Only in the past four years has that stigma begun to dissipate, as the culture has glocalized. Previous research has found evidence of this glocalization in Australian hip-hop culture (Masters, 2001; Maxwell, 2003). For example, many Australian MC's now rap in Australian accents and about Australian issues. However, to date, no research has investigated these effects of such glocalization on the consumption practices of what the press describes as the fastest growing youth culture in the nation (Donovan, 2004). Furthermore, no research has investigated the role of authenticity on youth subcultures despite its effect on increasing brand loyalty (Kates, 2004). In order to fill this gap this study examines the effect that the local interpretations of foreign brands and the glocalization of the Australian hip-hop culture have on the consumption practices of members, explores the reasons for such effects with a particular focus on authentic self-expression and draws some marketing implications.

> Arthur uses synthesis to outline what previous research has accomplished: evidence of glocalization.

> Arthur shows that in examining this synthesis, he finds that there has been no research on "consumption practices" or on the "role of authenticity." And it is these areas of research that his study will now go on to address.

From *Qualitative Market Research* (9.2), 2006.

Example 3: Literature Review, Debates in the Field, Sociology

The third example of a literature review focuses on debates within the field. Nearly all fields of inquiry have debates and disagreements, and a literature review can map this terrain. Here, author Peter Katel, a Sociologist, writes a literature review that asks, what are the main areas of disagreement and debate in hip-hop studies?

Excerpt from the Literature Review for
"Debating Hip-Hop: Does Gangsta Rap Harm Black Americans?" by P. Katel

Katel first identifies one position in the debate and provides an example.

Debates over hip-hop have taken place mostly within the black community. Some of hip-hop's fiercest critics, including black intellectuals and entertainers, argue that hip-hop presents a caricature of black America that damages how young black people view themselves and how they're viewed by others. Author and jazz critic Crouch has decried for years what he calls the ravages of hip-hop. In a 2003 column in the New York Daily News—one of dozens he has devoted to them—he lamented that ordinary African Americans were bearing the consequences of a genre in which "thugs and freelance prostitutes have been celebrated for a number of years." The result: "Thousands upon thousands…have been murdered or beaten up or terrorized. After all, the celebration of thugs and thuggish behavior should not be expected to bring about any other results." [18] …

Younger cultural critics, even those who partly agree with Crouch, reject such sweeping condemnations. Instead, they insist on distinguishing between mass-marketed hip-hop and what they see as a purer, original form, less tainted by the demands of the marketplace.

Now Katel shows how a younger generation of critics disagrees with the prior position, though not entirely, just in terms of "sweeping condemnations."

"I like conscious hip-hop and the stuff that you just dance to," says Lisa Fager, a former promotional specialist at commercial radio stations and record labels, "but I don't like stuff that demeans me as a black woman, or a woman, period—or degrades my community. People don't want to be called bitches, niggas, and hos."…

Rapper Banner doesn't dispute Fager on what gets played. "The labels don't want to deal with anything that creative," he says. "They don't want to develop an artist; they want the quickest thing people will buy. And as soon as one feminist gets mad, they back up."

From *Issues for Debate in Sociology: Selections from CQ Researcher*, 2010.

> Here, Katel integrates a third perspective, from someone who argues not over the condemnations, but who has the right (or not) to issue the condemnations.

But Banner reacts explosively to African Americans who attack hip-hop as degrading. Hip-hop mogul Simmons's proposal to ban offensive words is "stupid," Banner says. There was a time in history when we didn't have a choice about being called a nigger. Now that we're making money off it, it's a problem."

Goes on to talk about others who blame rappers for copping out or others who say hip-hop needs to be viewed as more than just about race.

Synthesis of application

One of the most common modes of synthesis involves applying one concept to another context or entity in order to yield a new understanding of that entity. Scholars apply theories, approaches, and concepts to new contexts in order to reaffirm, challenge, or otherwise expand or modify them. Sometimes this is called reading through a **critical lens** or reading from a critical perspective. Synthesis of application might be termed **thesis driven synthesis** (Jamieson) or **argumentative synthesis** (Carter) because it synthesizes in order to forward an argument. For instance, scholars in English might apply feminist theories to the reading of hip-hop lyrics, thereby creating a synthesis between hip-hop and feminist theory. Synthesis through application enables scholars to generate new questions: what happens if the ideas of x are applied to situation y or z? Importantly, synthesis through application often not only involves gleaning new insights about the idea or object to which a concept has been applied, but also invites readers to reconsider the concept being applied as well.

In this excerpt, James Stewart creates a synthesis by applying the ideas of Zora Neale Hurston, W. E. B. Du Bois, and Alain Locke to twentieth-century black popular music. This excerpt comes from Stewart's introduction. The remainder of the article goes on to apply in more detail the ideas of Hurston, Du Bois, and Locke.

Excerpt from "Message in the Music: Political Commentary in Black Popular Music from Rhythm and Blues to Early Hip-Hop" by J. B. Stewart

There are a variety of classical and more contemporary commentaries about the role of music in African American culture that provide useful insights for the development of a framework for understanding the political role of R & B. Early twentieth century perspectives advanced

From *The Journal of African American History* (90.3), 2005.

Stewart discusses Hurston and shows that he will extend (or apply) Hurston's ideas to political commentary in music lyrics.

by Zora Neale Hurston, W. E. B. Du Bois, and Alain Locke remain relevant for interpreting contemporary African American musical forms. Hurston insisted that African American folklore was the core component of authentic African American culture.[3] Extending this idea, the most authentic political commentary in music lyrics should originate in the organic everyday experiences of people of African descent. In *The Souls of Black Folk* Du Bois maintained that the "sorrow songs" provided one of the most useful documentations of the long history of oppression and struggle against that oppression.[4] Thus, this form of music became a bearer of historical memory, similar to the role of griots in many West African societies. In addition to the sorrow conveyed in these songs, Du Bois argued that there was also a "faith in the ultimate justice

Stewart suggests that R & B lyrics demonstrate the "shifts in moods and assessments" that Du Bois identified in "sorrow songs."

of things" and that "minor cadences of despair change often to triumph and calm confidence."[5] Similar shifts in moods and assessments can be observed in R & B lyrics. Philosopher Alain Locke went even further than Du Bois by proposing that changes in predominant African American musical genres were closely correlated with major transformations in the sociopolitical and economic milieu for African Americans.[6] Locke's views suggest that in the absence of external efforts to shape the content of African American music, changes in lyrical content should be correlated with changes in the social, political, and economic

Lastly, Stewart applies Locke's ideas to show that the political commentary impacted all Americans, not only African Americans.

circumstances for African Americans. Moreover, Locke emphasized that African American music was deeply ingrained in the American cultural fabric to the point that it "furnish[es] the sub-soil of our national music."[7] Locke's perspective suggests the need to explore political commentary in black music in terms of not only its impact on African Americans, but also on Americans of European and Asian descent.

Synthesis as interdisciplinarity

An extension of synthesis of application that deserves particular mention is synthesis as interdisciplinarity. This mode involves researchers actively drawing on and bridging the research methodologies and practices of multiple disciplines. Interdisciplinarity has been a feature of academic research across disciplines for years. In 1943, Henry Ozanne wrote about the phenomenon in his article, "'Synthesis' in Social Science":

> Sociological pilfering on the part of psychology is not a new form of scientific delinquency ... Dr. Kardiner [has] achieved ... a significant integration of two separate fields of social science, anthropology and psychology; or more specifically, culture and psychoanalysis. ... Six years ago [Kardiner] announced the attempt to "join the resources of psychology and those of sociology"...In his latest study Kardiner reapplies what he terms his operational tool, basic personality structure, to the analysis of three [cultures]. They are the Comanche,...the Alorese...and Plainville.... Kardiner insists repeatedly that his work is primarily a contribution in methodology. Two aspects of Ozanne's description bear noting: the concepts of "pilfering" and "methodology." Regarding the latter, Ozanne emphasizes that Kardiner's contribution is primarily methodological, which underscores the fact that interdisciplinary research yields contributions of content as well as methodology.

Second, Ozanne initially describes interdisciplinarity as a form of "pilfering," underscoring the tensions that can emerge as scholars blend methodologies. While tensions continue today, most fields now embrace interdisciplinarity. Disciplines such as American Studies, Women's Studies, and African and African American Studies are inherently interdisciplinary. Many institutions hire faculty who can work across disciplines and have established interdisciplinary studies departments or centers. Some areas of inquiry especially warrant interdisciplinarity. For instance, a committee from the National Institutes of Health created a book in which the second chapter argues for "The Potential of Interdisciplinary Research to Solve Problems in the Brain, Behavioral, and Clinical Sciences." Similarly, Stuart C. Carr and Malcolm MacLachlan argue for interdisciplinarity in the field of development economics: "The Millenium Development Goals (MDGs) focus on a range of human freedoms, and these reflect the inherent inter-disciplinarity of human poverty reduction." In the following excerpt, linguist H. Samy Alim describes his interdisciplinary approach to hip-hop studies. He outlines the many disciplines he has used for his book, *Roc the Mic Right*. Notice that, as we saw in Ozanne, Alim addresses the methodological contributions of this research.

In addition to offering an example of synthesis as interdisciplinarity, Alim's excerpt also shows another form of synthesis: code switching (DeBose). In code-switching, writers toggle between different types of speech patterns. In Alim's case, he code switches between more academic sounding language and language that is more of the style of hip-hop language itself. As you read, identify the moments where you see Alim engaging in code-switching.

Excerpt from *Roc the Mic Right* by H. Samy Alim

As an interdiscplinary area of inquiry [hip-hop studies] includes studies of language and language use from various methodological and theoretical perspectives. While studies are grounded in the streets, contributions come from cultural studies, communications studies, ethnic studies, literacy studies, philosophy, sociology, anthropology, sociolinguistics, poetics, literary analysis, and discourse analysis, among other approaches to the study of language. We begin with language as power, that is, the view that language *is* the revolution, a powerful discourse in and of itself. We know that the most powerful people in society tend to control speech and its circulation through mass media. We know, cuz the Wu-Tang Clans Rza told us, that "words kill as fast as bullets." Words are far more than parts of speech; they're weapons of mass culture to be deployed in the cultural combat that we, invariably, as humans, find ourselves in. Unfortunately, with teachers of young Hip-Hop Heads still sayin that the language of their students is the very thing tat they "*combat the most*," we learn this lesson very early on. In this sense of cultural warfare—the micro and macro forms of social control through culture—Hip-Hop Linguists are "combat linguists." Yeah, we know it's a war goin on, but don't get it twisted. We are never the aggressors. The task of the Hip-Hop Linguist is to both analyze and mediate the struggle …

> Alim identifies numerous disciplines that work together to inform hip-hop studies.

> Alim shows how an inquiry into language involves multiple disciplinary perspectives in order to fully appreciate its linguistic and cultural elements.

The hiphopography paradigm integrates the varied approaches of ethnography, biography, and social, cultural, and oral history to arrive at an *emic* view of Hip-Hop Culture. It is hiphopography that obligates [hip-hop studies] to directly engage with the cultural agents of the Hip-Hop Culture-World, revealing rappers as critical interpreters of their own culture. We view "rappers" as "cultural critics" and "cultural theorists" whose thoughts and ideas help us to make sense of one of the most important cultural movement of the late twentieth and early twenty-first centuries.

> Alim adopts the term "hiphopography" to name the multidisciplinary approach that combines culture, history, sociology, and language. He uses the term "emic" to suggest that this interdisciplinary approach evolves from a consideration of all the elements internal to hiphopography.

From *Roc the Mic Right*, 2006.

Synthesis as curation of collections

Academics synthesize materials into collections in many different modalities, from blogs and websites, to anthologies and museum or archive exhibits. This section offers three examples of how academics across disciplines synthesize while curating collections.

Example 1: Synthesis as Curating Collections, Blogs and Websites, African and African American Studies

Bloggers often synthesize what others have produced as material for their own blog; Jill Rettberg terms these "filter blogs." Similarly, people often curate websites or synthesize material about themselves on social networking sites such as Facebook, Twitter, and Instagram. The example, from the blog *NewBlackMan (In Exile)* by Mark Anthony Neal, shows a synthesis of events, ideas, and news. The blog, however, demonstrates synthesis not only with content, but also with form, combining print, images, and videos.

Excerpt from *NewBlackMan* by M. Anthony Neal

April 15, 2014:

HuffPost Live

> In this first example, Neal draws material from the Huffington Post about Nas.

Legendary hip-hop artist Nas joins HuffPost Live with Marc Lamont Hill to celebrate the 20th anniversary of his debut album, Illmatic. He reflects on his illustrious career, the state of hip-hop and what Illmatic XX means to him.

From *NewBlackMan*, 2014.

Excerpt from *NewBlackMan* by M. Anthony Neal

April 10, 2014: Hop, Grit, and Academic Success: Bettina Love at TEDxUGA

TEDx Talks

This impassioned talk explains how students who identify with hip-hop culture have been ignored or deemed deficient in schools because of mainstream misconceptions associated with hip-hop culture. Through hip-hop, these students embody the characteristics of grit, social and emotional intelligence, and the act improvisation—all of which are proven to be predictors

> This second example illustrates Neal drawing his blog followers' attention to a recent TEDx Talk about hip-hop culture.

From *NewBlackMan*, 2014.

for academic success. So where is the breakdown between formalized education and the potential for success for these students? Dr. Bettina Love argues that ignoring students' culture in the classroom is all but an oversight; it's discrimination and injustice that plays out in our culture in very dangerous ways.

Example 2: Synthesis as Curating Collections, Anthologies, Communication Studies, and African and African American Studies

Anthologies exist across all disciplines as a way of providing depth and breadth of knowledge: from the *Norton Anthology of Literature by Women* or *Environment: an Interdisciplinary Anthology* to *An Anthology of Theories and Models of Design* and *A Reader in Medical Anthropology: Theoretical Trajectories, Emergent Realities,* Anthologies also exist as explorations of single authors or concepts, as in *The Henry Louis Gates, Jr. Reader* or *Communicating Colonialism: Readings on Postcolonial Theory(s) and Communication.*

Anthologies rely on the work of synthesis. In all these instances, academic writers conduct curatorial work as editors, making decisions about what to include in an **anthology** and how to organize it. The synthesizing skills used in producing anthologies are summed up in this definition of synthesis by Anton Popovič and Francis Macri: "synthesis is … a configuration of texts according to the principles of combination, selection, and linking."

The example is from the promotional flyer for the 2nd edition of an anthology titled *New Book! That's the Joint! The Hip-Hop Studies Reader.* In this edition, the Editors Murray Forman and Mark Anthony Neal make a concerted effort at synthesizing old with new, to "conjoin essays from hip-hop's earlier phases with more recent scholarly interventions, facilitating a productive historical dialogue."

Excerpt from promotional flyer for *New Book! That's the Joint! The Hip-Hop Studies Reader,* M. Anthony Neal and M. Forman, eds.

I. Hip-Hop Ya Don't Stop: Hip-Hop History and Historiography

1. The Politics of Graffiti | *Craig Castleman*

2. Zulus on a Time Bomb: Hip-Hop Meets the Rockers Downtown | *Jeff Chang*

3. B-Beats Bombarding Bronx: Mobile DJ Starts Something with Older R&B Disks and Jive Talking NY DJs Rapping Away in Black Discos | *Robert Ford, Jr.*

Here is the selection of readings Murray and Neal chose for Part I (referred to in Murray's excerpt above). As you can imagine, there were likely a variety of possible choices, but their work of synthesis involved selecting which ones to include so that the historical dialogue would be as productive as possible.

From *NewBlackMan*, 2014.

This newly expanded and revised second edition of *That's the Joint!* brings together the most important and up-to-date hip-hop scholarship in one comprehensive volume. Presented thematically, the selections address the history of hip-hop, identity politics of the "hip-hop nation," debates of "street authenticity," social movements and activism, aesthetics, technologies of production, hip-hop as a cultural industry, and much more. Further, this new edition also includes greater coverage of gender, racial diversity in hip-hop, hip-hop's global influences, and examines hip-hop's role in contemporary politics.

> The final sentence indicates the difficulty of synthesizing large amounts of material. They chose to increase coverage of these areas in the second edition, in order, presumably, to address lesser coverage in the first edition.

Example 3: Synthesis as Curating Collections, Exhibits and Archives, Musicology

The work of synthesis in this domain (be it online, face-to-face, or blended) requires choosing what to include, how to organize it, and how to present it. Together, exhibits or archives provide viewers or visitors with a perspective on the topic. The excerpt is from a page of the hip-hop archive website, which is part of an archival collection at Harvard University.

Excerpt from "The Geoff Ward Collection"

The Hiphop Archive is proud to present our extensive "Geoff Ward Collection." Comprised of a large donation of hiphop-related periodicals and VHS cassette tapes, the collection provides a valuable historical account of hiphop culture from a popular perspective. Additionally, they give any student or researcher a glimpse of the issues and concerns surrounding the hiphop community throughout various periods of its development.

> Here, the curators of the archive describe the collection and its components. The collection is a synthesis of artifacts related to hip-hop.

The collection features an extensive range of magazine titles, ranging from mainstream publications like Vibe and Source to lesser-known magazines such as *4080, F.E.D.S.,* and *The Rap Pages. The Source* magazine is the most comprehensive title in the

From *hiphoparchive,com*, 2014.

collection with copies ranging from 1993 to 2003. A decade packed with fascinating and immensely important landmarks in the history of Hiphop, articles about the contentious "East Coast/West Coast" discussion (interviews with Ice Cube and Suge Knight), the first appearance and subsequent rise of contemporary artists (Nas, Mos Def, and Eminem), the contributions of hiphop's fallen stars (Notorious B.I.G., Tupac, and Big Pun), and many more can be found.

Write Now

Curating an exhibit relies on the ability of the curator to demonstrate what insights, ideas, or impressions might be newly generated from bringing various objects together. This work of curation becomes clear through the item descriptions in the exhibit; through these descriptions, curators can make visible the intersections and disparities between the items, as well as show how their being brought together yields new perspectives. Locate four or more images, artifacts, and/or items about a topic of interest to you, and create an mini-exhibit. You can do this with an online site such as Pinterest or through a different non-virtual format. Write captions and an overarching introduction to your exhibit that exemplify the synthesis informing the exhibit.

Synthesis of sources as evidence

Academic writers synthesize a variety of resources in order to generate an argument. The discipline of history offers a cogent example of this as historians synthesize a variety of sources and evidence to generate a fuller understanding of a person, era, or event. Historians make use of personal remembrances, artifacts, and other types of evidence. They synthesize them to generate conclusions and narratives.

In *A Pocket Guide to Writing in History*, Mary Lynn Rampolla emphasizes that historical questions "require [the exploration of] many different kinds of sources":

> [Historians] will read books and articles written by modern historians. [They] may examine maps, photographs, paintings, and pottery.... [H]istory often takes its practitioners into all manner of related disciplines: literary criticism, art history, and archaeology; political science, economics, and sociology."

Rampolla goes on to list the following as examples of the vast range of primary sources historians examine:

> {...} letters; diaries; newspaper and magazine articles; speeches; autobiographies; treatises; census data;...marriage, birth and death registers[;] art films, recordings, items of clothing, household objects, tools, and archaeological remains. For recent history, oral sources, such as interviews with Vietnam veterans or

Holocaust survivors and other such eye-witness accounts, can also be primary sources.

In addition to these primary sources, historians also work with secondary sources (i.e., other scholarship) and even tertiary sources such as encyclopedias and textbooks. The work of synthesis in history involves bringing this array of primary, secondary, and tertiary resources together, "mashing" them up, to generate a narrative and understanding of a particular historical period, person, or event.

The excerpt shows historian Derrick Alridge synthesizing several different kinds of primary and secondary sources to answer questions about the connections between the civil rights movement and hip-hop. Although this example is from history, academic writers use synthesis of resources across disciplines.

Writer Insights

How do you use synthesis in your writing?

I am a traveler, photographer, and writer. For me, writing travelogues is like drawing from wells of nostalgia buckets full of sights, sounds, smells and vapors of places that I have visited. Travel writing helps both my audience and me. It helps quench the measureless thirst of curious minds. But it also offers me an extraordinary chance to let the tide of old travel experiences ebb so that new ones may flow freely and spontaneously within me. My writing process is fairly straight-forward: I research extensively about a place or people before each trip. While on the road, I observe my surroundings keenly and take copious notes. Finally, I synthesize and organize my observations to create an original and personal memoir of my travel.

~Kartik, Travel Writer

Excerpt from "From Civil Rights to Hip-Hop: Toward a Nexus of Ideas" by D. P. Alridge

The most radical ideas often grow out of a concrete intellectual engagement with the problems of aggrieved populations confronting systems of oppression.

The preceding quotation from historian Robin D. G. Kelley captures the manner through which socially and politically conscious (SPC) hip-hop emerged from the social, economic, and political experiences of black youth from the mid- to late 1970s. Hip-hop pioneers such as Kool Herc, Afrika Bambaataa, and Grandmaster Flash and the Furious Five, among others articulated the post-civil rights generation's ideas and response to poverty, drugs, police brutality, and other racial and class inequities of postindustrial U.S. society. In many ways, early hip-hoppers were not only the progenitors of a new form of black social critique, they also represented the voice of a new generation that would carry on and expand upon the ideas and ideology of the civil rights generation.

> In both paragraphs, Alridge notes that hip-hop has emerged from a variety of resources, indicating that it synthesizes sources.

From *The Journal of African American History* (90.3), 2005.

Notice how Alridge links together Franti's lyrics with an interview and historical scholarship. Alridge synthesizes these sources in order to illustrate the political and ideological connections between hip-hop and the CRM.

Since the early years of hip-hop, SPC hip-hoppers have continued to espouse many of the ideas and ideology of the Civil Rights Movement (CRM) and Black Freedom Struggle (BFS), but in a language that resonates with many black youth of the postindustrial and post—civil rights integrationist era. For instance, on Michael Franti's 2001 compact disk (CD) *Stay Human*, Franti uses rap and reggae-style lyrics to critique U.S. capitalism, imperialism, racism, and globalization and to offer analyses of discrimination, prejudice, and oppression similar to those of activists and theorists of the CRM and BFS. In his song "Oh My God," Franti lays out what he believes are the hypocrisies of U.S. democracy by pointing out its discriminatory practices against the poor and people of color, its use of the death penalty, its indiscriminate bombing of other countries, and its counterintelligence activities that subvert the rights of U.S. citizens. He states:

> Oh my, Oh my God,
> out here mama they got us livin' suicide,
> singin' oh my, oh my God
> out here mama they got us livin' suicide....
> Stealin' DNA from the unborn
> and then you comin' after us
> 'cause we sampled a James Brown horn?
> Scientists whose God is progress,
> a four headed sheep is their latest project,
> the CIA runnin' like that Jones from Indiana,
> but they still won't talk about that Jones in Guyana…

In an interview with "underground" Atlanta rapper John Lewis, Jr., son of civil rights leader and icon John Lewis, Sr., Lewis, Jr. provides a firsthand account of the organic ideological connections between hip-hop and the CRM. In discussing the influence of his father and the CRM on his ideas and work, Lewis, Jr., recalled that:

> With me, I grew up around it [civil rights]. Like all I knew really was what was out here. Both of these worlds [civil rights and hip-hop] was [sic] together within me. You know it's hard as hell growing up in the house and, you know, you got pictures of your pops getting hit with billy clubs and getting dogs sicked on him, that shit goes into your head.

Lewis asserts that the stories he heard about the movement from his father are etched into his mind and have profoundly influenced his lyrics as a SPC rapper.

Synthesis as comparison

Writers across disciplines routinely invoke comparison, a well-known version of synthesis, in their writing. Some disciplines are even grounded in comparison, such as with Comparative Religions or Comparative Literature. Certain research methodologies also rely heavily on comparison, such as in anthropology where some ethnographers use fieldwork to compare cultures or peoples. Venn diagrams are one common visual form of comparison used in many subject areas. And, one might even suggest that in legal settings the use of precedent, looking to prior cases and their resolutions to inform decisions about current cases, illustrates yet another pervasive instance of synthesis as comparison. The genre of comparison and contrast as a form of writing may be well known to you as it is assigned across many subjects throughout all levels of education.

Comparison, as evidenced by its widespread usage, is a key strategy for people to use as they are seeking to understand concepts. This form of synthesis enables writers to identify both the intersections and the unique characteristics of the various entities being brought together for comparison.

Sometimes, however, people can approach a comparison-contrast essay without necessarily integrating a focus on what the outcomes are from having noticed these intersections and unique attributes. But for comparison to be most effective in the context of academic writing, it needs to accomplish more than just compare, or just contrast. In keeping with the ways in which synthesis hinges on the creation of something new, comparison should likewise yield new insights.

This excerpt shows a writer successfully using comparison as a form of synthesis, comparing digital music piracy in the U.S. with that in Japan in order to understand a problem and recommend a policy adjustment. Using comparison to yield policy recommendations, though, is but one possible outcome from this form of synthesis. Others could include using comparison with synthesis in order to yield explanations, definitions, or even critiques.

Excerpt from "Cultures of Music Piracy: An Ethnographic Comparison of the U.S. and Japan" by I. Condry

I begin with an ethnographic consideration of the music sharing in the U.S. to unpack the overly simplistic image that people are sharing music 'just to get something free.' A peer-to-peer perspective on popularity reveals that the boundaries between piracy, promotion, and sharing are far from clear. ... Then we turn to Japan, the second largest music market in the world, to consider what a cross-national comparison reveals about the intersections of culture, technology, legal setting, and business practices....

At the end of this paragraph, Condry conveys his purpose for synthesizing/comparing U.S. and Japanese digital music piracy. He aims to compare—to synthesize—in order to glean new understandings about the intersections between "culture, technology, legal setting, and business."

From *International Journal of Cultural Studies* (7.3), 2004.

Japan shows that the 'culture of piracy' transcends national boundaries, and does not depend on online peer-to-peer networks. In the U.S., the debate over music piracy largely revolves around peer-to-peer (p2p) file-sharing software, beginning with Napster, and later Kazaa, Bit Torrent, Freenet, and so on. But as of the beginning of 2004, Japanese record companies have largely avoided an online file-sharing epidemic. Sales have nevertheless plummeted more sharply than in the U.S. Yet Japan uses the law differently. By spring 2004, hundreds faced lawsuits in Europe (Lander, 2004), but Japan's legal action against file sharers is limited to three arrests. Instead some business leaders are taking a hard look at the intersection of fan attitudes and promotion strategies. Japan is also instructive becomes some Japanese popular culture industries, namely *manga* (comic books) and *anime* (Japanese animated movies), may have benefited substantially from copyright infringement that was not prosecuted.

> Condry outlines several similarities and differences, to find that Japanese businesses see digital piracy as yielding income (through promotion and other culture industries) even as it reduces sales. Note how Condry argues Japan is "instructive," again illustrating that synthesis as comparison yields new insights and generates recommendations for new "possible directions" in the U.S.

> Here, Condry shows that comparison demonstrates a widespread culture of piracy rather than it being representative of one national culture.

Then I return to the U.S. to analyze some possible directions for moving beyond the current impasses between record companies and recalcitrant pirates....

Synthesis as definition

Academic writers often invoke synthesis in order to define an idea or concept, showing how movements or ideas are often a synthesis of other related concepts. One might term this type of synthesis as **explanatory synthesis**. This mode of synthesis involves demonstrating the antecedents of a particular concept or movement in order to illustrate how the various parts combined together to create the new movement or concept. The purpose of this mode of synthesis is to gain a fuller understanding of the context surrounding ideas.

In the excerpt, Yvonne Bynoe explains how hip-hop itself emerged from a synthesis of various parts that combine to create hip-hop.

Excerpt from "Introduction" *Encyclopedia of Rap and Hip-Hop Culture* by Y. Bynoe

Hip-hop is not only music. It represents at least four different, interrelated art forms: MC-ing, or rap—the oral element; B-boying, break dancing, as it is commonly known—the dance element; DJing—the musical element; and graffiti, or aerosol art—the visual element. The acknowledged birthday of hip-hop is November 11, 1973, the date that Afrika Bambaataa, one of the most important hip-hop figures, established the Zulu Nation. This former Black Spades gang member formed a communal organization that intended to eradicate street violence by using the arts as a means to squelch rivalries. Under the Zulu Nation, street gangs transformed into crews, whose members vanquished foes in battles using superior turntable skills, dance, or lyrical talents instead of weapons....

————
From *testaae.greenwood.com*, 2006.

Synthesis in Bibliographic Essays

Bibliographic essays, often used in library studies, are another example of a synthesis of different materials. For example, in "The Kaleidoscope of Writing on Hip-Hop Culture," Gail Hilson Woldu "distinguish[es] three categories of writing about hip-hop—works by academics, works by journalists and cultural critics, and works by hip-hop's devotees." Similarly, in "'One Day It'll All Make Sense': Hip-Hop and Rap Resources for Music Librarians," Andrew Leach "provides descriptions of a wide array of resources relating to hip-hop culture and rap music," including works that define hip-hop, bibliographies of hip-hop, histories of hip-hop, scholarly literature, and biographies.

In the example, we see an academic writer in the discipline of librarian studies synthesizing the wide range of kinds of writing about hip-hop. Andrew Leach is librarian and archivist at the Center for Black Music Research at Columbia College Chicago.

Excerpt from "'One Day It'll All Make Sense':
Hip-Hop and Rap Resources for Music Librarians" by A. Leach

This bibliographical essay provides descriptions of a wide array of resources relating to hip-hop culture and rap music, and its final section is devoted to the collecting of hip-hop and rap materials by libraries.

> Here, Leach presents his purpose for the bibliographical essay and also discusses his choices for organization.

————
From *Notes* (65.1), 2008.

While the essay is primarily intended to serve as a guide for music librarians who provide reference service and library instruction, and to those with collection development responsibilities, it may also prove useful to educators, students, and those beginning to conduct research on hip-hop or rap.

Several...noteworthy essays and encyclopedia entries provide overviews of rap music. One such essay is "The Rap Attack: An Introduction," written by leading hip-hop scholar William Eric Perkins in the anthology for which he served as editor, *Droppin' Science: Critical Essays on Rap Music and Hip-Hop Culture*. Perkins's essay provides an excellent examination of rap music's early history and many of the musical origins of the rap tradition. Tricia Rose's essay "Rap Music," in *The Hip-Hop Reader*, provides another superb scholarly account of rap music's early years while taking into account its connections to culture, identity, gender, and technology. Rose's essay is based on an excerpt from her seminal book *Black Noise: Rap Music and Black Culture in Contemporary America*...David Toop's entry "Rap," in *The New Grove Dictionary of Music and Musicians* and in *Grove Music Online*, provides a useful overview of rap music, covering the genre's history from its beginnings to the present day and providing a short bibliography. Rob Bowman's succinct and well written entry "Rap" in *The Harvard Dictionary of Music* briefly discusses rap music's precursors in African and African American cultures, the use of turntables and samplers, copyright issues, political messages, censorship, and rap's broadening appeal among mainstream music listeners. Finally, the concise entry "Rap" in Bynoe's *Encyclopedia of Rap and Hip-Hop Culture* addresses rap's place within hip-hop culture, its musical antecedents, prior uses of the term "rap" within African American culture, and the music's origins and early history.

> Notice here that as Leach summarizes each article, he focuses on the ways in which each article approaches the same general topic (an overview of hip-hop) from a slightly different vantage point. The result is that the synthesis of all of them generates a deeper understanding of hip-hop.

Transferring Synthesis

The modes of synthesis addressed in this chapter represent only some of the many kinds of synthesis you will likely be asked to do across your undergraduate career. The very notion of synthesis, in fact, underpins transfer itself: synthesis invites you to apply, adapt, compare, overlay, reject, etc. what you learn about writing and learning when you move from one occasion to other occasions. Synthesis is grounded in advancing knowledge.

This chapter on synthesis has built upon the preceding chapters by providing strategies you can use as you pursue research questions, read others' texts, and deepen what you have learned from summarizing those texts throughout their reading encounters. Chapter 7, in turn, will expand this work by addressing a corollary strategy writers across disciplines can use—that of analysis. Where synthesis invites readers to combine ideas to create something new, analysis invites readers to break apart the component parts of concepts also to create something new, be it an insight, recommendation, definition, understanding, critique, or other sort of argument.

And, as you may be starting to discover, the sequence of concepts across Chapters 5, 6, and 7, which move from summary to synthesis to analysis, also equips you with increasing autonomy to contribute your own ideas and advance knowledge as you pursue research questions and engage with texts.

℮⟩ ℮⟩ ℮⟩

Chapter 6 Key Terms

Mashup	Critical lens	Anthology
Synthesis	Thesis driven synthesis	Comparison
Literature review	Argumentative synthesis	Explanatory synthesis
Background synthesis	Interdisciplinarity	Bibliographic essay

Write Away

Create your own mashup (synthesis) as a way of gaining a more nuanced understanding of how synthesis combines elements, ideas, or concepts in order to create something new.

Find a partner. Work in teams of two for this project as a way of enhancing the creative process through collaboration.

Choose a medium for your mashup. Together with your partner, you can decide to do a mashup in any medium you wish, provided you have relatively easy access to any needed materials or have the technological acumen necessary for the project. Media options for your mashup can include songs, videos, poetry, creative nonfiction, nonfiction, art, images, maps, clothing, objects, or any medium or combination of media that you want.

Create the mashup. Generate the mashup in whichever form you have chosen. As you generate the mashup, think deliberately about what you are hoping to accomplish from the mashup. *Why* are you combining these particular ideas, elements, or concepts? What larger purpose might this synthesis serve?

Generate a brief (100-150 word) summary and analysis of your mashup. Using the skills at summary you have learned from Chapter 5, and practicing in advance the skills at analysis you will gain in Chapter 7, write a brief (100-150 word) summary and analysis for your mashup. This brief text should accomplish the following aims: summarize the elements, ideas, concepts, etc. you chose to mashup, explain why you did so, and reveal, from your perspective, the "something new" generated by this mashup (synthesis). What new insights, critiques, illustrations, questions, etc. emerge from this mashup? Your brief written text should be modeled after the kinds of texts that can sometimes accompany art exhibits: brief, readable texts that provide a bit of background, general information, and often some small analysis or suggestions for interpretation. Since effective synthesis hinges on the "something new," be explicit about the "something new" generated by this mashup.

Share your mashup with the other teams. Share or present your mashup and your brief written text with the other teams, and learn about their mashups as well.

Reflect on transfer and synthesis. After having seen the other teams' mashups, and by invoking a comparative approach—itself synthesis—reflect in writing for ten minutes about what you have learned regarding transfer and synthesis: What skills with synthesis seem more or less important across different media? How did other teams go through the process of synthesis, and how do their processes compare with the process you and your partner followed? What do you now know about synthesis from having completed your own mashup project *and* from having seen other teams' mashups? What elements of synthesis do you anticipate transferring across occasions throughout your academic career?

Analysis

Moving from the synthesis addressed in Chapter 6, Chapter 7 focuses on analysis, where writers combine and also unbundle component parts to generate deeper understandings. Writers conduct and develop their research with and through analysis, using it to pursue the questions they pose, as well as to engage with the texts they read. To provide you with strategies for *analysis in transit*, this chapter addresses the following concepts:

- What Is Analysis?
- The Purposes of Analysis
- Types of Data Academic Writers Analyze
- Questions That Shape Analysis
- Criteria for Effective Analysis
- Modes of Analysis

Subsequent chapters, which focus on argument, extend knowledge about analysis by showing how writers move from analysis to constructing and shaping their arguments as effectively as possible.

$\mathcal{P}$etroglyphs, engravings carved into rock, can be found across the world, from New Mexico to Australia. Strategies for analyzing and calculating the age of petroglyphs have become a hotly contested issue. Depending on the strategy used, some scholars have suggested that petroglyphs in Pilbara, Australia, are among the oldest in the world, created as many as 60,000 years ago. Other scholars date most petroglyphs to, at most, 30,000 years ago (Pillans and Fifield; Watchman).

As with debates over the dating of petroglyphs, scholars also argue about how to interpret or analyze petroglyphs. Many scholars associate astronomical significance to some petroglyphs, hypothesizing that they depict solar entities or were designed with considerations about astronomical alignment. Ray P. Norris and Duane W. Hamacher describe some of these possible interpretations: "A 'bicycle-wheel' or 'sunburst' petroglyph…may represent the sun, or perhaps even a supernova…crescent shapes are also common, and may represent the moon." Norris and Hamacher, however, are careful to point out that such interpretations are speculative. Marinus Anthony van der Sluijs and Anthony L. Peratt surveyed petroglyphs in 139 countries around the world, noting that "all the sites allowed for the rock artist to look to the South Pole of the sky." They believe that abstract representations such as the sunburst above may actually be illustrations of intense auroral storms: "Auroras are centered on the poles. In this case, our observations suggest that an auroral storm of unprecedented proportions may have occurred over the South Pole. The light associated with such storms is unbearably bright and is called synchrotron radiation light."

Providing a different analytical perspective, other petroglyph research suggests that some "sites may have been places where medicine men, community, or spiritual leaders went to meditate to receive visions or guidance to lead or heal their people." Other research suggests instead that petroglyphs provide a visual "type of storytelling or recording of history & events [or a form of] artistic expression" ("About Petroglyphs"; Carr and Nevin).

Still other researchers focus on the spirituality of petroglyphs and argue that we should not spend time analyzing or interpreting petroglyphs as a way of maintaining respect and honor for petroglyphs. The National Park Service, for instance, resists interpretation: "We usually do not try and interpret the images or assign specific meanings. Some meanings were

not meant to be known or understood today. Some meanings were not meant to be known or understood by the uninitiated" ("Petroglyph").

As demonstrated by this wide range of interpretations and research about what petroglyphs may have symbolized or accomplished, scholars conduct analysis across an enormous variety of different data and texts, from geological analysis of rock to cultural or historical analysis of ancient images. This discussion of ancient petroglyphs illustrates that it is not only the objects or texts of analysis that vary broadly, but also the strategies for analysis (as in the dating methodologies) and the results of analysis (as in the many, often competing conjectures about the purposes and origins of petroglyphs).

The array of data academic writers analyze, the methods they use to analyze, and the outcomes of their analysis vary broadly as one can imagine. Paleontologists can choose to analyze fossils virtually, in person with chemical compounds, or by using other models. Scholars have been analyzing Shakespeare's plays for centuries and coming up with widely varying interpretations from their analysis. Two different economists might conduct gender analysis on CEO salaries, using different models and emerge with two markedly different assessments.

Analysis forms the basis of some of the most engaged debates and disagreements across all sorts of issues. Often, how we analyze, what we analyze, and the conclusions we reach from analysis provide the material writers use to make arguments, suggest policy, and convince decision makers. In this sense, analysis is not only widely variable, but also widely significant. In fact, analysis is one of the most significant elements of the research and writing process.

Write Here

Researchers disagree about how or whether to analyze the depictions on petroglyphs. What is your opinion? Why and under what circumstances might analysis of petroglyphs be inadvisable? When might petroglyph analysis be advantageous, and how can it be conducted in responsible manner? What can be gained from analyzing petroglyphs? Are there other kinds of texts or artifacts (contemporary or historical) that you think might sometimes be better left "unanalyzed"? Why or why not?

৩ ৩ ৩

What is Analysis?

Analysis occurs around you every day in ways that directly impact your life. Professionals at area water treatment plants analyze water samples to make sure drinking water is safe. Transportation specialists analyze traffic patterns to make adjustments in traffic light rotations. Police officers analyze crimes. You yourself likely engage in analysis on a daily basis with such everyday occurrences as deciding why you prefer one song over another, or as you try to better understand a friend's behavior.

In the broadest sense, **analysis** involves examining data closely, breaking down larger concepts, texts, images, events, and artifacts into smaller pieces. Through analysis, we then scrutinize these smaller components in order to notice patterns, anomalies, significant find-ings and observations. We also use analysis to draw conclusions and thereby arrive at a greater understanding of the data.

Analysis typically involves asking such questions like:

- What are the component parts of the data?
- What patterns do you notice?
- What tensions or contradictions can you identify?
- Are there any underlying assumptions in the data?
- What seems significant about the data?
- What is the context surrounding the data?

These general questions, however, blur the nuances and specifics of analysis within the disciplines. Definitions about analysis are highly contingent on disciplinary perspective and the specific writing occasion.

Chemists, for example, employ chemical analysis, defined by the Department of Chemistry at the University of Arizona as "the science of making chemical measurements and characterizations."

Philosophy provides an even more complex example of the contingent nature of analy-sis. The *Stanford Encyclopedia of Philosophy,* for example, provides eight different definitions of the term 'analysis,' and quotes more than fifty different people across history, from Plato to Clifford Geertz, each offering their own unique descriptions of the term. Michael Beaney explains the range of definitions for analysis in philosophy through variations in analytical method:

> Analysis has always been at the heart of philosophical method, but it has been understood and practised in many different ways. Perhaps, in its broadest sense, it might be defined as a process of isolating or working back to what is more fun-damental by means of which something, initially taken as given, can be explained or reconstructed.... This allows great variation in specific method, however. The aim may be to get back to basics, but there may be all sorts of ways of doing this, each of which might be called 'analysis.'

Part of what accounts for varying definitions for analysis, then, is that academic writers employ varying methods for analysis.

Many of these methods for analysis within disciplines require some measure of discipline-specific expertise. For instance, physicists use dimensional analysis, which the Department of Physics at the University of Guelph defines as "a useful method for deter-mining the units of a variable in an equation [and/or for] checking the correctness of an equation which you have derived after some algebraic manipulation."

Alongside these discipline-specific methodologies, however, academic writers across disciplines also employ more transferable types of analytic methods. Chemists, philoso-phers, and physicists, for example, also employ content analysis, depending on the writing occasion and their research questions.

Learning how to conduct and write analysis effectively requires recognizing the degree to which disciplinary perspective and writing occasion shape the analysis academic writers conduct. Effective analysis requires the flexibility to redefine what analysis involves as you move from one writing occasion to others across and among disciplines.

The Purposes of Analysis

Analysis can sometimes become the brunt of derision and resistance, as in the Urban Dictionary's definition of overanalyze: "to over think things to the point of it being annoying or ruining your relationships with people." Given that it can be difficult to discern definitively the point at which analysis becomes overanalysis, it becomes ever more important to keep in mind the purposes of analysis.

Analysis serves many vital roles in academic writing across disciplines and helps academic writers achieve a complex range of goals. Without analysis academic writers would not be able to sufficiently understand data, make arguments, or advance knowledge.

Analysis in academic writing can serve one or more of the following purposes:

- to understand data more deeply
- to explore relationships between two or more entities
- to explain data to oneself and/or others
- to draw conclusions from data
- to make decisions based on data
- to identify patterns or anomalies across and between data

Along with these general purposes, however, there are also discipline-specific purposes for analysis. These discipline-specific purposes are often connected to the very essence of foundational lines of inquiry within disciplines.

The Department of Chemistry at the University of Arizona, for example, explains that the purpose of chemical analysis is to answer four "fundamental questions about a substance or a sample of material. What is the identity of this substance? How can I separate the various components? How much of each component do I have? Is substance X present in the sample?"

Cultural anthropologists, by turn, have a particular purpose for conducting what they term cross-cultural analysis, also known as holocultural analysis. "The basic premise of Cross-Cultural Analysis is that statistical cross-cultural comparisons can be used to discover traits shared between cultures and generate ideas about cultural universals" (Kinzer and Gillies).

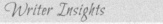

Writer Insights

How and why do you analyze data?

Part of my job is to analyze data about our campus writing center. I look at the number of visits in a semester, the ten most common student challenges, the most common courses tutored, the busiest times of day, and so on. I usually start by asking myself a research question, like "How often do students have MLA and APA citation questions?" Then, I use the search tool on my spreadsheet to check the tutor's reports for mentions of these terms. There are about 1,800 reports to sort through! I report my findings to the dean and the president's office.

~Brenna Dugan, College Administrator/ Writing Center Manager/English Professor, Ohio, U.S.

Often, academic writers have multiple purposes, some explicit and some implicit. But, as with most matters in academic writing, one should have some sense of aim or purpose when writing because it infuses academic writing with value and significance. Since academic writers can sometimes get mired within the component parts required by analysis, it is important to keep in mind the larger purposes for analysis, purposes that enable academic writers to achieve important disciplinary goals.

Write Now

Think about recent occasions when you have conducted analysis, both within and outside of school. Perhaps you analyzed choices while making a high-stakes decision in your life, such as where to work or go to school after you graduated from high school…Or perhaps you analyzed the interactions or behavior of a close friend…Or perhaps you analyzed the lyrics to a song…Or perhaps you analyzed an equation in a math course. Write for ten minutes about recent occasions in which you conducted analysis. What were you analyzing and what methods did you use for the analysis? What were your purposes for analyzing?

Types of Data Academic Writers Analyze

Academic writers analyze an enormously wide range of data. Nearly anything and anyone, in fact, can be analyzed. This list provides a glimpse into the many different types of data that academic writers analyze:

- **Visual:** photographs, images, art, graphics, observations
- **Aural:** music, spoken language, animal sounds, environmental sounds
- **Tactile:** physiological actions and reactions, forces, vibrations
- **Textual:** language in fiction, nonfiction, poetry, songs, criticism, websites, field notes, archives
- **Quantitative:** numbers, equations, statistics
- **Other:** liquids, solids, events, human or animal behaviors

These types of data often overlap. A film, for instance, has visual, aural, and textual components to it. Depending on your perspective, you might even argue that a film involves tactile data (viewers' responses) and quantitative data as well (costs, revenue, distribution, viewer attendance, length of availability).

To further illustrate the many different types of data that academic writers analyze, and how they work together to advance knowledge, examine this article from the magazine *Science News*. The section excerpted discusses the MERS and H7N9 viruses. It appeared as part of a larger article titled "Science News Top 25." The "Top 25" identified the top-ranked 25 articles from *Science News* across the year 2013. The excerpt here was #5, the fifth-highest ranked science news article from 2013.

The annotations point to the many types of data academic writers across disciplines might analyze in relation to this topic.

Excerpt from "A Double Dose of Virus Scares"
by T. Hesman Saey

Outbreaks of two deadly viruses captured the world's attention in 2013, but neither turned into the global pandemic expected to strike one of these years.

Scholars in public health analyze data sets about pandemics.

One of the viruses, known as MERS, causes Middle East respiratory syndrome. The other, H7N9, is a new bird flu virus from China. Each virus has infected fewer than 200 people, but both kill a sizable number of the people who contract them. Although the viruses have not spread far from where they started, the scientific effort to decipher and combat them has had global reach.

Engineers and computer scientists analyze data to determine which news stories from a given year are the most "popular."

Journalists analyze other news stories to understand how to research and write as effectively as possible.

Statisticians examine data about disease risk and death.

Scholars in English or Literature analyze data about "outbreak narratives" and "patient zero."

The MERS virus was first isolated from a patient in Saudi Arabia by an Egyptian physician who sent the sample to the Netherlands to be tested. The researchers in the lab of Ron Fouchier (who made headlines in 2012 for work on the bird flu virus H5N1) deciphered the MERS virus's genetic makeup. It turned out that MERS is a coronavirus related to SARS, a virus identified in 2003 as the cause of severe acute respiratory syndrome (*SN 3/23/13, p. 5*).

Geographers analyze data to produce maps representing the spread of disease.

Chemists and biologists analyze data sets about test samples and genetics.

Since it first appeared in people in 2012, MERS has sickened 163 people, killing 71. Most of the victims live in Saudi Arabia, Qatar or the United Arab Emirates, or had recently traveled to the Arabian peninsula.

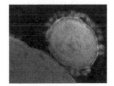

Scholars in visual studies analyze data sets consisting of medical images.

A transmission electron micrograph shows the Coronavirus responsible for Middle East respiratory syndrome in action.

From *Science News* (184), 2013.

H7N9, a new strain of avian influenza, began circulating in China in February. The outbreak peaked by early April, nearly halting after Chinese officials closed live poultry markets.

> Economists analyze data about the economic impact of closing live poultry markets.

Still, sporadic cases appeared in the summer and fall, raising concerns that the virus could make a resurgence in the coming flu season (*SN Online: 10/15/13*). By early December, of the 139 people with confirmed H7N9 infections, 45 had died.

It came as a surprise that this type of bird virus was seriously sickening and killing people. Experts have been worried for a long time that the H5N1 bird flu would sweep the globe as the 1918 Spanish flu did.

> Historians analyze data about the prior pandemics.

If H5N1 gained the ability to spread from person to person through the air while retaining its potency, it could potentially kill millions. But until this year, no serious human infections with H7N9 had ever been recorded.

As more and more cases of MERS and H7N9 infection appeared, scientists and health workers scrambled to investigate basic questions about the viruses: Where did they come from? How did they get into humans? How do they infect cells?

> Sociologists analyze data about surveillance and public health policy.

And perhaps most important, do they spread easily from person to person, becoming a candidate for a pandemic? Only partial answers have emerged, and some are not comforting.

Researchers found molecular handles on human cells that the MERS virus grasps during infection (*SN Online: 3/13/13*). One study revealed that H7N9 can grow well in human lung cells (*SN Online: 7/3/13*).

> Cultural anthropologists analyze data about human interactions and behaviors that can contribute to the spread of disease.

> Molecular biologists or biochemists analyze data about cells.

Studies of ferrets revealed that H7N9 can spread through the air from one of the animals to another, raising the possibility that it might also pass from person to person that way (*SN Online: 5/23/13*). But so far, the virus hasn't been easily transmitted between people. A few people may have spread the virus to their relatives, but most people probably caught it from chickens, ducks, pigeons or other birds at live poultry markets (*SN Online: 4/12/13, 4/15/13*).

> Ethicists analyze data about medical research on animals.

> **71**
> MERS deaths since September 2012
>
> **45**
> H7N9 deaths in 2013

> Mathematicians analyze data about the number of infections and deaths to generate mathematical models for the spread of and impact of disease.

But the MERS virus does spread from person to person, particularly among people who are elderly or have other health problems. Hospital dialysis wards proved important for at least one big outbreak (*SN Online: 6/19/13*).

Researchers have been using DNA data and old-fashioned health sleuthing to track down the source of the MERS virus. It probably originated in bats and may have spread to camels and other animals before infecting humans (*SN: 9/21/13, p. 18; SN Online: 8/8/13, 10/9/13*). Whatever its origin, MERS probably made the leap from animals to people multiple times (*SN: 10/19/13, p. 16*). New cases of the virus continue to emerge, and there is ongoing concern that it could become a worldwide problem.

> Those involved with veterinary science and evolutionary anthropology analyze data about bat and camel behavior.

> Scholars in public policy analyze data about pandemics in order to create policies for global pandemic cooperation.

> Psychologists analyze data about anxiety and concern among people.

Again, it is important to emphasize that academic writers from different disciplines often analyze the same types of data with different, but sometimes overlapping, approaches. For instance, while the economists in the example above might analyze agricultural market exchanges, they might also analyze the same data as psychologists do about anxiety; economists, though, might examine that same data to learn the economic impact of public anxiety. While no one individual academic writer has mastered analysis across all the different types of data, academic writers must nevertheless be equipped to analyze multiple different data types.

> ### *Writer Insights*
>
>
>
> **What analytical tools do you use?**
>
> With websites, there are four main technologies that can be used to collect data about website traffic, or "clickstream data": web logs, web beacons, JavaScript tags, and packet sniffing.
>
> ~Kyle James,
> *Internet Marketing and Web Development Consultant,*
> *Boston, MA, U.S.*

Write Now

Select a news article on a topic of interest to you. Using the previous excerpt as a model, annotate the article you have selected by noting the different types of data that could be analyzed in relation to that topic.

Transfer Hub: Contribute your summary and see what others have written at fountainheadpress.com/transferhub.

Questions that Shape Analysis

Learning how to conduct and write analysis requires posing and answering key questions about the writing occasion giving rise to the analysis.

Purpose

Are you hoping to understand a text in more depth? Or are you trying to predict an outcome of some sort? Are you testing a hypothesis? Note that this does not mean that you should have a pre-established agenda—this would warp your analysis. Nor does it mean that you need to have only one purpose—sometimes multiple purposes operate simultaneously. But, having greater clarity about why you are conducting analysis will help you conduct and write the analysis more effectively.

Disciplinary perspective

What is your disciplinary perspective for this writing project? While there is considerable crossover between disciplines, disciplinary perspective impacts your approach to analysis and the form in which the analysis appears in academic writing. In a scientific article, for instance, it would be less familiar (not unheard of, just less familiar) to see in-depth textual analysis; it would, however, be more familiar to see such textual analysis in a literary essay. Reading analyses from other articles in the discipline in which you are currently working helps provide a sense of disciplinary inflections and conventions regarding analysis.

Research questions

What are your research questions? The research questions driving a particular writing occasion also shapes the analysis you will conduct. If your research question is seeking statistical predictions, then you'll likely be including analysis of numerical data from a perspective that integrates a quantitative approach. By contrast, if you are seeking to explore the use of metaphor in Herman Melville's *Moby Dick*, you would likely be conducting textual analysis of passages in the novel and perhaps of other academic articles about the novel.

Collected data

What data to you have or still need? The type of data you are working with helps shape the analysis you will conduct. Many data types can be analyzed with multiple analytic approaches. Text, for instance, can be analyzed in quantitative ways (how many times do certain words or phrases occur?) or qualitative ways (what are the underlying assumptions of the textual passage?). But your data set will often help you determine the type of analysis.

Tools, technologies, and approaches

How are you going to approach your analysis? Sometimes analysis is conducted exclusively by thinking and in-depth reading practices, but many modes of analysis rely on tools, technologies, or specific theoretical approaches. In statistics, for example, academic writers might use "R" for analysis, a "language and environment for statistical computing and graphics" ("What is R?"); similarly, academic writers in a number of disciplines might use software such as NVivo or Provalis for qualitative coding. Still other fields rely on discovery and observer impression for analysis.

Disciplinary and publication context

What is the disciplinary and publication context of your writing occasion? Depending on the writing occasion for which you are conducting analysis, there may likely be discipline-specific or content-specific analytic questions that will help frame your analysis. For instance, if you are conducting a rhetorical analysis of an advertisement for an English course, you will ask questions about the Aristotelian appeals and about the rhetorical triangle. Similarly, if you are conducting a visual analysis of a website image for a cultural anthropology course, you will ask pointed questions about visual form and design. Once you have answered preliminary questions, you can more effectively conduct and write your analysis.

Criteria for Effective Analysis

Criteria for effective analysis are highly contingent on the writing occasion, disciplinary context, and individual purposes. Broadly speaking, though, certain aspects are present in effective analysis.

Connected to the data

Analysis must be connected to the data to show that a writer is drawing conclusions and making analyses based on evidence. While some disciplines or writing occasions warrant slightly more conjecture or inference than others, analysis should nonetheless be as closely connected to the data at hand as possible.

Thorough

Effective analysis reflects careful thinking, close reading, and deliberate attention. Analysis should illustrate that which would not be immediately obvious to someone who has spent less time examining the data.

Fully explicated

Although the person conducting the analysis might think much of the analysis is readily apparent to others, readers will likely need a thorough explication in order to understand an analysis. Offer full, expansive details in analysis.

Recursive and iterative

Effective analysis takes time and often repetition. It requires patience. Analysis happens at varying points in the research and writing process, and as new data comes in, analysis might shift accordingly.

Conducted to discover

If you approach a set of data with a predetermined, inflexible agenda, it is likely that you will miss important aspects of the analysis. Humans are curiously capable of finding what they want in data, perhaps by inadvertently (or explicitly) not noticing other details. Effective analysis should be open-minded and flexible. If you find contradictions in the data, address them as such rather than discounting one or more. Effective analysis should be conducted with a sense of discovery in order to maximize your likelihood of generating as effective an analysis as possible.

Aligned with disciplinary methods

Analysis should generally be linked to methods in the discipline in which you are writing. In English literature, scholars might analyze text through rhetorical analysis or discourse analysis. In mathematics, academic writers might use real or complex analysis. In sociology, academic writers might use dynamic network analysis or frame analysis. Find out the analytical methods of the discipline in which you are writing, and choose from among those for your analysis. If you are departing from accepted analytic methodologies or tools in a field, do so explicitly by stating why you are applying a somewhat less familiar analytical method.

Linked to argument and purpose

If you spend large amounts of time analyzing data, you'll likely have a considerable amount of material. When you write the analysis, you'll need to narrow your focus to include only the aspects of the analysis that are most relevant or significant for your current writing project's overall argument and purpose. Otherwise, you run the risk of veering off track and losing readers' attention.

Modes of Analysis

Numerous modes of analysis exist across and within academic disciplines. It would be nearly impossible to name, much less describe, all the modes of analysis that operate across disciplines. In the list provided, you will find overviews of the most common forms of analysis that you are likely to encounter in your undergraduate academic writing career:

- rhetorical analysis
- critical discourse analysis
- content analysis
- visual analysis

- scientific data analysis
- statistical analysis
- Big Data analysis

And, in keeping with the overarching line of inquiry in this chapter, each of the example readings is related to the *Science News* article excerpt that was first discussed.

Rhetorical analysis

Rhetorical analysis examines how text (written, verbal, or visual) influences readers. Nelson Graff, a writing faculty member at San Francisco State University, describes rhetorical analysis as follows:

> [R]hetorical analysis [means] examining not only what authors communicate but also for what purposes they communicate those messages, what effects they attempt to evoke in readers, and how they accomplish those purposes and effects. Rhetorical analysis often involves the study of rhetorical appeals (ethos, pathos, and logos), the purposes and aims of symbolic communication, and the structure of arguments.

When conducting and writing a rhetorical analysis, academic writers focus on the rhetorical situation, or the rhetorical triangle, as described in Chapter 4: Reading. That is, the analysis examines a combination of any of the following elements (described in brief here; for more expansive descriptions, see Featured In-Depth Reading Strategy: Reading Rhetorically in Chapter 4):

- **Author:** Who created/wrote the text? How might a person's background or circumstances inform the text?
- **Audience:** Who do you think are the primary readers/viewers of the text? Why?
- **Message:** What is the author seeking to communicate through the text? What is being argued or shared in the text? In what ways might metaphors, similes, and other figures of speech play a role in communicating that message?
- **Purpose:** What do you think are the primary aims or purposes of the text?
- *Ethos:* What kind of character does the writer construct?
- *Pathos:* How does the writer appeal to readers' emotions?
- *Logos:* How does the writer appeal to readers' sense of logic and reason?
- *Kairos:* How does the writer establish the timeliness of the text and address propriety through conventions and features of the text?

Academic writers conduct a rhetorical analysis on texts, speeches, artifacts, events, film, advertisements, and images. Rhetorical analysis can be applied to written, verbal, or visual texts, in print or digital environments.

To demonstrate how rhetorical analysis can be applied across a wide range of texts and to illustrate the significance of rhetorical analysis, two examples are provided.

Example 1: Rhetorical Analysis, Rhetoric

The first example comes from an article published in the *Rhetoric Review*, titled "The New Smallpox? An Epidemic of Words" written by Barbara Heifferon, a rhetorician at Clemson University. Heifferon uses rhetorical analysis to examine historical and contemporary medical rhetoric about smallpox vaccinations. Heifferon examines a variety of texts, including letters to the editor, seventeenth-century medical nonfiction, and contemporary advertisements.

The excerpt illustrates Heifferon's rhetorical analysis of visual discourse. The paragraphs come from a sub-section of her article titled "The Role of Visual Communication in Smallpox Vaccinations."

Excerpt from "The New Smallpox: An Epidemic of Words?" by B. A. Heifferon

On the December 11, 2002 airing of *60 Minutes* on CBS, the smallpox report included graphic pictures showing side effects of the complications resulting from smallpox vaccination. The pictures, in full color, represented the most extreme results and could easily scare even the most medically sophisticated citizens away from vaccinations. There was little mention of the fact that the vaccine itself does not result in smallpox (thus the graphic pictures were not of smallpox), but in a less harmful form of virus called vaccinia, … commonly referred to as cowpox. Yes, it too is ugly. But the results are less threatening and very much less common than infection with the actual smallpox virus in an epidemic. The rash occurs in very few people and is not life threatening. It would have given a more complete picture and been a better use of visual communication to show graphic pictures of smallpox itself, that is, what happens if one doesn't get vaccinated and contracts the disease.

> Heifferon describes the ways in which the *60 Minutes* report persuades viewers by way of *pathos,* evoking emotion—fear in this case.

> She emphasizes that the rhetoricians who designed the "graphic pictures" made choices designed to influence their audience to be fearful of the vaccinations.

Because smallpox has been eradicated in the world, what we have not seen or experienced recently has little valence for us. If active cases were part of our recent memory, as they are in Africa and other [locations around the world], we would have a more realistic context into which to place today's discussions. In other [locations] like Africa in which people remember smallpox cases in their not-so-distant past, there are graphic pictures in their memories of the suffering and disfigurement from this disease. In addition, constant reminders, often viewed daily, in the form of scarred bodies, still signal and visually communicate

From *Rhetoric Review* (25.1), 2006.

Heifferon discusses who the audience is and why they might be particularly susceptible to fear about vaccinations, namely because Americans do not have "recent memory" of the impact of smallpox itself.

the reality of smallpox, unlike the visuals we experience only through our media in this culture. ...

Thus our Western experience decontextualizes the disease itself. The corrective would be to visually communicate the experiences of smallpox in countries where the epidemic ended more recently, interview members of this population, or at least show graphic pictures of cases of smallpox on U.S. programs rather than graphic pictures of complications from vaccinia. However, because

At the end of this section, Heifferen reiterates her main point of this rhetorical analysis: the discourse creates fear about the vaccine instead of the disease.

our recent American experience does not include the visual and physical memories of active smallpox cases, the risk factors of the vaccination itself take center stage. Through such discourse more fear is created about the vaccine than about the disease itself.

As Heifferon's analysis demonstrates, audience plays a critical role. She makes the argument that the *60 Minutes's* rhetoric is only as effective as it is because most Americans who are watching *60 Minutes* lack a cultural memory of the devastation of smallpox to offset fears about vaccine-related side effects. In turn, understanding more about the role of audience in shaping meaning within a message enables readers or viewers to be more self-aware and reflective about the ways in which they might be influenced by subsequent messages.

Example 2: Rhetorical Analysis, Composition and English

Where Heifferon focuses on audience, this second example illustrates how advertising uses the Aristotelian appeals and *kairos* to influence consumers. In this article, Jessica Lundgren, an undergraduate at Pennsylvania State University, University Park at the time of her publication, conducts a rhetorical analysis on the "FreshFit" online Subway Restaurant advertising campaign. Through her examination of eight online advertisements that are part of this campaign, Lundgren pursues the question: how does Subway's "use of rhetoric...cause consumers to misunderstand the nutritional value of Subway's menu items?" She makes the argument that Subway's "use of rhetoric may cause consumers to misunderstand the nutritional value of Subway's menu items" by misguiding them into thinking that their items are healthier than they actually are.

Excerpt from "'Eating Fresh' in America: Subway Restaurant's Nutritional Rhetoric"
by J. Lundgren

No fast food restaurant has focused on the "healthiness" of its products to the extent that Subway Restaurant has over the past near decade. In 2000, the restaurant's famous "Jared" campaign first shared the story of Jared Fogle, who lost 245 pounds in one year by following a diet that consisted primarily of Subway sandwiches ("The Subway Diet"). ... While Subway's sales continue to grow rapidly (and with Jared still appearing in many of its commercials), America's obesity rates also are increasing at a shocking pace. ... To understand how restaurants like Subway influence the American diet, it is critical to examine their advertising strategies in order to ascertain specifically how their advertisements work to persuade potential customers....

> Lundgren establishes just how persuasive the campaign has been, showing that their rhetorical methods worked quite successfully. This discussion establishes *kairos* by showing how timely this inquiry is given the "obesity crisis."

For the purposes of my study, I define rhetoric as the persuasive methods applied by Subway Restaurant to entice television viewers to purchase its products. I specifically concentrate on ads that make a deliberate appeal to the nutritional and health concerns of the average television viewer; I designate this rhetorical focus as "nutritional rhetoric." ...

> Lundgren demonstrates that rhetorical analysis serves a valuable purpose by helping forge a link between advertising and nutrition. She coins the phrase "nutritional rhetoric" to describe this mode of communication.

Rhetoric of Comparison

MacArthur and Cuneo take note of the current trend of "comparative ads," which are used in attempts to demonstrate why one company's product is superior to a related company's product. ... The Fresh Fit campaign in particular uses comparison to present the argument that Subway's food is healthier than other restaurants' fast food options. ...

In an advertisement featuring Subway's Jared and the champion figure skater Kimmie Meissner, the announcer states that "the delicious Subway Foot-Long Club" has "less than half the fat of a Big Mac."

These comparisons establish the logos of the advertisements. They present the television viewer with negative images or facts related

> Rhetorical analysis involves looking at figures of speech, such as the comparisons in advertisements. In this case, Subway uses comparative language to suggest it provides healthier food than its competitors. Lundgren demonstrates that this is part of the *logos* of the advertisements— part of the way in which the message is effective at promoting Subway over others.

From *Young Scholars in Writing* (6), 2008.

to rival companies, and then contrast this information with the "better-for-you" nature of a specific type of Subway meal. This approach may influence a consumer to feel that he or she has received strong evidence that Subway Restaurant sells healthier food than other fast food restaurants. Equipped with this understanding, a person may feel that he or she is prepared to make informed and health-conscious decisions concerning future fast food meals....

Implied Undesirability of Weight Gain

The premise of several of the Fresh Fit commercials is that greasy fast food items will result in weight gain, and that this increased amount of body fat is undesirable primarily because of its physical appearance. The rhetorical nature of the perception of body fat in American culture is explored by Sonya Christine Brown, who asserts, "Body shape and size are aspects of physical ethos that Americans focus on" (10). She states: "Fat is . . . perceived as the visible, physical evidence that a body is likely to be unhealthy, unwell, unfit" (39), and adds that "to be fat is to be scorned." The relationship between fat and ethos clearly is a rhetorical basis of Subway's advertisements. In one ad, a man pulls up to a drive-through window and asks, "Can I get the love handles, double chin, and some blubber?" The female in his car requests the same, but substitutes for the blubber "thunder thighs and a badonkadonk butt." Another, similar advertisement is located in an office setting, where one character announces his intention to go to "Burger Town." He takes the orders of his coworkers, which include "the can-my-butt-look-any-bigger meal," "the extra-tight-pants combo," the "feel-so-bloated-I-just-want-to-sleep-for-three-days meal," and "a-bucket-of-please-keep-your-shirt-on."

> Lundgren builds on Brown's assertion about body shape contributing to the construction of *ethos*. Lundgren shows that Subway capitalizes on how other fast food restaurants contribute to this negative *ethos* of unhealthiness.

> By providing details about the focus on fat, Lundgren demonstrates how "the relationship between fat and *ethos* clearly is a rhetorical basis" for the advertising campaign.

In addition to its appeals to ethos, this aspect of Subway's advertisements employs pathos to get the consumer's attention by insinuating that (1) if people consume certain types of fast food, they likely will become overweight or obese and that (2) the consumer himself should fear becoming over-weight or obese and (3) as a way to protect himself from this fate, he should choose instead

> Lundgren demonstrates that the ads appeal to *pathos* by invoking fear of obesity and suspicion of other restaurants.

to eat the healthier fast food options that are offered at Subway. This approach attempts to plant in the consumer's mind suspicion regarding other fast food establishments, and then asks the consumer to consider that Subway actually can prevent him or her from acquiring "blubber."

Lundgren's deep rhetorical analysis shows the complex ways in which language can work to persuade consumers. While some may wonder if the creators of the advertising campaign were deliberate in invoking this "nutritional rhetoric," Lundgren's points about the significance of rhetorical analysis make questions about intentionality of less consequence. For Lundgren, the possible impact of the campaign on viewers, the potential for them to be misguided, and the continued prevalence of obesity in America make the rhetorical analysis meaningful. As Lundgren shows the many ways in which rhetorical appeals function in advertising, she also demonstrates the significance of rhetorical analysis as a means of understanding how language and images persuade consumers, often in subtle but powerful ways.

Write Now

Locate a website or advertisement about a topic of interest to you, perhaps involving medical rhetoric, or about some other area of inquiry. Practice conducting a rhetorical analysis on the website by focusing on the elements of rhetorical analysis described above in this section: author, audience, message, purpose, *ethos, pathos, logos,* and *kairos.*

Critical discourse analysis

Academic writers can define critical discourse analysis (CDA), also termed discourse analysis, quite differently. In *The Discourse Reader*, editors Adam Jaworski and Nikolaus Copeland offer eleven differently nuanced definitions of the term. Despite these different perspectives, however, many can agree that discourse analysis concerns itself, at heart, with the ways in which language reflects and shapes larger social, historical, and ideological forces. Put another way, CDA "explicitly draws our attention to issues of power and privilege" (Huckin, Andrus, and Clary-Lemon). Note also how the *Foundations of Qualitative Research* website from Harvard University defines CDA:

> Discourse analysis is based on the understanding that there is much more going on when people communicate than simply the transfer of information. It is not an effort to capture literal meanings; rather it is the investigation of what language does or what individuals or cultures accomplish through language. This

area of study raises questions such as how meaning is constructed, and how power functions in society.

Scholars deploy discourse analysis across a wide range of texts, including written and spoken. In *The Handbook on Discourse Analysis*, editors Deborah Schiffrin, Deborah Tannen, and Heidi E. Hamilton, all linguists, examine discourse analysis on political discourse, the media, and racism, as well as litigation discourse, medical discourse, educational discourse, and institutional discourse. Scholars can employ qualitative or quantitative approaches to discourse analysis.

The example demonstrates discourse analysis on the media and on medical discourse. The excerpt is from Priscilla Wald's book *Contagious: Cultures, Carriers, and the Outbreak Narrative*. In *Contagious*, Wald analyzes historical and contemporary discourse from media texts and medical journals to argue that they turn diseases and narratives about the outbreak of diseases into narratives with significant social implications, often involving stigmatization and hierarchical power divisions among certain social classes or ethnic groups.

In the chapter from which this segment emerges, Wald analyzes the way early twentieth-century media and medical journals wrote about Mary Mallon, an immigrant who worked as a cook in New York at the turn of the twentieth century and who was identified as the first person to carry typhoid without having symptoms of the disease herself. Wald argues that the outbreak narrative surrounding Mallon, also known as "Typhoid Mary" led to "society's blaming and stigmatizing immigrants because of their association with communicable disease (especially venereal disease)."

The excerpted reading demonstrates Wald's critical discourse analysis as she discusses the language in Dr. George Soper's early twentieth-century accounts of his investigation into Mallon and the typhoid outbreak.

Excerpt from *Contagious: Cultures, Carriers,
and the Outbreak Narrative* by P. Wald

Mary Mallon's recalcitrance, her reluctance to believe she was spreading typhoid and her unwillingness to meet with public-health officials became more central and elaborately recounted each time Soper told the story. With each version, Soper fleshed out the details of her life, shifting his emphasis from the detection of the carrier to a more comprehensive portrait of the woman. In his 1919 version, from an article titled "Typhoid Mary," Soper described the help that he had had in arranging a surprise interview with the reluctant cook from "a

> Here, Wald frames the analysis as reflecting a larger trend in Soper's narrative that added life details about Typhoid Mary.

From *Contagious: Cultures, Carriers, and the Outbreak Narrative*, 2007.

friend whom she often visited at night in the top of a Third Avenue tenement." Twenty years later, he would elaborate on their relationship, noting that at the end of her workday, Mallon retired "to a rooming house on Third Avenue below Thirty-third Street, where she was spending the evenings with a disreputable-looking man … [whose] headquarters during the day was in a saloon on the corner. I got to be well acquainted with him," Soper admits. "He took me to see the room. I should not care to see another like it. It was a place of dirt and disorder. It was not improved by the presence of a large dog of which Mary was said to be very fond." The dirt and disorder mark social margins and the hint of categorical breakdown, which Soper casts in sexual terms. Typhoid is not a sexually transmitted disease, but with his attention to the evident sexual activity of this unmarried Irish woman whose affection for her lover's dog adds to Soper's disgust, he summoned the conventions of a venereal-disease narrative. Mallon inhabited the spaces and indulged in the behavior of a fallen woman, and Soper's depiction implicitly coded her disease as a result of her illicit behavior.

> Wald analyzes Soper's text by pointing out how details like the dog, dirt, and disorder resonate with venereal disease narratives and position Mallon as a "fallen woman" who has somehow brought typhoid on herself.

Content analysis

Academic writers conduct **content analysis** across disciplines as a way of categorizing and organizing data in a wide variety of texts. Academic writers who conduct content analysis create categories, sometimes conceived of as conceptual "bins," for their data, and then "code" the data by placing parts of the data into these predetermined categories. Content analysis helps researchers understand the quantity of certain kinds of data and relationships across that data. Nearly any written or verbal content can be used for content analysis, from books and interviews to commercials and magazines.

Authors Stefan Timmermans and Steven Haas, both Professors of Sociology (UCLA and Penn State, respectively), use content analysis to analyze issues of a journal called *Sociology of Health and Illness* to point out a research gap in their discipline and to "argue for a sociology of health, illness, and disease." The excerpted reading discusses results from "a content analysis of the 10 most recent years of original articles published in *Sociology of Health and Illness* (1997–2006)." The authors likely created a coding schema for their research, identifying categories and key terms, and then identified which articles fit into particular categories.

Excerpt from "Towards a Sociology of Disease" by S. Timmermans and S. Haas

Timmermans and Haas use content to identify analysis how many original articles address a disease category.

The [underrepresentation in the literature of engagement by medical sociologists with diseases] can easily be found in the contributions to *Sociology of Health and Illness.* Between 1997 and 2006, 21 percent of original articles (82 out of 387 articles) published in SHI involved a specific disease category, meaning that the overwhelming majority did not deal with diseases. The most written-about diseases were HIV (16 articles) and various cancers (14 articles), stroke (6 articles), heart disease (5 articles), and depression (4 articles), followed by anorexia, asthma, and chronic back pain (3 articles). These figures do not necessarily mean that the authors paid attention to disease as a biological phenomenon because they included every possible topic related to disease such as, for example, the media representation or historical development of a disease classification. If we further limit the articles to those dealing with disease as a health issue for patients and/or clinicians, the pool shrinks to 16 per cent (60 out of 387).

Here, Timmermans and Haas have looked through each article to identify which diseases are mentioned the most. Such diseases as cancers, stroke, heart disease, etc. likely represent the disease categories they created in their content analysis.

From *Sociology of Health & Illness* (30.5), 2008.

Visual analysis

While visual analysis overlaps with several other modes of analysis (rhetorical analysis and data analysis in particular), it also merits a focused consideration because of its prevalence across disciplines. This section is also connected to the section on reading visual images in Chapter 4: Reading, and visual arguments in Chapter 10: Designing Arguments.

Visual analysis involves an in-depth consideration of the component parts of an image, be it a photograph, advertisement, painting, digital image, cartoon, graphic, or even a moving image such as a film, video game, documentary, performance, or video. Note that film studies and performance studies are entire disciplines with well-established modes of analysis. This section is intended to offer you a starting point, which you can then build, extend, and modify with more extended exploration in disciplines that rely heavily on the visual, such as those.

Visual analysis treats visual images as a form of text in that they contribute to (or form the foundation of) arguments in many of the same ways as written text. Visual images, though, also have unique features that warrant additional analytic tools.

For instance, when conducting a visual analysis, a writer might draw on the same rhetorical strategies described above. However, because of the unique features of visual images, visual analysis also asks that a viewer consider other questions in particular.

TABLE 7.1 Questions to consider for visual analysis.

What message is the visual image conveying?

What is the purpose of the visual image?

How does the visual image evoke emotions (*pathos*)?

How does the visual image appeal to viewers' sense of reason and logic (*logos*)?

How does the creator of the image (author) establish her credibility or construct her character?

How does the visual image establish *kairos*?

Who do you think is the primary viewer for this image? Why?

Who created the image? Why? How might his background impact our reading of the image?

What is in the foreground? How does it help the image achieve its aim?

What is in the background? Why do you think the image's creator included it?

What might be beyond the frame of the visual image? Why do you think the creator of the image chose to make the boundaries/frame in this way?

What is the relationship between the visual image and text (if there is text)?

What is the purpose of the visual image, in its original context and/or in a repurposed context?

Where are the visual images located in a text/document? How does that positioning impact their efficacy?

Where is the focal point of the image?

If there are humans in the image, where are they looking, and why?

What details do you notice about the objects in the image?

What details do you notice about the subjects in the image?

Conducting a thorough visual analysis with the kinds of questions in Table 7.1 requires significant time. As with written texts, those conducting in-depth analysis should be prepared to spend considerable time thinking about the image, returning to it many times, and allowing the analysis of it to percolate with time and deliberateness.

This visual analysis example comes from an article in which Anita Helle discusses photographer Dorothea Lange's photographs depicting rural health care during the Depression era. Helle is working in a branch of inquiry called narrative medicine, which bridges medicine and the humanities. In this article, Helle pursues the question, how did Lange's photographs work to shape and impact perceptions about New Deal health care initiatives?

Excerpt from "When the Photograph Speaks:
Photo-Analysis in Narrative Medicine" by A. Helle

Stricken with childhood polio, [photographer Dorothea] Lange was left with talipes equines ("drop foot"), a distorted leg, and an acknowledged desire, from an early age, for a "cloak of invisibility."[46] …[Linda] Gordon's biography [of Lange] helps us see … that Lange's body of photographic work, like her life, is "haunted by feet."[47] … The photographs depict feet splayed in dirt, feet dancing and playing, mothers' and children's feet, calloused feet against rough boards (with "healing" bracelet) seen at eye level (see figure 2), bare feet on donkey riders, feet seen from a distance and close up, feet from Lange's trips to Alabama and Mississippi as well as her later travels in Asia.

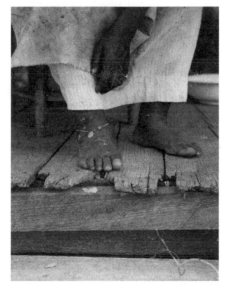

Helle shows through Figure 2 how the feet are the focus of the image. In this case, we have a greater sense of the significance of the focal point based on Lange's biographical history.

Figure 2.   Dorothea Lange. Fifty-seven year old sharecropper woman. Hinds County, Mississippi, 1937. Thin dimes around the ankles to prevent headaches. Library of Congress, Prints and Photographs Division, LC-DIG-fsa-8b32018.

…Consider another of Lange's photographs which bears directly on health care and rural poverty,… (see figure 3). This remarkable, neglected photograph appears in John Stoeckle and George Abbot White's collection, *Plain Pictures of Plain Doctoring: Vernacular Expression in New Deal Medicine and Photographs*…. The stakes of these photographs were

From *Literature and Medicine* (29.2), 2011.

high, sociologically, medically, ethically, artistically. While the administrators of rural "agrarian concerns" wished to build an archive of new health care initiatives as a "good thing," it becomes apparent to anyone who comes to this material for the first time, that the relationships between doctors (mostly from volunteer physicians' associations), nurses, and patients have more complex connotations.

The details, frames, and perspectives of the Klamath Falls photograph exceed the FSA-dictated neutral narrative documentary-style caption. We see a typical makeshift trailer, repurposed as the examining room (there are pictures of barns and storefronts in other photographs). A member of the co-op local physicians' association in a formal suit is examining a young girl, while in the background another figure identifiable in the sequence as the "camp nurse," also formally dressed, adjusts the clothing of a young boy sitting on a woman's lap (his mother perhaps) who has just been examined or is waiting his turn. In taking the picture from an angle that keeps the doctor's bulky figure high and in the foreground, Lange's eye has zeroed in on the power differential between doctor and patient. The girl, at three or four, a pale figure, is seated on an examining table—we see from a discrete angle, but can tell she is undressed. The examination table appears also to have been repurposed from a locker or sideboard. It is a delicate situation: the line of vision as the child looks up at the doctor, seeking eye contact as he looks down at her, is structured a priori by the visual template narrative of Madonna and child, a template often at play in Lange's work. In the months that I have studied this photograph, learning more about it, adding narratives and adjusting my vision, the photograph has continued to make me squirm.

Helle describes the photograph in significant detail, from the background to the clothing that the people are wearing.

Helle elicits the *kairos* of the photographs, showing that the photographs were part of a larger purpose of seeking to advance perceptions about New Deal health care initiatives by influencing viewer perceptions. Given that in 2011, when Helle published this article, debates about Obamacare were occurring, this focus on how public perceptions about health care are shaped has additional *kairotic* appeal.

Helle addresses the angle of the photograph and how that conveys a power differential.

Helle addresses the direction of the gaze of the child in the photograph as well, adding to the argument that the physician has complete control over her. This final sentence illustrates the *pathos* that Helle was experiencing as she considered the image. One can see that she has spent significant time studying the photograph, noticing new aspects over time.

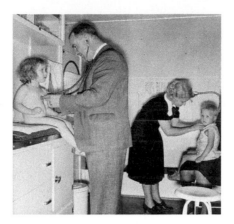

Figure 3. Dorothea Lange. Doctor Examining Child. Kalmath County, Oregon, 1937. Library of Congress Prints and Photographs Division, LC-USF34-021833.

The girl's look evokes the need for approval in a situation that demonstrates her social distance from the doctor, yet also opens up the moment to unfathomable possibilities of shame, embarrassment, confusion. The photograph for me has become more than a singular image, it has become a narrative screen, stirring my own memories of a first visit to the doctor in a different era, a small girl in another smallish, uninteresting room under the scrutinizing gaze of a strange, large man without anyone else anywhere near my size or state of undress or social standing. Perhaps a subliminal rage is stirred, too, because in the subset of photographs of which this one is a part are other photographs which depict makeshift waiting rooms crowded with people; it is all too easy to imagine that in the moments prior to the scene of examination, the small girl may have been among that crowd, having waited a long time for the suited gentleman to appear....

> Helle here refers to that which is outside the frame of the photograph, a waiting room crowded with people.

Write Now

Locate an image of your choice and practice conducting visual analysis by selecting several of the visual analysis questions in Table 7.1 and use them to sponsor your reading of the image.

Scientific data analysis

Academic writers in scientific fields such as Biology, Chemistry, and Physics analyze data using a wide range of approaches, tools, and methodologies, including the aforementioned content and discourse analysis, but also more specialized forms, many of which require technology, lab equipment, and mathematical and statistical knowledge.

In *A Practical Guide to Scientific Data Analysis*, David J. Livingston defines scientific data analysis as "mathematical and statistical procedures which scientists may use in order to extract information from their experimental data." Scientific data analysis often results in tables, graphs, and charts that offer a visual depiction of patterns, findings, and other relevant findings.

Each branch of science has multiple analytical methods, many of which overlap. In this example, we look more closely at data analysis in biology. According to Haixu Tang and Sun Kim, scientific data analysis in biology can be divided into two general approaches, hypothesis-driven or data-driven:

> Conventionally, biology knowledge was accumulated mainly through a hypothesis-driven approach, in which biologists conceive theory for a particular biological problem and then carry out an experiment to test it. In a hypothesis-driven approach, experiments are intentionally designed to collect data only relevant to the to-be-tested hypothesis.... [T]he...technology-driven or data driven approach...has several distinct features in comparing with the conventional "hypothesis-driven" approach: a high throughput technique platform, a blind collection of large amount of data, and a plan of free data sharing to the community. Tang and Kim develop the term *bioinformatics* as an important development in data-driven analysis in biology.

This example of analysis emerges from an article about how MERS spreads within various tissues. The team, led by Emmy de Wit, a lecturer and researcher in Earth and Life Sciences at VU University Amsterdam, analyzed tissue samples from rhesus macaques, small primates native to southern and southeast Asia. They argue that animal models "are instrumental for the development of prophylactic and therapeutic countermeasures."

According to their methods section, they used a combination of discipline-specific tests and analytical methods, including histopathology, transmission electron microscopy, microarray Data and Functional Analysis and Serum Cytokine and Chemokine Analysis.

Two segments are included, one excerpt from the "Results" section, and one excerpt from the "Discussion" section. Scientific articles often follow a structure known by the acronym IMRAD, which stands for Introduction, Methods, Results, and Discussion.

Excerpt from "Middle East Respiratory Syndrome Coronavirus (MERS-CoV)
Causes Transient Lower Respiratory Tract Infection in Rhesus Macaques"
by E. de Wit, et al.

Results

We have previously reported the presence of viral RNA and infectious virus throughout the
lungs of inoculated macaques, with viral load decreasing between 3 and 6 dpi…In addition to
the different lung lobes, we have previously analyzed several other tissues,
including tissues of the upper respiratory tract, lung lesions, and kidney…
Although there was some variation between the different macaques with
regard to the presence of viral RNA, we could consistently detect the virus
by qRT-PCR in the nasal mucosa, trachea, and mediasti-
nal lymph nodes on 3 dpi (Fig. 3). Furthermore, we could
detect viral RNA in conjunctiva, tonsils, oronasopharynx,
and in the left and right bronchus. Viral loads were lower
in these tissues by 6 dpi and viral RNA could no longer be detected in the nasal mucosa or
conjunctiva at that time (Fig. 3). Viral RNA could not be detected in kidney or bladder tissue samples.

de Wit, et al. note that they have previously conducted analysis on tissue samples. This suggests that they are operating from a hypothesis-driven approach to analysis where they are further testing a hypothesis about tissue samples and the presence of viral RNA and infectious virus.

de Wit, et al. present the results of their analysis, noting where they detected the virus across the various tissue samples.

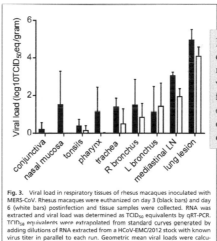

In Figure 3, de Wit, et al present the results of their analysis visually, in a graph form, which offers a corollary presentation of results to the textual description above.

Fig. 3. Viral load in respiratory tissues of rhesus macaques inoculated with MERS-CoV. Rhesus macaques were euthanized on day 3 (black bars) and day 6 (white bars) postinfection and tissue samples were collected. RNA was extracted and viral load was determined as TCID$_{50}$ equivalents by qRT-PCR. TCID$_{50}$ equivalents were extrapolated from standard curves generated by adding dilutions of RNA extracted from a HCoV-EMC/2012 stock with known virus titer in parallel to each run. Geometric mean viral loads were calculated; error bars represent SD. R, right; L, left; LN, lymph node.

Figure 3

From *Proceedings of the National Academy of Sciences* (110.41), 2013.

Discussion

In this rhesus macaque model, virus shedding as indicated by qRT-PCR occurred predominantly via the nose and, to a limited extent, the throat. In nasal swabs and BAL, viral loads were highest day 1 postinfection and decreased over time. However, at 6 dpi [days postinfection], two of three animals were still shedding virus from the respiratory tract. Although MERS-CoV was detected in the upper respiratory tract and the lymphoid tissue draining the lungs, replication of MERS-CoV was most prominent in the lower respiratory tract. MERS-CoV replicated predominantly in type I and II pneumocytes in the alveoli. These two cell types form the main component of the architecture of the alveolar space around the terminal bronchioles. This predominant replication of MERS-CoV in alveoli may explain the limited amount of virus shedding observed in our rhesus macaque model. In addition, the fact that human-to-human transmission so far seems limited to a few family clusters in Saudi Arabia (6), the United Kingdom (7), and Tunisia and nosocomial transmission in Jordan, Saudi Arabia (6), and France (9) might be explained by the propensity of the novel coronavirus to replicate deep down in the lower respiratory tract.

> Where the first excerpt presented the results of their analysis on the tissue samples, this section illustrates a second level of analysis performed on those results. They likely used statistical and mathematical analysis to generate these conclusions about which bodily tissues showed the greatest amount of viral replication.

Statistical analysis

Statistical analysis can be applied to nearly any data set. This mode of analysis involves not only choosing which statistical measures to generate from a data set, but also analyzing the results of those statistical tests. In his "Introduction to Statistical Analysis," David Rossiter, from the Department of Earth Systems Analysis in the International Institute for Geoinformation Science & Earth Observation (ITC), differentiates between two different kinds of statistical analysis, both of which he deems significant forms of the study:

1. Descriptive statistics: numerical summaries of samples (what was observed)
2. Inferential statistics: from samples to populations (what could have been or will be observed)

The example of statistical analysis is from an article on the European Centre for Disease Prevention and Control website titled "Epidemiological Update: Middle East Respiratory Syndrome Coronavirus (MERS-CoV)."

Excerpt from "Epidemiological Update: Middle East Respiratory Syndrome Coronavirus (MERS-CoV)" by the European Centre for Disease Prevention and Control

In June 2012, a case of fatal respiratory disease in a previously healthy 60-year-old man was reported from Saudi Arabia...The cause was subsequently identified as a new coronavirus that has been named Middle East respiratory syndrome coronavirus (MERS-CoV).

> Notice the focus on quantitative data nearly from the beginning of the article, signaling that statistical analysis will play a large role in the researchers' findings.

By 22 November 2013, 160 cases of MERS have been reported. All cases have either occurred in the Middle East or have direct links to a primary case infected in the Middle East....

As of 22 November 2013, the case-fatality ratio is 43% and is increasing with age. The male to female ratio is 2:1. Among the 155 cases with known age, the median age was 52 (IQR 39-64) and 142 (91.6%) were older than 19 years. We classified cases as primary or secondary based on the information provided publicly by WHO and KSA MOH. Primary cases were classified using the following criteria: no re-

> Here is an example of descriptive statistical analysis, sharing the demographic traits of MERS cases. Notice that the information in this paragraph is then depicted visually in the included graph.

ported exposure to other known cases, occurring in an area with no cases close in time and/or reported as primary case in a cluster. Secondary cases were classified based on the epidemiological link to other confirmed cases. Thirty-seven cases could not be classified based on the information available and they were left out from the analysis.

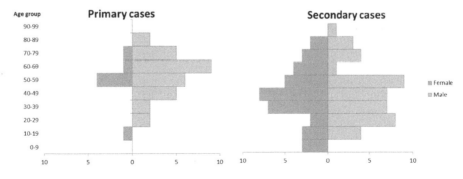

Figure 3. Distribution of confirmed cases of MERS-CoV by primary (N=39) and secondary cases (N=83) by gender and age group, March 2012 - 22 November 2013
*Among secondary cases, 3 cases were not included in the analysis due to unknown age.

From *European Centre for Disease Prevention and Control*, 2013.

Thirty-nine cases were classified as primary cases and of these, 79.5% (31/39) were male with a median age of 59 years (Table 1). The male to female ratio of 3.9 among primary cases is significantly differing from an even gender distribution (p=<10-3), reflecting potentially a gender related difference in exposures. Among the 83 secondary cases with documented age and sex, the median age is 45 years and the sex distribution does not significantly differs from an even distribution (p=0.44), with 38 (45.8%) cases being females. The more even male to female ratio of 1.2 among secondary cases, can be explained by the enhanced surveillance systems in tracing close contacts of the confirmed cases.

> This section layers an additional element of statistical analysis by examining gender alongside primary and secondary cases.

Table 1. Epidemiological characteristics of confirmed cases of MERS-CoV comparing primary (N=39) and secondary cases (N=83), March 2012 - 21 November 2013.

Epidemiological characteristics	Primary cases n=39 (%)	Secondary cases n=85 (%)	P value
Gender			0.004 a
Male	31 (79.5)	45 (54.2)	
Female	7 (17.9)	38 (45.8)	
Unknown	-	2	
Outcome			0.003 a
Dead	23 (59.0)	25 (29.4)	
Alive	16 (41.0)	60 (70.6)	
Comorbidities b			<0.001 a
Yes	27 (90.0)	39 (50.6)	
No	3 (10.0)	38 (49.4)	
Unknown	9	8	
Nosocomial transmission			<0.001 a
Yes	2 (5.7)	38 (50.7)	
No	33 (94.3)	37 (49.3)	
Unknown	4	10	

a. Two-tailed Fisher's exact test (unknown cases were excluded from the statistical analysis).

b. Comorbidities including, among others, diabetes, hypertension, chronic cardiac and chronic renal disease.

Big Data analysis

Big Data is a term gaining increasing prevalence across a wide variety of disciplines and economic sectors. It has particular applications in business and technology-driven fields, such as information technology and computer science. Rekha Mishra and Neeraj Kaushik define **Big Data** as follows:

> Big Data refers to relatively large amounts of structured and unstructured data that require machine-based systems and technologies in order to be fully analysed.… [W]hat turn[s] data into Big Data is the amount of information, and the speed at which it can be created, collected and analysed. They go on to say that Big Data can include such varying data as click streams, log files, retail transactions, mobile location information, and social media commentary.

In the Big Data analysis example, a research team of computer scientists and software engineers introduce a method for analyzing Big Data in relation to influenza. They address the ongoing question, how can we improve early detection, prevention, and treatment of influenza? This paper, published in the "Letters" section of the journal *Nature,* has led to a an ongoing debate in health care, public policy, and epidemiology about the use and value of what has now become known as Google Flu Trends.

The excerpt indicates the significance of their work and their methods for analyzing, showing where they get their Big Data from and how they analyze it.

Excerpt from "Detecting Influenza Epidemics using Search Engine Query Data"
by J. Ginsberg, et al.

> The authors first establish the significance and prevalence of the problem they are addressing, showing why it lends itself to Big Data analysis.

Seasonal influenza epidemics are a major public health concern, causing tens of millions of respiratory illnesses and 250,000 to 500,000 deaths worldwide each year. In addition to seasonal influenza, a new strain of influenza virus against which no previous immunity exists and that demonstrates human-to-human transmission could result in a pandemic with millions of fatalities. Early detection of disease activity, when followed by a rapid response, can reduce the impact of both seasonal and pandemic influenza. One way to improve early detection is to monitor health-seeking behaviour in the form of queries to online search engines, which are submitted by millions of users around the world each day. Here we present a method of analysing large numbers of Google search queries to track

> They introduce the Big Data they will use (Google search queries) and show that their contribution has been to develop a method to analyze it in order to "track influenza-like illness in a population."

From *Nature* (457.7232), 2009.

influenza-like illness in a population. Because the relative frequency of certain queries is highly correlated with the percentage of physician visits in which a patient presents with influenza-like symptoms, we can accurately estimate the current level of weekly influenza activity in each region of the United States, with a reporting lag of about one day. This approach may make it possible to use search queries to detect influenza epidemics in areas with a large population of web search users.

Traditional surveillance systems, including those used by the U.S. Centers for Disease Control and Prevention (CDC) and the European Influenza Surveillance Scheme (EISS), rely on both virological and clinical data, including influenza-like illness (ILI) physician visits. The CDC publishes national and regional data from these surveillance systems on a weekly basis, typically with a 1-2-week reporting lag.

> The authors show that although Big Data has been crucial in CDC work prior to this, the analysis has had a "1-2-week reporting lag," making their method, Big Data analysis, more timely and up to date.

In an attempt to provide faster detection, innovative surveillance systems have been created to monitor indirect signals of influenza activity, such as call volume to telephone triage advice lines and over-the-counter drug sales. About 90 million American adults are believed to search online

> They will be using online activity from 90 million American adults.

for information about specific diseases or medical problems each year, making web search queries a uniquely valuable source of information about health trends. Previous attempts at using online activity for influenza surveillance have counted search queries submitted to a Swedish medical website (A. Hulth, G. Rydevik and A. Linde, manuscript in preparation), visitors to certain pages on a U.S. health website, and user clicks on a search keyword advertisement in Canada. A set of Yahoo search queries containing the words 'flu' or 'influenza' were found to correlate with virological and mortality surveillance data over multiple years.

Our proposed system builds on this earlier work by using an automated method of discovering influenza-related search queries. By processing hundreds of billions of individual

> Here, Ginsberg, et al. describe their Big Data analysis, which involves aggregating queries by state and developing a list of "common search queries" related to influenza.

searches from 5 years of Google web search logs, our system generates more comprehensive models for use in influenza surveillance, with regional and state-level estimates of ILI activity in the United States.... By aggregating historical logs of online web search queries submitted between 2003 and 2008, we computed a time series of weekly counts for 50 million of the most common search queries in the United States. Separate aggregate weekly counts were kept for every query in each state. No information about the identity of any user was retained. Each time series was normalized by dividing the count for each query in a particular week by the total number of online search queries submitted in that location during the week, resulting in a query fraction.

Write Now

Based on a profession of interest to you, write down a number of possible sources of Big Data and their potential usefulness. What kinds of Big Data might be available to or of interest to people in this profession? Why do you think people in this profession might need (or not need) Big Data?

Transferring Analysis

Because analysis can include so many different modes, it is also important to note that academic writers do not necessarily need to become experts at all the modes, nor even in any particular mode of analysis. Instead, writers should aim to be able to recognize that disciplinary perspective and writing occasion shape the choices they make about analysis.

Building on Chapter 3: Posing Meaningful Questions, effective analysis hinges on learning how to pose the most precise and targeted questions in order to determine how best to analyze a given data type for a particular writing occasion. Analysis relies on that which has been addressed in the other preceding chapters as well in that it forms a vital part of the research and writing process, is grounded on in-depth reading, and often overlaps with summary and synthesis as a primary means of engaging with the work of others. Subsequent chapters extend these writerly skills by providing a focused view of how writers choose to shape and construct the arguments they set forth, and how those arguments hinge on the merits of the analysis they have conducted.

ℰↄ ℰↄ ℰↄ

Chapter 7 Key Terms

Analysis

Analytic methods

Rhetorical analysis

Critical discourse analysis (CDA)

Content analysis

Visual analysis

Scientific data analysis

Statistical analysis

Big Data analysis

Write Away

This activity asks that you engage in several different modes of analysis using the same object or text for analysis in order to gain insights into how different disciplinary contexts and different analytic modes yield different results from analysis.

Choose a somewhat brief or compact 'text' that you can analyze in multiple ways. As in other instances throughout *Writing in Transit*, the concept of 'text' should be as broadly construed as possible—an image, object, written text, etc.

Choose several analytic modes. Select from among those discussed in this chapter three or four different modes of analysis to use. For example, you might analyze an advertisement that includes written and visual elements by conducting a rhetorical analysis, a visual analysis, and a content analysis. If you choose as one of your modes of analysis one that requires additional expertise, such as, for example, scientific data analysis, you can opt to instead identify the various elements of the 'text' you would choose to analyze if you had more equipment and expertise, and ideas for how you might do so and what you would ostensibly learn.

Conduct and write the analyses. Conduct the different analytic approaches and write down what you discern—or think you would discern if you are analyzing in theory as opposed to reality—through each of these analyses.

Reflect on transfer and synthesis. After having had the opportunity to conduct multiple modes of analysis on the same 'text,' reflect for ten minutes in writing on how you transferred analytic skills across the different analyses: What were the intersections and differences between your analytic processes? What divergent or similar kinds of conclusions did you reach as you conducted the various analyses?

Framing Arguments

Namoratunga, located in Kenya, dates from 300 B.C.E. and is considered one of the oldest archaeoastronomical sites in sub-Saharan Africa. The location actually consists of two separate sites, both of which hold astronomical significance. Namoratunga pillars are aligned with astronomical precision, demonstrating that "an accurate and complex calendar system based on astronomical reckoning was developed by the first millennium B.C.E. in eastern Africa." The stones of Namoratunga track "the movement of seven constellations in relation to the lunar cycle" (Chwanya; Lynch and Robbins; Martin).

Many different scholars have engaged in arguments surrounding Namoratunga. While some of these focus on the age of the stones or interpretation of their design, much like the arguments we encountered regarding petroglyphs in Chapter 7, the vast range of arguments about Namoratunga reflect what is an enormously wide array of possible disciplinary perspectives within and across which arguments emerge.

Timothy Clack and Marcus Brittain, for example, draw on Namoratunga as a site to argue for a more ethical approach to archaeology, a "participative archaeology research framework in which accountability is directed toward common ground between multiple 'stake-holders.'" Another team of researchers, led by Astrophysicist Jarita Holbrook, include Namoratunga as one of several sites around which they have developed a research conference and publication about African archaeoastronomy. One of their primary arguments is that, contrary to popular conception, tribal populations and ancient herdsmen in Africa had sophisticated calendar and astronomical knowledge.

Meanwhile, Barbara P. Nash, Harry V. Merrick, and Francis H. Brown, a team with geological and engineering expertise, examine black, glass-like volcanic rock called obsidian at localities in and around Namoratunga as a means of arguing about "patterns of source utilization within the region during the Later Stone Age and Pastoral Neolithic times."

The many arguments surrounding Namoratunga—which engage, by turns, such issues as the discipline of archaeology, ethics, power dynamics, cultural knowledge, and history—illustrate the high stakes that often accompany arguments. Scholars develop and formulate arguments in order to advance knowledge, influence others, and draw attention to ideas that matter.

Although each argument about Namoratunga carries unique attributes, together they gesture toward two vital features of argument in academic writing worth emphasizing: significance and purpose.

These arguments show that even highly academic and somewhat nuanced topics, such as archaeological approaches or stone aging, have a larger significance and matter on a profound level. Similarly, while you might on occasion have the opportunity to argue in academic writing about a highly contentious issue such as the death penalty or abortion, it is far more likely that across your academic career you will be asked to develop arguments about issues that might seem on the surface much less polarizing, and perhaps initially somewhat less significant. Both occasions for argument have challenges: in the former, how do you convert opinion and emotion into a reasoned, effective, evidence-based argument? In the latter, how do you become intellectually and emotionally invested in less-contentious topics?

The Namoratunga arguments also convey a sense of what argumentative purpose may entail in the context of academic writing: namely that the purpose of arguments in academic writing is not usually to win so much as to advance knowledge. Joseph Joubert, an eighteenth-century French essayist, captures this version of argument quite well in a line from his famous text, *Pensées*: "The aim of argument...should not be victory, but progress."

As the Namoratunga arguments demonstrate, and as Joubert's quote argues, argument in the context of academic writing is more often about progress than victory. Whereas the concept of victory seems harnessed to a desire to vanquish an opponent, arguments aimed at progress instead help us learn and grow; they enable us to move forward with our goals and dreams, or reconsider our actions and change course when necessary.

Of course, progress itself is open to debate—progress according to one person might be lack of progress according to another—but Joubert's larger point is that argument should move our thinking along; it should advance knowledge by examining questions, listening to others' ideas, and communicating what you have learned.

Write Here

Reflect on why each of the arguments about Namoratunga might be important. What is at stake in these arguments? Why might they be significant? A different, perhaps brasher, way to ask this question would be, "So what?" What difference might these arguments make? Who is, or should be, invested in these arguments? Can you think of any other kinds of scholarly arguments that might emerge around Namoratunga? What might their significance be?

ᕦ ᕦ ᕦ

Correcting Common Myths about Arguments

Arguments are often affiliated with several common misconceptions that actually can be quite counterproductive to the construction of effective arguments. So let's begin by debunking some of these common myths about argument.

Myth #1: Arguments are about winning

As the opening section suggested, arguments in academic writing are not about winning, but about pursuing lines of inquiry, advancing knowledge, and making progress. Being focused on winning could have the negative consequence of making a scholar misinterpret evidence, or avoid considering certain evidence, or focus on winning at all costs.

Just because arguments are not about winning, though, does not mean that academic writers do not care very much about influencing or persuading others to think differently or take action (or cease action). For instance, academic writers across disciplines construct arguments about issues such as female genital mutilation or climate change and, in so doing, likely hope that their arguments will sway readers to modify behaviors and enact policy changes. Academic writers involved in social activism or social justice movements, similarly, may strongly advocate for certain positions on women's rights, minority rights, LGBTQ rights, or immigrant rights; they may hope to win more equality for groups of people based on their efforts. However, as they construct arguments about these issues, these academic writers are more than likely focusing on how they can persuade others or on what they are learning about particular experiences instead of winning.

Being overly focused on winning, therefore, can divert attention away from other, more important questions, such as what evidence and approach will persuade others to enact change or think differently? Or, what does the evidence and research indicate? Or even, what questions should I be asking? These questions, rather than one about winning, should reinforce effective academic arguments.

Myth #2: Arguments involve only highly debated issues

Some issues are so contentious as to be considered hot-buttons for arguments. The top ten arguments between parents and kids, for example, according to Nolan Katkowski, include grades/school (#1), money and privilege (#5 & #6), and driving (#9). The "10 Topics Guaranteed to Start an Argument," according to Listverse, include the existence of God (#10), freedom of speech (#4), and abortion (#1). These issues have high register value in that they are somewhat easily recognizable, have much available research at hand, and are issues about which people care deeply. But the truth is, people can argue about nearly anything. While academic writers do construct arguments about these kinds of hot-button issues, they also construct arguments about issues that may initially seem somewhat less divisive. For example, in the preceding chapters, we have seen academic writers constructing arguments about all sorts of ideas, from how ancient art should be preserved to how the media discuss vaccines. Arguments in academic writing can be about anything. The website *Useful Science* offers a glimpse into the range of arguments academic writers construct. Here are a few arguments posted on this website:

> When people held hot beverages (hot coffee), they perceived strangers as friendlier and warmer than when they held cold beverages (iced coffee).

> Swearing increases pain tolerance: people were able to hold their hand in ice water longer if they swore (this effect was reduced for people who swore frequently).

Red clothing may be a medium of sexual signaling: women expecting to meet an attractive man were more likely to select a red shirt than women expecting to meet an unattractive man.

Although it is unlikely that any of these arguments will ever make it to a top ten list of issues likely to start a debate, they matter, nonetheless, and carry with them a fair measure of significance for a number of stakeholders.

Myth #3: Arguments have only pro/con positions

While certain arguments may seem pro or con, they are actually more often than not much more complicated. Effective arguments generally take into account alternative perspectives, make concessions, and qualify the circumstances under which a position is most applicable. As an example, let's look more closely at the issue of "The Israel/Palestine question," which comes in, according to Listverse, as the ninth most likely topic to start an argument.

According to *ProCon.org*, the Israel/Palestine question is (somewhat ironically given the organization's name) not pro/con at all. The core question, according to *ProCon.org*, is, "What are the solutions to the Israeli-Palestinian conflict?" Within that question exist a number of other parameters to argue about: implications of one-state or two-state solutions, land disputes, refugees, international involvement, historical context. Each of these subcategories then have other elements, all of which can and need to be argued about and all of which do not fit neatly into a pro/con format. Arguments that adopt a pro/con perspective tend to diminish the complexity of an issue and overlook many important aspects related to that issue.

Myth #4: Arguments are based on opinion

While academic writers have opinions about the issues around which they construct arguments, academic arguments are more often based instead on research and evidence. Privileging opinion has the counterproductive impact of not really being an argument; how can anyone really argue that you do or do not have a particular opinion? And, how can your opinion influence anyone else? Why would people change their minds just because you have an opinion? Opinion lacks full sway unless you pair opinion with an appeal based on *ethos*, in which you establish your expertise and knowledge in such a way that people realize they should listen to you.

Privileging opinion can also have the negative consequence of delimiting the capacity of academic writers to examine evidence and reconsider positions. Perhaps you might even change your own opinion as you encounter others' arguments or new information.

A good example of the present but somewhat limited role of opinion in academic argument is the death penalty. Academic writers might have an opinion that the death penalty is warranted or not, in some cases more or less. But the academic arguments they construct will instead be based on answers to their research questions spurned from their preliminarily opinion. What is the impact of the death penalty on deterring crime? What demographic data exists about death penalty decisions? How is the death penalty carried out?

A final point about opinion being somewhat counterproductive as a frame for academic argument is that opinion does not necessarily translate into action or behavior. If someone's opinion is that the death penalty is unwarranted, that only goes so far; what carries farther is if an argument can influence someone not only to have a certain opinion but to take certain actions or engage in particular behaviors that will make an impact on that issue, such as legislation, additional research, or other forms of activism.

Myth #5: Arguments are about proving points

In the context of academic writing, an argument is not necessarily a final answer to a question. Instead, argument in academic writing might be conceived of as an occasion for a writer to communicate to others what he or she has learned by researching one or more questions. Then, as others continue to learn more, subsequent questions and arguments can continue to emerge. Arguments are, at heart, about inquiry.

Thinking about argument as inquiry challenges commonly held assumptions that argument involves proving a point. Instead, asking what argument is in academic writing requires asking what the questions are that have given rise to a particular argument.

What is Argument?

Now that we have argued against several myths about what argument is not, let's turn to exploring what argument is.

At the most basic level, an **argument** in academic writing is the position a writer takes in a particular writing project, the evidence he or she includes for that argument, and the way he or she chooses to structure and format the argument. The term argument brushes against several other related terms, some of which you may have encountered before: **claim**, **thesis**, **proof**, or **position**. These terms help situate argument within the context of academic writing and begin to illustrate how the notion of argument shifts slightly depending on disciplinary context. Though discipline-specific definitions most certainly overlap and fluctuate, disciplinary perspectives provide particular inflections on how argument is defined.

Sociologist Greta Krippner, for example, defines argument based on her disciplinary perspective of Sociology:

> Once you have developed a viable research question, your next task is to review the evidence in order to formulate an answer to your question. The answer to your question is your thesis, or your argument. Typically, researchers do original research at this point—they analyze statistical data, go to the field, administer surveys, conduct experiments, etc.

For Krippner, argument involves an answer to a research question based on original research. Arguments in the natural sciences, by contrast, might be defined more explicitly around evidence, accuracy, and logic:

> Taken together, the expectations generated by a scientific idea and the actual observations relevant to those expectations form what we'll call a scientific argument. This is a bit like an argument in a court case—a logical description of what we think and why we think it. A scientific argument uses evidence to make a case for whether a scientific idea is accurate or inaccurate.

Philosophy also has a discipline-specific definition of argument, perhaps one of the most extensive since philosophy is in many ways grounded on logic, argument, and reasoning. Matthew McKeon, a philosopher from Michigan State University, defines argument:

> [A]rgument [is] a collection of truth-bearers (that is, the things that bear truth and falsity, or are true and false) some of which are offered as reasons for one of them, the conclusion. [P]ropositions [are] the primary truth bearers. The reasons offered within the argument are called "premises," and the proposition that the premises are offered for is called the "conclusion."

Thus, in Philosophy, according to McKeon, argument should be understood in relationship to truth-bearers, propositions, **premises**, and **conclusions**.

While you will not be expected to understand argument as it is defined in each discipline, you should be prepared to encounter varying approaches to argument across disciplines. Recognizing that argument can carry disciplinary conventions and expectations will equip you with the awareness to learn more about argument within each new discipline and context you encounter.

Purposes of Argument

Academic writers construct arguments across disciplines for nearly as many purposes as there are arguments. The purpose of any given argument can be multiple and manifold, depending on the disciplinary context, the writer, and the writing occasion. As we will see later in this chapter, the structure of an argument also impacts purpose. For instance, Rogerian argument, emphasizes common ground and compromise, and these are therefore priorities of purpose for academic writers invoking Rogerian argumentation.

Disciplines also provide discipline-specific purposes for argument. Ian Johnston, of Malaspina University College in British Columbia, describes the purpose of argument in the context of Liberal Studies and English. Notice the emphasis on **persuasion**:

> Put most simply, an argument is an attempt to persuade someone of something. It is prompted usually by a disagreement, confusion, or ignorance about something which the arguers wish to resolve or illuminate in a convincing way.... The final goal of an argument is usually to reach a conclusion which is sufficiently persuasive to convince someone of something (a course of action, the reasons for an event, the responsibility for certain acts, the probable truth of an analysis, or the validity of an interpretation).

Writer Insights

How do you argue in your field?

In advertising you write more than you would ever expect; from proposals, to follow up emails, to copy for clients, it is all very reliant on words... the right words. I never considered how much I wrote. It was just a way to communicate ideas and generate interest resulting in sales. I am more [conscious] of it now that I have realized I am a writer. Sales is a thinking sport; researching clients and their industry, planning out what would be best for the client and executing. It is all strategic. Away from work, I have started writing a blog following my passion which is nutrition and the American food system.

~Cherie L. Dreves, Advertising Sales, Prescott Valley, Arizona, U.S.

Arguments can also have an important negative purpose: to convince someone that something is not the case. Other disciplines refer to argument not so much as about convincing others but about justification. In a paper investigating students' use of argument in engineering courses, Sibel Erduran and Rosa Villamanan argue that "the nature of arguments in the applied field of Engineering [involves] appeals to scientific principles [in order] to justify the design of an industrial product."

Despite the many varying purposes for argument across disciplines, some purposes do seem to be more widely embraced by academic writers. Some of the more commonly deployed purposes for arguments are:

- to persuade others to think or act
- to communicate research and conclusions
- to share and interpret evidence and data
- to define one or more terms or ideas
- to push against, critique, or counter another idea
- to explain a relationship or cause
- to propose a solution to a problem
- to suggest a policy or proposal for future action
- to generate consensus or mediate conflict
- to raise questions

These, however, are only a few of the possible purposes for arguments, and they are also often overlapping. As you encounter other writers' projects, the best way to consider purpose is to ask the writer to describe his purpose (if possible), read his text text to see if the purpose is explicit, and/or discern on your own what you take to be the writer's aims and purpose based on his text (see also Chapter 4: Reading).

Featured Purposes of Argument

Some purposes for argument are widespread enough that they warrant a more extensive discussion. This chapter addresses and illustrates three common purposes of argument: causal argument, proposal argument, and definitional argument.

Causal argument

A causal argument's purpose is to argue how something has become the way it is. Joseph Moxley at *Writing Commons* describes causal arguments as investigating the questions, "Why are things like this? What is the effect, or result, of this?" and, "What causes this?" Causal arguments appear in numerous ways across disciplines. These two examples can help illustrate causal arguments and their purpose.

Example 1: Causal Argument, Spanish Languages and Literature

This excerpt comes from a well-known book that critically examines the relationship between travel writing and colonialism, *Imperial Eyes,* by professor of Spanish Literature and Culture, Mary Louise Pratt. Pratt's line of inquiry asks, "what was the sociopolitical impact of travel writing in the twentieth century?" In the excerpt, Pratt presents a causal argument, in which she argues that European travel writing contributed to European colonization and expansionism.

Excerpt from *Imperial Eyes: Travel Writing and Transculturation* by M. L. Pratt

Pratt locates her causal argument as significant in that it participates in an ongoing effort to mitigate the long-term and ongoing impact of colonialism.

Here, Pratt specifies her causal argument. This strategy of naming her argument directly with the phrase, "I argue" is frequently deployed in disciplines dealing with languages and literature.

Pratt notes here how her argument emerges from inquiry, having asked "how travel writing made imperial expansion meaningful and desirable."

In the last decades of the twentieth century, processes of decolonization opened the meaning-making powers of empire to scrutiny, as part of a large-scale effort to decolonize knowledge, history, and human relations. This book is part of that effort. Its main, but not its only, subject is European travel and exploration writing, analyzed in connection with European economic and political expansion since around 1750. The book aims to be both a study in genre and a critique of ideology. Its predominant theme is how travel books written by Europeans about non-European parts of the world created the imperial order for Europeans "at home" and gave them their place in it. I ask how travel writing made imperial expansion meaningful and desirable to the citizenries of the imperial countries, even though the material benefits of empire accrued mainly to the few. Travel books, I argue, gave European reading publics a sense of ownership, entitlement and familiarity with respect to the distant parts of the world that were being explored, invaded, invested in, and colonized. Travel books were very popular. They created a sense of curiosity, excitement, adventure, and even moral fervor about European expansionism. They were, I argue, one of the key instruments that made people "at home" in Europe feel part of the planetary project; a key instrument, in other words, in creating the "domestic subject" of empire.

From *Travel Writing and Transculturation,* 1992.

Write Now

In the previous selection, Pratt uses several related terms to describe her project: argument, effort, subject, inquiry, and theme. How does Pratt differentiate between each of these terms? Based on her text, how is she articulating the difference, for example, between an argument and a subject? Between a theme and an inquiry?

Example 2: Causal Argument, Marine Biology

Where Pratt relies on rhetorical analysis for her causal argument, this second example, from Hamish Campbell, et al., uses quantitative evidence. In this article, Campbell, et al. ask how crocodiles travel long distances. Their causal argument is that surface currents enable crocodiles to travel greater distances.

Excerpt from "Estuarine Crocodiles Ride Surface Currents to Facilitate Long-Distance Travel" by H. Campbell, et al.

Here, the authors demonstrate that they are filling a gap in knowledge with their research because current research does not fully explain how crocodiles travel long-distances.

Many anecdotal accounts exist of large crocodiles being sighted in open-ocean, and on islands hundreds of kilometres from the nearest known population (Ditmars 1957; Allen 1974; Webb & Manolis 1989), yet their capacity for long distance ocean travel remains poorly understood and it is unknown if ocean voyages form part of their ecological repertoire or merely represent occasional mishaps of navigation....

The expansive geographical distribution of C. porosus suggests that long-distance ocean voyages are a regular occurrence between island populations. Certainly, large individuals have been sighted from vessels far out at sea (Ditmars 1957), but C. porosus cannot be considered a marine reptile, and primarily inhabits rivers and coastal systems. They live a low-cost energy lifestyle with limited capacity for sustained exercise (Pough 1980; Elsworth, Seebacher & Franklin 2003), and as such, their ability to purposefully traverse significant expanses of open-ocean seems extreme. This study provides an explanation as to how these remarkable feats of ocean travel may be achieved, by demonstrating that C. porosus adopt be-

This segment occurs in the discussion section, after the authors have presented their results. Here, they articulate their causal argument.

From *Journal of Animal Ecology* (79.5), 2010.

havioural strategies which utilise the momentum of surface currents to transport themselves long distances....

This study has shown that adult estuarine crocodiles dramatically increase their travel potential by riding surface currents. This observation has profound management applications because a problem crocodile translocated to an area where residual surface currents flow in the direction of the home-area will rapidly travel back home. Moreover, changes in coastal current systems, by either natural cycle or anthropogenically driven, may result in estuarine crocodiles travelling to locations without a recent history of their presence. Because adult estuarine crocodiles pose a significant risk to humans (Caldicott, et al. 2005), inshore current systems should be monitored in areas where humans and C. porosus may interact, and problem crocodiles should be translocated to areas where residual currents are not available for homeward travel.

> The authors emphasize again their argument in the first sentence of this paragraph and make its significance and applicability explicit, suggesting that demonstrating cause in this circumstance will help with crocodile management.

Proposal argument

Proposal arguments aim to offer a proposal for a problem or issue. These can include grant proposals or proposals for policies or other actions. While fields such as Business and Public Policy seem to lend themselves naturally to proposal arguments, many other disciplines also issue proposals. For instance, in English Literature, an academic writer might argue for a proposal that the field re-examine, or newly examine, an author, period, or genre of literature.

As with causal arguments, academic arguments whose main purpose is to create a proposal will often show how the proposal has broader applicability beyond the particular instance under consideration. Proposal arguments and causal arguments might also have some overlap, as academic writers making proposal arguments might also need to argue for what the causes of the current problems are or why the current arrangements are lacking in some way.

This example of a proposal argument comes from the field of Management Science. The authors argue in favor of a new proposal for how to determine time distribution models for emergency response vehicles. They articulate their purpose as follows: "We propose a new specification for the coefficient of variation, which decreases with distance. We illustrate how the resulting travel-time distribution model can be used to create probability-of-coverage maps for diagnosis and improvement of system performance."

Excerpt from "Empirical Analysis of Ambulance Travel Times: The Case of Calgary Emergency Medical Services" by S. Budge, A. Ingolfsson, and D. Zerom

The authors show how "past approaches" did not offer an adequate formula for predicting travel time. This background research establishes a need for a proposal.

Our paper provides the first thorough examination of the distribution of travel times in a way that can be easily incorporated into...models for EMS planning. Unlike the approach in this paper, past approaches often failed to account appropriately for the stochastic nature of travel time, which, even for a given origin and destination, will vary because of route choice, driver characteristics, traffic conditions, geographic aggregation of points into zones, and other known and unknown factors. This paper makes four main contributions. (1) We demonstrate that the KWH model for mean fire engine travel times is a valid and useful description of median ambulance travel times. We perform our validation by comparing the KWH function

The authors enumerate very clearly the "four main contributions" made by their proposal.

to the best-fitting nonparametric estimate of the median function; that is, we compare the KWH function to an infinite number of other possible functions, and find that it performs about as well as any of them. (2) We expand the KWH model to represent explicitly the full probability distribution of travel times conditional on travel distances. We propose a statistical model that allows the median travel time and its coefficient of variation (CV) to vary with distance, and we account for skewness and excess kurtosis (i.e., the distribution has a higher peak and fatter tails than a normal distribution). (3) We present and justify a parametric specification for how the CV varies with distance. (4) We show how our model of travel-time distributions can be used to create probability-of-coverage maps that facilitate decisions about where to locate stations and how to allocate ambulances to them.

The implications of this research extend beyond emergency services. Travel-time distributions are also critical in nonemergency applications, such as the routing of pickup and delivery vehicles...Delivery time is one of the operational dimensions on which private-sector firms compete...A familiar example is the delivery-time guarantees offered by companies such as Domino's Pizza.

The authors here demonstrate the more extended significance and applicability of their proposal argument.

From *Management Science* (56.4), 2010.

Definitional argument

A third especially frequent purpose for arguments across disciplines involves definition. **Definitional arguments** hold as their primary purpose defining a new term or concept, expanding the definition of an established term or concept, or challenging existing definitions.

One example of definitional arguments currently experiencing some measure of United States media coverage involves marriage, where many are arguing over the definition of what does or does not, should or should not, constitute the definition of marriage. Some argue that marriage is defined as between one man and one woman; others argue that marriage is a civil union. Some argue as well over who holds the power to define: should the state hold the power to define what marriage is or isn't? Other arguments in this arena of definition might argue for how dictionaries are defining the very word "marriage." All of these are examples of definitional arguments, and demonstrate that definitional arguments can hold significant impact.

The excerpted reading of a definitional argument comes from academic writer Yolanda Martínez-San Miguel, who argues for an expanded definition of the term "sexile."

Excerpt from "Female Sexiles? Toward an Archeology of Displacement of Sexual Minorities in the Caribbean" by Y. Martínez-San Miguel

> Martínez-San Miguel begins by offering what have been the more widely deployed definitions of the term "sexile." She therefore establishes that she will likely be challenging or expanding these definitions.

According to Manolo Guzmán, the term "sexile" refers to "the exile of those who have had to leave their nations of origin on account of their sexual orientation" (1997, 227). Yet sexile has a very different meaning for many contemporary university students in the United States. According to the Urban Dictionary, to sexile is "to banish a roommate from the room/dorm/apartment for the purpose of engaging in intimate relations with one's significant other/sex partner." It turns out that there is even an etiquette to sexiling, and some university newspapers have published articles educating students on the best way to sexile a roommate (Axelbank 2004). Proper warning, courtesy, timing, and consideration are among the most important elements in making sexile fall within the appropriate codes of conduct. In this sense, sexile is a paradoxical recognition of the ethical limits for negotiating a common domestic space. The other is excluded but only temporarily and as a result of an agreement, in order for sexual intimacy to take place. Thus, the other is complicit

---

From *Signs* (36.4), 2011.

with the self in the fulfillment of a desire that is not necessarily shared, and the other and the self negotiate the modes of appropriation and use of a common space.

Comparing some of the most common U.S. campus definitions of this notion, it became clear to me that "sexile," with its already double meaning, afforded an interesting point of departure in my study of the coloniality of diasporas in the Caribbean. In this essay I propose a working definition of sexile that refers to displacement in two simultaneous and complementary ways. The first is the displacement of subjects who are deemed misfits within the patriarchal, heteronormative discourses of collective identity formation in the Caribbean

> Martínez-San Miguel then offers her own working definition, which expands the term to include displacement and thereby apply the term to Caribbean sexual studies.

> At the end of this paragraph, Martínez-San Miguel explains the aim of her essay. Even though she frames it as a proposal, and it does have carryover with proposal arguments, her main purpose is to redefine a term. She also offers a sense of why this redefinition is important, and what the impact of it will be.

national states, neocolonial overseas territories, commonwealths, and departments that in many cases mimic the practices of exclusion found in the most traditional national discourses. The second form of displacement points to the negotiated and temporary exclusion of another from a shared communal space for the fulfillment of a diverging sexual desire. The aim of this essay is to extend the meaning of sexile as it has been used in Caribbean queer studies (Guzmán 1997; La Fountain-Stokes 2009): to propose it as a script to think about the configuration of alternative communal identities based on recent narratives that go beyond the heteronormative and homonormative matrixes (Martínez-San Miguel 2008).

As evidenced by these examples, argument purposes have considerable overlap. This is in part because arguments are complex and often carry multiple implications. When constructing your own arguments, you can determine your own purpose(s) by considering what you hope to accomplish through the writing project. Understanding what makes for an effective argument will help you identify and shape your purposes.

Write Now

For each of the examples included in the featured purposes section, identify what the argument is and evaluate it according to the criteria for effective arguments. Which criteria does it meet, and why? Are there any criteria it does not meet? If so, does this detract from the argument significantly? Based on each argument, can you identify any additional criteria that you think should be added to the list?

Criteria for Effective Argument

Given the immense variety of argument, it is nearly impossible to develop an exhaustive list of criteria for what makes an argument more or less effective. Many disciplines have particular discipline-specific measures of effective argument. In some approaches to rhetoric, for instance, an argument might be evaluated on the basis of whether it achieves an equal balance of the three **argumentative appeals** (*ethos, pathos, logos*). In the sciences, an argument is often deemed effective if it is valid, reliable, and replicable.

Some disciplines even argue about what constitutes effective argumentation. For instance, in philosophy, scholars argue about whether the concept of "soundness" is a criterion (or not) for effective argument. Complicating matters further is the fact that the purpose of an argument impacts and shapes the criteria by which it can be determined to be effective; if you are writing a proposal argument, then the proposal should be explained thoroughly and should address the problem and offer a viable solution. If instead you are writing a definitional argument, then your approach to definition should be well researched and widely applicable.

As we shall see in Chapter 9, the structure of arguments also creates certain criteria for efficacy. If you are writing a Rogerian argument, identifying common ground is a key criterion. Finally, as Chapters 10 and 11 will demonstrate, format and evidence likewise generate additional criteria. If you are writing an op-ed, it is more effective not to include extensive citations and quoted evidence. If, on the other hand, you are writing a scholarly argument, then this kind of evidence is of vital importance.

Still, amidst all the disciplinary and contextual variation, it is possible to identify several criteria for effective arguments that might be considered relatively applicable across contexts.

Complexity

Most arguments in academic writing should be sufficiently complex that they are not entirely self-evident and that they address meaningful questions and multiple avenues for exploration and research. As discussed earlier, arguments in academic writing are more often than not those that should move an ongoing conversation forward rather than function as the end-all finality of a point.

Contestable premises

Arguments generally involve issues about which reasonable people can disagree, not necessarily in pro/con ways, but in nuanced ways. Your argument should provide enough material that someone could reasonably launch a different or modified perspective.

Writer Insights

How do you convince others through your arguments?

In Argentina we use the verb *chamuyar* and the noun *chamuyo* a lot. With its origin in local slang and a broad meaning, these terms can imply, for example, telling lies, or improving a story you are telling, or even using pick-up lines with a girl. Of course you can do it when writing as well. Teachers here have to produce a lot of well-grounded planning that will be assessed by principals and inspectors. Peer assessment helps but *chamuyo* might save your day, not by lying but by putting some attitude and creativity into what you say. Dress up your words and bureaucracy will open its heavy gates for you.

~Fernando D. González Córdoba,
ESL Primary and Secondary School Teacher–Translator,
La Plata, Buenos Aires Province, Argentina

Evidence-based

Your argument should be connected to evidence. If you do not have the evidence to put forward your argument, then you should probably either find the evidence or change your argument.

Address rhetorical appeals

Argumentative appeals (discussed in detail in Chapter 4: Reading) provide the means for persuading your readers. In some contexts, an argument might call for an equal balance across all three appeals. Other contexts might privilege one or two appeals over another. Arguments generally, however, gesture in some meaningful way to each of the three appeals:

- *Ethos:* appeals made by establishing the character or image of the writer
- *Logos:* appeals based on evidence and reason
- *Pathos:* appeals to people's emotions and values

Demonstrate kairos

In Chapter 4: Reading, we addressed the dual meanings of *kairos*: appropriateness and timeliness. Effective arguments take into account appropriateness, demonstrating awareness of expectations and conventions in context in order to move an argument forward effectively. Effective arguments also show how and why they are significant and timely at this particular juncture.

Include qualifications

Hardly any arguments in academic writing are applicable across all circumstances. Effective arguments generally include qualifications. Qualifications are specifics about the circumstances under which an argument works, and when it might or will not work.

Framed within existing research

Arguments do not happen in a vacuum. They are situated within others' research and arguments, as part of a larger conversation. Arguments should be conceived of as making a contribution to an ongoing conversation, and in this way others can build on, modify, or extend your arguments as well.

Significant

While not everyone would agree about what constitutes significance, arguments should generally be about ideas that matter to you and, preferably, to at least some number of other people. Connect your argument to this larger significance.

Compliant with discipline and context

For every argument occasion, there are also likely discipline- and context-specific criteria. For philosophers, for instance, arguments should be valid or sound. In rhetoric, arguments are deemed more effective if they have a balance of three types of argumentative appeals: logical, ethical, and emotional ("The Three Appeals"). In evidence-based science disciplines, arguments are deemed more effective if they are replicable: "Scientists aim for their studies' findings to be replicable—so that, for example, an experiment testing ideas about the attraction between electrons and protons should yield the same results when repeated in different labs" ("Copycats"). Identify if there are any discipline-specific criteria for arguments so you can work to meet them.

Reasonable and logical

Whether something is reasonable or not is often more a matter of degree than a definite yes or no; and reason also depends on context. This criterion basically asks that the argument make sense and hold validity. Rhetoricians have developed a series of what they term logical fallacies to name common flaws in reasoning. Effective arguments avoid logical fallacies and display reasonable logic and evidence.

Featured Criteria for Effective Argument: Avoiding Logical Fallacies

Logical fallacies are a rhetorical term that denotes common flaws in reasoning that can often (though not always) make arguments less effective, or sometimes ineffective. According to Charles Hamblin, "a fallacious argument…is one that *seems to be valid* but *is not* so." Fallacies might diminish an argument's efficacy by distracting readers from the main point or by inviting what is often unnecessary disagreement and resistance from readers.

Aristotle originally developed 13 logical fallacies in his work *On Sophistical Refutations*. These, however, have since been expanded, with some sources naming as many as 150 unique logical fallacies. Because there are so many fallacies, they often overlap, have complex subcategories, or appear by varying names. For instance, the fallacies of *post hoc* and slippery slope both address false conclusions: the *post hoc* fallacy yields a false conclusion based on a cause and effect, while the slippery slope fallacy has a false conclusion based on loosely connected or unconnected statements.

Fallacies can also be confusing in that sometimes they seem closely connected with aspects of argument that are actually effective. For instance, one logical fallacy is termed "appeal to emotion" (also sometimes subcategorized into "appeal to pity" or "appeal to sympathy"). This fallacy seems (and is) closely connected to the Aristotelian appeal to *pathos*. However, in the fallacious use of emotional appeal, a writer will be overly sentimental, use emotion in contexts that do not warrant emotion, or use emotion at the expense of *kairos, logos,* and *ethos*. Therefore, as you encounter logical fallacies, be sure to evaluate the context in which they emerge to best determine if they are indeed fallacious or if it might be in fact efficacious.

Logical fallacies can occur across disciplines, but some disciplines might be more at risk for certain types of fallacies over others. For example, in disciplines such as development studies or human rights branches of public policy, academic writers might be particularly cognizant of how extensively they appeal to emotion. Since issues surrounding poverty, violence, and abuse are so inherently likely to evoke emotion in both readers and the researchers themselves, academic writers in these fields might need to work harder to remember to integrate appeals to *logos, ethos*, and *kairos* in order to make their arguments even more effective. This is not to say that these researchers should not also use *pathos*, but that their disciplinary context already holds *pathos* and so might warrant instead energy toward constructing arguments around *ethos, logos*, and *kairos*, as well as *pathos*.

Becoming familiar with logical fallacies and understanding more about how and when they emerge in arguments will help you avoid them in your own arguments as well as help you identify logical fallacies in others' arguments so you can contribute your own responses and ideas to ongoing debates in various fields. Take a look at several of the more common logical fallacies.

Hasty generalization

A **hasty generalization** fallacy is an overgeneralization based on incorrect, inadequate, or otherwise insufficient evidence. It may also describe an argument where "exceptions are overlooked and not properly taken into account" (Walton). An example of a hasty generalization might look something like this:

> Susan is writing a public policy brief on public perceptions about the common core curriculum in K-12 education. For her research, Susan surveys her two closest friends, both of whom dislike the common core. She concludes that everyone in the United States dislikes the common core.

Susan has made a hasty generalization because she surveyed only two people, both of whom were friends (perhaps of similar ages), and she therefore does not have enough evidence to justify her conclusion. Moreover, her argument that everyone dislikes the common core has neglected to consider exceptions—it would take only one person to say he or she likes the common core and Susan's argument would be discredited.

Ad hominem

Ad hominem arguments focus on a person's character. Sometimes arguments about character make sense, as when *ethos* matters: "Jones is not a fit candidate for public office, since he is a known embezzler" (Brinton). Other times, however, an *ad hominem* argument presents an irrelevant and/or overly venomous character attack, such as, "I refuse to listen to Senator Jones's proposals for amending the New Bank Bill; he cheats on his wife" (Hansen and Pinto). Note that some might still suggest that Senator Jones's marital fidelity is relevant, even for a bank bill. However, an *ad hominem* attack generally focuses on character at the expense of addressing other, more relevant aspects of the argument.

Straw Man

Straw Man fallacies involve a writer misrepresenting an opposing position in order to more easily refute it. Philosophers Robert Talisse and Scott F. Aikin argue that there are two forms of Straw Man fallacy: representation and selection.

Representation Straw Man

Representation occurs "in an adversarial argumentative context between two speakers (A and B), where the proponent (A) represents her opponent's (B's) position in an inaccurate way which facilitates or strengthens A's case against B." (Talisse and Aikin). An example of this type of Straw Man argument might be:

> "Senator Jones says that we should not fund the attack submarine program. I disagree entirely. I can't understand why he wants to leave us defenseless like that."

Selection Straw Man

Selection forms of Straw Man involve researchers choosing too selectively what evidence they will include based on an assumption that readers will be unaware of other evidence that might possibly work against their argument. Talisse and Aikin argue that the selection form of Straw Man is even more vicious than representation Straw Man because it takes advantage of reader ignorance: "(A) correctly presents (B's) argument and legitimately refutes it, but she fails to countenance stronger objections from other sources.... Unless her audience is familiar with the better counter-arguments proposed by (A's) opposition, then (A) succeeds in winning their assent." An example of a selection form of a Straw Man argument appears in the excerpted article, in which the authors claim that the American Society of Reproductive Medicine Practice Committee is guilty of a Straw Man argument by having based their message on selective evidence and assuming general ignorance on the part of the public and funding organizations:

> The American Society of Reproductive Medicine Practice Committee (ASRMPC) has suggested that DNA damage in spermatozoa should not be assessed because the correlation with pregnancy is inconsistent across independent studies. However this is a straw man argument. The reason why such assays should be undertaken is not just because they reflect the underlying quality of spermatogenesis but, more importantly, because the DNA damage they reveal may have detrimental effects on the developmental normality of the embryo and health of possible future children. (Aitken, et al.).

Some disciplines may lend themselves more readily to certain fallacies than others. In a field such as reproductive health, those making funding decisions (likely members of institutional or organizational administration or government) probably do not have the expertise that the members of the ASRMPC would have. Thus, these readers would be relying on the ASRMPC to provide a full consideration of the research, and a failure to include that evidence is considered a breach of trust. Aitken et al. claim that the ASRMPC is committing a Straw Man fallacy by refuting one justification for research when in fact another, better justification for research exists.

Other common logical fallacies

While the previous three are frequently occurring fallacies, there are a number of other logical fallacies, also worthy of your review and consideration.

Begging the Question: Using a conclusion that is already presumed to be true, or starting with an assumption that has not yet been proven

Many Questions: Posing numerous questions, some relevant, some irrelevant

False Dilemma: Suggesting that there is no middle ground and one position automatically negates or is in direct antithesis to the other position

Equivocation: Using words that have multiple meanings as a way of confusing readers

No True Scotsman: Refuting counterevidence by discrediting it entirely and completely

Missing the Point: Arriving at a conclusion that is unconnected (or not closely linked) to the evidence provided

Post Hoc: Assuming that because one thing followed another, then the second thing was caused by the first. For instance, if you wear a blue shirt and get in a car accident, *post hoc* fallacy would say that the blue shirt caused the car accident

Red Herring: Distracting readers by including an idea or concept that is irrelevant and therefore takes them away from the main issue

Slippery Slope: Stringing together a series of events and arriving at a conclusion that is extreme. For instance, a slippery slope argument would say that if you reduce fines for driving without a license, then more people will do so, and drunk driving will increase, and deaths from drunk driving will increase, until finally all civilian driving licenses will need to be revoked

Again, this is but a partial, overlapping list, and as you explore these fallacies in more depth, you will likely encounter more complex variations of them. The main point is for you to think carefully about the conclusions you draw and the claims you make to ensure that they are reasonable and relevant, and that they avoid these (or other) logical fallacies.

Write Now

Under most circumstances, academic writers try to avoid logical fallacies. But sometimes it's fun to purposefully create them if only as a way of better understanding how writers can accidentally fall into them. Review the logical fallacies discussed in this chapter, and do a quick Internet search to locate others. Then, practice... and then practice purposefully generating as many logical fallacies as you can for a general argument topic. For instance, with an argument about video games, a hasty generalization might be that all video games contain violence, or no video games contain violence.

Transferring Argument Frames

While arguments across contexts are enormously varied, they nearly all should strive to have a defined purpose, demonstrate effective criteria, and avoid logical fallacies. These elements, purpose, efficacy, and logical soundness, provide a strong frame for arguments across context. The specifics of each of these elements might shift, however, according to context.

Across contexts, arguments integrate nearly all the aspects of preceding chapters, from questions and reading to summary, synthesis, and analysis. This chapter is connected closely to the next two chapters, which will deepen your knowledge of argument by exploring, successively, particular argument structures (Chapter 9) and options for argument design (Chapter 10). By the end of Chapter 10, you will have a strong sense of argument in all its many complexities.

ℰ ℰ ℰ

Chapter 8 Key Terms

Argument	Conclusion	Logical fallacy
Claim	Persuasion	Hasty generalization fallacy
Thesis	Causal argument	*Ad hominem* fallacy
Proof	Proposal argument	Straw Man fallacy
Position	Definitional argument	
Premise	Argumentative appeals	

Write Away

Although you may feel relatively new to arguments, this activity asks you to take on an advanced role involved with publication: developmental editor. Developmental editors help authors (academic or not) prepare manuscripts for publication. These editors do not correct grammar but instead focus on ideas; they provide specific suggestions to authors for how to improve the content of their drafts-in-progress. You, as the developmental editor in this case, will work with an author to help make his or her somewhat lacking argument into a highly effective one.

Find a partner in your class.

Each partner chooses a discipline and a topic. Each person should choose a particular disciplinary perspective and a topic to focus on for this Write Away. Pretend you are a biologist, for example, working on plant photosynthesis. Or, pretend you are a cultural anthropologist studying agrarian societies.

Each partner writes a really "bad" argument. This is the fun part. Write the worst argument you can possibly imagine. Aim for an argument that is about as long as an abstract of 100-150 words. Try to include as many logical fallacies as possible, and stay as far away as possible from the criteria for effective arguments. Remember, though, developmental editors do not fix typos, so try to make your "bad" argument as grammatically accurate as possible.

Exchange "bad" arguments with your partner.

Developmental editors, get to work! Now it is time for you to assume your role as developmental editor. You are tasked with getting your partner's bad argument into shape. Revise, rewrite, and improve the "bad" argument to make it as effective as possible. This may require at times taking a few liberties with the original argument, which is fine in this case. Your author can always decide to decline your suggestions. For now, do not be shy, and make any and all changes you think the argument needs to become as effective as possible.

Trade arguments back, and reflect. Return the now-much-improved argument to the original author, and then examine your returned argument. Reflect for ten minutes about what you learned about argument from being a developmental editor and from seeing your "bad" argument become better. When providing and receiving developmental editing assistance, which changes made the biggest impact? What changes were deployed across both "bad" arguments? Which ones, if any, seem more particular to one instance than the other?

CHAPTER 9

Constructing Arguments

Pinpointing Chapter 9

This chapter extends the material about arguments introduced in Chapter 8 by examining how writers go about actually constructing arguments. Where Chapter 8 helped to frame what arguments accomplish and what makes them more or less effective, this chapter digs deeper to examine how writers structure their arguments. To provide you with strategies for *constructing arguments in transit*, this chapter addresses the following concepts:

- Questions that Shape Arguments
- Inductive and Deductive Reasoning
- Argument Structure
- Stasis Theory
- Classical Argument Structure
- Toulmin Argument Structure
- Rogerian Argument Structure

Chapter 10 builds on our exploration of argument by addressing the choices writers make regarding design and format, aspects that are, like structure, crucial to developing effective arguments.

In July 1911, explorer and Yale History Professor Hiram Bingham (who has since become the prototype for Indiana Jones) suddenly came across the Peruvian site now known as Machu Picchu and declared it the "lost capital" of the Incas. Constructed in the fifteenth century, Machu Picchu sits at an elevated point between two mountains. From the sky the structural layout resembles a condor sitting in its lofty nest (Heaney; Magli).

Since Bingham's re-discovery of Machu Picchu, the site has sparked numerous debates across academic disciplines. Some even debate Bingham's role as re-discoverer, arguing that those accolades should instead go to a 1910 German exploration team or to Peruvians themselves long before (Eisner).

Research about the purpose of Machu Picchu occupies some of the most contentious scholarly terrain. Because so much about the site demonstrates that the Incas paid deliberate, sustained attention to the structure of Machu Picchu—be it for geometrical, religious, astronomical, cosmological, or political purposes—scholars seek to find evidence for their arguments from Machu Picchu's structure itself.

Some scholars argue that it was primarily a royal retreat for a fifteenth century Inca ruler. Recently, evolutionary anthropologists conducted mtDNA analyses on skeletons Bingham had collected a century ago: "[Study] results support the hypothesis that the remains of residents of the Inca-period rural communities of Paucarcancha and Patallacta that were analyzed were native highlanders [and] we argue that they served roles of supporting the nearby Inca royal estate of Machu Picchu" (Verano).

Discrediting the notion of a royal retreat, other researchers argue that Machu Picchu served as an astronomical observatory. A team of Peruvian and Polish archaeologists used stone conservation and 3D documentation methods to argue that the building called El Mirador served as "a device used probably by a small group of Inca priest-astronomers for precise observations of the position of celestial bodies on the horizon, against the distinctive Yanantin mountain peaks." The Torreón structure, similarly, has been found to have a

window that opens in such a way as to track the solstices and equinoxes (Aveni; Dearborn and White; "New Archaeastronomical"; Reinhard).

Astrophysicist Guilio Magli argues that this astronomical function intersected with Machu Picchu's religious purposes: "[The geometry of the structural designs] lead[s] us to propose that Machu Picchu was intentionally planned and built as a pilgrimage center connected with the Inca "cosmovision." Travel blogger Julio Moreno explains how the archaeoastronomical planning might have impressed pilgrims as they arrived at Machu Picchu at particular points of the year: "[T]he sun rises exactly at a point between Machu Picchu Mountain, and the mountain next to it on June 21, the summer solstice. This is called the gateway of the sun, and the entrance to Machu Picchu is you come through the Inca Trail. During this day, some buildings are designed to cast shadows on altars or other religiously significant stones."

Constructing arguments across disciplines resonates with the mtDNA analyses conducted on the Machu Picchu skeletons. While the basic DNA building blocks of humans have universal, structural similarities, we all also have unique characteristics that make us more or less similar to one another and that ultimately make us each individual human beings. We can think of argument in the same vein; while there are nearly infinite opportunities for discipline-specificity, contextualization, and creativity for any given argument, there are also some structural similarities with argument construction that we can usefully identify across disciplines and contexts.

Drawing out the intersection between purpose and structure further, the scholars studying Machu Picchu create their very own arguments about the archaeological site with deliberate, sustained attention to structure. Their choices for how they construct arguments hinge not only on their disciplinary, historical, and individual context but also on whether their purpose is to affirm, compromise, debunk, hypothesize, or accomplish something else. Purpose deeply impacts choices made about construction, be it of an archaeological site or an archaeological argument.

Developing an awareness of the underlying structures for arguments as well as the ways in which they can be modified will help you recognize the choices academic writers make as they construct arguments and will help you make choices about constructing your own arguments.

Write Here

Identify an ongoing controversy surrounding Machu Picchu, and read an argument related to this controversy. Then, recreate that person's argument using objects (not words). To do so, find a variety of small objects that you can use to represent the various components of that person's argument, and arrange them in such a way as to represent that argument. Explain the argument, and your choices about constructional representation, in writing. Share your construction and your written account of it with your classmates and instructor.

꒰ ꒰ ꒰

Questions that Shape Arguments

Chapter 3 emphasized that posing questions is a key feature of academic writing across disciplines and contexts. As writers construct arguments, they often gradually move toward posing a somewhat more focused range of questions. Developing the most refined and precise question enables writers to thereby craft more effective, targeted arguments.

Research questions

What questions are you asking in relation to the argument? What do you need to learn or research in order to arrive at an argument? Well-defined questions will help shape your argument.

Disciplinary and publication contexts

What is the disciplinary and publication context of your writing occasion? Perhaps above all other questions to consider as you construct an argument are those pertaining to disciplinary and publication context. Readers carry different expectations across disciplines for what an argument looks like and what makes it more or less effective. Additionally, arguments look vastly different depending on whether they are published in contexts that are more academic, more public, or a combination of these. Of course, as you are learning in this text, writing contexts have overlap and we can transfer what we learn in one context to another. However, it is best, as you prepare to construct an argument, to review examples of argument in the context in which you are writing so you can model your approach on these, or, if not, at least break with or modify convention in an informed and deliberate way.

Purpose

What do you hope to accomplish by writing this argument? What would you like readers to do or think after having read your argument? Having a clearer sense of your aims and purpose will help you focus your argument. If your purpose is to provide a solution to a problem, then you'll want to focus primarily on defining the solution and demonstrating why this solution offers an advantage over other solutions. By contrast, if your purpose is to illustrate nuanced aspects of a text, then you'll want to focus mainly on analysis and interpretation of evidence.

Evidence

What is your evidence, or what evidence are you seeking? Since arguments in academic writing are linked to evidence, make sure you use your evidence to arrive at your argument. Sometimes writers review evidence and learn that they need additional evidence, or a different kind of evidence. In most cases, arguments should emerge from the evidence rather than the other way around. If you have to work hard to make your evidence fit with your argument, you are likely working with an argument that needs revision.

Assumptions

What assumptions will you make? Every writer makes assumptions. Perhaps these assumptions involve an assumed understanding of pre-existing knowledge or an assumption about how readers are likely to receive an argument. Some assumptions involve how we define terms, or what we value.

Davis Oldham, a writing professor at Shoreline Community College, suggests that **assumptions** can involve facts, values, or analysis. Daniel Kies, a writing Professor at DuPage University, argues that assumptions emerge from cultural, biological, intellectual, and idiosyncratic origins.

Not only should academic writers understand what their assumptions are, but they should also consider naming them explicitly so readers can see how the assumptions are functioning in an argument. "Every person is a learner," for instance, is an assumption named by the National Council of Teachers of English on their website.

Sometimes, through the process of naming an assumption, we realize that the assumption should be reconsidered. "Every person has traveled on vacation," for instance, could be an assumption based on one's own experiences and would need to be reconsidered to accommodate people with divergent experiences.

Audience

To whom are you directing your argument? While we cannot assume that we will always be able to reach our intended audience, nor that we can fully know our intended audience, nor that others outside of that audience might also be reading our writing, it is nevertheless a good idea to take into consideration those to whom you are directing your argument. Sometimes these readers can span across several different groups, each with varying levels of expertise, disagreement, or agreement with you. What do you hope they do with or think about your argument? What perspectives do you think they might have about your argument? How can you use this knowledge to shape your argument in such a way as to be more accessible, provocative, and/or effective?

Qualifications

What qualifications exist for your argument? Rarely are arguments universally applicable or valid in all possible circumstances. Holding arguments up to this expectation is unreasonable. Instead, academic writers qualify their arguments, or specify the circumstances for their argument and the instances where it makes sense. Avoid as much as possible making generalizations and trying to develop an argument that fits all occasions.

Alternative viewpoints

How might people disagree with your position or offer alternative viewpoints? Alternative viewpoints are sometimes termed counterarguments, but such a term can suggest that the only reason academic writers consider these arguments is in order to eliminate them. Instead, writers often take alternative views into consideration simply to acknowledge those views or to shape qualifications as we will see specifically in Toulmin argumentation. Disagreement can often be sustained productively.

Structure

What structure will best suit your argument? Deciding how to structure an argument is complex, enough so that there are entire books devoted to the challenge. Some arguments are better focused on compromise. Others focus more on debunking others' ideas, and others are best structured around a focus on one's own position nearly exclusively. Guidelines and examples for

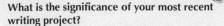

Writer Insights

What is the significance of your most recent writing project?

As a flute teacher, I create recital program notes to entertain, educate, and engage the audiences of my students. Listeners are more apt to connect with "Skip to My Lou" performed by a fledgling flutist if they know this popular American Frontier-era song encouraged the stealing of dance partners during its heyday. And what's the difference between a nocturne and a gavotte? The audience delights in such details. Writing is a valuable tool that I use to enhance the appreciation of music.

~June Newton, Flute Teacher and Freelance Musician, Augusta, Georgia, U.S.

various structures of argument will be provided in the latter portion of this chapter.

Credibility

How will you establish your credibility? Thinking deliberately about how you will gain and convey credibility about the argument will enable you to move beyond opinions into research-based evidence. What steps will you need to take in order to learn more about the ongoing scholarly conversation and debates centered around this area of inquiry? Sometimes this involves fieldwork, literature reviews, archival research, or some combination of these or other research methodologies (see Chapter 1 for more on research methodologies).

Format(s) or modalities

Should your argument appear in visual, verbal, multimodal, or written format? Is it a scholarly argument or a popular piece? Would it be better suited for multiple modalities? The format of arguments impacts what you argue and how you argue it. We will provide guidelines and examples in Chapter 10: Designing Arguments, for various formats and modalities of argument, including visual, written, and oral arguments that can emerge in print, digital, and/or in-person contexts.

So what?

This question is so important that it deserves to hold a power position as a final point of emphasis in this list of questions. While all of these questions are crucial, the "so what?" of your argument may be of most importance. This question invites you to identify why your argument matters. Why should people care about this argument? What important issues does it address? Not every argument is going to bring about world peace or end hunger, but every argument should have some larger significance to it. Articulate what this larger significance is for yourself, if not explicitly in your writing project as well.

Inductive and Deductive Reasoning

Arguments are developed through reasoning and proof. Chapter 8 already addressed reasoning in part through logical fallacies. But developing an effective argument entails deciding the way in which you will build your line of reasoning. Philosophers have created two general categories, or labels, for reasoning in arguments: inductive and deductive.

Inductive reasoning

Inductive reasoning involves moving from examples or observations (premises) to general assertions that are likely to be true (Figure 9.1). Economists Mikko Ketokivi and Saku Mantere describe inductive reasoning, and its challenges:

Inductive reasoning…runs…from particulars to generalizations. When one generalizes from data, one's inferences are always inductive…. [I]nduction is sometimes dubbed an ampliative form of reasoning (e.g., Salmon, 1966)—it "amplifies" our knowledge in that the conclusion is more than a restatement of the premises.

One can find inductive reasoning across disciplines. For example, Ketokivi and Mantere discuss inductive reasoning in the field of management and economics, where researchers collect data and then draw inferences and conclusions based on that data.

Deductive reasoning

In contrast to inductive reasoning, **deductive reasoning** moves from the general to the particular (Figure 9.1). Deductive reasoning has roots in the construction of hypotheses. For instance, if an academic writer develops a hypothesis to test, then she is approaching an argument through deductive reasoning. Deductive reasoning also presents challenges because it must be judged as being valid or invalid: if the premises (also termed evidence) hold truth, then the conclusion (also termed proof) will be true and the argument can be understood as valid.

Like inductive reasoning, deductive reasoning is woven throughout disciplines. Because of its emphasis on validity, Michal Ayalon and Ruhama Even argue that "deductive reasoning is often used as a synonym for mathematical thinking." Mathematicians, that is, might start a proof with a premise or law, and then apply it to a particular case in order to reach a conclusion. Offering another example of how deductive reasoning operates in a discipline, H. David Tuggle, Alex H. Townsend and Thomas J. Riley argue that the field of archaeology makes extensive use of deductive reasoning: "[the] identification of artifacts or features by archaeologists is accomplished by deductive reasoning."

Both forms of reasoning, therefore, have challenges and benefits, each affording academic writers with the opportunity to make claims based on premises and evidence and each having use across disciplines.

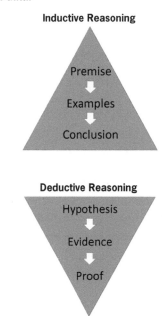

FIGURE 9.1 Inductive and deductive reasoning.

Write Now

Read an op-ed about an issue of interest to you. Write for 10 minutes about why you think the argument relies on inductive reasoning, deductive reasoning, or a combination of both.

Argument Structure

Although academic writers situate arguments uniquely within particular writing occasions, they also draw from a shared array of structures as they construct arguments. Argument structure helps determine how academic writers organize and emphasize certain shared features of arguments, such as introductions, conclusions, opposing viewpoints, evidence, and an articulation of a main position. Developing awareness of these common argument structures, as well as the ways in which they can be modified, will help you recognize the choices academic writers make as you encounter and respond to others', and generate your own arguments.

Four common approaches to argument structures that emerge across disciplines are Stasis theory, Classical argumentation, Toulmin argumentation, and Rogerian argumentation. Although each of these argument structures occurs across disciplines, certain structures might fit more readily in particular contexts. For instance, if you are working and writing in a field such as ethics or development studies, which often cover complex and ambiguous terrain, it might make sense to invoke Rogerian argument structure since Rogerian argument focuses on compromise. If you are writing in a field such as the Health Sciences and showing how a previous study reached a faulty conclusion, it might make sense to use the Classical structure because this structure emphasizes refuting others' arguments. In disciplines such as English Literature, History, or Cultural Anthropology, where writers often make use of deep analysis of texts to develop claims, the Toulmin argument structure might often make sense given that it provides guidelines for carefully connecting evidence to a main argument. Of course, a writer in History might use Classical argument structure to refute common perceptions about the narrative of a particular historical event. Still, it is important to consider how disciplinary context and writing occasion impact argument structure.

The upcoming sections introduce you to these four argumentation structures and provide examples of each. These examples demonstrate structure through written formats but can also be mapped onto and modified to other argument modalities, such as digital and in-person contexts, and for arguments that are visual or oral as well as written. Chapter 10: Designing Arguments will offer you the opportunity to think about how the platform and modality of an argument impacts the construction and design of an argument's structure. As you will also see, despite each of these structures having distinct features, they also have overlap, and academic writers often modify or blend these structures depending on the writing occasion. Thus, as you reflect on these structures, consider them not as strict templates, but as beginning points for constructing arguments.

Stasis Theory

Stasis theory provides a bridge between questions that shape an argument and argument structure. Where the questions in the prior section are more general in nature, stasis theory offers a structured set of questions—a heuristic—that can help you develop, refine, and shape your argument. It can be conceived of as a method of invention or discovery (or pre-writing, as we discussed in Chapter 2: Research and Writing as a Process), specifically geared toward argument. Stasis theory can essentially help structure any argument by helping you determine what the main issues are in an argument, how significant they are, what the implications are, and what you think next steps should be related to the argument.

After using the stasis questions to generate a range of possible approaches to an argument, academic writers can then make choices about which aspects they think are most significant and/or which ones they may want to focus on for a particular argument.

Stasis theory, also known as Issue theory, has its origins with "Hermagoras of Temnos, a rhetor of the second century B.C.E. [and] Hermogenes of Tarsus" [a rhetor of the second century C.E.] (Fernández-Garrido). Stasis theory initially emerged in the context of judicial deliberations as a way for lawyers and judges to discover and determine what issues were at stake pertaining to a particular legal case. Those in judicial circles could, ostensibly, go through the questions to gain clarity on whether a crime was committed, what that crime entailed, who was harmed, who was guilty, how significant the crime was, and what the punishment should be.

Now, stasis theory has found many realms of application beyond its legalistic, and arguably punitive, origins. For instance, Allen Brizee argues that stasis theory can help as a strategy for "workplace teaming and decision making." Kathryn Northcut has applied stasis theory to Paleontology. And Charles Marsh has applied stasis theory to crisis communication.

In terms of its application to argument structure, stasis theory invites you to pursue four main areas of questioning, or issue seeking, as a way of discovering the potential contours of an argument. Arguing for the universal applicability of these questions or issues, Cicero maintained that "There will always be one of these issues applicable to every kind of case; for where none applies, there can be no controversy."

The four stases, or issues, and their questions, are as follows:

Facts (termed 'conjectural'):
What has happened?
What has caused it?

Definition (termed 'definitional'):
Has harm been done?
What type of harm is it?
To whom or what has this harm been done?
Who is responsible for this harm?

Writer Insights

What are the purposes of your arguments?

I am a nonprofit professional.... As someone with nine years of experience in campaigns, communications, policy and philanthropy, I have an eye for detail, a drive to impact the world and a passion for leaving the earth, like a campground, better than I found it. I would like to think my writing is more than my work. The mission is always the same; I write to inspire, to teach, to share, to motivate, to communicate and to connect.

~Claire LaFrance, Nonprofit Professional, Washington, D.C., U.S.

Quality (termed 'qualitative'):
How severe is the harm or impact?
What is the degree of the harm or impact?

Policy (termed 'procedural'):
Should something be done?
What should be done?

Considering each of these questions helps writers determine the parameters of their argument. Arguments can emerge through one or more stases, depending on not only the particular issue, but also the writer, the context for the argument and discipline.

As an example of how stasis theory can work to shape arguments across disciplines, let's consider an academic writer who is interested in questions about climate change. He might pursue any of the following stases related to climate change:

Facts/Conjecture: Academic writers might argue over whether the climate is or is not changing, or about what is causing it. For instance, scholars David Stern and Robert Kaufman argue that "both natural and anthropogenic forcings cause temperature change."

Definition: Academic writers might also argue over what the impact is of climate change. For instance, Abigail Cahill and her coauthors argue in their article "How Does Climate Change Cause Extinction?" "Anthropogenic climate change is predicted to be a major cause of species extinctions in the next 100 years."

Quality: Those interested in examining the degree of the impact of climate change would be making an argument about issues of quality. For instance, in their article, "Climate Change Impacts on Marine Ecosystems," Doney, et al. argue about the severity of the impact of climate change, such as "shifts in the size structure...and...abundance of populations [and] altered species interactions."

Procedure: The stasis of procedure asks what policies should be enacted, what solutions can be achieved, or what behaviors should be developed. Guy Dauncey, for instance, focuses the majority of his book, *Stormy Weather*, on practical solutions to climate change that utilize available technology.

Many arguments span multiple stases, even sometimes all four stases, and other times writers will instead demonstrate why they are focusing on one particular stasis over others, having perhaps shown that other stases are less relevant, less significant, or already resolved.

In the excerpt from her book, *Kill the Messenger,* Maria Armoudian makes an argument about climate change and the media by systematically progressing through all four stases. In the text's annotations, I show how others could have argued alternative positions within each of the stases.

Excerpt from *Kill the Messenger: the Media's Role in the Fate of the World* by M. Armoudian

In 2007, political changes fueled more robust media coverage. With the climate on their agenda, Democrats gained control of both houses of Congress; the U.S. Supreme Court decided the EPA's role in regulating greenhouse gases; and California passed groundbreaking climate legislation, signed into law by actor-turned-governor Arnold Schwarzenegger. To disambiguate the science, former vice president Al Gore dispelled the myth of a scientific debate in his film, *An Inconvenient Truth.* ...

> Armoudian is arguing about the facts (conjecture), building a case as to what caused media to shift in 2007 to "more robust coverage" of climate change. Others might argue that different facts created this media shift, or that these facts tell only part of the story and that there are other facts leading to a conclusion that media coverage did not shift in 2007.

> Armoudian moves next to an argument of definition, arguing that the impact of this coverage generated a perception of "two sides to climate science." Others, presumably, could argue about a different impact.

Without checking the veracity of the naysayers' statements, many journalists gave equal footing to denialists and real climate scientists, ultimately framing an established climate science as "he-said-she-said" and creating an illusion that there were two sides to climate science....

> Armoudian now demonstrates the stasis of quality along with definition, arguing that the that this media coverage was severe in that it "unjustly tarnished climate scientists and misled the public." Those with different views could argue that this impact was not severe or problematic.

Eager for controversy, some journalists seized upon a handful of words that turned errors in judgment into evidence of a conspiracy that unjustly tarnished climate scientists and misled the public on the seriousness of global warming. ...

Media consolidation and concentration of ownership are the enemies of information diversity and pluralism, serving only media owners, not the public. To prevent narrow-minded discourse from dominating the public sphere, legal structures including antitrust laws, protections for net neutrality (unrestricted and unbiased Internet access and flow), treaties, and other thoughtful regulation are needed to help limit concentrated ownership and related forces that strangle the flow of independent information.

> Toward the end of her book, Armoudian moves to an argument of procedure. Here she argues for increased legislation to protect "information diversity and pluralism." Others might argue for different kinds of legislation.

From *Kill the Messenger: the Media's Role in the Fate of the World,* 2011.

Write Now

The preceding annotated example addresses climate, which seems to somewhat readily map onto the four stases because of its highly controversial and policy-driven nature. Choose another line of inquiry or discipline, perhaps one that seems less controversial, and develop questions and controversies for it based on the four stases. How would you develop stases, for instance, with arguments about sports psychology or the history of the plague?

Classical Argument Structure

Deployed since at least the fifth century B.C.E, the classical argument structure is most suitable when you are trying to make an argument convincing for readers who oppose your ideas, by addressing and refuting opposing viewpoints as a means of forwarding your own position. **Classical argument structure** may be familiar to you in the context of political debates, where candidates will argue for a particular agenda or approach, and in the process demonstrate why other candidates' approaches are less advantageous.

Classical argument has five primary components: introduction, narrative, confirmation, refutation and concession, and summary and conclusion.

Introduction

The introduction should accomplish several important objectives: secure the reader's interest, orient the reader to your argument, cultivate a positive relationship with the reader, and articulate your argument.

Securing readers' interest

Although your professors or teaching assistants are largely required to read your writing—it's part of their job—other readers have considerably more choice. Sometimes readers need encouragement to read, either because they may not know why an issue is important or interesting, or because they may be choosing from among a number of different options for research on a particular topic. Given all the options and choices readers have, what will encourage them to read your writing project?

You might consider this a hook for your readers, where you put a line out and hope they take a bite. Perhaps you can begin with something surprising, or a narrative anecdote, or a relevant quote or concept. Whatever it is you choose, be sure your hook is relevant in content, purpose, and tone to your overall argument.

Write Now

With a current writing project of your own, try developing at least three different possible hooks for readers. You might try a compelling sentence, a narrative anecdote, a significant fact or observation, a relevant quote, or some other way of capturing your reader's interest. Developing several different hooks will enable you to see that there is great variety in options for how writers go about securing readers' interest.

Orienting readers to the argument

Help readers prepare for the argument by providing key terms, the main line of inquiry, your approach, and any other relevant information you think they will need to adequately consider your argument. You may decide to expand on these aspects later in the argument, but offer a glimpse now of the main concepts under discussion.

Cultivating a positive relationship with readers

Creating a positive relationship between writer and readers involves presenting yourself as ethical, trustworthy, knowledgeable, and courteous. You might think of it as a performance of sorts, even if it is an honest performance. Erving Goffman argues in his well-known book, *The Presentation of Self in Everyday Life*, that all presentations are a performance:

> When an individual plays a part he implicitly requests his observers to take seriously the impression that is fostered before them. They are asked to believe that the character they see actually possesses the attributes he appears to possess, that the task he performs will have the consequences that are implicitly claimed for it, and that, in general, matters are what they appear to be.

Goffman's notion of performance can enable academic writers to think about the role they are playing in relationship to their readers, their presentation of self.

Articulating the argument (claim, thesis, position, etc.)

Articulate for readers as clearly as possible what your argument is. Your argument itself can consist of multiple sentences or one sentence, or even sometimes an entire paragraph; depending on the context, you might even say something like, "This article argues..." as a way of signaling to readers what the argument is.

Narrative

This second component of classical argument can be thought of as the story behind your argument. What other research has already been conducted about this issue? Why is your argument significant? Often this narrative section consists of the literature review (as discussed in Chapter 5: Summary, and Chapter 7: Analysis), where academic writers summarize and synthesize previous research. Include in this narrative section enough information for readers to feel fully apprised of the current state of research on a particular issue. One challenge of academic arguments is that readers often have varying levels of expertise. Writers must consider how they can bring those with less expertise up to speed and not condescend to or bore those with more expertise.

Confirmation

This aspect of classical argument provides readers with the main reasons and evidence supporting your argument. Using the evidence you have gathered, confirmations support your argument based on your narrative. This section might also include smaller arguments that are related to your overarching argument.

Refutation and concession

After offering evidence toward an argument, academic writers using classical arguments also address what are known as **counterarguments**. Academic writers anticipate what those with opposing views might argue, and they attempt to address, and counter, these views. Rather than dismissing them outright, though, academic writers often approach this through qualification or **concession**. A writer might acknowledge that an opposing view may have elements that are reasonable under certain circumstances. As we work to convince others to change their opinions, people rarely like to hear that they are completely wrong about something. More effective approaches will suggest that they are somewhat right, or that they are right under certain contexts.

Summary and conclusion

The final section of classical argument summarizes your argument and the main points you hope to have made. Think of this as the final opportunity to provide readers with your takeaway points: What do you want your readers to be thinking about as they finish reading your argument?

Effective conclusions tend to include certain components: a recap of the main argument, hints at future research, and a call to action.

Conclusions, unfortunately, sometimes get short shrift. Writers can find themselves with insufficient time to focus on a conclusion. Instead, writers should devote significant energy to conclusions because they are so important, holding the final opportunity for you to address your readers in that particular writing occasion.

Review or echo the main argument

While it is important to summarize your main argument (some busy readers may read only your conclusion!), you should avoid cutting and pasting text from earlier in the argument into the conclusion. Think about this conclusion as an echo of sorts, recasting the argument, but with just a slight variation in tone, content, or style.

Include ideas for future research and/or new questions

Since effective academic arguments contribute to ongoing conversations, furthering knowledge and making progress rather than providing the final say-so, effective conclusions should offer readers ideas for what still remains to be considered or researched.

Make a call to action of some sort (depending on context)

Now that readers have read your argument, what would you like them to do with what they have learned? Do you want them to think differently? Are you advocating for a policy or behavior of some kind? Provide readers with ideas for what they might do next.

In this example of a classical argument, David Corso, an undergraduate student majoring in biology and minoring in psychology at the University of South Carolina, Spartanburg, pursues the question, "What are the potential uses for video games in improving our lives?"

Corso perhaps adopts the classical style of argument because he anticipates that many readers will have opposing positions on video games, believing them instead to have deleterious effects on our lives. His strategy of refutation involves qualifying the context of others' research. This strategy of refuting others' claims based on methodology (what games they used in their experiments, for example) is a common strategy in the sciences and lends itself well to the Classical argument structure because it offers the opportunity to develop both refutation and concession.

Excerpt from "The Psychological and Physical Effects of Video Game Play" by D. Corso

From light and food to singing and dancing, our world is characterized by phenomena, events, and processes that have a physical and psychological effect on us. Our environment and our experience shape us—physically and mentally. Games work in a similar fashion. A game is any mental and/or physical activity that is defined by goals, rules, challenges, a feedback system, and voluntary participation (Game, n.d.; McGonigal, 2011; Prensky, 2001). A video game is a complex form of digital media that incorporates these gamic properties, and it requires the active interaction between a human and computer (Galloway, 2006; Wardrip-Fruin, 2009)....

> In the introduction, Corso provides a hook for readers, inviting us to think about light, food, singing, and dancing—universal human activities. The effect of this is also to link video games with other forms of enjoyment and leisure activities, thereby starting to link positivity with video games. Corso establishes goodwill and expertise by using a scholarly tone, and invoking current scholarship.

Video games are the popularized, digital form of games, and through their inherent properties, video games are a perfect tool to quantifiably measure a number of physical and mental capacities, capabilities, and characteristics.... We have to understand the cognitive and physiological effects of video game play in order to understand how these processes can be utilized to help us interpret and navigate our world. By understanding these effects, we can begin to develop games that facilitate our lives, e.g. constructing beneficial stratagems for education and public health....

> Corso's thesis, his main argument, appears here, where he argues that video games can help us "interpret and navigate our world" and "facilitate our lives." Thinking in terms of stases, Corso's argument would fall under definition and quality.

From *Caravel, Undergraduate Research Journal*, 2014.

Cognitive Effects

Video games exercise and train cognitive skills. Cognition is defined as the mental processes associated with memory, language, perception, attention, problem solving, decision-making, and reasoning (Goldstein, 2011). Video games create engaging environments that allow for cognitive growth and development in mental rotational skills, object location ability, attention, visual attention, targeting, iconic and verbal representation of processes, verbal fluency, executive control, and both short and long-term memory skills (Boyan & Sherry, 2011).… Through their intrinsic qualities, video games promote cognitive growth and development.

> This section marks the beginning of Corso's narrative, where he offers a literature review of video-game research. It is clear from the research he's citing that his disciplinary perspective is psychology and neuroscience. Corso uses summary and synthesis throughout this section.

> Corso blends narrative and confirmation, using Green and Bavelier as evidence for his own argument about the potential benefits of video games.

A 2003 study by Green and Bavelier demonstrated cognitive growth through video game play.… They conducted five experiments…

The State of Video Game Research: Problems and Solutions

Our lives and our world are characterized by complexity—the workings of a cell, law, quantum physics, etc.—and video games reflect these intricacies. … On the one hand, video games and video game play … have great utility in a number of areas, such as academia, research, and healthcare (Astle et al., 2011; Griffiths, 2002; Van Eck, 2006). On the other hand, video games and video game play create a number of problems that must be understood and resolved in order to utilize their full potential. … Through surveys, models, experimental tests, and correlational studies, video games have been shown to produce a number of negative effects (Carnagey et al., 2007; Gentile et al., 2012; Gentile et al., 2004; Wang et al., 2011). … Several studies have found correlation effects between aggressive behavior and video game habits (Gentile et al., 2004). …

> Corso now moves into refutation and concession, reviewing the literature that argues for the negative impact of video games. He summarizes and synthesizes fully, choosing not to refute it right away. This approach demonstrates judiciousness.

The major factor in a number of these studies is the nature of video game play: the content of the game, i.e. fighting and death, the context in which people play, i.e. a lack of supervision, and the amount of time spent playing.… Since we know that video games will create this effect under specific environmental influences, i.e. violent video games producing aggression and desensitization, then specific environmental influences on the other spectrum should be able to produce a different response, e.g. construction games producing cooperation and collaboration (Ito, 2009)....

Now Corso refutes the literature, conceding that these studies present solid evidence, but then stating that they address only certain types of video games. This approach qualifies the opposing point of view, showing that these arguments are valid, but only in certain circumstances.

The Potential Uses for Video Games

Corso now moves into a full section of confirmation, making specific points about how video games can facilitate "growth and success." He divides his confirmation into several categories (research, treatment/prevention, education), within which he argues that video games can have a strong impact.

Video games have enormous potential as tools to study human growth and development, as training simulators for various jobs and skills, for education at primary, secondary, and collegiate institutions, and so much more. ...

As Griffiths (2002) states, "Videogames can be used as research and/or measurement tools. Furthermore, as research tools, they have great diversity" (p. 47)....

Prevention and Treatment Strategies

Video games provide an effective prevention and treatment strategy for a variety of problems, such as with Alzheimer's and ADHD. ... Aart et al. (2007) report a number of problems that video game neurofeedback can be applied to as medication; these include alleviating attention and hyperactivity disorders, muscular tonicity recovery for cardiovascular patients, relaxation and meditation ...

Corso's confirmation continues, providing evidence for the positive impact and use of video games.

Educational Value

Video games are excellent pedagogical tools. As Gentile (2011) reports, video games can provide immediate feedback, motivate players, set specific goals, promote mastery, encourage distributed learning, teach for transfer, adapt themselves to the level of the learner, and provide various other teaching techniques. ...

Corso now moves into the conclusion, reminding readers of the contrasting positions as well but encouraging a "holistic" approach and inspiring readers about the many possibilities video games can confer. This opens the door for readers to pick up on this research and explore these potential uses in more depth.

Conclusion

Video games have measurable effects—physically and cognitively. Video games produce cognitive improvements, e.g. visual attention processes, as

211

well as physical changes, such as the brain areas responsible for processing and learning. However, video games also produce impairments that cause psychological deficits, e.g. inhibition and decision-making skills, from physical effects, i.e. prolonged stress mechanisms. As long as we approach video games in a holistic sense, we can design them to make us smarter and stronger while minimizing negative effects. There are no limits to the cognitive training and learning opportunities created by video games, and they can be developed to improve cognitive resources, such as memory, language, and problem-solving skills.

Toulmin Argument Structure

Toulmin argument structure emerged from a book by rhetorician and philosopher Stephen Toulmin (1922-2009) titled *The Uses of Argument* (1958). Toulmin arguments overlap with certain features of the Classical argument structure, such as an introduction and conclusion, but Toulmin focuses primarily on how writers use evidence to move their argument forward. Where Classical argument structures makes sense in contexts with oppositional readers, Toulmin argument structures might be applicable for more neutral contexts.

The Toulmin model involves six component parts: claim, evidence, warrant, backing, qualifier(s), and rebuttal.

Claim

The claim is the main argument or position of a writing project. Instead of labeling an argument a thesis, Toulmin refers to it as a claim. The word claim originates from the Latin route word of *clamare*, which can be translated as "to shout" or "to proclaim." Toulmin's terminology, then, illustrates that even in neutral contexts, writers should develop arguments that have significance, about which they feel compelled to "shout."

Evidence

Evidence works to move a claim forward or support a claim. Evidence, as we will see in Chapter 10, can include data, quotes, paraphrase, summary, and/or personal experience.

Warrant

This is the important connection between the evidence and the claim. The warrant enables the writer to explain how the evidence is connected to the claim.

Backing

Backing provides additional support for or explanations of the warrant.

Qualifier

Qualifiers indicate what the circumstances are when the argument works, or they indicate other limitations to the claim. This might be the moment also when an academic writer addresses the assumptions that are undergirding the argument.

Rebuttal

The rebuttal is much like the refutation or concession of the Classical argument structure. Rebuttals address counterarguments and are best approached by demonstrating which portions of counterarguments are accurate, or the circumstances under which counterarguments might be accurate rather than discounting them wholesale.

This example of a Toulmin-based argument is a literary analysis of George R.R. Martin's *A Game of Thrones*. Rebecca Jones, an undergraduate at the University of Wisconsin, River Falls, majoring in English, examines these questions: how are female characters depicted in Martin's novels?; and, how are female characters depicted in the television show?

Excerpt from "A Game of Genders: Comparing Depictions of Empowered Women between *A Game of Thrones* Novel and Television Series" by R. Jones

1. Introduction

The genre of fantasy has a long and sordid history in its depictions of women. Even today, female authors and positive female protagonists are still scarce. This is in part because the genre battles not only societal norms, but also the chivalric standards and gender roles of medieval times, which it often emulates. Knights and damsels-in-distress are often touchstones for male and female characters. Presently, "Feminist philosophy [...] sees chivalry as oppressing women by formulating a specific role that not all women want for themselves, and, further, by devaluing the role that women are supposed to play." Recent fantasy novels have started to counteract this trend through the writings of female and male authors alike, refuting the former chivalric expectations for women within the genre by allowing women greater prominence within their novels. In the novel, *A Game of Thrones* by George R. R. Martin, the modern reader encounters Cersei Lannister, Catelyn Stark, Sansa Stark, Arya Stark, and

> Jones situates her claim within an ongoing conversation about the role of women in fantasy novels. In so doing, she broadens her potential range of readers to include those interested in feminist theory, women's studies, and fantasy fiction, as well as those interested in *A Game of Thrones* more specifically.

From *Journal of Student Research* (1.3), 2012.

Daenerys (Dany) Targaryen … Each of the aforementioned women is empowered through her political rank within the world Martin creates, while also possessing a strength of her own, which manifests through the various trials she faces.… While the series is a close adaptation of the novel, by noting the variations in the depictions of … women, one sees the changing standards for women conveyed by the differences in portrayal between the two media, utilizing the lens of their respective archetypes. …

> Jones provides her claim at the end of this first paragraph in the final sentence. She argues that the archetypal portrayals in the novel and the show demonstrate an increase in power for female characters.

2. The Women

2.1. Cersei Lannister: Shadow Queen and Mother

Cersei Lannister is the most powerful woman in both novel and show, and by far the most feared.…

Four major scenes in the television show redefine Cersei's character and depict her as developed and complex, more so than Martin's presentation of her in the novel. The first of these scenes occurs in the episode "Kingsroad," when Cersei goes to the comatose Bran's room and consoles Catelyn telling of her own firstborn's death. The novel likewise mentions Cersei's first child, but much later and with a far different tone. When she tells Catelyn the story of her stillborn son in the show, it is with a quiet, somber voice. This change redefines her character and in the show's storyline gives her a different attitude and motivation than that of the poisonous, bitter Queen of the novel. This moment hints at the seeds of love she once had for Robert that have long since die: how there was a time when she bore his children, and rather than intentionally killing the child, as she does in the novel, he is already dead, and foreshadows the fate of her love for Robert. This moment gives the viewer some ground upon which to understand Cersei's later actions, as well as presenting her character as that of a Mother figure not just the Queen …

In the show, [Cersei] is calm the entire time and in control. The novel, however, paints a different picture. She is still the strong woman but she shows her anger …

> Jones includes backing here as she provides information about Cersei's history with Robert that helps readers understand the warrant and evidence.

> Jones includes evidence here for the show's depiction of a more complex character in the "Kingsroad" scene.

> Here, Jones provides the warrant for the evidence by demonstrating why this change is so significant in strengthening Cersei's character.

> Jones offers a qualification to her argument, by admitting that Cersei also displays strength in the novel, just not as much as in the show.

While the show presents her as strong, unashamed, and un-afraid…, Martin presents her as pathetic, disgusting, and [subordinate] in the novel. The differing lines in the novel and the actions presented in the show are what shape the difference between Cersei's two representations and allow her to be stronger in the show….

Jones concludes this section by re-emphasizing her claim: that the show presents Cersei as a stronger, more complex female character than the novel does. In subsequent sections, Jones provides evidence, backing, and warrants about the other female characters in A Game of Thrones.

3. Conclusion

Jones here offers a rebuttal to the counterargument that women are depicted in problematic ways in fantasy fiction shows and novels. Rather than suggesting this position is wrong, Jones instead reframes it by illustrating the opportunity for progress.

Fantasy has not always been kind in its depictions of women, such as its damsels-in-distress, passive ladies who do little but fill in the background space of the castle, or serving only as possessions who produce heirs for their lords. However, as society changes, so too must the literature it produces. Martin has already established strong and empowered women in his novel, yet in the show adaptation these women have often gained more strength, as fifteen years later he is now catering to a society whose standards for television have changed and is now able to have leading women who are strong, without objectifying them…. Allowing for [these changes], Martin reveals how society is more open to strong women, and looks for complex characters… In the end, [Martin] shows that while our culture has changed over the past fifteen years, there is still plenty of progress to be made …

Jones qualifies her argument by acknowledging that women are strong and empowered in the novel already, even though the show takes it to a greater degree. And, she further qualifies her argument by showing that more progress is yet to be made.

Rogerian Argument Structure

Rogerian argument, developed by psychologist Carl Rogers (1902-1947), is founded on compromise and understanding, resting on the premise that an argument should reach resolution. Rogerian argument focuses more explicitly on the refutation or rebuttal components of argument, and with more of a goal of compromise, than do the Classical or Toulmin argument structures. Approaching common ground and compromise may be more realistic or appropriate in some contexts. In the prior two examples, common ground might have been achieved if Corso had argued for increased regulation of violent video games even as he also argued for the positive impacts among other video games. For Jones, compromise might have emerged by exploring in more detail the lack of power among female characters in the show, or the lack of power among female characters in another show.

Rogerian argument is comprised of four components: catching the reader's interest, presenting the opposition's viewpoint, presenting the writer's viewpoint, and establishing common ground.

Catching readers' interest

As with other argument structures, Rogerian argument begins with an introduction that captures reader interest.

Presenting the opposing side's position

Rogerian argument offers an extended discussion of opposing views and emphasizes understanding and acknowledgement rather than criticism.

Present the writer's position

As with the other argument structures, Rogerian asks for a full discussion of the writer's point of view or position. Evidence and reasons should be included here, relying on appeals to *ethos, pathos, logos*, and also *kairos* as appropriate for the context.

Finding common ground

Where other argument structures might lean more heavily toward concluding with the writer's position, Rogerian asks for an emphasis on common ground and compromise.

The example of Rogerian argument comes from Eva Orbuch, who wrote this article while an undergraduate at Stanford University where she majored in Urban Studies and minored in Education. In the article on microfinance, published in the *Journal of Politics and Society*, Orbuch takes up the question, "[W]hat approach to service delivery is most effective in helping [microfinance institutions (MFIs)] achieve a balance between financial well-being and social impact?" She explores the debate between two approaches to MFI service delivery: a financial approach or an integrated approach. While Orbuch ultimately advocates for an integrated approach, she forges a compromise with those who advocate for a financial approach.

Excerpt from "Toward an Integrated Approach to Microfinance:
Sustainability in Bolivia and Peru" by E. Orbuch

Microfinance is a concept that has greatly expanded in meaning and practice since its inception. ... One group of MFIs chooses to provide only financial products to their clients, primarily in the form of small loans, in order to maximize operational efficiency. This strategy contrasts with MFIs that choose to [use an "integrated approach"] and consider additional means of economic and social development ... such as life insurance products, educational programs, and direct healthcare.

> Orbuch outlines the two positions here: one focused on "financial products" and the other, an "integrated approach." Orbuch does not malign or elevate either approach.

Current literature has called into question the previously touted effectiveness of microfinance and many in the microfinance community acknowledge the difficulty of fighting poverty through micro-loans alone. ... Based on contemporaneous literature and on the perspectives of MFI leaders and employees, I conclude that the integrated service approach provides the best framework through which to balance the demands between financial sustainability and social impact.

> Orbuch captures reader interest by noting that the effectiveness of MFIs is being called into question.

> Orbuch here conveys her argument for the integrated approach, but, in Rogerian fashion, introduces the idea that this offers a "balance" between financial and social interests.

Literature Review

... In 2005, the MIT Poverty Action Lab undertook a randomized evaluation of the impacts of introducing microcredit in a new market.... The results revealed that the introduction of microcredit has some varied and significant effects on business outcomes and the composition of household expenditure.... In a 2003 paper, researchers ... give the rationale that many other interventions such as employment, education, and healthcare depend on people's access to financial services, and that improvements in these other areas can only be maintained when households have increased control over financial resources.

> Orbuch offers a literature review of the financial approach, Notice there is no rebuttal or concession here, but, in a Rogerian manner, Orbuch is establishing common ground.

From *Journal of Politics & Society* (22), 2011.

While research focusing specifically on the effects of integrated microfinance is relatively rare, the work done has largely confirmed the positive nature of its impact. Institutions like Freedom from Hunger (FFH)…have performed several useful studies…. The results indicated that recipients of both credit and education services displayed greater business acumen and higher revenues than those who received only credit services….

Next, Orbuch outlines the integrated approach, building on the common ground by showing that the integrated approach actually enhances the financial outcomes.

[S]ome organizations are being pressured into… leaving out non-credit products. There are also additional pressures for MFIs to "install complex accounting and managerial systems."… These pressures squeeze current practitioners of the integrated approach and discourage new MFIs from adopting service integration… Yet, as I will discuss later, my interviews also indicate that a strong social mandate and well-defined organizational policies could allow MFIs to continue to pursue their stated goals rather than face "mission drift," i.e., the gradual abandonment of the poverty-reduction aims of the microfinance sector…. I

Orbuch acknowledges the challenges involved with adopting the integrated approach, demonstrating a keen awareness of opposing viewpoints.

Orbuch establishes a "both/and" approach rather than an "either/or," suggesting that the integrated approach provides equilibrium and balance.

argue that this sought-after equilibrium between the banking and development aspects of MFIs can be translated into a more general balance between financial sustainability and social impact in the microfinance sector. While agreement among those interviewed was not unanimous, I believe that this balance is possible and the tradeoff is not inevitable.

Orbuch's methodology also achieves a Rogerian equanimity as she specifically sought out MFIs delivering through both perspectives.

Project Methodology

To ensure a general amount of representation of the two sectors and a variety of service delivery approaches, … I visited thirteen MFIs and conducted interviews with thirty-one different MFI managers and employees,

Organizational Benefits to Service Integration

1) Financial Sustainability and Cost-Effectiveness

Secondary data confirms the cost-effectiveness of the service integration approach…. Data from the Consortium of Private Organizations for the Promotion of Small and Micro-Enterprise (COPEME), a microfinance umbrella organization, shows that every Peruvian integrated organization studied had reached financial and operational sustainability.

As Orbuch moves to present her own position, she first discusses the financial sustainability of the integrated approach. This organization places emphasis on the financial aspects and forges a compromise with opposing perspectives. This section is then followed with more evidence about how the integrated approach increases organizational competitiveness and client loyalty.

Social Benefits of Service Integration

1) Client Health

Orbuch continues to offer evidence for her own position, but continues to speak in terms of financial benefit, showing how even health care offers financial reward.

...My interviews strongly suggest that health training and direct health interventions improve client health.... [H]ealth education and direct delivery of health services are not only beneficial for clients, but also for the organization delivering them. According to Carmen Velasco, "Even if you don't care about the social component of the program of what you do, if you're clever, you don't want to kill your clients..."

3) Economic Improvement

The final social benefit of integrated microfinance is the added economic progress for the clients. ... [C]lients in solidarity loan groups are graduating out of their small group loan products, demonstrating that they are financially prepared to access a larger individual loan for their business....

Orbuch's final evidence returns to the common ground: financial improvement.

Under What Circumstances Does Microfinance Integration Work?

This section is key for Orbuch's Rogerian approach as she suggests that the financial approach might in fact be more effective in some contexts.

Integrated microfinance will not work effectively in every context.... Integrated microfinance can work well in countries that have consumer protections in the form of interest rate caps, but that have the flexibility to allow the rates required by integrated programs. Integration may not be possible in countries with rigid interest rate regulations, such as Venezuela....

Conclusion

...This paper argues that one of the most effective ways for MFIs to maintain [their] original social mission while also remaining financially sustainable is through a deliberate mix of financial and non-financial services.

> Even in her conclusion, Orbuch continues to establish common ground by showing that one can have an approach that is simultaneously social and financial.

Transferring Argument Construction

This chapter has built on the preceding chapter by deepening our consideration of argument, helping you discover how writers shape and construct arguments. Specifically, this chapter has provided guidance for how you might decide what to argue, what approach to reasoning you might use, and what structure will likely best suit your argument. These decisions will shift dramatically across writing occasions, with different situations inspiring you to tailor these choices in response to their circumstances.

Chapter 10 continues our exploration of argument by addressing the importance of format and design in shaping argument. As we will see, there are many modalities and formats—print, digital, and in-person, visual, written, or oral—within which arguments can emerge and which also shape writers' decisions about structure. Then, Chapter 11 continues to help you learn how to develop arguments by addressing how academic writers across disciplines integrate evidence. And, finally, Chapter 12 completes this foray into argument by providing guidelines on how to cite evidence effectively, again with an explicit focus on how writers actively engage in transferring their knowledge about citation across contexts.

Chapter 9 Key Terms

Assumptions	Stasis theory	Toulmin argument
Inductive reasoning	Classical argument	Rogerian argument
Deductive reasoning	Counterargument	
Credibility	Concession	

Write Away

One of the best ways to improve your own ability to construct effective arguments is to unpack the structures of others' arguments. This activity asks you to do so with one area of argumentation across several different instances so you can begin to see the ways in which writers customize general structures for argument as demanded by particular writing occasions. This activity also enables you to gain an advance perspective on argument design and format, the next chapter's area of focus.

Decide on a general area of argumentation. Choose a general area of argumentation you would like to investigate. This can be any area in which you have an interest.

Select three to four different arguments in this area to examine. Locate three or four different examples of arguments in this area, being careful to choose different argument formats. For instance, if you are examining arguments about refugee issues, you might choose one peer-reviewed scholarly article, one YouTube video, and one op-ed. Or, you might choose a blog post, a homepage of a website, and a policy brief.

Identify the argument's structure. Carefully examine each of the arguments and identify the structure. The concept of a reverse outline, the revision method introduced in Chapter 2, can also be applied to examining others' arguments: Identify what each paragraph is accomplishing with a key word or phrase. What does the writer do first, then, next? After developing the reverse outline for each argument, see if you can discern the argument structure. Does it seem to resemble Classical, Toulmin, or Rogerian structure, or some combination of those, or a different structure altogether? What area of the stases do you see each argument operating within? What kinds of reasoning do you notice in the arguments?

Reflect on transfer and argument structure. Having seen several different arguments and their structures, reflect in writing for ten minutes about how writers tailor and customize argument structures for particular writing occasions. Did you notice that the writers employ, modify, or challenge one of the structures identified in this section? How and why do you think the writers chose their structures? In what ways do you think argument format and writing occasion might impact the choices writers make about argument structure?

Designing Arguments: Formats and Modalities

Several well-known Hollywood films, including *Raiders of the Lost Ark* and *Journey to the Center of the Earth*, have made use of archaeoastronomical features, elements, and designs. In one such film, *Castaway*, the lead character, Chuck Noland (played by Tom Hanks), becomes stranded on a Pacific Island for four years. He marks the passage of time by designing a measurement device called an analemma, carving it as an image onto a wall in the cave in which he sleeps. An analemma, a device emerging from ancient mathematics, tracks time by marking the sun's passage through the sky on a stationary object ("Archaeoastronomy").

Fictional though Noland's analemma is, moviegoers and film critics take matters of design seriously. Those with knowledge of analemmas have charged Noland's analemma with several design inaccuracies. Their commentary demonstrates that design is not merely a matter of surface-level aesthetic preference, but instead shapes and reflects meaning.

Posters to the website *science.blog*, for instance, have noted that the shape of Noland's analemma is inaccurate given his location in the Pacific: "Anyone who saw [*Castaway*] with Tom Hanks would now recognize the error in the analemma drawn on the cave wall as being too vertical. Hanks's character was stranded on a tropic island, and the analemma should have been nearly horizontal."

Meanwhile, contributors to a discussion on *NavList*, an online community "devoted to the preservation and practice of celestial navigation and other methods of traditional position-finding," take issue with whether Noland would have even had the expertise to etch the analemma onto the cave wall in the first place. One *NavList* contributor argues that the analemma would have required Noland be able to differentiate between "Local Apparent Time" and "Mean Time," and then to have known how to read the analemma within the context of these varying notions of time. These online discussions about the intricacies of Noland's analemma may seem somewhat nitpicky, but they actually illustrate the importance of intentional design. Whether within the film, in which the character Noland hopes to rely on precise measurements to track time, or outside of the film, where accurate measurements really do take on even higher stakes, the analemma's design impacts perception and conveys meaning.

Analemmas thereby illustrate the ways in which design impacts the very nature of the argument itself. Change the analemma from horizontal to vertical, and the record of time shifts; design the analemma according to "Local Apparent Time," instead of "Mean Time," and, again, the way we understand the analemma, and its meaning, changes.

Just as Noland's analemma provides an illuminating perspective into argument by demonstrating that design shapes meaning, it also illustrates how design intersects with context to determine modality. Analemmas incorporate, simultaneously, several modes of communication—visual, written, mathematical, temporal, and even cultural and religious. Through this confluence of modalities, knowledge emerges.

So, too, with academic arguments. Academic writers can—and often should—make use of multiple modalities for their arguments in order to convey them as robustly as possible, and also to reach as many potential people, each with different learning styles, as possible.

Websites provide an apt example of the value of multiple modalities. The People for the Ethical Treatment of Animals website, *peta.org*, for instance, argues for animal rights through multiple modalities, from photographs and videos to written arguments. Photographic essays, likewise, often argue by relying on the interplay between the written and visual. One of the most well-known examples of this form is James Agee and Walker Evans's photographic essay, *Let Us Now Praise Famous Men*, in which they argue through photographs and written text about the hardships endured by Depression-era tenant farmers in the southern United States.

Another more recent example of the value of overlapping modalities is a *YouTube* video that enjoyed some viral exposure in 2012, "The Ivy-League Hustle (I Went to Princeton, Bitch)." In this video, which combines written, visual, and verbal modalities, creator Nikki Muller makes the following arguments: "a college degree doesn't necessarily lead to a six-figure salary" ("Ivy League…Rap Pokes") and "[s]mart women are threatening to men and are expected to tone it down to be socially successful."

These examples of arguments using multiple modalities show that argument designs, as was the case for Noland's Pacific island location and the analemma, intersect deeply with context. Different contexts impact the choices writers make about how to most effectively design their arguments. An argument advocating for HPV vaccines designed for a print journal such as the *Journal of the American Medical Association*, for example, should include different components than would the same argument designed as a photographic essay of people receiving, refusing, or delivering the vaccines. The very same argument would again incorporate different features if one redesigned it, by turns, as a TEDx Talk, a print ad, or a public-service announcement.

As illustrated by analemmas, websites, viral *YouTube* videos, and print journal articles, the choices writers make about design shape the arguments themselves and are deeply connected to the contexts in which the arguments will be developed and delivered. Far from being a small matter for afterthought, design should occupy a central, formative role for academic writers as they construct their arguments.

Write Here

Outline designs for two different versions of a research report on analemmas written for people unfamiliar with analemmas. Your options for design platforms include: verbal presentation, website, scholarly article, visual image, or moving image. Or you can design using a different or combined platform. What different design features would you include in each of the two platforms?

ॐ ॐ ॐ

Written Modalities of Argument:
Scholarly, Public Scholarship, Popular Scholarship

Chapter 4 described how academic writing exists along a continuum ranging from popular to public scholarship to scholarly. Written arguments also emerge along every segment of this continuum.

Scholarly

Scholarly formats for written argument include peer-reviewed research, as in the examples in Chapter 9. Scholarly arguments of this sort use a full range of citation and research, as appropriate for the disciplinary context in which the text appears. Some written scholarly arguments are intended for particular readers, such as other experts in the field, while others are intended for a broader range of educated experts. The examples we read in Chapter 9, because they were published in multidisciplinary undergraduate journals, were likely directed toward a broader range of readers. By contrast, an article that appears in the *Quarterly Journal of Economics* is likely directed more toward other economists.

Public scholarship

Written arguments can also appear in the form of public scholarship, perhaps as an op-ed or blog. Op-eds (opinion pieces that appear in newspapers or news websites), for instance, rely on the expertise (*ethos*) of the writer, but do not have the same rigor of citation or the expectation for quotes, data, and research. One example is Chelsea Carmona's July 6, 2012 op-ed that appeared in *The Washington Post*, "How AA Fails to Support Young Addicts." Carmona, who drafted the piece in conjunction with the "Op-Ed Project," begins with this captivating sentence: "I was 20 when I attended my first Alcoholics Anonymous meeting." She makes the argument that "some of the techniques that work for adults are much more challenging for the 46 percent of patients at substance abuse treatment centers who are age 18 to 24." Her evidence includes personal experience, which might also be included in a more scholarly version of her argument but would appear so alongside scholarly published research as well.

Writer Insights

What formats or modalities do you use as a writer?

Letters, words, sentences, school essays, poems (deliberately stopped in early 20s: one must be a great poet—or silent), diary, letters, a short story (polished by editor, never published), exam papers, a play (read by a troupe, never performed), sketches performed for students by students, emails, Honours project, scientific articles, Ph.D. thesis, forum posts, personal blog (still going), Wikipedia articles and discussions, instant messages, conference theses, review, scientific articles again, paid professional blog contributions, media articles, molecular biology e-book (post-production stage), applied feminism book draft…some years later—epitaph.

~Victoria A. Doronina, Molecular Biologist,
Manchester, Lancashire, U.K.

Popular Scholarship

Written arguments can also appear in more popular forums, often distinguished by a more narrative quality, though they often still include research and evidence. For instance, in "The Case Against Summer Vacation," published in *Time Magazine*, author David Von

Drehle, argues that summer vacation has a negative impact on economically disadvantaged children:

> Dull summers take a steep toll, as researchers have been documenting for more than a century. Deprived of healthy stimulation, millions of low-income kids lose a significant amount of what they learn during the school year. Call it "summer learning loss," as the academics do, or "the summer slide," but by any name summer vacation is among the most pernicious—if least acknowledged—causes of achievement gaps in America's schools.

Von Drehle's argument includes research (and he goes on to mention studies by researchers at Duke University and Johns Hopkins University), but the research is primarily presented as summary, without citations. Von Drehle also includes a number of photographs throughout the article, designed to maintain reader interest and enhance the reading experience of the argument.

Visual Arguments: Thinking Visually

Visual argument involves the use of visual components to make an argument. Sometimes visual arguments might include what Susan Hagan terms "visual/verbal collaboration," where images and text work together to "clarify, contradict, or challenge common understanding." But visual arguments can also be stand-alone arguments comprised only of visual elements such as photographs or animation. And, visual arguments also include those texts that incorporate key visuals, tables, charts, graphics, and other infographics as a substantive part of the argument. While some disciplines such as Art or Photography or Visual Studies seem to be particularly close to visual arguments, visual arguments appear across all disciplines.

Visual arguments should be approached with the same considerations as discussed in Chapter 7 regarding visual analysis. However, visual arguments also ask that academic writers engage in the art of **visual thinking**, which invites them to consider the certain kinds of questions as they design visual arguments.

Visual options

Media options include animation, video, photography, and audio (although audio is technically not visual, it often accompanies a visual experience). Visual options also include charts, graphs, infographics, tables, and other visual elements. Those engaging in visual thinking will embed in their creation process a phase devoted to brainstorming and experimenting with various forms of media so they can choose which medium is most advantageous for their purpose. Digital storytelling, for instance, often involves a storyboard element, where the writer brainstorms script and media components in side-by-side columns.

Purpose of visual components

If you are designing a visual argument, the visual elements should serve a substantive function in advancing the argument itself. If the visual elements are solely a matter of enhancing reader engagement, then the argument is probably not a visual argument. Instead, the visuals should feature strongly as part of the argument itself.

Relationship between visual and written components

Do the visuals reinforce what the written text argues? Or, are the visuals such that they extend, challenge, or otherwise build on the written text? Another way of thinking about this would be to reverse the question and ask how the written text challenges, counters, or supplements the visual. A related aspect to consider is what the balance will be between the written and the visual. Will your text be mostly visual, mostly written, or balanced between the two? All of these involve choices that academic writers should consider as they embark on designing and constructing visual arguments.

Location of visual components

Choosing where in an argument to include visuals, both spatially and sequentially, shapes the direction of the argument. At what points will the visual elements be included and why? Where will they go?

Common Forms of Visual Arguments across Disciplines

Since visual arguments come in so many different forms, from advertisements to public service announcements, photographic essays to tables, we've included several of the most common forms: photographic essays, graphics, academic posters, and presentation software.

Since visual arguments are so varied and complex, however, you should continue to explore and create other varieties of visual arguments as you move through your academic career.

Write Now

What forms of visual argument do you have experience creating or encountering? What forms of visual argument would you be interested in exploring further? If you have generated visual forms of argumentation, why did you do so? What kinds of argumentative occasions seem to warrant visual argument? Why do you think writers turn to visual argument in some instances and not in others?

Photographic essays

A **photographic essay** is an argument that emerges in the form of photographs. Often these photographs are documentary in nature. Photographic essays can stand alone as arguments, or they can be paired with written arguments. An example of a photographic essay is "Strong and Beautiful," by Brooke Kantor, Helen Clark, and Lydia Federico. They have constructed a written argument along with a photographic essay.

The written component, titled "An Exercise in Body Image," makes the claim, "Our society lacks a significant space for body positivity. Fortunately, one area that has the potential to provide this space for young females is in women's athletics—in particular, the sport of rugby." The photographic essay that accompanies the argument includes a series of images, with brief captions, of members of the Harvard University women's rugby team (Figure 10.1).

HOT WON'T STOP BIG SQUAT MASTER
#feeling HUGE HEY QUADS Open Heart

BIG HUGE RIPPED

FIGURE 10.1 Images from "Strong and Beautiful," a photographic essay.

Being presented as a photographic essay separate from, though connected to, the written argument enables these photographs to make their own argument about athletics and female body positivity.

Graphics

The use of **graphics**, like the use of photographs in a photographic essay, can enable academic writers to construct an argument with particular efficacy. Graphics can be part of a written argument, such as the use of tables, charts, and other visuals, or they can stand alone. See these two brief examples of the use of graphics in visual arguments. In the first, Renee Farrar uses graphics as the arrangement for her poem, "Apple (a poem)," to make the argument that the icon for Apple participates in the disempowerment of the consumer (Figure 10.2).

Apple (a poem) | Renée Farrar

FIGURE 10.2   Graphic poem "Apple (a poem)."

The second example of graphics as visual argument demonstrates how graphics can participate as a critical aspect of a written argument. In the excerpt, undergraduate Benjamin Weia (Rice University) uses a chart for integral evidence in his argument that "bottled water is just as likely to have the same level of harmful chemicals as that of tap water, containing between 20,000 to 200,000 bacterial cells, and lack any beneficial minerals depending on water source."

Excerpt from "Do You Know Your Bottled Water?" by B. Weia

In terms of mineral composition, the amount of mineral content in bottled and tap water largely depends on source and treatment....

Three specific minerals important for a healthy body are calcium, magnesium, and sodium. Adequate calcium intake is important to maintain and restore bone strength for the young and to prevent osteoporosis in the old. Insufficient consumption of magnesium has been associated with heart disease including arrhythmias and sudden death. On the other hand, overly high sodium intake is well associated with high blood pressure and death from heart disease. The intake of all three of these minerals can be ensured by drinking water high in calcium, high in magnesium, and low in sodium. In fact, magnesium in water is absorbed approximately 30% faster than magnesium in food.

A comparative study in 2004 examined these three minerals in bottled and tap water across major U.S. regions. It concluded that drinking two liters per day of tap ground-water in certain regions or bottled mineral water of certain brands can significantly supplement a person's daily intake of calcium and magnesium (Figure 1).... While tap water sources showed wide variations in calcium, magnesium and sodium content, mineral levels of bottled water were more consistent from category to category. In general, tap water from groundwater sources had higher levels of calcium and magnesium than those from surface water sources....

> Weia includes the figure so that readers can begin to look at it, but notice that he does not actually refer to the figure until the next paragraph. This demonstrates how the graphic itself needs to offer a clear demonstration of the evidence or argument.

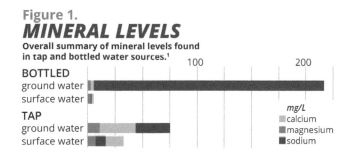

Figure 1.
MINERAL LEVELS
Overall summary of mineral levels found in tap and bottled water sources.[1]

From *Catalyst* (7), 2014.

> **Weia spends considerable space explicating the graphic, necessitating that the reader examine the graphic in some detail.**

Amongst the bottled waters, spring water consistently contained low levels of all three minerals, while mineral waters contained relatively high levels of all three minerals (Figure 1). Ozarka® spring water, produced in Texas, provides less than 2% of the three minerals' DRIs. In contrast, one liter of Mendocino® mineral water supplies 30% of the calcium and magnesium DRIs in women, and one liter of Vichy Springs® mineral water provides more than 33% of the recommended maximum sodium DRI. Based on these percentages, drinking bottled "mineral" as well as tap water from groundwater sources in certain cities can supplement food intake to fulfill calcium and magnesium DRIs.

Academic posters

Academic posters are a visual representation of an academic argument. These can be created using a software program such as PowerPoint and then printed (a large-scale poster commonly runs 36" high and 48" wide), or they can appear as digital posters, with interactive elements that users can control, like the Prezi presentation interface. Academic posters are common in academic conferences, where researchers create a poster and display it at what is often termed a "poster session." Although conferences across disciplines include poster sessions, they are especially common in disciplines throughout the natural sciences and STEM disciplines.

During a poster session, the writer stands by his or her poster, and other scholars review the poster and then can ask questions of the writer about his or her argument. Posters have the challenge of presenting complex amounts of information in readable, visually organized ways.

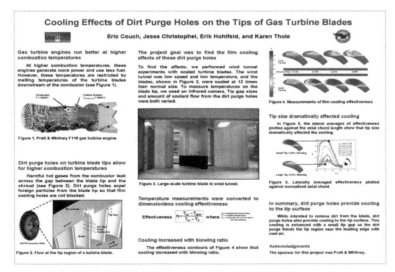

FIGURE 10.3 Academic poster design.

The academic poster in Figure 10.3 is so successful in part because Couch, Christophel, Hohlfield, and Thole have made careful use of white space and color. They included only the most essential elements on the poster, avoided crowding the information, and included graphics and images. For more information on designing academic posters, you can find a number of resources that provide templates for how to arrange the material and how to decide what sections to create for the poster.

Presentation software

Though **presentation software** might have been included in the section on verbal presentations, presentation software increasingly stands alone as an argumentative medium apart from the actual presentations that it might have originally accompanied. Designing the visual component of a presentation requires careful planning about how much to include on each slide or section, what order to arrange the material in, and how to integrate it with the presentation itself.

Several years ago, presentation software rarely appeared unless accompanied by the presentation. In that way, the presentation software was seen as a visual aid and did not have an expectation of presenting a full argument but operated as a supplement or visual enhancement to the main content of the presentation. Presentation software is now commonly posted online as an academic argument in and of itself. This adds a challenge in that academic writers must now balance between not adding so much information as to be overcrowded and inscrutable, while still including enough information that viewers can understand and appreciate the argument in all of its complexity.

Figure 10.4 offers an example of such an argument. Prezi is a cloud-based online presentation tool that has rapidly gained popularity in the classroom and in business settings. Tanja de Bie argues in her Prezi that communities serve a vital role in the educational aspect of MOOCs and also present several key challenges. de Bie's Prezi, therefore, operates as an argument without the actual verbal presentation component, even if she had at some point made a presentation about this argument.

FIGURE 10.4 Prezi presentation software example.

Visual arguments, again, can emerge in many different modalities beyond photographic essays, graphics, academic posters, and presentation software, though these are likely among the formats you will encounter throughout your academic career. Explore visual arguments on your own to learn more about how to effectively design and construct visual arguments for your areas of interest and course assignments.

Write Now

What are your experiences using or viewing presentation software? What do you think accounts for their being more or less effective? If possible, try to recall an instance where you saw a presentation that used presentation software with particular efficacy. Describe what this person did to make it so effective.

Verbal Arguments

As prevalent as visual modalities are for argument across disciplines, so too are **verbal modalities.** Having the opportunity to share arguments verbally through in-person encounters (even if in-person is virtual but live) provides academic writers with the opportunity to exchange ideas with others and advance not only others' thinking, but their own. While verbal arguments can sometimes emerge in a debate format, where a scholar is prepared to present and defend his or her argument at all costs, verbal arguments often have the characteristic of being exchanges, where scholars have an open mind to reconsider their own argument or take other viewpoints into consideration for future iterations of the argument.

Verbal arguments can occur at various stages of the writing and research process, from an interim stage where scholars share works-in-progress to a more polished stage where the end result is a verbal argument. Nearly all disciplines hold academic conferences where scholars present their arguments in a verbal manner.

Common Forms of Verbal Arguments across Disciplines

Learning how to present verbal arguments effectively requires attention to such components as body language, voice, and eye contact, as well as visual elements. Many good resources are available for effective verbal presentations. This section will provide an overview of several of the most common forms of verbal presentations that you might encounter during your academic career: academic presentations, elevator speeches, public service announcements/advertisements, and film.

Academic presentations

Academic presentations can appear in many forms, either through conversation, flash rounds, or in an extended verbal presentation of 10 minutes, 20 minutes, or longer. TEDx Talks are another manifestation of presentations, where speakers have a relatively brief amount of time to deliver an argument about an issue and, often, call others to action. Typically these occasions for presentation will optimize the presence of others through opportunities for interaction, either in paving the way for questions at the end, asking questions of the audience themselves, or otherwise engaging with the audience in an immediate, dialogic way. (While it is possible to engage with an audience through comment features on a written blog, for example, this is often a delayed interchange rather than an immediate back-and-forth.)

Elevator speeches

People in some industries, such as those involved in startups, business, or nonprofit work, might do well to practice what can be termed the **elevator speech**, whereby you imagine that an individual who has the power to finance your project is in an elevator with you. How do you present your argument in 90 seconds? While it may be unlikely that you'll ever be called upon to give a formal elevator speech, you may find yourself offering informal ones to peer reviewers or in the event of a class discussion.

Public service announcements/advertisements

Public service announcements (PSAs) offer a brief opportunity to convince viewers about your arguments. Similarly, advertisements seek to convince consumers or viewers about a topic or commodity. They are very brief verbal opportunities to whittle down your arguments to the most essential elements and make sure you are reaching as broad a range of viewers as possible.

Film and videos

Film and videos offer broad opportunities for arguments across disciplines. From feature-length documentaries to film shorts, one can construct an argument through this medium. Earlier in this chapter we referred to the YouTube video "The Ivy-League Hustle (I Went to Princeton, Bitch)," which makes an argument through video, lyric, and music. Throughout the text, films have been referenced in many of the example readings; take particular note of Morgan Spurlock's argumentative nutritional film, *Super Size Me*, that uses his personal experience as evidence (Chapter 11, p. 244–45).

Write Now

Using a recent argument that you have written, spend 10 minutes reflecting in writing on how you would transform it into a verbal argument in the form of a video or film. What might you include in your video or film? How would you construct your argument differently with this modality than you did for a written context?

Other Modalities for Argument

While the overlapping modalities, which primarily fuse written, visual, and verbal modes of communication, offer a large array of possible formats for argument, others also exist across disciplines and contexts. For instance, performance artists and choreographers construct arguments through dance and performance; musicians construct arguments through sound, lyrics, and music; architects make arguments through materials and structural design. Even silence or darkness can make an argument.

With so many design options available for arguments, you can at times have the freedom to be highly creative in approaching the construction of arguments, even as you also stay attuned to disciplinary conventions and expectations.

Transferring Argument Design

Chapter 10 builds on prior chapters by continuing our exploration into argument. Where Chapter 8 introduced a framework for approaching argument and Chapter 9 addressed the construction of arguments, this chapter focused on how writers design arguments. As integral as matters such as reasoning, significance, and structure are to argument, so too is design. The formats and modalities writers use to convey arguments have a deep impact in how their arguments are shaped. Writers must choose carefully how to design their arguments and what format to use by taking into consideration the writing occasion and the argument itself. And, while each design format carries particular considerations, writers also have the opportunity to transfer key skills and approaches to design across the many modalities and formats they may deploy.

Subsequent chapters extend our work with argumentation by focusing on, respectively, the integration of evidence and citation practices. These elements enable writers to fully develop their arguments and make them as effective as possible, whatever their particular purpose, structure, or designs are.

❧ ❧ ❧

Chapter 10 Key Terms

Modalities

Scholarly

Public scholarship

Popular scholarship

Visual argument

Visual thinking

Photographic essay

Graphics

Academic poster

Presentation software

Verbal modalities

Academic presentation

Elevator speech

Write Away

This activity invites you to transfer an argument currently shaped for one modality into several other different formats. Doing so will help you experience how design choices impact argumentation and how you can work to transfer the art of designing arguments across different argument occasions.

Locate an argument. Locate an argument that is of interest to you. It can be in any format you choose: a written one in the form of a peer-reviewed scholarly essay, a print advertisement, a YouTube video, or any argument you want so long as it is clear to you what the main claim is of that argument.

Choose two to three alternative design formats. Select two to three other formats or modalities, different from the one in which the argument currently appears, that you can use for this argument. For instance, you could decide to transfer a written scholarly argument into a song and a photographic essay. Or, you could transfer a YouTube video into an op-ed and a verbal presentation.

Whatever you choose, these should be design formats with which you would be interested in experimenting and which seem to lend themselves particularly well to the particular argument with which you are working.

Transfer the argument to each of those alternative design formats. Transfer the argument you have chosen to each of the other design formats. To transfer the argument, you will need to make decisions about which aspects of the argument should be transferred, and how. You may also be called upon to introduce additional elements for the new formats. If so, do so to the best of your ability. Since you will be using the work of another, even as you transfer that argument to a different format, be sure to attribute the argument properly to the original author at some point in the new format, indicating that you have adapted the original argument to the new format.

Reflect on your design process. Reflect in writing for ten minutes about this experience: Why did you choose the formats you chose for this argument transfer? Why did you think they might lend themselves especially well to the particular argument with which you were working? Which, if any, elements of the argument became reshaped as you moved from one format to others? What elements did you carry over or modify from one format to the others? What did you learn about designing arguments from this experience? What did you learn about transfer from this experience?

Share your argument formats and reflections with others. Share your arguments in their different formats, as well as aspects of your reflection (as relevant) with others.

Transfer Hub: Contribute your ideas and see what others have written at fountainheadpress.com/transferhub.

Choosing and Integrating Evidence:

Quotes, Paraphrases, Visual Materials, and Data

Pinpointing Chapter 11

Having explored in Chapters 8, 9, and 10 the various choices writers make in developing, structuring, and designing arguments, Chapter 11 focuses in depth on the hearty substance that drives argument: evidence. The evidence writers choose to advance their arguments, and the ways in which they integrate evidence into their arguments, enable them to accomplish the purposes they set out to achieve with their arguments. To provide you with strategies for *choosing and integrating evidence in transit*, this chapter addresses the following concepts:

- What is Evidence?
- Purposes for Integrating Evidence
- Questions that Shape Integration of Evidence
- Criteria for Effectively Integrating Evidence
- Featured Strategy for Integrating Evidence: the MEAL Plan
- Examples of Integrating Evidence

Chapter 12 will then build on these aspects of evidence by addressing citation practices surrounding evidence. For writers, citation works in concert with the selection and integration of evidence as a way of conveying to readers as robustly as possible a full record of their research and the disciplinary perspective informing their approach.

I was there entirely alone. Not a soul stood even on the road below.... I was literally astounded. The light began as a thin pencil and widened to a band of about 6 in. There was so much light reflected from the floor that I could walk around inside without a lamp and avoid bumping [against]...the stones. It was so bright I could see the roof 20 ft above me.... I expected to hear a voice, or perhaps feel a cold hand resting on my shoulder, but there was silence. And then, after a few minutes, the shaft of light narrowed as the sun appeared to pass westward across the slit, and total darkness came once more. (Michael J. O'Kelly, 1967)

*S*o describes Professor of Archaeology Michael J. O'Kelly of the moment he confirmed the local legends he had long been hearing about the mysterious illumination that purportedly transpired at Newgrange on each winter solstice. O'Kelly had witnessed a remarkable event at this Neolithic structure in Ireland where, at precisely, and only on, the winter solstice, for a period of approximately 17 minutes, a swath of direct sunlight enters through an opening in a small "roof-box" and "penetrate[s] down the passage to [fully] illuminate the central chamber." Tourists now flock to Newgrange each December to witness for themselves the annual winter solstice that so brilliantly marks the onset of winter (McKenna-Lawlor; Murphy).

The precise alignment visible each year at the winter solstice demonstrates keen Neolithic astronomical ability. Once thought to be exclusively a burial mound, Newgrange features a large, dome-shaped roof and a striking triple spiral design located at the entrance. Newgrange was constructed over 5,000 years ago, in approximately 3200 B.C.E., by a "farming community that prospered on the rich lands of the Boyne Valley." Nearby, "wattled huts" remain, providing evidence for how these Neolithic settlers and their forebears also hunted salmon, eels, and waterfowl from nearby rivers (McKenna-Lawlor).

Farming and hunting as it turns out, connect deeply to the winter solstice and help explain why those who built Newgrange did so with such archaeoastronomical precision. Some maintain that Neolithic farmers may have honored astronomical events such as the winter solstice and "worshipped...sky power" as a way to curry favor with the Gods and therein "ensure better food supplies."

Other researchers have found evidence attesting to the hypothesis that food might have motivated ancient astronomical alignments (Munson). Archaeologist Maria Reiche, for instance, has found such evidence at the Nazca Lines in Southern Peru: "The geometric drawings [at Nazca] are directed toward horizon points marking the rising and setting of the heavenly bodies…[They] most likely served to mark the sowing and harvest time, and [guide the more conservative] distribution of food during the dry period of the year." Likewise, the winter solstice illumination at Newgrange may have served as a harbinger of winter for the hunters and farmers, signaling them to prepare for winter, store food, and adjust farming techniques to accommodate the change in season.

Each winter solstice, therefore, the ancient Neolithic people of Newgrange read evidence from the solstice alignment to conclude that the winter had begun. Today the archaeological evidence from Newgrange and the excavations of other such sites yield evidence suggesting that the archaeoastronomical alignments may have been part of ancient traditions affiliated with hunting, farming, and food storage and preparation.

Exploring the evidence surrounding food and the Newgrange winter solstice actually generates a productive lens through which to consider evidence more broadly, as in the context of academic writing. Evidence in this broader context retains a metaphoric affiliation with food: it fuels arguments, sustaining, nourishing, and generating them, and thereby enabling scholars to continue learning and advancing knowledge. Moreover, and resonating with the Newgrange winter solstice alignment, evidence draws connections, sponsors unique alignments, drawing lines between concepts in order for writers to convey, reflect, and shape their insights, ideas, and arguments.

Considering evidence through the metaphor of food helps illuminate several additional and important features of evidence as well. One such feature pertains to the level of depth with which academic writers integrate evidence in their texts. Across and within different writing occasions, academic writers will sometimes examine evidence in an exceptionally in-depth manner, closely reading and analyzing evidence, digesting evidence morsel by morsel, inside and through, as when one bisects an apple. At other times, in ways that seem to more closely resemble a bushel of apples, academic writers will **integrate** evidence in more sweeping ways, glossing quickly over a large quantity or range of research, or by referencing in a text only in the briefest of ways another's work.

Another way in which food serves as an apt metaphor in an examination of evidence is that evidence should be **sandwiched** effectively within the writer's ideas. That is, when academic writers integrate evidence, be it charts, images, tables, graphs, quotes, or paraphrases, they should position that evidence within their own argument, providing material before and after the evidence that helps readers understand the purpose of the evidence. The sandwich concept enables evidence to be nested between layers of bread that can effectively frame and interpret the evidence for readers. The top piece of bread introduces the evidence, helping readers understand why it is being included, what the evidence is, and how it relates to the point the writer is making. The bottom piece of bread further explicates the evidence, highlighting what the writer wants readers to notice. Without these pieces of bread, evidence remains unframed (sometimes referred to as orphaned), and readers may not understand how that evidence is forwarding an argument or participating in the writer's larger aim.

And, variety is a crucial aspect of integrating evidence. Without variety, food would likely be somewhat boring; so too with evidence. Effective academic writing includes a variety of different voices and perspectives and offers readers a sense of the complexity and range of thinking for any particular line of inquiry. Academic writers integrate many different types of evidence, often from many different contexts. The best academic writers also deploy variety in the ways in which they integrate evidence into any given piece of writing, varying where they place evidence in the text and how they frame it.

Write Here

Although most contemporary people probably do not change their food gathering, distribution, or consumption practices across seasons as drastically as these Irish predecessors might have 5,000 years ago, it is likely that you do nonetheless make some such adjustments to your diet. Reflect for 10 minutes in writing on your own food practices as they are connected to the seasons. Do you eat more or less of certain kinds of food in particular seasons? Do you notice an abundance or scarcity of certain kinds of food across the seasons? Do you notice that you crave or desire different kinds of foods across seasons?

What is Evidence?

Evidence is the material academic writers draw from to advance their arguments. Evidence can take many forms, some quantitative (or numerical) and others text-based, field-based, or visual. Fieldnotes, survey responses, interviews, experiment results, photographs, passages from texts, graphs, tables, charts, artifacts, objects, numbers…any of these (and more) might be considered evidence.

Evidence can serve many purposes in an argument, from being that which a writer analyzes, to supporting an argument, or by offering a counterpoint or contrasting view to an argument.

Evidence is situated deeply within disciplinary and publication context. Readers in particular disciplines or in particular publication contexts form certain expectations—tacit and overt—about what kinds of evidence they expect to encounter and how that evidence is generally integrated into a writing project. Do readers of a particular writing project expect peer-reviewed scholarship or more popular evidence? Does your intended audience prefer long quotes or paraphrase? Are tables and charts customary for a particular context? These are all discourse conventions that shape the ways in which academic writers integrate evidence into academic writing.

The range of evidence from which academic writers draw falls along the kinds of research described in Chapter 2: Research and Writing as a Process. In that chapter, we discussed several different types of research: quantitative, qualitative, mixed-methods, and we also discussed primary and secondary sources. Academic writers choose from among these options and generate evidence for their arguments.

Another area that shapes the evidence from which academic writers draw is the continuum of secondary materials discussed in Chapter 4: Reading. In this chapter, we discussed how academic writers choose what to read, which is essentially their choice about what evidence to develop and consider. Academic writers read primary and secondary materials; secondary materials exits along a continuum ranging from popular and public scholarship to scholarly secondary materials. All of this together serves as the range of evidence from which academic writers draw.

>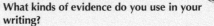
> ### Writer Insights
>
> **What kinds of evidence do you use in your writing?**
>
> As a historian, I like to employ two different types of "evidence" in my own writing. The first type of evidence I like to use is quotes. Quotes are easy to find and can help me "instantly" build theories in a reliable way. My second favorite type of evidence is anecdotes. When anecdotes are used carefully, they can help illustrate important points in a colorful way. Also, anecdotes help my readers connect emotionally to my scholarly thoughts about the people, places, and things of the past, which is pretty powerful.
>
> *~Derek L. Zboran, Writer, Rolla, Missouri, U.S.*

Chapters 6 and 7 also play key roles in establishing how academic writers work with evidence. Scholars conduct careful analysis and synthesis on data in order to make use of their evidence. Using these scholarly skills enables academic writers to transform data (text, images, artifacts, numbers) into evidence that forwards an argument or supports a position.

There are several ways in which evidence commonly appears in academic writing across disciplines: quotations, summary, paraphrase, visual evidence, data, and personal evidence.

Quotations

The use of **quotations** happens most frequently in the humanities and the social sciences. However, writers in the natural sciences also use quotes, especially in the popular versions of their scholarship. Quotes appear in many different ways, from partial words or phrases to full sentences or paragraphs. Longer quotes, those typically longer than four printed lines of text, are often referred to as block quotes. Shorter quotes are integrated directly into an academic writer's own writing and are referenced using in-text citations (specifically discussed in Chapter 12).

Summary

In Chapter 5, we discussed summary. Summary appears as evidence most frequently as writers provide a literature review of prior scholarship. Summary can serve as evidence for an argument as a writer perhaps summarizes prior research in order to build on ideas or develop new questions.

Paraphrase

Paraphrase involves borrowing the ideas of another and rephrasing them in your own words. Unlike quotations, paraphrases are not the actual language of others' work. Unlike summary, it is a particular moment in a text or work rather than condensing an entire project into less material. Paraphrase occurs throughout all disciplines.

Visual evidence

Visual evidence appears in many forms, from art and photographs and drawings, to charts, tables, and graphs. Visual evidence also includes artifacts of various kinds, either depicted through drawings or photos (as in scrolls) or in the form of objects, as in archaeological evidence. All visual evidence must be integrated carefully into the text.

Data

Data include the results of research, and often take the quantitative forms. Data as evidence can overlap in some ways with visual evidence because data can be represented visually in the form of charts, tables, and graphs. Data, which can include enormous quantities of information, are often interpreted and selected in order to serve as evidence for a particular argument.

Personal evidence

There is considerable disagreement about the use of personal opinion or experience as evidence. Some disciplines rely more extensively on the use of personal perspective, others not at all. Some writing occasions also make more extensive use of the personal, such as in blogs or op-eds, which are forms of public scholarship and academic writing. The personal is also becoming more apparent in scholarly writing as well. Composition Professor Candace Spigelman argues about the use of the personal in academic writing:

> Personal writing can do serious academic work; it can make rational arguments; it can merge appropriately with academic discourse. Indeed, this "blended genre" is starting to appear in…professional literature…Nevertheless, the problem of the personal remains controversial.

Interviews are another moment when the personal is relevant, as in historical writing or some social science inquiries. In one well-known example of the use of the personal related to food, documentary filmmaker Morgan Spurlock ate only McDonald's food for 30 days as research for his documentary film *Super Size Me*. Here's a quote from Spurlock citing personal evidence:

> [I]n only thirty days of eating nothing but McDonald's I gained twenty-four and a half pounds, my liver turned to fat and my cholesterol shot up sixty-five points. My body fat percentage went from eleven to eighteen percent, still below the national average of twenty-two percent for men and thirty percent for women. I nearly doubled my risk of coronary heart disease, making myself twice as likely to have heart failure. I felt depressed and exhausted most of the time, my mood swung on a dime

and my sex life was non existent. I craved this food more and more when I ate it and got massive headaches when I didn't.

Spurlock's argument, that McDonald's food is unhealthy is also bolstered by other kinds of evidence, but his personal testimony goes far in providing evidence for his claim. From an example like Spurlock's then, we learn three caveats about the use of personal evidence.

Use with other evidence

Academic writers generally combine personal evidence with other forms of evidence when using them in scholarly work. Because readers vary in their receptivity to personal evidence, it is likely best in most writing occasions to use it in conjunction with other evidence rather than as stand-alone evidence.

Personal evidence is not personal opinion

Instead, personal evidence is drawn from experiences and generally appears as narrative accounts of experience. As we discussed in Chapter 8: Framing Arguments, academic writers do have personal opinions, and it is important to reflect on and acknowledge opinions in order to understand potential bias or perspective. However, academic writers must ground any opinions in evidence-based research in order to construct arguments effectively. Ideally, scholars also are open to the ways in which the evidence they find might enable them to revisit and possibly change their own personal opinions.

Disciplinary context matters

While disciplinary context matters across many dimensions of academic writing, it bears particular impact on the use of personal evidence. Some disciplines rely very heavily on personal evidence (Cultural Anthropology, History) and others nearly always exclude personal evidence (Engineering, Chemistry). As with all such elements of academic writing, it is best to familiarize yourself with the discourse conventions present in each writing occasion so you can be sure that you are adhering to them or, if you are challenging them, that you are doing so from a position of deliberateness.

Write Now

What kinds of evidence have you used in your academic writing (quantitative, qualitative, popular, scholarly)? How have you presented evidence in your academic writing (quotes, paraphrase, summary, visual, personal)? Are there any other kinds of evidence you have used? Which kinds do you find it easier to work with? Harder to work with? Why?

Purposes for Integrating Evidence

Academic writers use evidence for a variety of purposes, many of which operate simultaneously in any given writing project. Generally speaking, academic writers across disciplines integrate evidence in order to accomplish certain goals.

Build on the work of others

If others have already made particular contributions to an ongoing area of inquiry, then you should integrate their evidence so that you can build on it and make your own contribution. Sometimes your contribution is to apply or extend or replicate, and other times it will be more along the lines of reconsidering or critiquing, or otherwise modifying the work of others.

Situate writing in relationship to existing work

Academic writers use evidence to show that their own work exists within, alongside, and against the work of others. Knowledge does not happen in a vacuum. Sometimes this work of others involves others in the same field, or in other fields. By connecting their work to ongoing conversations they can advance knowledge and also can demonstrate the significance of their research, insofar as it raises questions or speaks to concerns shared by others.

Transform research into evidence

Integrating evidence enables scholars to communicate effectively the research they have conducted. Communicating evidence relies on the author's interpretation, synthesis, or analysis of the evidence. Without interpretation, evidence is not used in the service of arguments; instead, it is what is known as "raw data" or "unprocessed data." Scholars must then analyze, interpret, synthesize, and otherwise do the intellectual work involved with examining evidence and using it to advance knowledge.

Shape, illustrate, and advance arguments

As we discussed in Chapters 8 and 9, arguments emerge from evidence. Evidence enables academic writers to draw conclusions and shape arguments.

Infuse credibility and authority

While personal opinion and personal experience can have a place in academic writing in some disciplines, scholars make use of evidence from research and from others in order to lend credibility and authority to their own work. They can show that they have considered the work of established and respected

---

Writer Insights

Why does personal experience help you convince others?

Living in Malaysia, my students come from different backgrounds and most of them learn English as a second language. It isn't easy for them to express their thoughts in English so in class I would show them my blog posts or Facebook posts where I write about my experiences in life or at work. Through my writing, I'd like to inspire them to write, starting with themselves and gradually about the people and things around them. A love for writing can be nurtured. Like a gardener tending to his plants, I am committed to unearth the writer within my students with tender loving care.

~Chiew yen Dwee, English Language Teacher, Batu Pahat, Johor, Malaysia

scholars. Importantly, however, even the most established and respected of scholars also use evidence from others.

Add variety

Integrating evidence enables academic writers to infuse their writing with the voices of others. Even if these voices appear in the form of summary or paraphrase, it nevertheless adds stylistic variety and diversity to a particular writing project.

Questions that Shape Integration of Evidence

Each writing occasion offers its own particular demands for integrating evidence. This discussion of questions builds on the questions provided for prior chapters, especially for how to critically read, how to analyze, how to synthesize, and how to summarize.

All of these moves together enable academic writers to make sense of their data and research. Integrating it into a particular writing project requires another set of related strategies.

Elements of context that help determine the answers to effective integration of evidence include your primary questions, your arguments, disciplinary context, publication context, and other matters of the rhetorical triangle described in Chapter 4: Reading (purpose, audience, author). Integrating data effectively into your own work will involve your asking and considering certain questions for each particular writing project.

Choose effective evidence

Does your research demand qualitative or quantitative data? Should you draw from more scholarly sources, popular sources, or public scholarship? Do you need fieldwork, images, interviews? Your line of inquiry and the purpose for your writing project will help you determine which kinds of evidence you need to include. Perhaps your evidence is visual in nature. As addressed in Chapter 7: Analysis, scholars often use visual evidence for their arguments.

Explicate evidence accordingly

How much explanation does my evidence require? Some evidence warrants extended explication and analysis, whereas other forms of evidence can be integrated in a quicker way.

Evaluate location of evidence

At which junctures in your argument is evidence necessary? Generally, writers integrate evidence throughout a writing project, but deciding exact locations will also be something necessary. One way of evaluating this is to examine where you make claims or assumptions that need to be evidenced.

Determine appropriate amount of evidence

How much evidence do particular writing opportunities require? Depending on the claim, length of writing project, and your purpose, writers make different determinations about how much evidence is needed. Some writers may have heard about the requirement of three sources. This is an arbitrary number. The amount of evidence you need depends on how much evidence is needed to successfully forward your argument. This varies across context.

Decide how to present evidence

When is it best to use quotes, paraphrases, summary, or visual? Is it preferable to use a table, chart, graph, image? Should you use a long quote or a short quote? Your decision about how to present the evidence is determined by what you hope the evidence accomplishes as well as considerations about the disciplinary and publication context in which you are writing. Sometimes it is advisable to include evidence in multiple forms in order to make that evidence accessible to readers with different learning preferences (visual, aural, written, etc.).

Choose credible evidence

How credible is my evidence? Evidence should be credible. Determining what makes something credible, though, hinges on writing context. If you are writing about the history and reception of a particular restaurant, then posts on a message board from the general public are credible. If, however, you are writing about the state of hunger in developing countries, then more credible evidence will be found in the form of government reports and scholarly, peer-reviewed research.

Choose current evidence

How recent should my evidence be? Some fields develop knowledge rapidly and writers are expected to integrate evidence that is as current as possible. Often this is considered to be evidence from within the past five years, though sometimes even more recent. Many disciplines make use of historical evidence, and the evidence in this case should be historical.

Balance integration of evidence

Do I have the right balance of evidence across my writing project? Effective integration of evidence hinges on having the right amount of evidence (not too much, not too little) especially as seen in relationship to your own ideas. This varies across writing projects. For a synthesis in a literature review, the balance will lean much more heavily toward the work of others. For many kinds of writing in the sciences, writers will also have much space in their writing devoted to the evidence. For some other kinds of arguments, such as an analysis of a text, writers should include evidence but spend more of their writing space articulating their own conclusions and interpretations. But for an original argument, writers often spend more space in their writing with their own arguments.

Criteria for Effectively Integrating Evidence

As with criteria in the other aspects of academic writing across disciplines, what makes effective integration of evidence in one writing context does not necessarily map onto all writing contexts. The National Council of Teachers of English describes the ways in which disciplines impact the efficacy of integrating evidence in a policy brief:

[T]he assessment of whether evidence "counts" also depends upon how a writer uses evidence to support an argument. Writers carefully select evidence based on their chosen stance, purpose, and audience. Then writers use their chosen evidence to warrant, or justify, their stance. In literary analysis, for example, evidence from a literary text counts when citations include specific details that support a particular argument about the literature and when the writer sufficiently connects the textual evidence with his or her stance. In historical writing, too, determining the quality of evidence is equally about how well the writer analyzes and interprets its significance.

Thus, what counts or what is effective in one context does not necessarily apply to all contexts. Still, although disciplines and writing projects vary widely in the kinds of evidence used and the way that evidence should be integrated, it is possible to identify some important criteria for effectively integrating evidence.

Use evidence accurately

While it's perfectly fine to include only portions of evidence (and in fact we must always make these choices), the portions we include should not be taken out of context. As indicated in Chapter 5: Summary, imagine that the author of the evidence is reading your work. Would he or she agree that you have accurately represented the evidence? If someone examined your entire dataset, would that individual agree that you have, to the extent possible, accurately represented your evidence? Accuracy also means that you have attributed the evidence appropriately and cited it correctly. Accuracy also means that you have not ignored counter-evidence or other data that would work against conclusions.

Accuracy of evidence is particularly important because readers rely on your conclusions and arguments by assuming your evidence is correct. Some disciplines, such as science, emphasize with particular significance the importance of accuracy related to evidence:

> Falsification in science is loosely defined as publishing or reporting misleading facts associated with a study, research or experimentation. Scientific falsification can be considered as: Falsifying data; Falsifying evidence; Fabricating data; Fabricating evidence; Plagiarism. ("Scientific Falsification")

After explaining more about each of these types of evidence falsification and citing some well-known cases of falsified evidence, the authors of this article offer an injunction against inaccuracy in scientific evidence: "Scientific falsification goes against everything that the scientific method stands for. It is unethical, immoral and dangerous. It is one of the worst acts that anyone in research can commit. It is severely punished."

Select evidence appropriately

Even as we accurately portray evidence, writers must also appropriately select it. We do this by selecting which evidence to include based explicitly on writing goals. A discussion about popular diet plans in the United States, for example, would benefit from including evidence in the form of both scholarly and popular sources to illustrate how much consumer research goes into the creation of diet fads. Such a study would have to especially consider which forms of visual evidence will be most impactful; the writer may have to choose between analysis of advertisements or nutritional science graphs depending on the study's goal. In quotes, we might use brackets, ellipsis, and abridgement to note specific components of a source.

Analyze evidence sufficiently

Evidence relies on a writers' work analyzing, synthesizing, interpreting, and explicating. The intellectual work involved with evidence rests on the extent to which a writer can show readers why evidence leads to a particular argument or conclusion.

Distinguish evidence from opinion

Academic writers certainly have opinions, but their arguments are generated with research-based evidence. Historian Elizabeth Shown Mills, for instance, describes the rigor that historians use as they work with evidence, and why it matters:

> As history researchers, we do not speculate. We test. We critically observe and carefully record. Then we weigh the accumulated evidence, analyzing the individual parts as well as the whole, without favoring any theory. Bias, ego, ideology, patronage, prejudice, pride, or shame cannot shape our decisions as we appraise our evidence. To do so is to warp reality and deny ourselves the understanding of the past that is, after all, the reason for our labor.

Mills' point is that historians, and researchers from other disciplines, must use critical observation, analysis, and synthesis as they consider evidence. Otherwise, they run the risk of treating evidence erroneously. While all humans have opinions, biases, and subjective perspectives, researchers must try as much as possible to differentiate these from the evidence they are using and be transparent about their own agendas, assumptions, and perspectives.

Contextualize evidence

As much as possible, sandwich your evidence in such a way that readers understand where your evidence is coming from and what the important elements of context are for that evidence. Introduce evidence clearly with what is called a "signal phrase." The Writing across the Curriculum program at Loyola University New Orleans describes signal phrases:

> Effective use of quotations requires that you include quotations in your paper in a way that allows the reader to understand the relevance of the quoted material to your own argument. You should never drop a quotation into your paper unannounced and apparently unrelated to the ideas around it. The quotation must always be embedded into one of your own sentences.

A common way to do this is to use a signal phrase that incorporates the quotation smoothly into your writing and, just as importantly, provides context for the material.

Very often a signal phrase will also name the author of the quoted material, thus serving at once to include the quotation smoothly and to attribute the idea to its source. ("Quotations")

Although they connect signal phrases explicitly to quotations, I would suggest that the idea of embedding evidence into a writing project in a way that introduces the evidence and describes its relevance applies more broadly, to paraphrase, summary, and visual evidence as well.

Relate evidence to writing purpose

Evidence must be related to the overall aims and purpose of your writing project. This connection is termed "warrant" under Toulmin's conceptualization of claims, as discussed in Chapter 9: Constructing Arguments. Different writing occasions demand varying approaches to evidence, but in general academic writers must work to explicitly connect evidence through explication, analysis, synthesis, or other interpretation. While it might on occasion be reasonable to add an image or visual without explicitly referring to it, most other forms of evidence (quotes, paraphrase, summary, tables, charts, figures, etc.) must be discussed explicitly as they are integrated into a writing project. Sometimes this means that sources should be recent, sometimes historical.

Attend to discipline and context

Different writing occasions carry different discourse conventions. In scientific papers, for instance, readers are not accustomed to seeing large amounts of quoted text. Similarly, in the humanities, readers might be less familiar with tables and graphs. Neither occasion excludes the use of these, but writers should be aware of the discourse conventions that define the particular writing occasion.

Publication context also impacts the evidence writers use and the ways in which that evidence is integrated. If you are seeking publication in a scholarly journal, you should integrate scholarly evidence, even if you also use personal or popular evidence. By contrast, if you are instead writing a blog post, you might be more authorized to rely exclusively on personal experience. Being aware of discipline-specific and context-specific criteria, however, does not mean that one cannot sometimes challenge convention. Some of the most exciting scholarship is that which brings in new and different kinds of evidence to a question that has previously been primarily addressed through a different angle. Often, though, those who challenge conventions in these ways do so explicitly and by addressing why the other, more discipline-specific and context-specific kinds of evidence have limitations.

Vary evidence appropriately

In an essay for English literature, for instance, one might include some block quotes, some shorter quotes, and some paraphrases. In a sociology essay, a writer might include a review of the literature, as well as more in-depth charts and data depictions.

Manage ratio of evidence to original content

Different writing occasions warrant different ratios between evidence and a writer's own contributions around that evidence. This also means that readers can discern with relative ease which portions of your essay are evidence from research and which are your own contributions and arguments based on that evidence.

Ensure credibility

Often, the writing context will dictate what is or is not credible evidence for a particular writing project. Sometimes personal anecdotes and opinions, on the part of the writer or from his or her research, are credible. Other times, writers need to rely on scholarly evidence that is deemed credible in that it has been published in a peer-reviewed journal or conducted with research methodologies that are valid. Much has been said about the credibility of online sources. Rather than generating a global argument about whether online sources are or are not credible, which is complicated by the question of what constitutes online sources (Online research databases? Blogs? Online newspapers? Wikipedia?), it might be more fitting to suggest that writing occasion dictates credibility. Read the texts of others who have published in your field and look to see what sources they have deemed credible for their research. It's fine to depart from convention, but always do so with full knowledge that you are making a departure, and explicate why you are doing so.

Featured Strategy for Integrating Evidence: the MEAL Plan

One strategy for integrating evidence is through what is referred to by many writing centers with the acronym MEAL, or more colloquially as the MEAL plan. The MEAL plan (which coincidentally also works perfectly within our ongoing food metaphor) provides a way of organizing paragraphs with evidence. The MEAL plan consists of the Main idea, Evidence, Analysis, and Link.

M: Main Idea

The main idea is the focus of the paragraph. Paragraphs generally have one main idea in order to be considered unified. Paragraphs might be thought of as individual, perfectly proportioned bites of food—enough to chew on and enjoy, and not so much as to be overwhelming or so little as to be frustrating. If a writer puts too many ideas in a paragraph, then readers have a difficult time processing the information. If a writer has one main idea, but hasn't explored that idea effectively, then a reader may be left feeling dissatisfied and the argument will not be sufficiently advanced.

E: Evidence

Evidence, in the MEAL plan, comes after the main idea. This entails the writer sufficiently introducing and framing the evidence, directing readers' attention to the important aspects of the evidence.

A: Analysis

Analysis occurs next, where a writer explicates more fully what is significant or compelling about the evidence.

L: Link

Finally, the Link enables the writer to link the evidence and analysis to the main idea of the paragraph and, more broadly, to the main idea of the larger writing project.

As with many writing guidelines, strategies such as the MEAL plan are meant to be a beginning structure which writers can further develop to fit their own purposes and writing projects. Sometimes, paragraphs have one primary piece of evidence, sometimes multiple; sometimes the analysis and the link are combined. And sometimes several paragraphs in a row will have the same main idea. Some writers will also opt to include in their writing on occasion a paragraph that consists entirely of only one main idea and nothing else. Doing so can, at times and when done so sparingly, be effective at drawing readers' attention to that idea.

One aspect that might usefully be added to MEAL as well is a transition at the beginning of a paragraph, rendering our acronym, more fittingly, T-MEAL. Transition sentences, the first sentence of a paragraph must accomplish several critical aims: to move the reader from what was discussed in the prior paragraph to what is coming in the new paragraph; to provide a topic sentence or overview of the new paragraph; and to connect the new paragraph to the larger claim of the writing project so readers can see how the paragraph is advancing the argument.

As an example of the T-MEAL plan, please see the third paragraph of Example 1, which includes annotations according to T-MEAL.

Examples of Integrating Evidence

This section provides examples of integrating evidence across disciplines. Since evidence is in so many ways like food, it seems apropos to use food as the multidisciplinary anchor to show how academic writers across disciplines select and integrate evidence for their arguments about food. This section contains examples from seven different disciplines.

Example 1: History

The excerpt comes from an article in a peer-reviewed scholarly journal about the use of taste in historical research. The authors, Gerald J. Fitzgerald and Gabriella M. Petrick make the argument that taste helps historians understand culture. The paragraphs show Fitzgerald and Petrick integrating evidence from a variety of sources: primary historical sources and scholarly secondary sources. You will see them using also a variety of formats for their evidence, from block quotes to paraphrase and summary.

Excerpt from "In Good Taste: Rethinking American History with Our Palates"
by G. J. Fitzgerald and G. M. Petrick

Good food writing can make the mouth water, the nose tingle, and the stomach growl. It invites readers to reconstruct a dish or a meal so that they may reflect on or imagine its taste, flavor, and texture. M. F. K. Fisher is probably the best known of the literary gourmands who helped spark gustatory imaginations and linked words to taste. In her book *An Alphabet for Gourmets*, she evokes the essence of a pea. "I watched the head-waiter, as skilled as a magician, dry peas over a flame in a generous pan, add what looked like an equal weight of butter, which almost visibly sent out a cloud of sweet-smelling hay and meadow air." In describing her own perfect garden peas she wrote,

> Small brown roasted chickens, the best ones I have ever eaten, done for me that afternoon…and not chilled since but cooled in their own intangibly delicate juices. There was salad of mountain lettuces. There was honest bread…. But what really mattered, what piped the high unforgettable tune of perfection, were the peas, which came from their hot pot onto our thick china plates in a cloud, a kind of miasma, of everything anyone could ever want from them, even in a dream.[1]

What is striking about Fisher's work is that she not only places the reader at the table with her, but engages all the reader's senses to evoke taste. To convey the perfection of the peas, she relies on the readers' previous experiences with the foods (and their imagination of what they could be), conjuring the sensuality of peas freshly picked from the garden, cooked for only the briefest moment in boiling water, and brought steaming to the table with all their vegetal sweetness bursting in our mouths. Although only Fisher and her table mates actually tasted the peas and knew the delight they brought and

Sidebar (left): Fitzgerald and Petrick here introduce a primary source: Fisher. They provide her full name and her book title as part of their signal phrase. They also show that they are integrating Fisher in order to illustrate their point about how food writing can "spark gustatory imaginations."

Sidebar (right): Notice that the authors choose to include one quote that is shorter and a block quote as well. They have inserted ellipses in the text, which indicate that they are omitting certain words that are less relevant for their point. Even though they have omitted words, though, they have not taken the quote out of context or misrepresented the quote.

Sidebar (lower left): After the quote, the authors explicate the words, highlighting for readers the exact parts of the quote that offer evidence for their claim. Notice that the quote itself is shorter than the explication of the quote.

From *The Journal of American History* (95.2), 2008.

while her description assumes a universal experience with taste that is unlikely to exist, her vivid descriptions and attention to flavor can evoke a simulacra of the peas based on readers' previous experiences, especially if those readers share a common gustatory heritage. Rather than arguing for some universal or a historical sense of taste, we are suggesting that reading and writing with a sense of taste, one that is both sensitive to context and experience and also infused with historical imagination, can help historians think through the contingent nature of taste and its historical meanings.

Transition and Main Idea: The phrase "historians of food and taste" forges a transition from the prior paragraph; the phrase "previous gastronomic experiences" both provides a topic sentence for the paragraph and serves as the paragraph's main idea.

As historians of food and taste, we find that we depend on our previous gastronomic experiences to try to taste the past. Whether we are reading a grandmother's cryptic recipes, a technical paper, a cookbook, tasting panel notes, or a dietary survey, when it comes to food, we try to taste it in our minds if we can, and sometimes one of us, Gabriella M. Petrick, even prepares foods to give us a better understanding of the techniques used to produce them and of their flavor.... Tasting allows historians to place the sensory experience in historical context and to utilize an often-ignored analytical tool: the body's senses. Just as historians of art or music use their senses to analyze material, so too can historians of food and taste.

Evidence: This list of details serves as the evidence for the paragraph, along with the evidence of Petrick preparing food.

Analysis: The writers now analyze the evidence, discussing what the tasting affords them as scholars.

Link: Lastly, the writers provide the link here: linking the evidence to their overall claim and to the paragraphs main idea.

However, using the sense of taste to investigate the past has its limits (we will never know what Fisher's peas really tasted like), but exercising historical imagination while attending to how people described past flavor experiences can help us approximate the nature of taste historically.[2]

In short, to understand a culture, past or present, we should endeavor to understand how a society feeds itself. It is the ubiquity and everydayness of eating that makes understanding it historically so important. The taste and flavor of food play an important part in social relationships, and a food's taste can embody meanings well beyond what is put into the mouth. It is only within the past ten years or so that food history—and the access it allows us to the history of taste—has become a field of inquiry. Many of the

Here the authors summarize the relevant literature that is mentioned again in a footnote at the end of the text. The sentence makes a claim about pre-1990s histories and the footnote provides evidence for that claim.

> Since they are building on Mintz's work more deliberately than on the work of the other scholars they mention, they take time to quote his argument.

books written before the 1990s were popular histories tracing the origins and dissemination of dining rituals, culinary traditions, and foodstuffs.[3] Historians who wrote academic texts about food in the 1980s, including Sidney W. Mintz, Harvey A. Levenstein, and Warren J. Belasco, asked complex questions about food's relationship to industrialization. In *Sweetness and Power*, Mintz explored the nexus between the metropolis and the colony through Britain's desire for sweetness. By focusing on sugar as an export commodity, Mintz examined how political and economic power was wielded in interactions between the colonial West Indies and Britain from the seventeenth to the nineteenth centuries. According to Mintz, the rise of the British factory system reinforced Caribbean sugar production. He explained that "cheaper sugar came at a time when its increased consumption was guar anteed not by the sugar habit itself, but by the factory world and machine rhythms which were the background of its use." Mintz concluded that readily accessible cheap calories (in the form of sugar) fueled industrial economies. Furthermore, this proliferation of sweetness ultimately transferred control over the foods workers ate to large corporations, thus transforming not only the British working-class diet but also the country's palate by separating the source of food production from the locus of its consumption.

[1] M. F. K. Fisher, *An Alphabet for Gourmets* (New York, 1949), 135, 138-39.
[2] For a critical examination of sensory history, see Mark M. Smith, "Producing Sense, Consuming Sense, Making Sense: Perils and Prospects for Sensory History," *Journal of Social History*, 40 (Summer 2007), 841-58.
[3] Good examples of the pre-1990 popular literature are Margaret Visser, *Much Depends on Dinner: The Extraordinary History and Mythology, Allure and Obsessions, Perils and Taboos of an Ordinary Meal* (Toronto, 1986); and Reay Tannahill, *Food in History* (New York, 1973). Notable popular food histories from the early 1990s include Raymond Sokolov, *Why We Eat What We Eat: How the Encounter between the New World and the Old Changed the Way Everyone on the Planet Eats* (New York, 1991); and Martin Elkort, *The Secret Life of Food: A Feast of Food and Drink in History, Folklore, and Fact* (Los Angeles, 1991).

Write Now

Fitzgerald and Petrick, like many academic writers, use footnotes in multiple ways. In the example, readers see them using footnotes as a form of citation (see Chapter 12) as well as a space to provide additional scholarship for readers to consider. Reflect on your experiences encountering footnotes. Do you often read them? Under what circumstances are you more or less inclined to read them? What kinds of readers do you think are interested in reading particular footnotes?

Example 2: Biology

The excerpt comes from an article in a peer-reviewed scholarly journal that is investigating the question, "What causes food hoarding in animals?" The authors have written a review of the literature, a synthesis of prior research, in order "to integrate what is known about the neuroendocrine mechanisms" related to food hoarding and food foraging. They make use of several published secondary scholarly sources and, in keeping with the purpose of a historical review of scholarly literature, they begin with sources that are from earlier in the twentieth century.

Excerpt from "Physiological Mechanisms for Food-Hoarding Motivation in Animals"
by E. Keen Rhinehart, M. J. Dailey, and T. Bartness

Since Wallace Craig is the person who has initiated the field of inquiry, the authors devote more space to his work, not only summarizing it, but also outlining several of his contributions.

Ingestive behaviour has a long history of study and currently has a place in the fields of animal behaviour, learning and memory, psychology, physiology and neuroscience. In 1918, Wallace Craig, an animal behaviourist, coined the terms 'appetitive' and 'consummatory' for the two-part sequence of behaviours required for eating, drinking and reproduction (Craig 1918). More specifically, he defined appetitive behaviours as motivated, species-specific behaviours involved in seeking a goal object (e.g., food, water, a mate), ultimately bringing the animal into physical contact with the goal object (Craig 1918). By contrast, the consummatory behaviours (from consummate not consume) are reflexive, stereotyped and are the final act once the goal object has been obtained (Craig 1918), in the case of ingestive consummatory behaviour—eating.

The primary purpose of this review is to focus on the appetitive ingestive behaviour of food hoarding, and to a lesser extent, food foraging, and attempt to integrate what is known about the neuroendocrine mechanisms controlling these behaviours.... More specifically, we will focus our review on the offspring of wild trapped animals that are considered 'natural food hoarders' because they are documented hoarders in nature, but have been studied in the laboratory, such as Syrian hamsters (Mesocricetusauratus; Murphy 1985) and Siberian hamsters (Phodopus sungorus). Occasionally, we will supplement this information with studies of laboratory rats, which are not natural hoarders (Pisano &

In this series of sentences, the authors cite prior studies that have researched various kinds of animals, such as the five studies of laboratory rats cited here.

From *Philosophical Transactions: Biological Sciences* (365), 2010.

Storer 1948; Calhoun 1962; Lore & Flannelly 1978; Takahashi & Lore 1980; Whishaw & Whishaw 1996), but instead carry food from the source to a safe place to eat. A paper by Wolfe in 1939 (Wolfe 1939) opened the door to the laboratory study of food hoarding by demonstrating that it was quantifiable. Several years later, Morgan et al. (1943) generated a 'deficit hypothesis' that continues to guide many hoarding studies today. The deficit hypothesis proposes that animals hoard owing to a growing energetic deficit that eventually reaches a threshold that triggers food hoarding (Morgan Stellar & Johnson 1943).

> As earlier in the excerpt, when the authors refer to a groundbreaking study, they spend more space, introducing the study directly in the text and summarizing in more detail the research.

Example 3: International Development

This excerpt comes from a scholarly book that is investigating the question, "How [will we] feed a growing global population in the face of a wide range of adverse factors, including climate change?" In the excerpted section, Gordon Conway, a Professor of International Development at Imperial College London, is examining what hunger is and how it is calculated. Specifically, he is discussing the spike in food costs from 2007-08. He cites the work of Anthony Young who has critiqued data that suggests arable land is increasing. Notice also how Conway integrates visual evidence into his argument, positioning it alongside his own ideas and explicating it carefully for readers.

Excerpt from *One Billion Hungry: Can We Feed the World?* by G. Conway

> Conway is building on the work of Young, showing that, like Young, he believes the earlier estimates about the growth of cultivable land are in error.

Yet these [data about expansions in arable land and crops] seem to be overestimates. The results have been trenchantly criticized by Anthony Young, who has a long and extensive experience of soil and land surveys.[58] He believes the estimates suffer from the following flaws:

- Overestimation of cultivable land (not accounting for features such as hills and rock outcrops when the maps are reduced in scale)
- Underestimation of presently cultivated land (illegal land occupation; e.g., forest incursions, not recorded)
- Failure to take sufficient account of land required for purposes other than cultivation (underestimates of human settlements and industrial use)

From *One Billion Hungry: Can We Feed the World?*, 2012.

A more recent [Food and Agriculture Organization of the United Nations (FAO)] analysis in 2000 accepts these criticisms [about flawed estimates of cultivable land] as possibly valid and acknowledges that much of the cultivable but uncultivated land is under rainforest or needed for purposes such as grazing land and ecosystem services. [59]

> Here, Conway adds his own evidence to the evidence from Young, drawing on FAO reports.

Probably the most telling data is the area harvested over time. Total cropland has increased by only 10 percent over the past fifty years, while population has grown by 110 percent. [60] Given the pressures to increase food production, we would expect to see much greater land expansion if it were readily available. The only exceptions are for oil crops (Figure 1.7). Soybeans and oil palms have each increased by over 300 percent in area and by over 700 percent and over 1,400 percent, respectively, in production over the past fifty years. Presumably this is a result of clearing the Cerrado in Brazil and rainforests in the Amazon, Africa, and Southeast Asia. Permanent meadows and pastures (the land used to grow herbaceous forage crops) have increased somewhat, by nearly 9 percent in an area from 1961 to 2008. [61]

> In this paragraph, Conway continues to build the evidence he is using to show that cultivable land has not grown. He introduces the chart next.

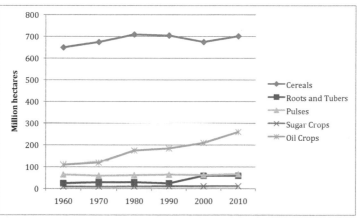

> Conway has preceded this chart with an explication of some of the figures, even explaining the one anomalous line.

Figure 1.7 Trends in harvested area for selected food cropss, million hectares.[62]

> Following the chart, Conway continues to discuss the prospect of creating more cultivable land. What follows are the footnotes citing the sources Conway uses as evidence in this section.

More land could be brought into cultivation by clearing tropical rainforests, but this would be at the expense of biodiversity and would add considerably to greenhouse gas emissions…A further factor in the equation is the large amount of land being degraded as a result of erosion, loss of fertility, and desertification.

[58] Young, A. 1994. *Land degradation in South Asia: Its severity, causes and effects upon people.* FAO World Soil Resources Report 78. Rome: FAO

Young, A. 1998. *Land resources: now and for the future.* Cambridge, UK: Cambridge University Press.

Young, A. 1999. "Is there really spare land? A critique of estimates of available cultivable land in developing countries." *Environment, Development and Sustainability* 1:3-18.

[59] FAO. 2000. World soil resources report 90. Land resource potential and constraints at regional and country levels. Based on the work of Bot, A., Nachtergaele, F., and Young, A. Rome: FAO

[60] Heldt, M. 2010. Science and innovation can help farmers meet global challenges. Presentation given at Investing in Science. London: Chatham House, 22 November

[61] FAO. 2009. Statistical yearbook, 2009. Rome: FAO

[62] FAO. 2010. FAOSTAT

Example 4: Engineering

The preceding example shows an author integrating a graphic and explicating it in detail. In Chapter 7: Analysis, we saw Anita Helle closely analyzing several photographs as evidence. Scholars also integrate evidence as a form of illustration, as in the example excerpted here, which is from an engineering article written by Parisa Pouladzadeh, Shervin Shirmohammadi, and Rana Al-Maghrabi. In this article, the authors are proposing a food imaging system that can use an image of food to identify how many calories and other nutritional elements are in the food. This is part of a larger inquiry into how technology and imaging can facilitate healthier living.

Excerpt from "Measuring Calorie and Nutrition From Food Image"
by P. Pouladzadeh, S. Shirmohammadi, and R. Al-Maghrabi

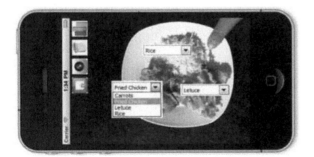

Fig. 6. SVM module verifies with the user the type of foods it has determined [18].

The authors use the image as an example, or illustration of how the interface will look to users. Demonstrating the interface as being user friendly and effective is key for the authors since this is a proposal argument. Notice that they refer to Fig. 6 in the text and describe it, so the image is a crucial component that works in concert with the text.

In our proposed method,... the feature vectors of each food item, extracted during the segmentation phase, will be used as the training vectors of

From *IEEE Transactions on Instrumentation and Measurement* (63.8), 2014.

SVM. For increasing the accuracy, after the SVM module has determined each food portion type, the system can optionally interact with the user to verify the kind of food portions.

For instance, it can show a picture of the food to the user, annotated with what it believes are the portion types, such as chicken, meet, vegetable, and so on, as…shown in Fig. 6. The user can then confirm or change the food type….

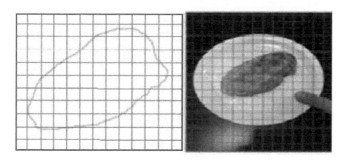

Fig. 7.   Methodology for food portion area measurement.

To calculate the surface area for a food portion, we propose to superimpose a grid of squares onto the image segment so that each square contains an equal number of pixels and, therefore, equal area. Fig. 7 shows an example with an actual food portion. The reason for using a grid is twofold. First, compared with other methods, the grid will more easily match with irregular shapes, which is important for food images because most of the food portions will be irregular…. Second, depending on the processing capabilities of the user's mobile device…, we can adjust the granularity of the grid…

Here too the image plays a crucial role as a behind-the-scenes demonstration of the food imaging system's grid methodology. Again, the authors refer directly to Fig. 7 in the text so readers can toggle between reading the text and viewing the images. The images are also clearly labeled, though, so that readers can see which images is under discussion at a given moment in the text as well as to make it easier for readers who are interested only in the images to skim through the text.

Example 5: Literature/Women's Studies

The excerpt comes from a scholarly article that is investigating the question, "In what ways did community cookbooks shape and reflect cultural mores?" In the excerpt, Ferguson is conducting an analysis of a primary source, a community cookbook from 1878 in some depth, selecting particular portions of the text to provide evidence for her argument.

Excerpt from "Intensifying Taste, Intensifying Identity:
Collectivity Through Community Cookbooks" by K. Ferguson

Ferguson first outlines the claim that these community cookbooks "reinforce various class boundaries." Then Ferguson introduces in detail, with contextual information, the cookbook that will provide evidence for this claim.

One aspect of class difference is woven into the very egression and distribution of recipes. The sale of such cookbooks often served to raise funds for the impoverished and destitute, but the cookbooks themselves were aimed at those with the resources to make new, even unusual, foods (the main culinary attempts for which one needs direction). They thus create and reinforce various class boundaries, both in their purpose and in their instruction. One early community cookbook, written in 1878 not by a large community but by a committee of three women, epitomizes this ironic juxtaposition. Profits from *The Home Messenger Book of Tested Receipts*, the first page announces, benefited the Detroit Home of the Friendless. The authors warn, however, that in using the recipes, the lady of the house should "*stand by* her cook, to see that she follows them" (Steward, Sill, and Duffield 1878, ii, iv). [14]

The authors follow this with a notional dialogue:

Do you understand how to make muffins, Bridget?

I do that, mum. I makes illegant muffins; they're just as loight, as loight, etc. (iv)

This (conspicuously Irish) cook's muffins may be "loight," the authors warn, but this is likely because they are "poisoned with baking powder, and they taste like saw-dust and overeffervesced soda water" (iv). One must, they repeat, "stand by" one's cook to make sure she performs each step correctly; this, more than cooking itself, is the proper role of the lady of the house.

Ferguson explicates in the next two paragraphs the quoted material in depth to show readers how this evidence proves her claim.

What is being instructed, here? Not the cooking itself, although it is presumed that a supervisor should always be able to do the menial task being overseen. Instead, it is the proper way to engage and to assign one's servants—to keep them properly in line. Although this cookbook, like others of the time, is made up mostly of food recipes, these textual instructions are surrounded by a reticulation of authority and propriety; how to oversee and how to delegate are often presented as more important than how to cook.

[14] Italics in original. The title page also notes that the recipes therein apportion "TOTAL ABSTINENCE."
Stewart, Isabella G. D., Sally B. Sill, and Mary B. Duffield, comps. 1878. *The Home Messenger Book of Tested Receipts*. 2nd ed. Detroit: E. B. Smith.

From *Signs: Journal Of Women In Culture And Society* (37.3), 2012.

Example 6: Sustainability, Environmental Research Organization

The excerpt comes from a magazine article printed in a Worldwatch Institute publication and reposted on their website. Worldwatch Institute is an environmental research organization. Their mission statement as quoted on their website specifies their goals:

> Through research and outreach that inspire action, the Worldwatch Institute works to accelerate the transition to a sustainable world that meets human needs. The Institute's top mission objectives are universal access to renewable energy and nutritious food, expansion of environmentally sound jobs and development, transformation of cultures from consumerism to sustainability, and an early end to population growth through healthy and intentional childbearing.

This excerpted article investigates the question, "What is the Slow Food Movement and what is its impact?" Brian Halwell uses primarily personal evidence from his visit to a diner to help define Slow Food and why people adhere to it.

Excerpt from "The Argument for Local Food" by B. Halwell

Stop in at the Farmers Diner in Barre, Vermont, and you have landed in the middle of a revolution, although you might not see it at first glance.... Twelve green vinyl stools line the white linoleum countertop in this 60-seat eatery.... A pass-thru window to the kitchen frames the cooks as they flip omelettes and pancakes and push burnt bits of hash-browns and bacon towards the grill's gutter. Not too different from the original diner that opened in this long and narrow building 70 years ago.

The place has its early morning regulars—a retired farmer, a couple of state highway maintenance workers, electricians, plumbers, and other assorted craftsmen—who on this gray winter morning are already cradling their bulky white coffee mugs by 7 a.m. Booths are illuminated by 1930s style pendent lights....

Linger a bit longer, though, and you find that this isn't any ordinary diner. The milk in the blenders and dispenser is certified organic, which means the cows it came from weren't given shots of antibiotics, and weren't given feed grown with chemical fertilizers and pesticides. It's also from a local dairy, which means it didn't arrive in a tank truck from a place most of the folks in Barre have never seen.

From *World Watch Magazine* (16.3), 2003.

The eggs in the omelettes are local too. The berries and flour in the muffins and pies are from local berry patches and wheat fields. The diner cuts all its own French fries and grinds all its own hamburger meat—the beef too coming from local farms. In fact, while most of the food that Americans eat travels at least 1,500 miles from farm to plate, most of the food served in this place was grown within 50 miles, and Murphy's goal is 100 percent....

> Notice that because this is a popular publication, Halwell does not provide citations for his evidence about how far most of the "food that Americans eat travels."

I notice that the menu covers feature pictures of the farmers who supply the food. (Who would have thought that the food you eat in a restaurant could come from individual people?) The plastic place-mat reads like a Who's Who of radical thought on the state of the modern food system, which is decidedly not about individually responsible people. I chuckle at the quote from Columbia University nutritionist and suburban homesteader Joan Gussow: "I prefer butter to margarine because I trust cows more than chemists." There is Wendell Berry's famous declaration that "eating is an agricultural act." And there's a quote from Murphy himself: "Think Locally, Act Neighborly." He tells me he won't hold it against anyone for acting or thinking globally, but it seems too complex to him. "Acting neighborly is something we know," he says.

> Halwell invokes the use of the personal voice here, using "I" and relaying his experience and conversations. Again, Halwell does not cite the quotes on the placemats because this is a popular publication format.

Write Now

Halwell's article makes use of personal evidence. What impact does the use of personal evidence have on you as a reader? What other kinds of evidence might Halwell need to include and integrate alongside (or instead of) the personal evidence in order to influence your perceptions about the Slow Food movement?

Example 7: Anthropology

Ethnography is a research methodology that is a subset of Anthropology. As a discipline interested in individual cultures and their customs, personal evidence is often utilized as a component to ethnographers' research. Ethnographer Brian Hoey describes the ways in which ethnographers use the personal as follows:

> Ethnographers generate understandings of culture through representation of what we call an emic perspective, or what might be described as the "insider's point of view." The emphasis in this representation is thus on allowing critical

categories and meanings to emerge from the ethnographic encounter rather than imposing these from existing models.

The excerpt comes from an article, an ethnography, of Alaska, specifically of the Arctic National Wildlife Refuge. Ganapathy pursues the questions, "What is the role of place in culture?" and, "What role does the Arctic Refuge play in understanding the culture of the people who engage with it?" Ganapathy discusses food as a particular aspect of her ethnography. Notice how Ganapathy blends personal evidence with critical perspective and other forms of scholarly secondary evidence.

Excerpt from "Imagining Alaska: Local and
Translocal Engagements with Place" by S. Ganapathy

In August of 2010, during the course of fieldwork in the village of Vashraii K'oo, Alaska, I was casually speaking to Jeanie—a Gwich'in Athabascan woman whose family I was staying with—about our recent berry-picking endeavors.[1] On the previous day, I had joined Jeanie and four other women to pick wild blueberries from the expanses of tundra surrounding the village. To access the most productive patches, we arranged for someone to ferry us across an adjacent river and then hiked for about a mile over rough terrain, picking plump berries along the way. Jeanie and I chatted about the previous day's outing, our bountiful harvests as well as the unfortunate berry-picking injuries I had sustained: sore knees, achy ankles, and an eye nearly swollen shut from a poorly placed mosquito bite. Jeanie also recounted stories from her youth of berry picking and being out on the land and mentioned that she now tries to encourage young people in village to maintain these activities....

> Ganapathy provides personal evidence in the form of a narrative anecdote about berry picking. Where she could have instead offered a statistic about how many blueberries are picked by Gwich'in Athabascan women, Ganapathy instead depicts the scene more vividly.

This brief anecdote serves as a starting point to further examine the concepts of "space" and "place" as well as processes of place-making from afar—and, more specifically, to consider how "local" populations engage with places that are, in large part, translocally constituted. Alaska is an ideal location for examining concepts of space and place across multiple scales. For Native communities in Alaska, surrounding landscapes have long been imbued with cultural, spiritual, and economic significance (Catton 1997; Nelson 1973;

> Ganapathy uses the personal evidence as a way into formulating her claim, and she also begins to insert relevant secondary materials as additional evidence for how landscapes in Alaska hold "cultural, spiritual, and economic significance."

From *American Anthropologist* (115.1), 2013.

Peter 1981; Thornton 2008).... The Arctic Refuge is one case in point. Adjacent Native groups, specifically Gwich'in Athabascan communities located to the south and west of the refuge and Inupiaq Eskimo settlements along the northern coasts, have engaged with surrounding landscapes for millennia in the pursuit of customary subsistence activities, seasonal migrations, trade, and sociability (Burch 1998; Chance 1990; McKennan 1965; Nelson 1972, 1973; Peter 1981)....

The Arctic Refuge exemplifies a place of translocal contestation.... The Arctic Refuge is sometimes portrayed as "America's Serengeti" (evoking colonial fantasies of distant exotic landscapes) or a place that is "too special to drill." The Gwich'in are presented through essentializing (albeit strategic) tropes as one of the last surviving subsistence cultures, whose members depend on the Arctic Refuge for food, clothing, and meaning in their lives. These narrative framings of the Arctic Refuge and the Gwich'in circulate widely. For instance, while at muliticulturalism festival in Stevens Point, Wisconsin, in May of 2011, I attended a featured lecture and photo presentation about a local resident's recent travels through the Arctic Refuge and his Arctic Refuge environmental activism. The striking images, descriptions of rugged landscape and encounters with bears, and portrayals of the Gwich'in as authentically traditional Native Americans captivated the attendees and enabled them to connect to a place and cause that would otherwise be well outside their frames of reference. Such narrative framings, in conjunction with extensive lobbying, have been successful in forestalling development for over 20 years.

> Ganapathy again draws on personal evidence to show how the Arctic Refuge is often framed as a place that the Gwich'in people rely on for "food, clothing, and meaning."

[1] The majority of my ethnographic vignettes derive from fieldwork conducted in Alaska between 2005 and 2010....

Transferring Evidence

As with many aspects of academic writing, integrating evidence affords academic writers across disciplines a wide variety of choices. Prior chapters examined these choices from the perspective of argument—why we argue, how we argue, how we construct arguments, and how we design arguments. But even the most efficacious decisions in these domains would be hampered without also making keen decisions regarding evidence.

Evidence, as with these other aspects of argumentation, is also one of the most varied. Writers can choose from numerous potential sources for evidence, from data and visual images to prior scholarship, primary evidence, and personal evidence. Amidst this great variety of options for what evidence to choose and how to integrate it, one habit of evidence writers can transfer across writing occasions is to always base those decisions on careful discernment of what you are claiming, how you are structuring that argument, and the format which you are using to shape that argument. Doing so will help your evidence be as effective as possible for whatever the particular context is in which you are currently arguing.

This consideration of how to choose and integrate evidence, though, would be incomplete without also examining the practicalities of how writers cite evidence. Citation practices, then, will be the area of focus for Chapter 12.

ез ез ез

Chapter 11 Key Terms

Integrate   Evidence   MEAL plan
Sandwiched   Quotations

Write Away

This activity asks you to work together in a small group with a round-robin of evidence integration so you can consider how you will transfer the art of choosing and integrating evidence across diverse writing occasions.

Form a small group, consisting of approximately four people.

Collaborate to create an argumentative claim. Together with your group members, collaborate on an argument that you can set forth, perhaps even one about an aspect of food (sustainable food practices, hunger and food, dietary trends, health and food). It might be the case that not all members of the group fully agree with the argumentative stance, but that is fine. Your task is merely to develop a claim for the purposes of this Write Away.

Refine the argument according to disciplinary perspective and writing occasion. Together determine a disciplinary perspective for the argument and decide details about the writing occasion. What is the publication context? What format are you using? What disciplinary perspective is informing the argument? These decisions are critical for the next step since they will impact the kinds of evidence you and your group members choose.

Assign each group member a different form of evidence to choose and integrate. Each group member should be responsible for choosing and integrating evidence towards that argument, but each group member should do so with one primary form of evidence. For example, one person could use personal evidence, another visual evidence, and another previous scholarship.

Using the MEAL plan as a format, each group member composes one evidence-based paragraph. Using the MEAL plan and the assigned form of evidence as determined by your group, each group member develops a paragraph of evidence. This will include choosing the evidence for that paragraph and integrating it as effectively as possible. For example, if one group member is responsible for including personal evidence, he or she will decide what kind of personal evidence to draw on (which experiences, how much, what sorts, etc.) and create a paragraph that advances the argument by integrating that personal evidence.

Repeat the entire cycle one or two more times. Using different arguments and rotating the forms of evidence each group member is responsible for, repeat the cycle one or two more times so that every group member gains experience with a few different kinds of evidence and a few different arguments.

Reflect on evidence and transfer. Reflect for ten minutes about the process of choosing and integrating evidence across contexts: What did you learn about choosing evidence and how it is nested within the disciplinary context and writing occasion? What forms of evidence seemed easier or harder to find and integrate? In what ways did the MEAL plan apply across writing occasions? Did you find it necessary to modify your approach in any ways? If so, describe these modifications.

Citing Resources

Pinpointing Chapter 12

Chapter 11 focused on how writers choose and integrate evidence into their writing. Chapter 12 continues addressing evidence by providing specifics for how writers cite the evidence they have chosen and integrated. Far from being a logistical afterthought, citation actually makes it possible for writers to pursue questions, advance arguments, and offer credit to those who have contributed prior research to any given field. To provide you with strategies for *citation in transit*, this chapter addresses the following concepts:

- What is Citation?
- Purposes for Citation
- Questions that Shape Citation
- Criteria for Effective Citation
- Examples of Citation across Disciplinary Perspectives
- Citation Practices in the Twenty-First Century: Digital and Visual Formats and Materials
- Citing Your Own Work
- Crafting Acknowledgments

With this final chapter of *Writing in Transit*, which builds on the features of writing in transit explored in the preceding chapters, you will now be equipped to continue strengthening your acumen with writing transfer as you embark on your own academic explorations, engaging with the work of others, contributing your ideas to ongoing conversations, and advancing knowledge within and about the world around you.

Beijing, China, features two exceptional archaeoastronomical sites: the Ancient Beijing Observatory and the Forbidden City.

The Forbidden City, also known as the Imperial Palace or the Purple City, emerged during the Ming Dynasty in 1404 C.E. designed to signify an alignment between astronomical power and imperial power:

> the Forbidden City...was approached along the meridian, directly toward the north celestial pole, which was seen as the very heart of the heavens.... [S]ubjects permitted to visit the emperor...were required...to approach his throne—the center of the earthly realm—from due south.

Mirroring the Forbidden City's meticulous alignment, the Ancient Observatory, built during the fifteenth century, yielded such accuracy that lead astronomer Guo Shou Jing could "establish the length of the tropical (seasonal) year with an error of only twenty-six seconds" ("Chinese Astronomy").

Curiously, these Beijing sites stand apart in some ways from the dominant Western framework often invoked to categorize archaeoastronomical research: the "'green' v. 'brown' methodological debate," so named in reference to the different colored covers binding two separate volumes of research papers delivered at the 1981 Oxford archaeoastronomical conference (Carlson, et al.; Ruggles).

According to the green/brown debate, green archaeoastronomers research European sites and, since these sites often lack robust historical and cultural records, tend to focus on statistics and mathematics. Brown archaeoastronomers, meanwhile, research sites in the Americas and, since these sites often have more extensive records, tend to rely on ethnography and historical evidence (Ruggles, "Lecture 7"; Dalgleish).

Because Beijing is neither located in Europe nor the Americas, sites such as the Forbidden City and the Ancient Observatory exemplify how alignments can be not only divisive and unifying, but also exclusionary. Where and with whom would those researching Beijing archaeoastronomy align their methodological approaches?

The answer, likely, is that archaeoastronomers probably move with more flexibility across methodological lines than the green/brown debate would suggest, and that categories nearly always have seepage. But, considered from this perspective, these Beijing sites are

noteworthy not only for their astronomical alignments but also because they raise important questions about research and alignment: When scholars cite evidence, whom do they align themselves with—and why? How do they make those alignments visible? What are the implications? Who gets included? Who gets excluded?

These questions signal the underlying, complex power dynamics that often motivate academic writing citation practices. Too often, citation seems a matter of rules, indicating how writers should format a document or whether they should use endnotes or footnotes. Fortunately, though, learning citation is not so much about memorizing rules (many resources are available to help with the rules). Instead, learning about citation demands a conceptual understanding of why writers cite, why citation styles vary across disciplinary and publication context, and why decisions about citation can have high stakes.

Scholars decide with each writing occasion whom to cite and how to cite, and in so doing align themselves with particular discourse communities (and differentiate themselves from others). Contrary to what the green/brown debate might suggest, scholars actually have numerous different discourse communities from which to choose and blend, and therefore can also select from among many different citation styles. Each of the acronyms and names depicted here, in fact, represents a different citation style.

These citation styles, though, and the choices writers make about which citation style to use for any given writing occasion, are not arbitrary. Rather, the values and priorities within a discourse community shape citation styles. Writers deploy a particular citation style so their readers can clearly discern the key bibliographic information they will need in order to extend, challenge, or otherwise modify the arguments they encounter.

While some writers may often write within one particular discourse community or citation style, most writers move among discourse communities, and thereby also use different citation styles for different writing projects, depending on the disciplinary and publication context of any given writing occasion.

Although citation styles and discourse communities can at times create division, as suggested by the green/brown debate, they can also be much more productive. Deployed in the most effective ways, citation enables academic writers to reach out, connect with others' research and writing, forge new intersections, and disrupt unproductive alignments as they explore instead those alignments that might be more illuminating and enriching for their research and writing.

Write Here

Locate a peer-reviewed article on the Forbidden City or the Ancient Observatory. Looking only at the references, hypothesize whether the article would be categorized as "brown" or "green" archaeoastronomy, as a mixture of the two methodological approaches, or as something different altogether. What scholars and prior research are being cited? What disciplinary frames do you see motivating the author's approach in the article?

☙ ☙ ☙

What is Citation?

Citation involves attributing the words of others in academic writing. Different disciplines typically use different strategies for citation; these strategies are referred to as citation styles, citation guides, or schools of citation. While there are many citation styles, and disciplines do not map rigidly into particular citation styles, review some of the more often-used citation styles, along with the disciplines with which they are commonly affiliated.

Modern Language Association (MLA)
Often used in English, Literary Studies, Performance Studies, and Art

American Psychological Association (APA)
Often used with social sciences such as Public Policy, Sociology, and Psychology

American Anthropological Association (AAA)
Often used with Cultural Anthropology

American Sociological Association (ASA)
Often used with Sociology

Council of Science Editors (CSE)
Often used in Health Professions

American Chemical Society (ACS)
Often used with Chemistry, Physics, and Biology

Institute of Electronics and Electrical Engineers (IEEE)
Often used with Engineering

Chicago Manual of Style (CMS)
Often used with Economics, History, and some social sciences

Although each citation style offers unique guidelines for how to cite, all generally provide guidelines for these three aspects of academic writing: document format, bibliographic citations, and in-text citations.

Document format

Matters of document format include specifications about where to put page numbers, title, author name, margin size, font size, placement of appendices, etc. It also determines what a writer calls the resources section (references, works consulted, bibliography, works cited, etc.).

Bibliographic Citations

Bibliographic citations are the materials that appear as footnotes or endnotes, or sometimes as a separate bibliographic section.

In-Text Citations

In-text citations are the occasions within the actual text (as opposed to the references section) when academic writers integrate evidence, quoting or paraphrasing others, or summarizing relevant research. Whenever this occurs, academic writers cite where the information came from in order to make their research trail visible to readers. Some citation styles rely on author last name and page number (i.e., Comer 220), others require author last name and year of publication (i.e., Comer, 2014). In-text citations are connected to the bibliographic citations; readers use in-text citations to quickly recognize the attribution without getting distracted from what they are reading, and then they can go to the bibliographic section to learn the full bibliographic information, should they need or want it.

Citation styles are developed and maintained by members of varying governing organizations of disciplines. For instance, in the case of the MLA citation style, a committee of individuals involved with MLA, likely academics from a broad range of institutions, will periodically examine and, as needed, modify, the MLA citation style. They then publish these guidelines in a guide called the *MLA Handbook for Writers of Research Papers*. These citation styles are updated as research and writing practices change, and new, updated editions emerge periodically. For instance, older editions of the *MLA Handbook* had very little guidance on how to cite electronic references because, at the time, few academic writers used websites or electronic versions of articles. Now, of course, guides such as the *MLA Handbook* have large sections on how to cite electronic sources.

The rules, conventions, and guidelines for citation and formatting, however, are not arbitrary. Instead, they are deeply embedded in the knowledge-making practices that shape disciplinary inquiry. For example, scholars in Biology may use the CSE citation style, which asks for author last name and year of publication to be included in the text whenever a source is referenced. In biology, it is of crucial importance to know what year a study was published so readers can discern how current the research is.

By contrast, scholars in English Literature often use the MLA citation style, where references in the text usually include a quote, followed by the author last name and

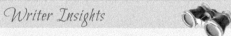

Writer Insights

What is important about citation in your discipline?

Switching my career from finance to stress management, I felt something was missing. I didn't know what…. Instead of figures, I write words now, and I learned to write psychological and neuroendocrine research in a clear way. I became such a fan I plan to spend a lot more time on writing about stress management. Therefore, I gladly invested many hours on the APA school of citation.

~Karin de Wulf, Health Coach,
Fabas Ariège, France

TABLE 12.1 In-text citation comparison.

Modern Language Association (MLA)	David Bartholomae illustrates the challenges students face with writing in the disciplines: "Every time a student sits down to write for us, he has to invent the university for the occasion" (273).	Ken Hyland conducted research on citation practices across disciplines: "Writers in the humanities and social sciences employed substantially more citations than scientists and engineers, and were more likely to use integral structures, to employ discourse reporting verbs, and to represent cited authors as adopting a stance to their material."
American Anthropological Association (AAA)	David Bartholomae argues, "Every time a student sits down to write for us, he has to invent the university for the occasion" (1986:273).	As Ken Hyland notes, "Writers in the humanities and social sciences employed substantially more citations than scientists and engineers, and were more likely to use integral structures, to employ discourse reporting verbs, and to represent cited authors as adopting a stance to their material" (1999:1).
American Sociological Association (ASA)	Students "invent the university" each time they write. (Bartholomae 1986:273).	"Writers in the humanities and social sciences employed substantially more citations than scientists and engineers, and were more likely to use integral structures, to employ discourse reporting verbs, and to represent cited authors as adopting a stance to their material" (Hyland 1999:1).
American Psychological Association (APA)	According to David Bartholomae (1986), "Every time a student sits down to write for us, he has to invent the university for the occasion" (p. 273).	According to Ken Hyland (1999), "Writers in the humanities and social sciences employed substantially more citations than scientists and engineers, and were more likely to use integral structures, to employ discourse reporting verbs, and to represent cited authors as adopting a stance to their material" (p. 1).
Council of Science Editors (CSE)	David Bartholomae (1986) outlines the challenges students face as they write in the disciplines.	Ken Hyland (1999) identifies different citation practices across the humanities, social sciences, sciences, and engineering.
American Chemical Society (ACS)	Students face many challenges trying to figure out how to write within disciplines (Bartholomae, 1986).	Scholars in different disciplines deploy different citation practices (Hyland, 1999).
Institute of Electronics and Electrical Engineers (IEEE)	Students face many challenges learning how to write within disciplines [1].	Disciplinary discourse conventions shape citation practices [1].
Chicago Manual of Style (CMS)	David Bartholomae illustrates the challenges students face writing in the disciplines.[1]	Ken Hyland's research demonstrates divergences in citation practices across disciplinary context.[1]

page number specified in the parenthetical citation. While the year of publication matters, and is included in the works cited at the end of a paper, scholars affiliated with MLA are often interested in language and words, and therefore emphasize quotation and page numbers. Moreover, scholars in biology do not normally include quotations in their academic writing; it is much more customary for them to summarize others' research findings and then include the author last name and year of publication.

To briefly illustrate in-text citation and how it shapes knowledge making, Table 12.1 offers the same two sentences as they might appear in several different citation systems.

Please note that Table 12.1 offers only a general sense of in-text citations. Citation styles shift across time, and particular contexts change the ways in-text citation looks. Some publishing houses also create "in-house" citation styles that are geared toward either simplifying or standardizing citations across multiple texts. Writers should also become familiar with citation style guidelines for block quotes (defined differently according to citation style, but essentially larger portions of quotes). And, in-text citations in MLA, as another example, change with or without signal phrases and depending on whether a citation is the first or a subsequent reference to a particular resource (see Questions that Shape Citation for more discussion about this). Finally, individual writers may choose from a variety of options for how to frame a citation, even within a citation style.

Still, as these examples illustrate, citation styles are quite varied and emerge from a set of practices that reflect the way knowledge is created among various disciplines.

Write Now

Which citation styles have you used for your research and writing? What do you find challenging about citation? In what writing occasions have you found citation to be most valuable?

Purposes for Citation

Chapter 11 discussed why academic writers integrate evidence; this chapter extends those ideas by discussing why academic writers cite that evidence. The purposes for citing the work of others all enable academic writers to advance knowledge.

Map for other scholars

Academic writers read others' research so they can build, expand, adapt, modify, reconsider, or otherwise make use of it for their own research. As academic writers read others' research, they rely on those academic writers to provide bibliographic and citation information so that they too can then build, respond, counter, or modify those ideas as well. Sometimes readers use your citations in order just to get a fuller sense of the shape of research in a particular field.

Citations can reveal a considerable amount about your project; they can communicate to readers what disciplinary perspective you are using. They also, in a collective way, work to bring certain research into more prominence than other research. If enough scholars cite a particular person's research or a particular research paper, then that person and his or her work become more central to research in that field. After time, one notices that, if a scholar is working on a certain subject, he or she is likely to cite a particularly prominent scholar or important research. Some disciplines refer to this as impact, meaning how significant the impact of that particular research has been. Higher impact means that more people have cited that scholar's work. Some research databases even provide statistics on how many others have cited a particular text.

Consistency for readers

Adhering to a sanctioned citation style, one which readers are likely accustomed to, enables readers to process the research more readily. It would be highly distracting for readers if they had to learn a new style of citation when they encountered each new text. Busy researchers come to recognize what citations look like and they can quickly find what they are looking for in others' research.

Acknowledge others' work

When you cite properly, you are acknowledging the work of others. Most people want to be recognized for the work they have done, and in research that is no different. Citing the work of others enables you to engage ethically by awarding them credit and recognizing their contributions. In the same way, when others cite you, they will be recognizing your contributions.

Avoid plagiarism

Plagiarism is using the work of others without attributing it. This includes words, ideas, images, visuals, audio recordings, music—anything that is the work of someone else. Academic writing is reliant on creating a community of high ethics so that researchers build on the work of others rather than steal from the work of others. Citing properly enables academic writers to attribute what is the work of others and to differentiate that from their own research contributions. Improper or absent citation is plagiarism—stealing. It carries with it severe consequences, including academic suspension or expulsion at many campuses. In academic communities, plagiarism also has severe consequences, including professional loss of career and public humiliation.

Write Now

Imagine a circumstance where you learned that someone else had plagiarized your writing. How would you feel about someone using your work without attributing it to you? What impacts do you think plagiarism has on authors?

Differentiate others' ideas from your own

Citations within the text signal to readers that you are using the work of others. That which is not cited is understood to be your contribution to research. Scholars want to differentiate their ideas from others' ideas so that it is clear how their writing projects are building and advancing knowledge.

Questions that Shape Citation

Don't believe you need to memorize the specific rules for various styles of citation—there are too many specifics and they change so frequently that it would be challenging to stay up to date. However, gaining a familiarity with schools of citation will help you approach citation in your own academic writing. Beyond that, these questions will help you determine which style of citation to use for a particular writing project.

Disciplinary context

What is the disciplinary context of your project? Some disciplines use multiple citation styles, while some rely primarily on a single style. As you encounter writing projects in a discipline, familiarize yourself with citation styles commonly deployed in that discipline. Most libraries affiliated with postsecondary education provide guides that specify which disciplines typically follow which citation style.

Publication context

What is the publication context within which you write? Publication context impacts the citation style as well, in part in terms of how popular or academic the context is. Editors of scholarly journals will also tell authors which citation style to use; these are often found in a section on the journal website labeled author guidelines or submission guidelines. Some journals even create individual citation styles.

Citation style

Has a citation style been specified for your project? Most professors will let you know what citation style you should use for a particular writing project. If you are unsure, just ask.

> ### *Writer Insights*
>
> **Why is citation important in your field?**
>
> As a technical writer, I rely heavily on style guides to ensure that my writing is interchangeable with the writing of others on my team. When our writings are merged together into one user manual, our styles, grammar, and voices need to appear as one. This may sound difficult to achieve, but its success lies in the preparation. The technical writing field frequently relies on the Chicago Manual of Style, and each project will then set additional style guidelines relevant to the company or industry we are working with (healthcare, manufacturing, etc.). These additional style guides may address acronyms and their use or colloquial terms.
>
> ~Stacey Wagner, Software Technical Writer,
> Seattle, Washington, U.S.

Resources

What kinds of resources are you citing? Each citation style provides guidelines for how to cite print resources, digital resources, and visual resources. They also often provide guidelines for citing a variety of other kinds of resources, such as performances, archives, interviews, and surveys. Be aware that each different type of resource usually carries with it a slightly different citation structure. As you work with different types of resources and evidence, review the citation styles for those specific types of resources.

Citation guides

What citation guides do you plan to use? Once you know which citation style to use, you'll want to locate one or more resources to use in following that citation style. There are numerous resources available for citing the works of others, and more continue to emerge.

Citation style guides

Each citation style has an official style guide, often in print and online. MLA, for instance, publishes its guidelines in the *MLA Handbook for Writers of Research Papers*. The Chicago citation style publishes its guidelines in the *Chicago Manual of Style*. These style guides provide the most current and official guidelines. Be sure, though, to secure the most recent edition of the style guide since that will include the most up-to-date and accurate information.

Library and writing center websites

Most libraries and writing centers offer guidelines for citing the work of others; many of these are available publicly online. Beware that not all websites are updated, though, to reflect new editions of citation styles, so as you use these resources, look to see when the site was updated and try to discern how reliable the site is. For more on the reliability of sources, see Chapter 11: Choosing and Integrating Evidence.

Research and library databases

Many research databases (i.e., JSTOR, Google Scholar, ScienceDirect, etc.) will have an icon on the page near an article that enables a citation pop-up and provides options for various styles of citation, which you can then copy and paste into your document. Beware, however, that not all research databases provide accurate citations, so be sure to proofread them in consultation with a more official citation style guide.

Citation management software

These software programs enable you to enter bibliographic information into the program so that it stores your sources in an organized manner. Many of these programs, such as Endnote or Zotero, can also generate citations in the citation style you specify. As with research and library databases, these programs are not always accurate with the citations they generate; sometimes they do not include pertinent information, and other times, since they are reliant on user input, they include inaccurate information. Always proofread if you use a bibliographic citation manager.

Amount of referenced material

How much material from a particular reference are you citing? If you are quoting a larger portion of text, you would use what is termed a block quote. Block quotes are defined differently across citation style. For instance, in ASA, block quotations are any quotation longer than 40 words. ASA asks writers to set block quotes apart from the text and single space them. MLA, however, defines block quotations as more than four lines of prose or three lines of verse. MLA asks writers to indicate block quotations by indenting the block quote one inch from the margin and double spacing it along with the rest of the text.

The amount of material you cite also impacts whether you will use a particular page number for a citation (if you quote or paraphrase from one page), or if you are summarizing an entire article, in which case you instead refer to the entire reference without a page number.

Signal phrases

Have you included an appropriate signal phrase before a citation? Some citation styles provide different guidelines for in-text citation depending on whether you use a signal phrase when you integrate a reference within the text. **Signal phrases,** as discussed in the Fitzgerald and Petrick example in Chapter 11: Choosing and Integrating Evidence, explicitly name the author and/or the text within the framing material.

> **MLA In-Text Citation, with Signal Phrase**
> David Bartholomae illustrates the challenges students face with writing in the disciplines: "Every time a student sits down to write for us, he has to invent the university for the occasion" (273).

However, writers sometimes choose not to use a signal phrase, and in these cases the in-text citation must therefore include the author and page number in the parenthetical citation so readers can still identify the resource.

> **MLA In-Text Citation, without a Signal Phrase**
> Students face many challenges when writing. Among them is that they need to "invent the university for the occasion" (Bartholomae 273).

In some disciplinary and citation style contexts, it is exceedingly rare to use signal phrases. Please review the discourse conventions for the context in which you are writing to get a sense of how writers handle signal phrases.

First and subsequent reference

Is this citation the first time I've referenced this source, or is it a subsequent reference? Some citation styles shift guidelines depending on whether it is the first or a subsequent reference to a resource. For instance, in MLA, the first time a writer refers to a resource, he or she uses the resource's first and last name.

MLA In-Text Citation, first reference to a resource

David Bartholomae illustrates the challenges students face with writing in the disciplines, explaining, "Every time a student sits down to write for us, he has to invent the university for the occasion" (273).

However, the signal phrase looks different if a writer has already referred to the reference at some point in the text. In this case, the writer refers to Bartholomae only by last name (unless the writing project includes multiple resources by authors with the same last name, and the first initial is needed in order to avoid reader confusion).

MLA In-Text Citation, second or subsequent reference to a resource

Bartholomae illustrates the challenges students face with writing in the disciplines, explaining, "Every time a student sits down to write for us, he has to invent the university for the occasion" (273).

In some disciplinary and citation style contexts, it is exceedingly rare (or even forbidden) to use author first names. Please review the discourse conventions for the context in which you are writing to get a sense of how writers handle multiple references to the same resource within a text.

Criteria for Effective Citation

While the previous chapters often included several criteria regarding efficacy, there really are only two criteria for effectively citing resources.

Accurate

Whichever style of citation you choose, be sure you are using it accurately. Check and double check, and allow time for it. Avoid waiting until the end of a writing project to cite things because you may forget where you located certain information.

Accurate citations should include the correct scholar, bibliographic information, and text. Find out for certain what the year of publication is and make sure you are spelling the author's name correctly. Be sure to attribute ideas to the correct author.

The correct format according to the citation style, including location of the citation for in-text citations, must be utilized. While you may think it shouldn't matter whether a comma appears inside quotes or whether the year of publication appears after an author's name or at the end of a reference, these matters are important in helping provide consistency among a community of researchers so they can read one another's work without being distracted by how to find the information they need.

Appropriate for the writing occasion

Make sure you have chosen a style of citation that is appropriate for the given context of the writing project. Your professor will likely tell you what style of citation to use. If not, choose one that matches similar writing in that field. The importance of attending to discourse conventions in the context in which you are writing is further illustrated in the next section, which discusses citation practices in online publication platforms.

Examples of Citation across Disciplinary Perspectives

To illustrate how citation styles vary and the impact they have on academic writing, this section provides examples of citation styles, many of which cross disciplinary contexts:

- Institute of Electrical and Electronics Engineers (IEEE), Physics
- American Psychological Association (APA), Information Science
- Modern Language Association (MLA), English Literature
- Chicago Manual of Style (CMS), History of Science
- American Chemical Society (ACS), Chemistry
- American Anthropological Association (AAA), Archaeology
- American Sociological Association (ASA), Sociology
- Chicago Manual of Style (CMS), with Digital Resources Art
- Chicago Manual of Style (CMS), with Images, Art

As you explore these different examples, keep in mind that citation guidelines may have shifted since the time when a particular author was preparing his or her manuscript. Thus, these examples are not necessarily intended to show you how to cite so much as to help you learn why people cite, what citation entails, and how to locate the resources that will enable you to accurately and appropriately cite the work of others. Keep in mind as well that hardly any citation style is exclusively connected to one particular discipline. For example, Chemists might often use ACS, but they are also likely to use other citation styles as well, such as APA or CSE. Consider these examples, then, as a beginning point for you to consider how academic writers approach citation and how citation looks across contexts and disciplines.

Example 1: Institute of Electrical and Electronics Engineers (IEEE), Physics

In this example, Physicist Sidney Redner is pursuing the question, "how often is a paper cited?" He examines the impact factor of citation, and how that impact, or frequency of citation, is calculated. Faculty gain more prestige if they have an article that is distributed and cited more widely, so Redner is researching how papers get distributed and what the implications are of that popularity. He is using the IEEE citation style, primarily because he is publishing it in a journal that asks for that citation style, but also because he is a faculty member in Physics, which makes use of IEEE at times.

Excerpt from "How Popular is Your Paper? An Empirical Study of the Citation Distribution" by S. Redner

Redner uses brackets with the numbers 1 and 2 to show that he is referring to research in references 1 and 2, as indicated in his references section. If readers want to read that research, they can then go to the references section and find items 1 and 2.

Redner names the study and the author in a signal phrase. Notice that Redner includes citations right after the author's name, a feature of IEEE.

I consider a question which is of relevance to those for whom scientific publication is a primary means of scholarly communication. Namely, how often is a paper cited? While the average or total number of citations are often quoted anecdotally and tabulations of highly-cited papers exist [1,2], the focus of this work is on the more fundamental distribution of citations, namely, the number of papers which have been cited a total of x times, $N(x)$. In spite of the fact that many academics are obliged to document their citations for merit-based considerations, there have been only a few scientific investigations on quantifying citations or related measures of scientific productivity. In a 1957 study based on the publication record of the scientific research staff at Brookhaven National Laboratory, Shockley [3] claimed that the scientific publication rate is described by a log-normal distribution. Much more recently, Laherrere and Sornette [4] have presented numerical evidence, based on data of the 1120 most-cited physicists from 1981 through June 1997, that the citation distribution of individual authors has a stretched exponential form, $N(x) \propto \exp[-(x/x0)\,\beta]$ with $\beta \approx 0.3$. Both papers give qualitative justifications for their assertions which are based on plausible general principles; however, these arguments do not provide specific numerical predictions. Here, the citation distribution of scientific publications based on two relatively large data sets is investigated [5].

Notice that the references from the end of Redner's paper include some discursive information as well as citations. Citations appear with the author's first initial and then the last name.

IEEE does not call for article titles, and it makes extensive use of abbreviations. For instance, item 3 is citing an article written by William Shockley titled "On the Statistics of Individual Variations of Productivity in Research Laboratories." It appeared in the proceedings of the IRE (Institute of Radio Engineers).

[1] See e.g., Science Citation Index Journal Citation Reports (Institute for Scientific Information, Philadelphia) for annual lists of top-cited journals and articles (web site: http://www.isinet.com/welcome.html).

[2] For example, current lists of top-cited articles in high-energy physics are maintained by the SPIRES High-Energy Physics Database at SLAC (web site http://www.slac.stanford.edu/find/top40.html).

[3] W. Shockley, Proc. IRE 45, 279 (1957).

[4] J. Laherrere and D. Sornette, cond-mat/9801293.

[5] The PRD data was provided by H. Galic from the SPIRES Database. The ISI data was provided by D. Pendlebury and H. Small of the Institute for Scientific Information. These two data sets and related citation data are available from my web site http://physics.bu.edu/~redner.

From *The European Physical Journal B-Condensed Matter and Complex Systems* (4.2), 1998.

Example 2: American Psychological Association (APA), Information Science

Michael Levin and his team examine here how large research databases learn to differentiate between authors of the same name, known by the phrase "author disambiguation." The authors use APA citation style.

Excerpt from "Citation-Based Bootstrapping for Large-Scale Author Disambiguation" by M. Levin, et al.

The authors include a footnote for the Web of Knowledge, a research database. They choose not to include it in the references section at the end because it is not a research study, but a database.

Large bibliographic databases often fail to distinguish authors with similar names. Consider "J. Lee," attributed with over 56,000 articles in Thomson Reuters' Web of Knowledge[1], or "Kim, J.H.," with over 11,000. Clearly there is not just a single J. Lee or J.H. Kim who published all of these articles. But although distinguishing the different authors with similar names is important for any research that makes use of networks of scientific publications, the task is quite difficult. Publication databases are huge, requiring methods that can scale up to millions of articles, and methods must be capable of handling partial and conflicting metadata. ...

There have been three classes of algorithms for author disambiguation.[2] Methods relying on supervised machine learning train classifiers (support vector machines, random forests, etc.) on a hand-labeled training set containing pairs of articles where similarly named authors are identified as being the same or different persons (Han, Giles, Zha, Li, & Tsioutsiouliklis, 2004; Huang, Ertekin, & Giles, 2006; Kanani, McCallum, & Pal, 2007; Chen, Kalashnikov, & Mehrotra, 2007; Culotta, Kanani, Hall, Wick, & McCallum, 2007; Yang, Peng, Jiang, Lee, & Ho, 2008; Treeratpituk & Giles,

The first line of the second paragraph has another footnote; though it is citing a study, it is also communicating additional information, so the authors chose to include it as a discursive footnote, and they also include the study in the references section.

On the bottom of the page in the publication appear what are known as discursive footnotes. As opposed to bibliographic footnotes, discursive footnotes add extra information to what appears in the text itself. They are almost like parenthetical asides that direct readers to additional literature or to further explain points. Writers generally decide what can or cannot go in a discursive footnote based on how central the information is to the actual argument. These can also sometimes be organized as endnotes, which appear at the end of a text, instead of footnotes at the bottom of pages.

The authors name several studies that refer to "supervised machine learning train classifiers" and their year of publication. Notice that APA calls for a list of multiple authors to include a comma and an ampersand before the final name in the list, followed by the year. According to current APA guidelines, if there are one to five authors, they are all named; if there are six or more, the citation includes just the first author's name plus the phrase et al. (and others).

[1] http://www.webofknowledge.com/
[2] See Smalheiser and Torvik (2009) for a comprehensive summary of this literature.

From *Journal of the American Society for Information Science and Technology* (63.5), 2012.

2009). Supervised algorithms require large handlabeled training sets, especially for huge databases like MEDLINE or Web of Knowledge that contain tens of millions of articles. Such large quantities of manually annotated training data are not easily available, would be hard to make representative, and would be expensive to collect. For this reason, supervised algorithms may not be the best solution for such databases….

Although these previous studies have shown that high precision features may be useful for bootstrapping, a number of open issues remain. It is not clear how effective feature based bootstrapping is on large-scale collections—only Torvik and Smalheiser's (2009) study was large scale, and they combined feature-based bootstrapping with additional hand-labeled training data, so it is not possible to see the effect of feature-based bootstrapping alone. It is also unknown whether existing findings about feature-based bootstrapping will hold with very large datasets—for example, contrasting with the work of Bhattacharya and Getoor (2007) and Ferreira et al. (2010) on smaller datasets, our results will show that coauthorship is not effective for bootstrapping author disambiguation on Thomson Reuters' Web of Knowledge.

Here, the authors focus on specific studies, naming them within the body of the text as they hold more important findings relevant for their research. The Ferreira study, because it includes et al., indicates that that study included six or more authors.

This is partial listing of the references, which illustrate that APA asks for references to have the last name, followed by the first initial, then the year. Titles capitalize only the first letter, and this citation style includes more publication information than does the IEEE. Notice that references appear with a "hanging indent," whereby the second and subsequent lines of each entry are indented. This is so that busy readers can quickly scan through the names to find the reference they are looking for. Notice that references are alphabetized rather than appearing in chronological order of publication or of when they appeared in the text.

References

Andrew, G., & Gao, J. (2007). Scalable training of l1-regularized log-linear models. In *Proceedings of the 24th International Conference on Machine Learning (ICML '07)* (pp. 33–40). New York: ACM Press.

Bagga, A., & Baldwin, B. (1998). Algorithms for scoring coreference chains. *Recall*, 5(1), 2.

Banko, M., & Brill, E. (2001). Scaling to very very large corpora for natural language disambiguation. In *Proceedings of the 39th Annual Meeting of the Association for Computational Linguistics* (pp. 26–33). Stroudsburg, PA: Association for Computational Linguistics.

Bhattacharya, I., & Getoor, L. (2006). A latent dirichlet model for unsupervised entity resolution. *In Proceedings of SIAM International Conference on Data Mining* (pp. 47–58). New York: ACM Press.

Bhattacharya, I., & Getoor, L. (2007). Collective entity resolution in relational data. *ACM Transactions on Knowledge Discovery from Data*, 1(1), 5.

Example 3: Modern Language Association (MLA), English Literature

In this example, Amy Robillard poses the inquiry, "how do scholars make use of student writing in scholarship about writing studies and what are the implications?" Robillard uses the MLA citation style; she is publishing in a journal called *College English*.

Excerpt from " 'Young Scholars' Affecting Composition: A Challenge to Disciplinary Citation Practices" by A. E. Robillard

In their article, "When Peer Tutors Write about Writing: Literacy Narratives and Self Reflection," Heather Bastian and Lindsey Harkness demonstrate that composition scholars have constructed "an image—a critical image—of students," and that such critical images of students are further supported by the type of student the discourse community of composition chooses to discuss in their essays. Struggling or poor writers remain the focus. The preoccupation with "poor" and "struggling" students establishes these writers as the norm and disregards other students, such as competent college writers (81).

> Robillard provides a signal phrase here by naming the full article title and the authors' first and last names. She includes a parenthetical citation at the end of this section, indicating to readers that all the sentences preceding the citation are from Bastian and Harkness's article. She combines paraphrase with quotation, all from page 81 of their article.

Bastian and Harkness suggest that students ought to be provided opportunities "to engage in the rhetoric of the composition field, so that they can create more accurate representations of themselves" (91), a suggestion that makes sense when one considers the extent to which composition studies—unlike, say, astronomy or biology or economics—has relied upon student writing as the subject of so much of its research.... In WPA-L listserv discussions, Doug Downs, Christina Fisanick, and Elizabeth Wardle advocate a focus in first-year composition courses on the very questions underpinning composition studies itself—especially student empowerment. This small trend represents a shift in the central question of composition studies, as John Trimbur notes in his article "Changing the Question: Should Writing Be Studied?" In the 1960s and 1970s, the central question of composition studies

> Here, Robillard continues to cite their article, this time with a longer quotation from page 91; notice that she includes the parenthetical citation directly after the quoted material, even though it is not the end of the sentence. This signals a shift from the ideas of Bastian and Harkness to her own ideas. The material after the parenthetical citation is Robillard's analysis. MLA does not call for year of publication in the in-text citation.

> Robillard now turns her attention to another scholar whose work applies to her research: John Trimbur. Again, Robillard names him and includes the full title of his article.

From *College English*, 2006.

Throughout this paragraph, as with the former one, Robillard includes page numbers after quotes and names authors and their works within her sentences. Notice how much more frequently Robillard addresses particular quotes and passages in the texts she's citing. This is characteristic of research in MLA citation style.

was "Can writing be taught?" (16). The process movement, in what Trimbur calls "a kind of trickster operation," revised the question to "How can writing be learned?" shifting the subject of the question from teacher to student and leading to "a proliferation of answers with no end in sight" (22). The question that seems now to be at the forefront of composition studies is "Should writing be studied?" and the answer that the process movement, with the writing workshop at the center of undergraduate writing instruction, seems to be providing is a resounding "no" (22). Trimbur cites the pedagogical imperative—on the part of not just teachers but also students who expect to become better writers through classroom practice—as the reason the question "Should writing be studied?" has met with such negative responses. The pedagogical imperative fixes writing as a verb, whereas Bastian and Harkness's work—and the publication of *Young Scholars in Writing* more generally—forces us to see writing as a noun, an object of study for students as well as for teachers. More recently, Nancy Dejoy argues in her book, *Process This: Undergraduate Writing in Composition Studies*, that engaging students in the questions of composition studies is essential to reconceiving students' current positions as consumers of composition's disciplinary knowledge and seeing them as participants in and contributors to such knowledge.

MLA asks for a Works Cited section instead of References or Bibliography. Each entry has a hanging indent, and the full name of each author (rather than an initial) is included. Traditionally, MLA Works Cited pages are double spaced.

Works Cited

Bardies, Roland. "The Death of the Author." *Image, Music, Text*. Trans. Stephen Heath. New York: Noonday, 1977. 142-48.

Bastian, Heather, and Lindsey Harkness. "When Peer Tutors Write about Writing: Literacy Narratives and Self Reflection." *Young Scholars in Writing* 1 (2003): 77-94....

Example 4: Chicago Manual of Style (CMS), History of Science

Yves Gingras explores in this article how scholars define "impact" regarding a scientific publication. Gingras writes in the CMS style.

Excerpt from "Revisiting the 'Quiet Debut' of the Double Helix:
A Bibliometric and Methodological note on the 'Impact' of Scientific Publications"
by Y. Gingras

In the field of the history of molecular biology we have observed, over the past ten years, a tendency to "revisit" the dominant narrative that made the double helix papers of 1953 by Watson and Crick a crucial event that transformed modern biology. Soraya de Chadarevian recently wrote: "it is now widely accepted that James Watson and Francis Crick's model of the structure of DNA did not make immediate impact"[1] Though the term "impact" is not defined, her statement is backed by a reference to a brief paper by Robert Olby published in *Nature* on the occasion of the 50th anniversary of the publication of the DNA structure and to the author's own previous work where she argued, on the basis of interviews, press coverage and archival documents that the discovery of the DNA structure was not considered important until the 1960s. She writes, for example, that "a letter addressed to the secretary of the MRC by Bragg at the end of the 1950s confirms the relative oblivion surrounding Watson and Crick's work on the double helix."[2]

Though it may be true that DNA was not a big thing in Bragg's laboratory, one can hardly generalize from such a local reaction to the whole community. In the same vein, Robert Olby titled his contribution "Quiet debut for the double helix." Its headline stated that "the historical record reveals a muted response by the scientific community to the proposal of [the DNA's] structure in 1953."[3] Three months later another historian, Bruno Strasser, repeated the same message that "we usually think that the double-helix model acquired immediate and enduring success" but that "on the contrary, it enjoyed only a 'quiet debut,'" the author then referring the reader

> Gingras includes quotes, but CMS has the citations as footnotes. These footnotes indicate the pages where the quote appears.

> In CMS, footnotes usually have the full bibliographic citation the first time a resource is cited. This journal has modified CMS slightly (which journals often do) and includes only an abbreviated reference here.

> Gingras makes use of signal phrases here but most often includes only the author's first and last name, omitting the titles of the works.

> Footnotes appear at the bottom of each page and are used with superscript numbers.

[1] de Chadarevian, 2006, p. 707.
[2] de Chadarevian, 2002, p. 243, our emphasis.
[3] Olby, 2003, p. 402

From *Journal of the History of Biology* (43.1), 2010.

to Olby's piece.[4] Finally, a few years later, biologist Peter A. Lawrence, in an opinion piece criticizing "the mismeasurement of science" based on citation analysis, took that new wisdom as a fact and wrote that "the most important paper of the 20th century was cited rarely for the first ten years" again send was cited rarely for the first ten years" again sending the reader to Olby's piece in Nature for the "proof of that assertion.[5]

> Whereas the footnotes contain the individual page citations, or in-text citations, the References section contains full bibliographic information. The year appears directly after author name. As with the other citation styles, books and journal titles appear in italics. In this citation style, articles appear with quotation marks.

References

de Chadarevian, S. 2002. *Designs for Life: Molecular Biology After World War II.* Cambridge: Cambridge University Press.

---- 2006. "Mice and the Reactor: The 'Genetics Experiments' in the 1950s Britain." *Journal of the History of Biology* 39: 707-735.

Olby, Robert. 2003. "Quiet Debut for the Double Helix." *Nature* 421: 402-405.

[4] Strasser, 2003, pp. 803-804, our emphasis.
[5] Lawrence, 2007, pp. R584-R585, our emphasis.

Example 5: American Chemical Society (ACS), Chemistry

This fifth example comes from an editorial section of the *Journal of Medicinal Chemistry*. Editors Georg and Wang are discussing plagiarism as it relates to their journal. In the sciences, plagiarism can be complicated since many researchers publish multiple papers based on one large research project. These editors are clarifying the question, "what is self-plagiarism?"

Excerpt from "Plagiarism" by G. I. Georg and S. Wang

At the *Journal of Medicinal Chemistry*, the annual number of suspected plagiarism cases is very low, which we credit in part to the thorough reviews of our Associate Editors and reviewers but most especially to the self-vigilance of our authors. We are pleased that our authors remain upstanding scientists and are being careful to avoid such egregious errors.

As Editors of the *Journal of Medicinal Chemistry*, we wish to provide our readers, authors, and reviewers with some guidance. Plagiarism is defined as the "wrongful appropria-

From *Journal of Medicinal Chemistry* (56.1), 2013.

tion or purloining and publication as one's own, of the ideas, or the expression of the ideas ... of another".[1] Many instances of plagiarism are committed because of authors' unfamiliarity regarding what constitutes plagiarism. It is on this topic we wish to provide additional information, specifically on self-plagiarism.

Georg and Wang quote the Oxford English Dictionary definition of plagiarism and include a footnote for the reference.

The *Journal of Medicinal Chemistry* publishes original research; therefore, authors should not include lengthy discussions of their prior work. Authors should include only as much material as necessary to make the reported work clear and understandable.

(1) Whereever possible, new language should be used to present material rather than copying from previous publications.

(2) Partial or whole sentences taken from a prior publication should be placed in quotes and the reference given. This does not mean that large amounts of information should be repeated from other publications.

(3) It is acceptable to reuse figures as long as permission and acknowledgment has been received from the copyright owner. If the American Chemical Society is the sole owner, permission is not needed to publish in an ACS journal as long as credit is given to where the figure originally appeared in the ACS journal. If credit is given to another source in the figure caption, permission must be obtained from that source.

(4) As it is difficult to create unique ways to describe procedures and equipment, it is acceptable to reproduce language for these items in the experimental section.

(5) If you are in doubt as to whether or not material would be considered self-plagiarism, it is best to reword the text.

Because of the serious nature of the plagiarism, we continue to take all suspected cases very seriously. Allegations of plagiarism are thoroughly investigated according to established best practices (http://publicationethics.org/resources/guidelines). When we have reasonable concern, we ask authors to respond. If a satisfactory response is not forthcoming and there is adequate evidence to establish

Here, the editors refer to another text and again include a footnote for the reference.

that self-plagiarism or plagiarism has occurred, we proceed per definitions and guidelines stated in the Ethical Guidelines to Publication of Chemical Research, American Chemical Society.[2]

References

(1) *Oxford English Dictionary*, 2nd ed.; Oxford University Press, Oxford, U.K., 1989.
(2) Ethical Guidelines to Publication of Chemical Research; American Chemical Society: Washington, DC, 2012; http://pubs.acs.org/userimages/ContentEditor/1218054468605/ethics.pdf.

> In these references, the page numbers are included for the entire article, not just the particular page from which the citation was pulled.

Example 6: American Anthropological Association (AAA), Archaeology

This example comes from Scott Hutson, an Archaeologist, who is writing an inquiry into gendered citation practices in archaeological journals. Hutson makes the argument that "citations serve as a measure of structural inequalities, but may also act to reproduce or transform such structures." He examines citations spanning 10 or more years in four academic journals in his field, finding that in several of the journals, women are cited less frequently than men, and that this "under-referencing of women might imply a devaluation of women's archaeological labor."

Hutson also makes the important point that some citation systems make gender inequities less visible than do others: "Because patterns in citations can be subtle, not easily detectable without tally sheets and statistics, they can operate below the level of awareness." For instance, in the AAA citation style in which Hutson is writing, first names are not included in the references, but only initials. While it is not possible to detect gender from first names all the time, sometimes one can, and omitting first names reduces the level of awareness of the gender of those who are cited.

Excerpt from "Gendered Citation Practices in American Antiquity and Other Archaeology Journals" by S. R. Hutson

Personal networks might also be expected to affect the frequency at which women are cited. For example, Margaret Nelson (1994:201) reports that female archaeology graduate students "do not form peer groups that include women within their graduate departments"…and, therefore, "feel isolated and unable to gain answers to professional, non-academic questions." Roundtable discussions for women at the SAA annual meetings

> Hutson includes in the parentheses the year of Nelson's text, a colon, and the page number from which the ensuing quote comes. Notice that AAA calls for the page number prior to the quote rather than after.

From *American Antiquity* (167.2), 2002.

In the parenthetical citation of Ford, Hutson is paraphrasing something from page 72 of Ford's text. When Hutson refers to Kehoe, he uses only the year because he is summarizing the entire publication on citing circles rather than a specific idea on a specific page.

and at other conferences allow women to gain a network of female colleagues that might be reflected in their citations (e.g., also Ford 1994:72). Of course, other forms of networking, such as that which occurs between one's peers and professors at graduate school, have significant though not always gendered effects on citation (see Kehoe 1992 on citing circles). The existence of citing circles reminds us that citation is also a form of communication. By citing certain writers and not others, authors communicate, consciously or unconsciously, their alliances, alignments, and scholarly self-identities. Furthermore, citation may obliquely flatter...or affront.

References Cited [abridged]

In these references, the authors do not include page numbers, but they do include all the other relevant citation information.

Ford, A.

> 1994 Women in Mesoamerican Archaeology: Why are the Best Men Winning? In *Women in Archaeology*, edited by C. Claassen, pp. 159-172. University of Pennsylvania Press, Philadelphia.

Kehoe, A.

> 1992 The Muted Class: Unshackling Tradition. In *Exploring Gender through Archaeology*, edited by C. Claassen, pp. 23-32. Prehistory Press, Madison, Wisconsin.

Nelson, M. C.

> 1994 Expanding Networks for Women in Archaeology. In *Equity Issues for Women in Archaeology*, edited by M. Nelson, S. Nelson, and A. Wylie, pp. 199-202. Archaeological Papers of the American Anthropological Association No. 5.

Example 7: American Sociological Association (ASA), Sociology

In the example, authors Nina C. Heckler, David R. Forde, and C. Hobson Bryan examine how assignment design potentially reduces the likelihood of plagiarism among students, specifically in digital environments. They use a combination of print and digital sources, and are writing in the ASA citation style.

Excerpt from "Using Writing Assignment Designs to Mitigate Plagiarism" by N. C. Heckler, D. R. Forde, and C. H. Bryan

In sum, faculty have the most important role in mitigating plagiarism in higher education (Van Gundy et al. 2006). To the topic of this research, the first line of defense for faculty is

From *Teaching Sociology* (41.1), 2013.

course design. In fact, some authorities maintain that faculty can and should be "designing out" plagiarism (Gannon-Leary, Trayhurn, and Home 2009:446).... Numerous researchers point to course design as a potentially important factor in preventing plagiarism (e.g., Compton and Pfau 2008; Gannon-Leary et al. 2009; Parameswaran and Devi 2006; Samuels and Bast 2006). Among the most integral elements of course design are assignment strategy and structure. Specific strategies include designing assignments for collaborative work (Hart and Friesner 2004; Kasprzak and Nixon 2004; McCord 2008; Pedersen 2010), having students turn in the actual sources used in research assignments (McCord 2008; Samuels and Bast 2006; Sterngold 2004), collecting students' field notes (Pedersen 2010), having students submit work through plagiarism detection software (Batane 2010; Gannon-Leary et al. 2009; Walker 2010), having students turn in progressive work products for large projects (Gibson et al. 2006; McCord 2008; Samuels and Bast 2006), varying the nature and frequency of assignments (Batane 2010; Bernardi et al. 2008; McCord 2008; Sutherland-Smith 2008), and developing assignments that require evaluation and reflection of material rather than collation of materials (Batane 2010; Howard and Davies 2009; Sutherland-Smith 2008).

> ASA calls for the author-date form of in-text citations; notice in the Gannon-Leary, Trayhurn, and Home citation that the authors have included a specific page number because they quoted a phrase directly from the text as opposed to just referring to it generally.

References [abridged]

Gannon-Leary, Pat, Deborah Trayhurn, and Margaret Home. 2009. "Good Images, Effective Messages? Working with Students and Educators on Academic Practice Understanding." *Journal of Further and Higher Education* 33(4):435-48.

Gibson, Jane Whitney, Charles W. Blackwell, Regina A. Greenwood, Ingrid Mobley, and Raquel Whitney Blackwell. 2006. "Preventing and Detecting Plagiarism in the Written Work of College Students." *Journal of Diversity Management* 1(2). Retrieved March 20, 2011 (http://journals.cluteonline.com/index.php/JDM/ article/view/5033).

McCord, Alan. 2008. *Improving Online Assignments to Deter Plagiarism.* Paper presented at the Proceedings of the 12th Annual Technology, Community & Colleges Worldwide Online Conference. Retrieved April 12, 2011 (http://etec.hawaii.edu/proceedings/2008/Mc-Cord2008.pdf).

Van Gundy, Karen, Beth A. Morton, Hope Q. Liu, and Jennifer Kline. 2006. "Effects of Web-Based Instruction on Math Anxiety, the Sense of Mastery, and Global Self-Esteem: A Quasi-Experimental Study of Undergraduate Statistics Students." *Teaching Sociology* 34(4):370-88.

> Several of the sources are from electronic versions, noted by the inclusion of websites in the references. In Gibson, the authors write "retrieved" and include the database from which they retrieved the article; in McCord, the website is the address where the papers are available.

Example 8: Chicago Manual of Style (CMS), with Digital Resources Art

The excerpt appears in an article documenting "how The Phillips Collection, a small museum of modern and contemporary art [in Washington, D.C.], desired to share its reputation as a welcoming and comfortable environment with remote audiences by launching a grassroots-style blog." The author, Sarah Bender, describes the deliberations involved in deciding about citation practices for the blog. They use Chicago style of citation, but notice how many different kinds of resources they are citing in this section, from conference papers and published papers to blogs, emails, and even a personal conversation.

Excerpt from "History, Identity, and Twenty-First Century Skills: Experiments in Institutional Blogging" by S. O. Bender

The blogs that served as a model for the Phillips Collection were the Los Angeles County Museum of Art's Unframed, the San Francisco Museum of Modern Art's Open Space,[9] the Brooklyn Museum's blog, and the Smithsonian American Art Museum's blog Eye Level.[10]

Bender cites the blogs that informed their approach to blog development. CMS requires footnotes, so the actual blogs are cited in the footnotes according to the standards laid out in the *Chicago Manual of Style* for blogs.

Based on this research, contact was made with fellow museum professionals who oversaw some of the blogs on the spreadsheet. Amy Heibel, then director of Web and Media Strategy for LACMA, provided generous insight and support.[11] She emphasized the value of staying non-promotional in building an authentic relationship

Bender cites a conversation she had with Heibel, again, using CMS guidelines.

9. See Rebecca Nath, "Social Media Tool Case Study: The San Francisco Museum of Modern Art's Blog, Open Space" (paper presented at the California Association of Museums Conference, San Jose, California, March 3–5, 2010), http://www.calmuseums.org/_data/n_0001/resources/live/FINAL_RNathSFMOMA.pdf.

The Gates article, though published in a collection of papers, was retrieved by Bender from archimuse.com, a website called *Archives and Museum Informatics,* which provides resources for members of those fields. CMS asks for the full website to be provided.

10. See Jeff Gates, "Case Study: New World Blogging within a Traditional Museum Setting," in Museums and the Web 2007: Selected Papers from an International Conference, ed. Jennifer Trant and David Bearman (Toronto, Ontario: Archives & Museum Informatics, 2007), http://www.archimuse.com/mw2007/papers/gates/gates.html; Jeff Gates, "Clearing the Path for Sisyphus: How Social Media is Changing Our Jobs and Our Working Relationships," Museums and the Web 2010: Selected Papers from an International Conference, ed. Jennifer Trant and David Bearman (Toronto, Ontario: Archives & Museum Informatics, 2010), http://www.archimuse.com/mw2010/papers/gates/gates.html; Jeff Gates, "Confessions of a Long Tail Visionary," Life Outtacontext (blog), consulted August 14, 2013, http://outtacontext.com/articles/confessions/.

CMS specifies that references appear as footnotes at the bottom of the page on which the citation appears. In this article, there is no separate references section at the end of the document.

11. Amy Heibel (vice president, Technology, Web, and Digital Media at the Los Angeles County Museum of Art), in discussion with the author, October 15, 2010.

From *Art Documentation: Journal of the Art Libraries Society of North America* (33.1), 2014.

Bender cites an email from Gates. Since Bender is not using quotation marks, this indicates that she is paraphrasing his ideas rather than quoting.

with readers, especially art critics and bloggers who would be likely to promote blog content if it offered a fresh perspective, but not if it echoed marketing materials. … Jeff Gates,[12] lead producer of New Media Initiatives at the Smithsonian American Art Museum and managing editor of its blog, was also a valuable resource, offering two gems of wisdom in particular. In response to concerns, chiefly from curatorial staff, regarding citations on the blog, Gates clearly distinguished the venue of the blog from that of a scholarly publication. On the blog, the content is more conversational, and simply noting a source's title is sufficient. If a point needs a more detailed citation, it is an indication that either the post's tone is inappropriate for the blog or the content is better suited to a more formal article or essay. Regarding the intention to make the Phillips Collection blog media-heavy and low on article-length posts, Gates alleviated concern over access to enough quality photography. He said that images on the blog didn't necessarily have to be "beautiful"; what was important was that they be "interesting."[13] This straightforward perspective was liberating and inspiring on many levels related to content creation (72).

Citing another conversation, Bender now uses quotation marks, indicating that these were Gates's words.

12. Jeff Gates (lead producer, New Media Initiatives at the Smithsonian American Art Museum, and managing editor, Eye Level), in e-mail message to the author, February 2, 2011.
13. Jeff Gates, in conversation with the author, October 21, 2010.

CMS specifies exactly how to cite a conversation and an email, as well as many other kinds of resources that academic writers might use in their scholarship.

Example 9: Chicago Manual of Style (CMS), with images, art

The final example of this segment will offer you a glimpse of citation with images. Citation with images depends on the context in which the image is included. Often, if the image is included as an illustrative figure, then authors will attribute the image source near the actual image, but not necessarily include the image in the References section. The example demonstrates this mode of citation with images. Here, Alexander Watkins is arguing for the citation tool Zotero as a strong tool for image resource management, which can help users organize, manage, and cite their personal image collections.

Excerpt from "Zotero for Personal Image Management" by A. Watkins

Each different type of item in Zotero has its own metadata schema, though many fields are shared between item types. Zotero's artwork item type has fields for the most important image data (Figure 2). The ability to document images fully makes the program much more than a way to store and view images. It becomes a place to keep important information, generate citations, and make the data available for analysis. Zotero's metadata for images is strong compared to other image-management software programs, but it is less robust than full-featured digital asset management systems. It lacks the complexity of a schema like VRA Core or the ability to integrate vocabularies (305-6).

Watkins includes a screen shot of Zotero, and labels it as a Figure. He does not include a bibliographic citation for the image, but earlier in the article he did have a footnote directing readers to the Zotero website: "1. Readers unfamiliar with using Zotero as a citation manager can get a quick introduction here: "Quick Start Guide [Zotero Documentation]," https://www.zotero.org/support/quick_start_guide."

Figure 2. Artwork item type metadata in Zotero.

From *Art Documentation: Journal of the Art Libraries Society of North America* (32.2), 2013.

Citation Practices in the Twenty-First Century: Digital and Visual Formats and Materials

It is useful to keep in mind that citation practices have evolved considerably over the last twenty years to integrate the increasing prevalence of digital formats for academic writing and the increasing preponderance of digital and visual materials.

Most scholarship in the twentieth century emerged in either print or verbal formats, and relied on print resources. Since so much academic writing now appears in digital formats, from webpages and op-eds to online journals, academic writers need to be particularly attuned to citation practices related to these digital environments. Moreover, with increased access to digital materials of all sorts, writers must likewise be savvier at learning how to cite across many different kinds of materials.

Digital materials

All evidence and resources must be cited, including digital materials. Each citation style provides guidelines for how to cite a variety of kinds of materials, from an email or listserv posting to a photograph, whether it appears in an archive, a blog, or a website.

Still, because online contexts develop more quickly than the regular update cycles for citation styles, you should be prepared to encounter a resource at some point that a citation style does not address or does not fully address. In this case, you will need to adapt citation style guidelines to fit the resource. Do this in consultation with your professor and other writing-related resources, such as your institution's writing center, similar writing in that field, and/or reliable, official online writing guides.

Publishing online

Academic writers must use citation whether they are publishing in a peer-reviewed journal, a blog, or a website. Still, the specific strategies for citation can shift across these various platforms.

Some digital platforms, for example, cite by using weblinks instead of standard academic in-text citation formats. In the excerpt, from an article titled "The Play's The Thing," published in the online journal *Hybrid Pedagogy*, author Sarah Heidebrink-Bruno embeds several links, reprinted here in blue, in much the same way that they appear in the online article (though without the live link).

> When reading aloud in class, always do the voices. I know, you don't want to be "that teacher," but trust me, do the voices. Do you remember the first time someone read to you, or you listened to an audio book, and you heard a voice so wonderful, so adaptable that it made the storytelling come alive for you? Chances are, so do your students. If they haven't had that moment yet, create it for them. Be their Alan Rickman.

The first of the links brings readers to a YouTube video featuring an audio book: *The Hobbit*, read by Nicol Williamson (Haamurabi). The second link takes readers to a YouTube video featuring Alan Rickman reading Shakespeare's Sonnet 130 (Kedavra). Heidebrink-Bruno is providing examples of strong reading voices.

In a print journal, these citations may have instead appeared as discursive footnotes where Heidebrink-Bruno might have offered readers examples of strong reading voices with something along the lines of:

> For examples of the power generated from strong reading voices, see Alan Brickman's reading of Shakespeare's Sonnet 130 and Nicol Williamson's reading of *The Hobbit*.

Then, in her works cited or references, Heidebrink-Bruno would have included full bibliographic citations for these two audio texts. However, because Heidebrink-Bruno is publishing in an entirely digital platform, she instead opts to link out directly to these sites.

Heidebrink-Bruno's article also illustrates another feature of academic writing in digital platforms through its approach to citation more broadly. While, as indicated earlier, many online peer-reviewed journals maintain the same discourse conventions for citation as in print publications, using one of the citation styles exemplified in the section toward the end of this chapter, some online publication formats require a modified approach to citation. *Hybrid Pedagogy*, in particular, adopts citation practices that might seem more characteristic of a blog, web-based article, or a more popular print article. That is, Heidebrink-Bruno does not include bibliographic citations at the end of her text. Instead, any resources she uses are attributed through embedded links in the text.

As an example of her modified approach to citation, Heidebrink-Bruno discusses at one point a photographic image as an instance of how students will enjoy examining and creating captions for visual images as a writing activity. Heidebrink-Bruno includes the image along with a caption (Figure 12.1).

**"In 1937, two women caused an accident
by wearing shorts in public for the first time."**

FIGURE 12.1 Example of an image and caption.

Importantly, Heidebrink-Bruno does not include a text-based citation for the photograph. She instead includes a live link embedded within the image leading readers to the source where she found the image (a *Tumblr* blog titled *stability.tumblr.com*, run by blogger and photographer Nick Avallone).

In this case, the original photograph is an archival image located in the City of Toronto archives. The *Huffington Post* reported on the photograph, documenting that it went viral after a blogger posted it with the caption on *Reddit* because of the way the caption blames the women instead of the driver. Heidebrink-Bruno includes the photograph, but her embedded link does not take readers to the City of Toronto archives, nor to the initial *Reddit* posting, nor even to the *Huffington Post* article discussing the photograph. Instead, the link takes readers to another blogger on *Tumblr* who had reposted the photograph. This kind of networked approach to citation reflects the discourse conventions present in some (not all) digital environments and contrasts with citation practices in print-based scholarly contexts.

Photo credits in online platforms provide another distinctive feature of citation practices when publishing online. Heidebrink-Bruno includes another image in her article, with the following photo credit, again with embedded links (depicted in blue here): "[Photo, Minimalism outside by 55Laney69, licensed under CC BY 2.0.]" This approach enables Heidebrink-Bruno to attribute her resources, but not necessarily in accordance to any specific citation style as enumerated by, for instance, MLA, CMS, or APA.

By contrast, the bibliographic citations, excerpted from an article by Anita Helle (also excerpted in Chapter 7: Analysis), show how photographs are cited in a print-based scholarly format:

> Lange, Dorothea. Doctor examining children in trailer clinic. FSA (Farm Security Administration) mobile camp, klamath County, Oregon. Washington, DC: Library of Congress. http://www.loc.gov/pictures/item/fsa2000005393/PP/ (accessed September 9, 2011).
> ———. Fifty-seven year old sharecropper woman. Hinds County, Mississippi, 1937. Washington, DC: Library of Congress, Prints & Photographs Division, LCDIg-fsa-8b32018.

Despite the different citation approach illustrated in Heidebrink-Bruno's article, though, she is still attributing her resources; she is just doing so from within the established discourse conventions of the context an in accordance with the editorial guidelines of that journal.

Write Now

Find an online publication context and examine the citation approach. How is the author attributing and referencing resources in this online format?

Transfer Hub: Share your ideas and see what others have written at fountainheadpress.com/transferhub.

Citing Your Own Work

Though it may seem surprising, if you borrow ideas from work that you have previously produced, you need to cite yourself. This is alternately termed **self-citation** or self-reference. Citing yourself achieves the same purposes as citing others: it awards credit, offers a bibliographic trail for readers to follow, and enables academic writers to situate their current writing project within a larger, ongoing conversation. In educational settings, if students draw from prior writing projects they have produced, they must cite their prior writing projects (citation style guides even provide guidelines for citing unpublished writing).

An example of self-citation can be found within the article by David Corso on video games. Corso uses an idea from another of his writing projects, and therefore cites it:

> If we maintain a holistic approach when dealing with video game play, we can investigate these effects and provide instruction on their implementation, i.e. incorporate less violence in video games while maintaining competition or making the player cognizant of these violent effects (Corso, 2013).

From the references section included with the article, readers learn that the work Corso cited was his honors college thesis:

> Corso, D. (2013). Holistic gaming: Using the physical and psychological effects of video games to better our lives. (Unpublished Honors College thesis). The University of South Carolina, Columbia.

Citing your own prior work is in many ways a positive strategy. Academic reputations with regard to publications can be in part determined by how many other articles have cited a particular publication. The more your text is cited, the more reputable it is (for more discussion about this phenomenon, known as impact factor, and the ensuing complexities, see Example 1). In scientific disciplines, where writers often publish multiple articles from one research project, the necessity for citing your own work becomes more complex. Citing their own work ensures that each publication has an original contribution rather than repeating the ideas of other prior publications.

Crafting Acknowledgments

Many academic texts include an acknowledgments section as well as a references or works cited section. These sections enable academic writers to acknowledge the ways in which others around them have shaped the text, even if they might not have done so explicitly as in the case of evidence and actual works cited. Writers will often use this space to acknowledge, for instance, feedback they have received from readers, editorial suggestions from editors, research assistance from librarians or archivists, and also funding support from grants or organizations.

Example 1: Acknowledgments

Excerpt from "'It's Medically Proven!': Assessing the Dissemination of Religion and Health Research" by S. M. Frenk, S. L. Foy, and K. G. Meador

Acknowledgments

The authors would like to thank Joe Mann, Director of the Rural Church Division at The Duke Endowment, Mary Piepenbringin, Director of the Health Care Division at The Duke Endowment, and Gene Cochrane, President of The Duke Endowment for financial support of the Caring Communities Health Ministries Assessment from which these data are drawn. The authors would like to thank Alexis T. Franzese and Whitney Arroyave for their assistance with the Caring Communities Health Ministries Assessment Project and Wendy Cadge, Linda K. George, and Harold Koenig for reviewing the manuscript. Finally, the authors thank the congregations that participated in the study. The content of this article is solely the responsibility of the authors and does not reflect the views or opinions of The Duke Endowment.

> The authors thank the people at the various sites they studied for their field research as well as the funder of their research. They also thank those who reviewed the manuscript.

From *Journal of Religion and Health* (50.4), 2011.

Example 2: Acknowledgments

Excerpt from "Responding to the Work of Others: There's a Better Way for Us to Live" by D. Wong

Acknowledgments

I'd like to thank Joav and Zach for their comments on my draft. Their input was very helpful in my revision. Their feedback on how I should add in a second rewrite at the end of the piece was insightful, and their encouraging comments gave me more confidence in writing my final draft. They did a

> Wong, an undergraduate when he published this article, expresses appreciation for his peers who read the draft, as well as a writing center tutor.

From *Deliberations* (9), 2008.

very thorough reading of my second draft, so I really appreciate their hard work. I'd also like to thank Timothy Wright from the Writing Studio, who gave me valuable feedback on ways I could improve my draft, especially with regard to my introduction.

Example 3: Acknowledgments

Excerpt from "History, Identity, and Twenty-First Century Skills: Experiments in Institutional Blogging" by S. O. Bender

Acknowledgments

I wish to express my gratitude to Amy Heibel and Jeff Gates who, as is evident in this article, provided early and essential guidance and support to this project. My unending thanks go to former public relations manager Cecilia Wichmann who, by bringing her blog idea to me, forever enhanced my relationship to my colleagues and my institution, and changed my belief in social media and its power to tell stories worth sharing.

> Bender thanks those who contributed intellectual inspiration and support to her project and those who influenced her thinking.

From *Art Documentation: Journal of the Art Libraries Society of North America* (33.1), 2014.

Transferring Citation

Citation practices build on the concepts covered in nearly all the preceding chapters. Citation makes it possible for writers to pursue questions, engage with the texts they read, develop arguments, and integrate evidence. While it may be true that accurate citation practices enable scholars to avoid plagiarism, a more productive approach to citation involves considering citation as a way of demonstrating your knowledge and of helping other researchers (your readers) build knowledge as well.

Transferring citation practices across writing occasions acknowledges that citation contributes to and reflects academic writing culture more broadly. Citation also has high political implications, due to its power to establish, reinforce, or damage reputations across disciplines. Transfer is the essence of citation since citation practices exemplify the dynamic nature of academic writing.

❧ ❧ ❧

Chapter 12 Key Terms

Citation styles   Document format   Plagiarism

Citation guides   Bibliographic citations   Signal phrase

Schools of citation   In-text citations   Self-citation

Write Away

Because you will be called upon throughout your undergraduate education and beyond to cite within different contexts, you should gain familiarity with how to transfer citation practices across writing occasions. This activity invites you to do so by transferring citation styles for the same text across disciplines and formats in order to reflect on citation and transfer.

Choose a two-page segment from a peer-reviewed text that includes citations. Choose a text you can use as an original citation starting point. The text you choose can be from any disciplinary perspective, and in any citation style. Once you have selected the text, choose a two-page segment of it that you can use to transfer citations.

Identify the text's current citation style. Using a library resource, citation guide, or authoritative online resource, identify which citation style the article is currently adopting. Be careful as some citation styles look similar to one another, and you might have chosen one that is a journal-specific citation style (which is fine). To discern citation style, look at both in-text citations and bibliographic information.

Choose two to three additional citation styles you can use for the transfer. Select two or three citation styles different from the one currently being deployed in the text you have chosen. If your text is using a journal-specific form of citation, just choose two or three other citation styles that look quite different from the current one. Aim to secure a mix of citation styles that ask you to examine citation from several different perspectives.

Transfer the citations across citation styles. Transfer the citation style from the original version to the other citation styles, one at a time. First, transfer all the citations in that two-page segment (in-text and any related bibliographic entries) into one of the other citation styles you have selected. Then, repeat that transfer for the second citation style, and the third if you chose three. You may find that in the process of transferring citation styles you will be called upon to reduce quoted material or change the style of signal phrases. Use a library resource, citation guide, or authoritative online resource to make sure you are citing as accurately as possible.

Transfer citations to a citation style for a weblinked blog. As a final transfer move, paraphrase the two-page segment of text as though you were posting the paraphrase to an online blog. As would be customary in that setting, opt as much as possible for weblinks instead of full in-text citations. Be sure to also cite that you are adapting/paraphrasing an article so that your own citation attribution is accurate.

Reflect on citation and transfer. Reflect in writing for ten minutes on what you learned about citation and transfer from having completed this activity. Which citation styles seemed more difficult for you? Which ones fit better with the kind of disciplinary perspective you were using? What elements of citation carried over from one version to another? Which elements were drastically different?

Moving Forward with Writing Transfer

Writing in Transit has provided you with a transfer-based approach to writing, inviting you to approach each new writing occasion by considering the disciplinary and publication context, drawing on your prior experiences with writing, and cultivating and fortifying your writing-related strengths. By exploring *Writing in Transit*, and to invoke once again Chapter 1's Chaco Canyon, your own Writing Great House has now become more expansive and nuanced as you have learned more about the key aspects of academic writing that transverse disciplinary contexts:

- Research and writing as a process
- Posing meaningful questions
- Reading
- Summary
- Synthesis
- Analysis
- Framing arguments
- Constructing arguments
- Designing arguments
- Choosing and integrating evidence
- Citing resources

Just as each of these aspects of academic writing move within and across disciplinary contexts, emerging as aligned, inflected, and distinctive, so too will you as a writer move throughout the varied terrain of academic writing, pursuing your curiosity and discovering new ideas.

The transfer-based approach featured in *Writing in Transit* empowers you to write with deep awareness and reflection, to survey and recognize that which you might apply, extend, reconsider, reject, or otherwise transfer from one writing and learning occasion to others. Challenging as this can be, you will likely have many opportunities to invoke and build on these transfer-based strategies throughout your undergraduate experience and beyond. In this way, *Writing in Transit* has prepared you to move forward with writing transfer, empowering you to make a difference and cultivate your aspirations as you encounter complexity, learn from and about yourself and others, advance knowledge, and otherwise contribute to the world around you.

"About Alignments." *Exploratorium*. Exploratorium, n.d.

"About Petroglyphs." *Zion Canyon Offerings*. Zion Canyon Offerings, n.d.

"About Stonehenge." *stonehenge.co.uk*. 3 Oct. 2014.

"Abstracts." The Writing Center at UNC Chapel Hill. *writingcenter.unc.edu*.

Adelson, Glenn, ed. *Environment: an Interdisciplinary Anthology*. New Haven: Yale UP, 2008.

Agee, Jane. "Developing Qualitative Research Questions: A Reflective Process." *International Journal of Qualitative Studies in Education* 22.4 (2009): 431-47.

Aitken, R. John, et al. "The Source and Significance of DNA Damage in Human Spermatozoa; a Commentary on Diagnostic Strategies and Straw Man Fallacies. *Molecular Human Reproduction* 19.8 (2013): 475-85. *Oxford Journals*.

Aleghfeli, Obaid Rashed. "Video Games." *Undergraduate Research Journal for the Human Sciences*. 11 (2012): n.p. *kon.org*.

Alexander, Jeffrey. *Classical Attempt at Theoretical Synthesis*. Berkeley: U of California P, 1983.

Alim, H. Samy. *Roc the Mic Right: The Language of Hip Hop Culture*. New York: Routledge, 2006.

Anderson, Craig A., Douglas A. Gentile, and Katherine E. Buckley. *Violent Video Game Effects on Children and Adolescents: Theory, Research, and Public Policy*. Oxford: Oxford UP, 2007.

Archaeoastronomy. Web.

"Archaeoastronomy." *scienceclarified*.

Aristotle. *On Sophistical Refutations*. 350 B.C.E. Trans. Arthur Wallace Pickard-Cambridge. Blacksburg, VA: Virginia Tech, 2001.

"Assumptions about Learners and Teachers." *Position on the Teaching of English*. 1988-89. *ncte.org*.

Australia. Attorney General's Department. *Literature Review on the Impact of Playing Violent Video Games on Aggression*. Barton, Au.: September 2010. *classification.gov.au*.

Aveni, Anthony F. "Archaeoastronomy in the Ancient Americas." *Journal of Archaeological Research* 11.2 (2003): 149-91. *ProQuest*.

---. "Zapotec Astronomy: Reconsideration of an Earlier Study." *Archaeoastronomy* 18 (2004): 26-31. *Academic Search Complete*.

Aveni, Anthony F., and Robert M. Linsley. "Mound J, Monte Albán: Possible Astronomical Orientation." *American Antiquity* 37.4 (1972): 528-531. *JSTOR*.

Ayalon, Michal, and Ruhama Even. "Deductive Reasoning: In the Eye of the Beholder." *Educational Studies in Mathematics* 69.3 (2008): 235-47. *edumatec.mat.ufrgs.br*.

Babcock, Rebecca Day. *A Synthesis of Qualitative Studies of Writing Center Tutoring*, 1983-2006. New York: Peter Lang, 2012. *books.google.com*.

Barmé, Geremie. *The Forbidden City*. Harvard UP, 2008.

Bartholomae, David. "Inventing the University." *Journal of Basic Writing* 5.1 (1986): 4-23. *wac.colostate.edu*.

Baudo, Renato, Gianni Tartari, and Mohiuddin Munawar, eds. *Top of the world environmental research: Mount Everest-Himalayan ecosystem*. Leiden: Backhuys, 1998. Print.

Bazerman, Charles. *Shaping Written Knowledge: The Genre and Activity of the Experimental Article in Science*. Madison, WI: U of Wisconsin P, 1988. Print.

Beach, King. "Consequential Transitions: A Developmental View of Knowledge Propagation Through Social Organizations." *Between School and Work: New Perspectives on Transfer and Boundary-Crossing*. Ed. Terttu Tuomi-Gröhn and Yrjö Engeström. Bingley, UK: Emerald Group, 2003. 39-61. Print.

Beaney, Michael. "Analysis." *The Stanford Encyclopedia of Philosophy* (Summer 2014). Ed. Edward N. Zalta. 25 March 2014. *plato.stanford.edu.*

Becker, Ben. "PAX EAST 2012 Queue Room – Fisheye." Photograph. 7 Apr. 2012. *flickr.com.*

Bitzer, Lloyd. "The Rhetorical Situation." *Philosophy and Rhetoric* 1.1 (1968): 1–14. *JSTOR.*

Bolker, Joan. *Writing your Dissertation in Fifteen Minutes a Day: A Guide to Starting, Revising, and Finishing your Doctoral Thesis*. New York: Macmillan, 1998. Print.

"Boudhanath Stupa, Kathmandu." *sacred-destinations.com.* n.d.

Brinton, Alan. "The *Ad Hominem*." *Fallacies: Classical and Contemporary Readings*. Ed. Hans V. Hansen and Robert C. Pinto. University Park, PA: Penn State UP, 1995. 213-21. *books.google.com.*

Brizee, H. Allen. "Stasis Theory as a Strategy for Workplace Teaming and Decision Making." *Journal of Technical Writing and Communication* 38.4 (2008): 363-85. *Metapress.*

bubble.us.

Bunn, Mike. "How to Read Like a Writer." *Writing Spaces: Readings on Writing*. Ed. Charles Lowe and Pavel Zemliansky. Vol. 2 Anderson, SC: Parlor P, 2011. 71-86. atleegoesto11.pbworks.com.

Burnette, Jeni L., Jeffrey M. Pollack, and Donelson R. Forsyth. "Leadership In Extreme Contexts: A Groupthink Analysis Of The May 1996 Mount Everest Disaster." *Journal Of Leadership Studies* 4.4 (2011): 29-40. *Business Source Complete.*

Bushman, Brad J., and L. Rowell Huesmann. "Twenty-Five Years of Research on Violence in Digital Games and Aggression Revisited: A Reply to Elson and Ferguson (2013)." *European Psychologist* 19.1 (2014): 47-55. *PsycINFO.*

Cahill, Abigail, et al. "How Does Climate Change Cause Extinction?" *Proceedings of the Royal Society of Biological Sciences* 280.1750 (2013): n.p. *RoyalSocietyPublishing.org.*

Canniford, Robin, and Avi Shankar. "Purifying Practices: How Consumers Assemble Romantic Experiences of Nature." *Journal of Consumer Research* 39.5 (2013): 1051-69. *JSTOR.*

Carlson, John B., David S. P. Dearborn, Stephen C. McCluskey, and Clive L. N. Ruggles. "Astronomy in Culture." *Archaeoastronomy* 14.1 (1999): 3-21. *honors.umd.edu.*

Carmona, Chelsea. "How AA Fails to Support Young Addicts." *The Washington Post*. 6 July 2012. *thewashingtonpost.com.*

Carr, Kurt, and Paul Nevin. "Petroglyphs of Pennsylvania." *Pennsylvania Historical & Museum Commission*. Pennsylvania, 2014.

Carr, Nicholas. "Is Google Making Us Stupid?" *The Atlantic Monthly* 107.2 (2008): 89-94. *Wiley Online Library.*

Carr, Stuart A., and Malcolm MacLachlan. "Interdisciplinary Research for Development: A Policy Paper." *globalhealth.tcd.ie*. Global Development Network. n.d.

Carroll, Laura Bolin. "Backpacks vs. Briefcases: Steps toward Rhetorical Analysis." *Writing Spaces: Readings on Writing*. Vol. 1. Ed. Charles Lowe and Pavel Zemliansky. Anderson, SC: Parlor P, 2010. 45-58. *1112dual.pbworks.com.*

Carter, Cassie. "Introduction to Syntheses." *msu.edu.*

Carter, David. "Computer & Video Game Archive." *lib.umich.edu.* University of Michigan.

Carter, Michael. "Ways of Knowing, Doing, and Writing in the Disciplines." *College Composition and Communication* 58.3 (2007): 385-418. *JSTOR.*

Center for Reviews and Dissemination (CRD). *Systematic Reviews. CRDs Guidance for Undertaking Reviews in Health Care*. 2009. *york.ac.uk.*

Chakrabarti, Amaresh, and Lucienne TM Blessing. *An Anthology of Theories and Models of Design*. London: Springer, 2014. *SpringerLink.*

The Chicago Manual of Style. Chicago: U of Chicago P, 2010. Print.

"Chinese Astronomy." n.d. *what-when-how.com*.

Ching, Frank, Mark Jarzombek, and Vikramaditya Prakash. *A Global History of Architecture*. Hoboken, N.J.: John Wiley, 2010. *books.google.com*.

"Chaco Culture." *World Heritage Center*. Unesco, n.d.

Chwanya, Matengo. "Namoratunga Like the Nabta Playa." *streamafrica.com*.

Clack, Timothy, and Marcus Brittain. "Place-Making, Participative Archaeologies and Mursi Megaliths: Some Implications for Aspects of Pre- and Proto-History in the Horn Of Africa." *Journal Of East African Studies* 5.1 (2011): 85-107. *Political Science Complete*.

Clark, Liesl. "Who Built the Pyramids?" *NOVA*, 1997. pbs.org.

Corso, David. "The Psychological and Physical Effects of Video Game Play." *Caravel, Undergraduate Research Journal* (2014): n.p. *caravel.sc.edu*.

Cox, Trevor. "Was Stonehenge Built for Rock Music?" *ShortCutsBlog*. *The Guardian*. 5 Mar. 2014.

Cultural Treasures of Nepal. Nepal Tourism Board, 2011. *Welcomenepal.com*.

Daily, Gordon. "Comment." 28 August 2009. "Starts with a Bang." Ethan Siegel. 26 Aug. 2009. *scienceblogs.com*.

Dalgleish, Hannah. "Delving into Archaeoastronomy." n.d. *thetribeonline*.

Dauncey, Guy. *Stormy Weather: 101 Solutions to Global Climate Change*. Gabriola Island, BC: New Society P, 2001. *books.google.com*.

Dearborn, David S. P., and Raymond E. White. "The Torreón of Machu Picchu as an Observatory." *Archaeoastronomy*. 14.5 (1983): 37-49. *ProQuest*.

DeBose, Charles. "Codeswitching: Black English and Standard English in the African-American Linguistic Repertoire." *Codeswitching*. Ed. Carol Eastman. Clevedon: Multilingual Matters, 1992. 157–67. *books.google.com*.

"Dimensional Analysis." *Department of Physics*. University of Guelph, n.d.

"Discourse Analysis." *Foundations of Qualitative Research in Education*. Harvard University, 2008.

Doescher, Ian. *William Shakespeare's Star Wars: Verily, A New Hope*. Philadelphia, PA: Quirk, 2013. *amazon.com*.

Doney, Scott C., et al. "Climate Change Impacts on Marine Ecosystems." *Annual Review of Marine Science* 4 (2012). 11-37. *annualreviews.org*.

Drehle, David Von. "The Case Against Summer Vacation." *Time Magazine*. 22 July 2010. *content.time.com*.

edge.org. John Brockman, 1996.

Eisner, Peter. "Who Discovered Machu Picchu?" *Smithsonian Magazine*. March 2009. *smithsonianmag.com*.

Erduran, Sibel, and Rosa Villamanan. "Cool Argument: Engineering Students Written Arguments about Thermodynamics in the Context of the Peltier Effect in Refrigeration." *Educación química* (2009): 119-25.

Evans, Walker, and James Agee. *Let Us Now Praise Famous Men*. (1941) Boston: Houghton Mifflin, 2001. *books.google.com*.

"Executive Summary." University Writing Center. Texas A&M University. 2011. *writingcenter.tamu.edu*.

"Fajada Butte." *Evaluating Models of Chaco: A Virtual Conference*. University of Colorado. University of Colorado, 1997.

Fall, A., et al. "Sliding Friction on Wet and Dry Sand." *Physical Review Letters* 112 (175502): 2014. *journals.aps.org*.

"Fallacies: Alphabetic List (Full List)." *changeminds.org*.

Farrar, Renée. "Apple (a poem)." *Digital America*. 24 April 2014. *digitalamerica.org*.

Fazenda, Bruno. "Acoustics of Stonehenge." *University of Salford*. Acoustics Research Centre, University of Salford, 2012.

Fernández-Garrido, Regla. "Stasis-theory in Judicial Speeches of Greek Novels." *Greek, Roman, and Byzantine Studies* 49.3 (2009): 453–72. *Greek, Roman, and Byzantine Studies*.

Fichter, Darlene. "What is a Mashup?" *Library Mashups Exploring New Ways to Deliver Library Data*. Ed. Nicole Engard. Medford, NJ: Information Today, 2009. 3-17. *books.infotoday.com*.

"For Teachers: 1001 Assignments." *Department of English*. Louisiana State University. 23 July 2013.

Game Over: Gender, Race & Violence in Video Games. dir. Nina Huntemann. Media Education Foundation, 2002. Film.

Garcia, Nelly Robles. "Land Use in the Environs of Monte Albán and Mitla." *The Management of Archaeological Resources in Mexico. Oaxaca as a Case Study. Society for American Archaeology.* Society for American Archaeology, 2000.

Gates, Henry Louis, Jr., and Abby Wolf. *The Henry Louis Gates, Jr. Reader.* New York: Basic Civitas, 2012. *amazon.com.*

"General Information: Chichen Itza, The Great Ball Court." *American Egypt.* Mystery Lane Press, 2009.

Gentile, Douglas A., ed. *Media Violence and Children: A Complete Guide for Parents and Professionals.* Westport, CT: Praeger, 2003. *psychology.iastate.edu.*

Gere, Anne Ruggles, et al. "Using Evidence in Writing. A Policy Brief Produced by the National Council of Teachers of English." Urbana, Ill: NCTE, 2012. *ncte.org.*

Gibaldi, Joseph. *MLA Handbook of Research for Writers.* 7th ed. New York: MLA, 2009. Print.

Gibson, Karen. "All Roads Lead to Chaco Canyon." *Cobblestone* 20.6 (1999): 26. *General OneFile.*

Gilbert, Sandra M., and Susan Gubar. *Norton Anthology of Literature by Women: The Tradition in English.* New York: Norton, 1985. Print.

"The Giza Plateau." *sca-egypt.org.* Supreme Council of Antiquities. n.d.

Goffman, Erving. *The Presentation of Self in Everyday Life.* Garden City, NY: Doubleday, 1959. Print.

Good, Byron J., et al., eds. *A Reader in Medical Anthropology: Theoretical Trajectories, Emergent Realities.* Chichester, West Sussex, UK: Wiley-Blackwell, 2010.

Gore, Albert. *An Inconvenient Truth.* Hollywood, Calif.: Paramount, 2006.

Graff, Nelson. "Teaching Rhetorical Analysis to Promote Transfer of Learning." *Journal of Adolescent & Adult Literacy* 53.5 (2010): 376-85. *ProQuest.*

Grahame-Smith, Seth. *Pride and Prejudice and Zombies: The Classic Regency Romance—Now with Ultraviolent Zombie Mayhem.* Philadelphia, PA: Quirk, 2009.

Graves, Roger, Theresa Hyland and Bob M. Samuels. "Undergraduate Writing Assignments: An Analysis of Syllabi at One Canadian College." *Written Communication.* 27.3 (2010): 293–317. *sagepub.*

"Great Ball Court." *Chichen Itza.* Chichen Itza, 2014.

Greitemeyer, Tobias. "Intense Acts Of Violence During Video Game Play Make Daily Life Aggression Appear Innocuous: A New Mechanism Why Violent Video Games Increase Aggression." *Journal of Experimental Social Psychology* 50.1 (2014): 52-56. *PsycINFO.*

Grossman, Dave, and Gloria DeGaetano. *Stop Teaching Our Kids to Kill: A Call to Action against TV, Movie & Video Game Violence.* New York: Crown, 1999. Print.

Gtaforums.com. GTANet.

"Guide to Boudhanath." *thelongestwayhome.com.* n.d.

Guinness World Records 2014: Gamer's Edition. London: Guinness World Records, 2013. Print.

Haas, Christina, and Linda Flower. "Rhetorical Reading Strategies and the Construction of Meaning." *College Composition and Communication* 39.2 (1988): 167-83. *JSTOR.*

Haamurabi. " 'The Hobbit', Audio Book-Part I of III." Online video. *YouTube.* YouTube, 16 Feb. 2011.

Hagan, Susan M. "Visual/Verbal Collaboration in Print: Complementary Differences, Necessary Ties, and an Untapped Rhetorical Opportunity." *Written Communication* 24.1 (2007): 49-73. *SageJournals.*

Hamblin, Charles. *Fallacies.* London: Methuen, 1970. *scribd.com.*

Hansen, Hans V., and Robert C. Pinto, eds. *Fallacies. Classical and Contemporary Readings.* University Park, PA: Penn State UP, 1995. 213-21.

Harder, Jeff. "How Synthesizers Work." *howstuffworks.com.*

Hawkins, Gerald S. "Stonehenge Decoded." *Nature* 200 (1963): 306-8. *nature.com.*

Heaney, Christopher. *Cradle of Gold: the Story of Hiram Bingham, a Real-Life Indiana Jones, and the Search for Machu Picchu.* New York: Palgrave Macmillan, 2010. Print.

Heidebrink-Bruno, Sarah. "The Play's The Thing: Lessons from Preschool Storytimes for College Classrooms." *Hybrid Pedagogy.* 29 May 2014. *hybridpedagogy.com.*

Hempstead, Colin A. and William E. Worthington, eds. *Encyclopedia of 20ᵗʰ-century Technology.* New York: Routledge, 2005. Print.

Herodotus. *"The Histories"—The Great Pyramid.* Transl. A.D. Godley. Cambridge: Harvard UP, 1920. *blog.worldmysteries.com.*

"Historic Centre of Oaxaca and Archaeological Site of Monte Albán." *whc.unesco* UNESCO, n.d.

"History & Culture." *Chaco Culture.* National Park Service, n.d.

"History of Stupas." *Shambhala Mountain Center.* Shambhala Mountain Center, n.d.

Hoey, Brian A. *brianhoey.com.*

Holbrook, Jarita C., R. Thebe Medupe, Johnson O. Urama, eds. *African Cultural Astronomy: Current Archaeoastronomy and Ethnoastronomy Research in Africa.* Berlin: Springer, 2009.

Holmes, John. "LibGuide." University of Washington Libraries. *guides.lib.washington.edu.* University of Washington.

Horning, Alice S. "Reading across the Curriculum as the Key to Student Success." *Across the Disciplines 4.* 14 May 2007. *wac.colostate.edu.*

Huckin, Thomas, Jennifer Andrus, and Jennifer Clary-Lemon. "Critical Discourse Analysis and Rhetoric and Composition." *College Composition and Communication* 64.1 (2012): 107-29. *ProQuest.*

Hyland, Ken. "Academic Attribution: Citation and the Construction of Disciplinary Knowledge." *Applied Linguistics* 20.3 (1999): 341-67. *Oxford Journals.*

---. "Writing in the Disciplines: Research Evidence for Specificity." *Taiwan International ESP Journal.* 1.1 (2009): 5-22. *tespa.org.tw.*

Ingram, Laura, James Hussey, Michelle Tigani, and Mary Hemmelgarn. "Writing a Literature Review and Using a Synthesis Matrix." *writingcenter.fiu.edu.*

Institute of Medicine. Committee on Building Bridges in the Brain, Behavioral, and Clinical Sciences. "The Potential of Interdisciplinary Research to Solve Problems in the Brain, Behavioral, and Clinical Sciences." *Bridging Disciplines in the Brain, Behavioral, and Clinical Sciences.* Ed. Terry C. Pellmar and Leon Eisenberg. Washington, D.C.: National Academies P, 2000. *ncbi.nlm.nih.gov.*

"Introduction and Overview of The Great Pyramid of Giza." *gizapyramid.com.* n.d.

"Ironyca Stood in the Fire." *ironyca.wordpress.com.*

"Israeli-Palestinian Conflict." 1 May 2014. *procon.org.*

James, Kyle. "Four Types of Web Analytic Data." *doteduguru.com.* 27 Oct. 2008.

Jamieson, Sandra. "Synthesis Writing." *users.drew.edu.*

Jarus, Owen. "Photos: Amazing Discoveries at Egypt's Giza Pyramids." 21 Jan. 2014. *livescience.com.*

---. "Stonehenge: Facts & Theories About Mysterious Monument." *livescience.com.* 15 Sept. 2014.

Jaworski, Adam, and Nikolaus Copeland. *The Discourse Reader.* New York: Routledge, 1999. Print.

Johnson, Burke, and Larry Christenson. "Writing Quantitative Research Questions. Table 3.7." *Educational Research. Qualitative, Quantitative, and Mixed Methods.* 4ᵗʰ ed. Thousand Oaks, Calif.: Sage, 2010. 8 Feb. 2007.

Johnson, Ralph H. "ISSA Proceedings 1998—The Problem of Truth for Theories of Argument." *Rozenberg Quarterly* n.d. *rozenbergquarterly.com.*

Joubert, Joseph. *Extracts from the Pensées of Joubert.* 1925. Trans. Katharine Lyttelton. Pittsburgh, PA: Laboratory P, 1925. Print.

Juul, Jesper. *A Dictionary of Video Game Theory.* *half-real.net.*

Kak, Subhash. "Visions of the Cosmos: Archaeoastronomy in Ancient India." *Journal of Cosmology* 9 (2010): 2063-77. *journal of cosmology.com.*

Kantner, John. "Rethinking Chaco as a System." *Kiva* 69.2 (2003): 207-27. *JSTOR.*

Kantor, Brooke, Helen Clark, and Lydia Federico. "An Exercise in Body Image." *Harvard Political Review.* 28 June 2014. *harvardpolitics.com.*

---. "Strong and Beautiful." *Harvard Political Review*. 28 June 2014. *harvardpolitics.com*. Web.

Katkowski, Nolan. "Top Arguments with Parents over School, Chores, and Curfew." 10 May 2005.

Kedavra, Avada. "Alan Rickman Reads Shakespeare's Sonnet 130." Online video. *YouTube*. YouTube. 20 May 2013.

Kendall-Tackett, Kathleen. "Silence that Inner Critic and Start Writing!" *Meditations and More*. February 2009. *kathleenkendall-tackett.com*.

Ketokivi, Mikko, and Saku Mantere. "Two Strategies For Inductive Reasoning In Organizational Research." *Academy Of Management Review* 35.2 (2010): 315-33. *Business Source Complete*.

Kies, Daniel. "Underlying Assumptions." *The HyperText Books*. Department of English. College of DuPage. 10 Jan. 2012.

Kinzer, Heath, and Judith L. Gillies. "Cross-Cultural Analysis." *Department of Anthropology*. The University of Alabama, 2009.

Krakauer, Jon. *Into Thin Air: A Personal Account of the Mt. Everest Disaster*. New York: Villard, 1997. Print.

Krippner, Greta. "Making a Sociological Argument." 28 Sept. 2000. American Sociological Association. *asanet.org*.

Krupp, Edwin C. *Echoes of the Ancient Skies: The Astronomy of Lost Civilizations*. Mineola, NY: Dover, 2003. Print.

Lamott, Anne. *Bird by Bird: Some Instructions on Writing and Life*. New York: Random House, 2007. Print.

Leach, Andrew. " 'One Day It'll All Make Sense': Hip-Hop and Rap Resources for Music Librarians." *Notes* 65.1 (2008): 9-37. *JSTOR*.

Lee, Carol D., and Anika Spratley. "Reading in the Disciplines. The Challenges of Adolescent Literacy." New York, NY: Carnegie, 2010. *carnegie.org*.

Leung, Rebecca. "Can a Video Game Lead to Murder? Did 'Grand Theft Auto' Cause One Teenager to Kill?" *60 Minutes*. 17 June 2005. *cbsnews.com*.

Levin, Henry, dir. *Journey to the Center of the Earth*. Twentieth Century Fox, 1959. Film.

Liu, Ziming. "Reading Behavior in the Digital Environment: Changes in Reading Behavior over the Past Ten Years." *Journal of Documentation* 61.6 (2005): 700–12. *ProQuest*.

Livingstone, David. *A Practical Guide to Scientific Data Analysis*. Chichester, U.K.: Wiley, 2009. Print.

"The Logic of Scientific Arguments." *Understanding Science*. University of California Museum of Paleontology. Berkeley. *undsci.berkeley.edu*.

"Logical Fallacies." *logicalfallacies.info*.

lolmythesis. Angie. Dec. 2013.

Lopata, Peg. "Chichén Itzá." *Faces: People, Places, and Cultures*. July-Aug. 2008: 28+. *General OneFile*.

Lotan, Gilad. "Big Data for Breaking News: Lessons from #Aurora, Colorado." SocialFlow. 1 Aug. 2012. *blog. socialflow.com*.

Lowe, George, and Huw Lewis-Jones. *The Conquest of Everest: Original Photographs from the Legendary First Ascent*. New York: Thames & Hudson, 2013. Print.

Luongo, Giuseppe, et al. "Impact of the AD 79 Explosive Eruption on Pompeii, II. Causes of Death of the Inhabitants Inferred by Stratigraphic Analysis and Areal Distribution of the Human Casualties." *Journal of Volcanology and Geothermal Research* 126 (2003): 169-200. *Science Direct*.

Lynch, B. Mark, and Lawrence H. Robbins. "Namoratunga: the First Archaeoastronomical Evidence in Sub-Saharan Africa." *Science* 200 (1978): 766-68. *JSTOR*.

Madson, John. "The Deadliest Day on Everest: May 10, 1996." *Glide Magazine* 4 Mar. 2003. Web. *glidemagazine. com*.

Magli, Giulio. "Akhet Khufu: Archaeo-Astronomical Hints at a Common Project of the Two Main Pyramids of Giza, Egypt." *Nexus Network Journal* 11.1 (2009): 35-50. *ProQuest*.

---. "At the Other End of the Sun's Path: A New Interpretation of Machu Picchu." *Nexus Network Journal* 12.2 (2010): 321-41. *ProQuest*.

Major, Ted. "Rhetorical Triangle." Photograph. *flickr.com*.

Malville, J. McKim. "Prehistoric Astronomy in the American Southwest." *The Astronomy Quarterly* 8 (1991): 1-36. *ScienceDirect*.

Mangen, Anne. "Hypertext Fiction Reading: Haptics and Immersion." *Journal of Research in Reading* 31.4 (2008): 404-19. *onlinelibrary.wiley.com.*

Marcus, Joyce. "The Iconography of Militarism at Monte Albán and Neighboring Sites in the Valley of Oaxaca." In *The Origins of Religious Art and Iconography in Pre-Classic Mesoamerica.* Ed. Henry. B. Nicholson. Los Angeles: UCLA Latin American Center, 1976. 123-39. Print.

---. "The Origins of Mesoamerican Writing." *Annual Review of Anthropology* (1976): 35-67. *JSTOR.*

Marsh, Charles. "The Syllogism of Apologia: Rhetorical Stasis Theory and Crisis Communication." *Public Relations Review* 32.1 (2006): 41-6. *ScienceDirect.*

Martin, Denise. "Reflections on African Celestial Culture." *African American Consciousness: Past and Present.* Ed. James L. Conyers. New Brunswick, N.J.: Transaction, 2012. 109-26. *books.google.com.*

---. "Reflections on African Celestial Culture." *African American Consciousness: Past and Present.* Ed. James L. Conyers. New Brunswick, N.J.: Transaction, 2012. 109-26. *books.google.com.*

Martin, George R. R. *A Game of Thrones.* New York: Bantam, 1996. Print.

"Mayan Ball Game." *ChichenItzaRuins.* chichenitzaruins.org, 2013.

McCauley, Marissa. "Probing Question: How Were the Egyptian Pyramids Built?" *Penn State.* Penn State, 15 April 2014.

McColm, Gregory. "Analysis, Synthesis, and Doing Homework."

McCullough, Jessica. "Identifying and Finding Scholarly Sources: A Web Tutorial." George Washington University. 7 Dec. 2009. *gwu.edu.*

McKenna-Lawlor, Susan M. P. "Astronomy in Ireland from Earliest Times to the Eighteenth Century." *Vistas in Astronomy* 26.1 (1982): 1-13. *ScienceDirect.*

McKeon, Matthew. "Argument." *Internet Encyclopedia of Philosophy. iep.utm.edu.*

MedicineNet.com. MedicineNet, 1996-2014.

Michael. "Violent Video Games – What Does the Research Say?" Podcast. The Psych Files. *thepsychfiles.com.*

Mills, Elizabeth Shown. *Evidence Explained: Citing History Sources from Artifacts to Cyberspace.* Baltimore: Genealogical P, 2007. *amazon.com.*

Mishra, Rekha, and Kaushik, Neeraj. "Big Data: An Analysis." *International Journal of Science, Engineering and Computer Technology* 3.1 (2013): 29-31. *ProQuest.*

"Monte Albán." *ancient-wisdom.*

Moreno, Julio. "10 Questions You Never Had about Machu Picchu." *travelworldheritage.com.* 26 Aug. 2013.

Muller, Nikki. "The Ivy-League Hustle (I Went to Princeton, Bitch)." *YouTube.* 20 May 2012. *youtube.com.*

Munson, Gregory E. "Mesa Verde Archaeoastronomy." *Handbook of Archaeoastronomy and Ethnoastronomy.* Ed. Clive N. Ruggles. New York: Springer, 2014. 565-75. *link.springer.com.*

Murphy, Anthony. "The Ancient Astronomers of Newgrange." mythicalireland.com. *mythicalireland.com,* 2002.

Nash, Barbara P., Harry V. Merrick, and Francis H. Brown. "Obsidian Types from Holocene Sites around Lake Turkana, and Other Localities in Northern Kenya." *Journal of Archaeological Science* 38.6 (2011): 1371-76. *ScienceDirect.*

NavList.

Naydler, Jeremy. *Shamanic Wisdom in the Pyramid Texts: The Mystical Tradition of Ancient Egypt.* Rocherster, Vt.: Inner Traditions, 2005.

Neal, Mark Anthony. *NewBlackMan (In Exile).* n.d.

"Nepal: Everest Base Camp Trek." *National Geographic Expeditions.* National Geographic, n.d.

"New Archaeoastronomical Alignments Found at Machu Picchu." *ancienthistoricalresearchfoundation.com.* 8 Oct. 2013.

Newell, William H. "The Role of Interdisciplinary Studies in the Liberal Arts." *LiberalArtsOnline* 7.1 (2007): n.p. *liberalarts.wabash.edu.*

"Newgrange." *newgrange.com.*

Norris, Ray P., and Duane W. Hamacher. "Astronomical Symbolism in Australian Aboriginal Rock Art." *Rock Art Research* 28.1 (2011): 99-106. *Art & Architecture Complete.*

Northcut, Kathryn M. "Stasis Theory and Paleontology Discourse." Sept. 2007. *MoSpace.*

O'Dell, William. "Top 10 Arguments That Can't Be Won." *toptenz.net.* 13 Nov. 2008.

Oldham, Davis. "Assumptions." *Shoreline Community College.* shoreline.edu.

OMICS Publishing Group. "Peer Review Process." *omicsonline.org.*

"One Billion Hungry. Can We Feed the World?" *cornellpress.com.*

"Overanalyze." *Urban Dictionary.* 23 May 2008.

Ozanne, Henry. " 'Synthesis' in Social Science." *Sociometry* 8.2 (1945): 208-15. *JSTOR.*

Patton, Michael Quinn. *Qualitative Research and Evaluation Methods.* Thousand Oaks, Calif.: Sage, 2003. Print.

Pauwels, Luc. "Visual Sociology Reframed: An Analytical Synthesis and Discussion of Visual Methods in Social and Cultural Research." *Sociological Methods & Research* 38 (2010): 545-81.

"Petroglyph National Monument New Mexico." *National Park Service.* National Park Service, n.d.

physics.org. Institute of Physics, n.d.

Pillans, Brad, and L. Keith Fifield. "Erosion Rates and Weathering History of Rock Surfaces Associated with Aboriginal Rock Art Engravings (Petroglyphs) on Burrup Peninsula, Western Australia, from Cosmogenic Nuclide Measurements." *Quaternary Science Reviews* 69 (2013): 98-106. *ScienceDirect.*

Popovič, Anton, and Francis Macri. "Literary Synthesis." *Canadian Review of Comparative Literature.* 4.2 (1977): 117-32. *ejournals.library.ualberta.ca.*

Porter, James E. *Audience and Rhetoric: An Archaeological Composition of the Discourse Community.* New York: Prentice Hall, 1992. Print.

Pratt, Mary Louise. "Arts of the Contact Zone." *Profession* (1991): 33-40. *JSTOR.*

Prelli, Lawrence J. "Stasis and the Problem of Incommensurate Communication." *Rhetoric and Incommensurability.* Ed. Randy Allen Harris. West Lafayette, IN: Parlor P., 2005.

"Primary and Secondary Sources." Education Psychology Library. University of California, Berkeley. 2013. *lib.berkeley.edu.*

"Quotations: Using Signal Phrases to Integrate Quotations into Your Writing." *Writing Across the Curriculum.* Loyola University. *loyno.edu.*

Rampolla, Mary Lynn. *A Pocket Guide to Writing in History.* Boston: Bedford/St. Martin's, 2007. *books.google.com.*

Rao, N. Kameswara. "Astronomy with Buddhist Stupas of Sanchi." *Bulletin, Astronomical Society of India* 20 (1992): 87- 98. *adsabs.harvard.edu.*

Reed, Frank. "The Analemma in Castaway." *NavList.* NavList. 10 Dec. 2006.

Reinhard, Johan. *Machu Picchu: Exploring an Ancient Sacred Center.* Los Angeles: Cotsen Institute of Archaeology, U of California, 2007. Print.

"Religion of Nepal." *Royal Mt. Trekking.* royaltibet.com. n.d.

Rettberg, Jill. *Blogging.* Cambridge, UK: Malden, 2008. Print.

Richardson, Robert, et al. "The 'Djedi' Robot Exploration of the Southern Shaft of the Queen's Chamber in the Great Pyramid of Giza, Egypt." *Journal of Field Robotics* 30.3 (2013): 323-48. *onlinelibrary.wiley.com.*

Roberts, David. "Romancing the Stones." *Smithsonian* 33.4 (2002): 86-94, 96. *ProQuest.*

Rossiter, David. "An Introduction to Statistical Analysis." *itc.nl.* International Institute for Geo-information Science & Earth Observation (ITC). 9 Jan. 2006.

Rottenberg, Annette, and Donna Haisty Winchell. *The Structure of Argument.* New York: Macmillan, 2011. *books.google.com.*

Ruggles, Clive L.N. *Ancient Astronomy: An Encyclopedia of Cosmologies and Myth.* Santa Barbara, Calif.: ABC-CLIO, 2005. Print.

---. "Lecture 7: The Rise of American Archaeoastronomy and the 'Green' v. 'Brown' Methodological Divide." 2003. *le.ac.uk.*

---. "Stonehenge for the 1990s." *Nature* 381.6580 (1996): 278-79. *ProQuest.*

Saint-Germain, Michelle A. "PPA 696 Research Methods Data Collection Strategies II: Qualitative Research." *csu.edu*.

Samuels, Holly. "Brainstorming Research Questions. Tip Sheet 10." *CRLS Research Guide*. 2004. Web. *www.crlsresearchguide.org*. 21 Mar. 2014.

Schiffrin, Deborah, Deborah Tannen, and Heidi E. Hamilton, eds. *The Handbook of Discourse Analysis*. Malden, MA: Blackwell, 2001.

"Scientific Falsification." *explorable.com*. 5 Aug. 2010.

Schwartz-DuPre, Rae Lynn. *Communicating Colonialism: Readings on Postcolonial Theory(s) and Communication*. New York: Peter Lang, 2014. *amazon.com*.

Shelby, Karen. "The Stupa." *Smart History*. Khan Academy, n.d.

Shmueli, Efraim. "How is Objectivity in the Social Sciences Possible?: A Re-Evaluation of Karl Mannheim's Concept of 'Relationism.'" *Journal for General Philosophy of Science*. 10.1 (1979): 107-18. *JSTOR*.

Sipiora, Phillip, and James S. Baumlin, eds. *Rhetoric and Kairos: Essays in History, Theory, and Praxis*. Albany, NY: SUNY P, 2012. *books.google.com*.

Sollaci, Luciana B., and Mauricio G. Pereira. "The Introduction, Methods, Results, and Discussion (IMRAD) Structure: A Fifty-Year Survey." *Journal of the Medical Library Association* 92.3 (2004): 364-371. *ncbi.nlm.nih.gov*.

Sparavigna, Amelia Carolina. "Maria Reiche's Line to Archaeoastronomy." *Archaeoastronomy and Ancient Technologies* 1.2 (2013): 48-54. *arXiv.org*.

Spence, Kate. "Ancient Egyptian Chronology and the Astronomical Orientation of Pyramids." *Nature* 408.6810 (2000): 320-324. *ProQuest*. 9 Sept. 2014.

Spielberg, Steven, dir. *Raiders of the Lost Ark*. Paramount, 1981. Film.

Spigelman, Candace. *Personally Speaking: Experience as Evidence in Academic Discourse*. Carbondale, Ill.: Southern Illinois UP, 2004.

"Spinal Tap's Nigel Tufnel on Why Aliens Didn't Build Stonehenge." *Stonehenge Decoded*. National Geographic Channel. 2007. Television. *natgeotv.com*.

Springen, Karen. "This is your Brain on Alien Killer Pimps of Nazi Doom." *Newsweek* 148.22 (December 11, 2006): 48. *ProQuest*.

Spurlock, Morgan, and Steve Horowitz, Dir. *SuperSize Me*. New York: Hart Sharp Video, 2004.

Stern, David I., and Robert K. Kaufmann. "Anthropogenic and Natural Causes of Climate Change." *Climatic Change* 122.1-2 (2014): 257–69. *SpringerLink*.

Storm, Darlene. "Not Again: Stop Blaming Violent Video Games for Mass Shootings." 18 Sept. 2013. *blogs.computerworld.com*. Computer World.

"Super Size Me Quotes." *imdb.com*.

"Synthesis." *Biology Online*. 14 April 2011.

"Synthesis." *Oxford English Dictionary*.

Talisse, Robert, and Scott F. Aikin. "Two Forms of the Straw Man." *Argumentation* 20.3 (2006): 345-52. *ProQuest*.

Tang, Haixu, and Sun Kim. "Bioinformatics: Mining the Massive Data from High Throughput Genomics Experiments." *Analysis of Biological Data A Soft Computing Approach*. Ed. Sanghamitra Bandyopadhyay, Ujjwal Maulik, and Jason T L Wang. *Science, Engineering, and Biology Informatics*. Vol. 3. 3-24. *worldscientific.com*.

Thom, Alexander. "Stonehenge." *Journal for the History of Astronomy* 5.2 (1974): 71-90. *SAO/NASA Astrophysics Data System*.

"Title Summary." Sale, Richard, and George Rodway. *Everest and Conquest in the Himalaya: Science and Courage on the World's Highest Mountain*. Barnsley: Pen & Sword Discovery, 2011. *library.duke.edu*.

Toulmin, Stephen. *The Uses of Argument*. Cambridge: Cambridge UP, 2003. Print.

Tuggle, H. David, Alex H. Townsend, and Thomas J. Riley. "Laws, Systems, and Research Designs: A Discussion of Explanation in Archaeology." *American Antiquity* 37.1 (1972): 3-12. *JSTOR*.

Twenge, Jean M. "Yes, Violent Video Games Do Cause Aggression." *Psychology Today*. 21 Dec. 2012. *pscychologytoday.com*.

U.S. Wisconsin Department of Public Instructions. "Literacy in the Discipline and Disciplinary Literacy: A Place for Both." 2012. *standards.dpi.wi.gov.*

United States. Department of State. Bureau of Democracy, Human Rights and Labor. *Nepal 2013 Human Rights Report.* 2014. *state.gov.*

Urcid, Javier, and Arthur Joyce. "Early Transformations of Monte Alban's Main Plaza and Their Political Implications, 500 BC-AD 200." *Mesoamerican Plazas: Arenas of Community and Power.* Ed. Kenichiro Tsukamoto and Takeshi Inomata. Tucson: U of Arizona P, 2014. 149-67.

Useful Science. usefulscience.

Van Der Sluijs, Marinus Anthony, and Anthony L. Peratt. "Searching For Rock Art Evidence For An Ancient Super Aurora." *Expedition* 52.2 (2010): 33-42. *Academic Search Complete.*

Vassallo, Paul. "The Knowledge Continuum: Organizing for Research and Scholarly Communication." *Office of Information Services. United States Department of Commerce. National Institute of Standards and Technology.* Web. *nist.gov.*

Venner, Ed, Barny Revill, and Ed Wardle, dir. *Everest: Beyond the Limits.* Discovery Channel, 2006-2009. Film.

Verano, John W. "Human Skeletal Remains from Tomb 1, Sipan (Lambayeque River Valley, Peru); and their Social Implications." *Antiquity* 71.273 (1997): 670-82. *ProQuest.*

"Violence in the Media — Psychologists Study TV and Video Game Violence for Potential Harmful Effects." *apa. org.* Nov. 2013.

Walker, Janice R. "Everything Changes, or Why MLA Isn't (Always) Right." *Writing Spaces. Readings on Writing.* Anderson, S.C.: Parlor P, 2011. 257-69. *wac.colostate.edu.*

Walton, Douglas. *Fundamentals of Critical Argumentation.* New York: Cambridge UP, 2006.

Ward, Christine. "The Bluff Great House. On the Periphery of the Chaco World." *Expedition* 45.3 (2003): 9-14. *penn.museum.*

Watchman, Alan, Paul Taçon, and Maxime Aubert. Correspondence on "Erosion rates and Weathering History of Rock Surfaces Associated with Aboriginal Rock Art Engravings (Petroglyphs) on Burrup Peninsula, Western Australia, from Cosmogenic Nuclide Measurements" by Brad Pillans and Keith Fifield. *Quaternary Science Reviews* 69: 98–106. *Quaternary Science Reviews* 91 (2014): 70-73. *ScienceDirect.*

Weaver, Teresa K. "Maya Angelou's Final Chapter." *Palm Beach Post-Cox News Service.* 5 May 2002. *racematters.org.*

Weber, Karin. "Outdoor Adventure Tourism: A Review of Research Approaches." *Sport & Tourism: A Reader.* Ed. Mike Weed. New York: Routledge, 2007. 57-71. Print.

WebMD. WebMD, 2005-14.

Welfare, Simon, John Fairley, and Arthur C. Clarke. *Arthur C. Clarke's Mysterious World.* London: Collins, 1980. *knowth.com.*

"What is English Studies?" *Department of English.* Illinois State U., 2009.

"What is Chemical Analysis." *Department of Chemistry.* University of Arizona. n.d.

Wikipedia: WikiProject Video Games. en.wikipedia.org.

Woldu, Gail Hilson. "The Kaleidescope of Writing on Hip-Hop Culture." Notes. 67.1 (2010): 9-38. *Academic OneFile.*

Wolf, Mark J. P., ed. *Encyclopedia of Video Games: The Culture, Technology, and Art of Gaming.* Santa Barbara, Calif.: Greenwood, 2012. *ProQuest ebrary.*

"Women In Shorts (Maybe) Cause Car Crash In 1937 (PHOTO)." *Huffington Post.* 15 Mar. 2013. *huffingtonpost.com.*

"Writing a Synthesis Essay." *Northern Virginia Community College.* n.d.

Youngblood, Dawn. "Multidisciplinarity, Interdisciplinarity, and Bridging Disciplines: A Matter of Process." *Journal of Research Practice* 3.2 (2007): n.p. *jrp.icaap.org.*

Zemeckis, Robert, dir. *Castaway.* Twentieth Century Fox, 2000. Film.

Acknowledgments

Chapter 1

Sun Dagger image courtesy of Karl Klernberger/© Solstice Project.

Chapter 2

Krieger, Katharine. "Google Earth's Role in Marine Conservation through Biologging." *Deliberations. 2011. twp. duke.edu/deliberations.*

Chapter 3

Excerpt from "Evaluation of Corrective Measures Implemented for the Preventive Conservation of Fresco Paintings in Ariadne's House (Pompeii, Italy)"by Paloma Merello, Fernando-Juan Garcia-Diego, and Manuel Zarzo. *Chemistry Central Journal* 7 (2013): 87.

Excerpt from "Before Pornography: Sexual Representation in Ancient Roman Visual Culture" by John R. Clarke. *Pornographic Art and the Aesthetics of Pornography.* Edited by Hans Maes. New York: Palmgrave, 2013.

Excerpt from "Imperial Decadence: The Making of the Myths in Edward Bulwer-Lytton's 'The Last Days of Pompeii'" by William St Clair and Annika Bautz. *Victorian Literature and Culture* 40.2 (2012): 359-396.

Excerpt from "Painted Birds at Pompeii"by Brian A. Sparkes. *International Journal of Osteoarchaeology* 7 (1997): 350–353.

Chapter 4

Aleghfeli, Obaid Rashed. "Video Games." *Undergraduate Research Journal for the Human Sciences.* 11 (2012): n.p. *kon. org.* Reprinted with permission.

Chapter 5

Excerpt from "Fatal Attraction" by Alistair Scott. *The New York Times,* May 18, 1997.

Excerpt from "Why Climb a Mountain? It's There, and It's Hard to Do" by Susan Stewart. *The New York Times,* November 14, 2006.

Excerpt from *"Review of The Conquest of Everest: Original Photographs from the Legendary First Ascent"* by Margaret Heilbrun. *Library Journal* 138.7 (2013).

Excerpt from "Review of *Top of the World Environmental Research*" by Sebastian Interlandi. *Quarterly Review of Biology* 75.2 (2000): 209-10.

Morrison, Shawnda A., Jurij Gorjanc, and Igor Mekjavic. "Mount Everest and Makalu Cold Injury Amputation: 40 Years On." *High Altitude Medicine & Biology* 15.1 (2014): 78-83.

Excerpt from "Books on History and Exploration, with a Focus on Central Asia … [and] The History of Climbing and Mountaineering" by Bill Buxton. billbuxton.com, 2014.

Excerpt from "United States. Department of State. Bureau of Democracy, Human Rights and Labor." Nepal 2013 Human Rights Report. 2014. state.gov.

Excerpt from "Introduction." *Sport & Tourism: A Reader,* edited by Mike Weed. New York: Routledge, 2007. 1-6.

Excerpt from "Climbing Mount Everest: Women, Career and Family in Outdoor Education" by Linda Allin. *Australian Journal of Outdoor Education* 8.2 (2004): 64-71.

Excerpt from "The Mallory Mount Everest Expedition of 1924: An Irish Perspective" by Justyna Pyz. *History Ireland* 19.5 (2011): 42-43.

Excerpt from "Confetti of Empire: The Conquest of Everest in Nepal, India, Britain, and New Zealand" by Peter H. Hansen. *Comparative Studies in Society and History* 42.2 (2000): 307-332.

Excerpt from "Death and Anger on Everest" by Jon Krakauer. *thenewyorkeronline.com*, Apr. 21, 2014.

Chapter 6

Excerpt from "Hip Hop, Health, and Human Papilloma Virus (HPV): Using Wireless Technology to Increase HPV Vaccination Uptake" by Tami L. Thomas, Dionne P. Stephens, and Beverlee Blanchard. *The Journal for Nurse Practitioners* 6.6 (2010): 464-70.

Excerpt from "Authenticity and Consumption in the Australian Hip Hop Culture" by Damien Arthur. *Qualitative Market Research* 9.2 (2006): 140-156.

Excerpt from "Debating Hip-Hop: Does Gangsta Rap Harm Black Americans?" by Peter Katel. *Issues for Debate in Sociology: Selections from CQ Researcher*. Thousand Oaks, CA: Pine Forge P, 2010.

Excerpt from "Message in the Music: Political Commentary in Black Popular Music from Rhythm and Blues to Early Hip Hop" by James B. Stewart. *The Journal of African American History* 90.3 (2005): 196-225.

Excerpt from *Roc the Mic Right* by H. Samy Alim, New York: Routledge, 2006.

Excerpts from *NewBlackMan* by M. Anthony Neal. http://newblackman.blogspot.com/.

Excerpt from "The Geoff Ward Collection." hiphoparchive.org.

Excerpt from "From Civil Rights to Hip Hop: Toward a Nexus of Ideas" by Derrick P. Alridge. *The Journal of African American History* 90.3 (2005): 226+.

Excerpts from "Cultures of Music Piracy: An Ethnographic Comparison of the U.S. and Japan" by Ian Condry. *International Journal of Cultural Studies*. 7.3 (2004): 343-363.

Excerpt from "Introduction" *Encyclopedia of Rap and Hip Hop Culture* by Yvonne Bynoe. Westport, CT: Greenwood P, 2006. testaae.greenwood.com.

Excerpt from "'One Day It'll All Make Sense': Hip-Hop and Rap. Resources for Music Librarians" by Andrew Leach. *Notes* 65.1 (2008): 9-37.

Chapter 7

Excerpt from "A Double Dose of Virus Scares" by Tina Hesman. *Science News* (2013): 18–35. 23.

Excerpt from "The New Smallpox: An Epidemic of Words?" by Barbara A. Heifferon. *Rhetoric Review* 25.1 (2006): 76-93.

Excerpt from "'Eating Fresh' in America: Subway Restaurant's Nutritional Rhetoric" by Jessica Lundgren. *Young Scholars in Writing* 6 (2008): 110-117.

Excerpt from *Contagious: Cultures, Carriers, and the Outbreak Narrative* by Priscilla Wald. Durham, NC: Duke UP, 2007.

Excerpt from "Towards a Sociology of Disease" by Stefan Timmermans and Steven Haas. *Sociology of Health & Illness* 30.5 (2008): 659-676.

Excerpt from "When the Photograph Speaks: Photo-Analysis in Narrative Medicine" by Anita Helle. *Literature and Medicine* 29.2 (2011): 297-324.

Dorothea Lange. Fifty-seven year old sharecropper woman. Hinds County, Mississippi, 1937. Thin dimes around the ankles to prevent headaches. Library of Congress, Prints and Photographs Division, LC-DIG-fsa-8b32018.

Dorothea Lange. Doctor Examining Child. Kalmath County, Oregon, 1937. Library of Congress Prints and Photographs Division, LC-USF34-021833.

Excerpt from "Middle East Respiratory Syndrome Coronavirus (MERS-CoV) Causes Transient Lower Respiratory Tract Infection in Rhesus Macaques" by Emmie de Wit, et al. *Proceedings of the National Academy of Sciences* 110.41 (2013): 16598-16603.

Excerpt from "Epidemiological Update: Middle East Respiratory Syndrome Coronavirus (MERS-CoV)." *European Centre for Disease Prevention and Control.* Nov. 23, 2013.

Excerpt from "Detecting Influenza Epidemics using Search Engine Query Data" by Jeremy Ginsberg, et al. *Nature* 457.7232 (2009): 1012-4.

Chapter 8

Excerpt from *Imperial Eyes: Travel Writing and Transculturation by Mary Louise Pratt.* New York: Routledge, 1992

Excerpt from "Estuarine Crocodiles Ride Surface Currents to Facilitate Long-Distance Travel" by Harnish Campbell. *Journal of Animal Ecology* 79.5 (2010): 955-964.

Excerpt from "Empirical Analysis of Ambulance Travel Times: The Case of Calgary Emergency Medical Services" by Susan Budge, Armann Ingolofsson, and Dawit Zerom. *Management Science* 56.4 (2010): 716-723.

Excerpt from "Female Sexiles? Toward an Archeology of Displacement of Sexual Minorities in the Caribbean" by Yolanda Martinez-San Miguel. *Signs* 36.4 (2011): 813-836.

Chapter 9

Excerpt from *Kill the Messenger: the Media's Role in the Fate of the World* by Maria Armoudian. Amherst, NY: Prometheus Books, 2011.

Excerpt from "The Psychological and Physical Effects of Video Game Play" by David Corso. *Caravel, Undergraduate Research Journal* (2014): n.p. Reprinted with permission.

Excerpt from "A Game of Genders: Comparing Depictions of Empowered Women between *A Game of Thrones* Novel and Television Series" by Rebecca Jones. *Journal of Student Research* 1.3, (2012). Reprinted with permission.

Excerpt from "Toward an Integrated Approach to Microfinance: Sustainability in Bolivia and Peru" by Eva Orbuch. *Journal of Politics and Society* 22, (2011). Reprinted with permission.

Chapter 10

Kantor, Brooke, Helen Clark, and Lydia Federico.. "Strong and Beautiful." *Harvard Political Review.* 28 June 2014. *harvardpolitics.com.* Reprinted with permission.

Farrar, Renée. "Apple (a poem)." digitalamerica.org. Reprinted with permission.

Excerpt from "Do You Know Your Bottled Water?" by Benjamin Weia. *Catalyst* 7 (2014): 7-8.

Couch, Eric, Jesse Christophel, Erik Hohlfeld, and Karen Thole. "Cooling Effects of Dirt Purge Holes on the Tips of Gas Turbine Blades." (2003). In Alley, Michael. *The Craft of Scientific Presentations. Critical Steps to Succeed and Critical Errors to Avoid.* 2nd ed. New York: Springer, 2013.

de Bie, Tanja. "MOOC Community. More than Weblectures." 24 Mar. 2014. *Prezi.com.*

Chapter 11

Excerpt from "In Good Taste: Rethinking American History with Our Palates" by Gerald J. Fitzgerald and Gabriella M. Petrick. *The Journal of American History* 95.2 (2008): 392-404. Reprinted with permission.

Excerpt from "Physiological Mechanisms for Food-Hoarding Motivation in Animals" by Erin Keen-Rhinehart, Megan J. Dailey, and Timothy Barness. *Philosophical Transactions: Biological Sciences* 365 (2010): 961-975.

Conway, Gordon. Excerpt from *One Billion Hungry. Can We Feed the World?* Ithaca: Cornell UP, 2012. Reprinted with permission.

Excerpt from "Measuring Calorie and Nutrition From Food Image" by Parisa Pouladzadeh, Shervin Shirmohammadi, and Rana Al-Maghrabi. *IEEE Transactions on Instrumentation and Measurement* 63.8 (2014): 1947-1956.

Excerpt from "Intensifying Taste, Intensifying Identity: Collectivity Through Community Cookbooks" by Kennan Ferguson. *Signs: Journal Of Women In Culture And Society* 37.3 (2012): 695-717.

Excerpt from «The Argument for Local Food" by Brian Halwell. *World Watch Magazine.* 16.3 (2003): 20-27.

Excerpt from "Imagining Alaska: Local and Translocal Engagements with Place" by Sandhya Ganapathy. *American Anthropologist* 115.1 (2013): 96-111.

Chapter 12

Excerpt from "How Popular is Your Paper? An Empirical Study of the Citation Distribution" by Sidney Redner. *The European Physical Journal B-Condensed Matter and Complex Systems* 4.2 (1998): 131-134. *Cornell University Library*. Web. 27 July 2014.

Excerpt from "Citation-Based Bootstrapping for Large-Scale Author Disambiguation" by Michael Levin, et al. *Journal of the American Society for Information Science and Technology* 63.5 (2012): 1030-1047.

Excerpt from «»Young Scholars» Affecting Composition: A Challenge to Disciplinary Citation Practices» by Amy. E. Robillard. *College English* (2006): 253-270.

Excerpt from "Revisiting the 'Quiet Debut' of the Double Helix: A Bibliometric and Methodological note on the «Impact» of Scientific Publications" by Yves Gingras. *Journal of the History of Biology* 43.1 (2010): 159-181.

Excerpt from "Plagiarism" by Gunda I. Georg and Shaomeng Wang. *Journal of Medicinal Chemistry* 56.1 (2013): 1. *ACS Publications*.

Excerpt from "Gendered Citation Practices in American Antiquity and Other Archaeology Journals" by Scott R. Hutson. *American Antiquity* 167.2 (2002): 331-342.

Excerpt from "Using Writing Assignment Designs to Mitigate Plagiarism" by Nina C. Heckler, David R. Forde, and C. Hobson Bryan. *Teaching Sociology* 41.1 (2013): 94-105.

Excerpt from "History, Identity, and Twenty-First Century Skills: Experiments in Institutional Blogging" by Sarah Osborne. *Art Documentation: Journal of the Art Libraries Society of North America* 33.1 (2014): 69-80.

Excerpt from "Zotero for Personal Image Management" by Alexander Watkins. *Art Documentation: Journal of the Art Libraries Society of North America* 32.2 (2013): 301-313.

Image from Heidebrink-Bruno, Sarah. "In 1937, two women caused an accident by wearing short in public for the first time." *Hybrid Pedagogy*, May 29, 2014.

Excerpt from ""It's Medically Proven!": Assessing the Dissemination of Religion and Health Research" by Steven M. Frenk, Steven L. Foy, and Keith G. Meador. *Journal of Religion and Health* 50.4 (2011): 996-1006.

Excerpt from "Responding to the Work of Others: There's a Better Way for Us to Live" by Daniel Wong. *Deliberations* 9 (2008): 4-7.

Excerpt from "History, Identity, and Twenty-First Century Skills: Experiments in Institutional Blogging" by. Sarah Osborne. *Art Documentation: Journal of the Art Libraries Society of North America* 33.1 (2014): 69-80.

Index